SIXTY-SIX BOOKS

Presented by the Bush Theatre in association with the
King James Bible Trust and supported by the National
Lottery through Arts Council England, Foyle Foundation,
Westminster Abbey, the National Theatre, Southbank Centre
and Sound and Music

Sixty-Six Books received its world premiere on 14th October
2011 at the Bush Theatre

The Bush Theatre would particularly like to thank

SIXTY-SIX BOOKS

By

Kwame Kwei-Armah, Neil Bartlett, Caroline Bird, Yemisi Blake,
Billy Bragg, Moira Buffini, Sam Burns, Suhayla El Bushra,
Anne Carson, Matt Charman, Brian Chikwava, Elinor Cook,
Laura Dockrill, Carol Ann Duffy, Stella Duffy, David Edgar,
Helen Edmundson, David Eldridge, Adam Foulds, Naomi Foyle,
Salena Godden, Chris Goode, James Graham, Trevor Griffiths,
Suheir Hammad, Nathalie Handal, Nancy Harris, Daisy Hasan,
DC Jackson, Jackie Kay, Luke Kennard, Maha Khan Philips,
Deirdre Kinahan, Nancy Kricorian, Neil LaBute, Nick Laird,
Mandla Langa, Toby Litt, Lachlan Mackinnon, Marks & Gran,
Ian McHugh, Anne Michaels, Helen Mort, Kate Mosse,
Andrew Motion, Paul Muldoon, Molly Naylor, Nick Payne,
Wena Poon, Anya Reiss, Tim Rice, Michael Rosen, Amy Rosenthal,
Kamila Shamsie, Owen Sheers, Christopher Shinn, Wole Soyinka,
Jack Thorne, Enda Walsh, Zukiswa Wanner, Steve Waters,
Rowan Williams, Jeanette Winterson, Anthony Weigh, Tom Wells
and Roy Williams.

All writers are generously waiving their royalties for the production
and publication, with the funds going towards the Bush Theatre's
Writers Development Programme.

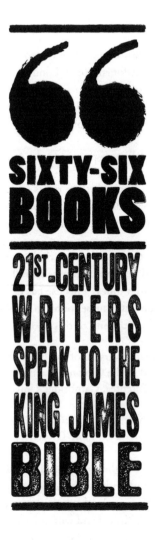

SIXTY-SIX BOOKS

21ST-CENTURY WRITERS SPEAK TO THE KING JAMES BIBLE

bush theatre

OBERON BOOKS
LONDON

WWW.OBERONBOOKS.COM

First published in 2011 by Oberon Books Ltd
521 Caledonian Road, London N7 9RH
Tel: +44 (0) 20 7607 3637 / Fax: +44 (0) 20 7607 3629
e-mail: info@oberonbooks.com
www.oberonbooks.com

A catalogue record for this book is available from the British Library.

ISBN: 978-1-84943-227-6

Printed and bound by CPI Group (UK) Ltd, Croydon, CR0 4YY.

Creative Team

Sixty-Six Books is brought together by **Artistic Director Josie Rourke in collaboration with Christopher Haydon, Rachel Holmes and Ben Power.**

Directors Hannah Ashwell-Dickinson, Philip Franks, Peter Gill, Chris Goode, James Grieve, Titas Halder, Tamara Harvey, Robert Hastie, Olly Hawes, Christopher Haydon, Alice Lacey, Michael Longhurst, Róisín McBrinn, Joe Murphy, Nessah Muthy, Gbolahan Obisesan, Mark Rosenblatt, Josie Rourke, Richard Twyman, Charlotte Westenra, Philip Wilson, Abbey Wright and Madani Younis.
Designer Amy Cook
Lighting Designer Will Evans
Sound Designer Matt McKenzie
Casting Director Sam Chandley
Company Stage Manager Helen Gaynor
Associate Director Robert Hastie
Associate Producer Lucy Oliver-Harrison
Assistant Director Josh Seymour
Design Assistants Sarah Booth, Guy Burnett, Hebe George, Claire Harrison, Tori Jennings, Natalie Moggridge
Assistant Lighting Designer Nic Farman
Assistant Sound Designer Tom Meehan
Deputy Stage Managers Rachel Gillard, Rachael Miller
Assistant Stage Managers Elisabeth Donaghy, Kathryn Linnell, Phillip Richardson, Penny Salway
Stage Management Intern Ingeborg Ugland

Thank you to Sky Arts as Media Partner, RADA, Almeida Theatre, Stratford East, National Youth Theatre, English Touring Theatre, Donmar Warehouse, Honeyrose Products LTD, Fulham Library, Bertie Watkins

The Bush Theatre

'These are great times for the Bush Theatre…the new building already looks like a winner'
Charles Spencer, *Telegraph*

Since its inception in 1972, the Bush Theatre has pursued its singular vision of discovery, risk and entertainment from its home on the corner of Shepherds Bush Green. That vision is valued and embraced by a community of audience and artists radiating out from our distinctive corner of West London across the world. The Bush is a local theatre with an international reputation. From its beginning, the Bush has produced hundreds of groundbreaking premieres, many of them Bush commissions, and hosted guest productions by leading companies and artists from across the world. On any given night, those queuing at the foot of our stairs to take their seats could have travelled from Auckland or popped in from round the corner.

What draws them to the Bush is the promise of a good night out and our proven commitment to launch, from our stage, successive generations of playwrights and artists. Samuel Adamson, David Eldridge, Jonathan Harvey, Catherine Johnson, Tony Kushner, Stephen Poliakoff, Jack Thorne and Victoria Wood (all then unknown) began their careers at the Bush. The unwritten contract between talent and risk is understood by actors who work at the Bush, creating roles in untested new plays. Unique amongst local theatres, the Bush consistently draws actors of the highest reputation and calibre. Joseph Fiennes and Ian Hart recently took leading roles in a first play by an unknown playwright to great critical success. John Simm and Richard Wilson acted in premieres both of which transferred into the West End. The Bush has won over 100 awards, and developed an enviable reputation for touring its acclaimed productions nationally and internationally.

Audiences and organisations far beyond our stage profit from the risks we take. The value attached to the Bush by other theatres and by the film and television industries is both significant and considerable. The Bush receives more than 3,000 scripts every year, and reads and responds to them all. This is one small part of a comprehensive playwrights' development programme which nurtures the relationship between writer and director, as well as playwright residencies and commissions. Everything that we do to develop playwrights focuses them towards a production on our stage or beyond.

We also run an ambitious education, training and professional development programme, bushfutures, providing opportunities for different sectors of the community and professionals to access the expertise of Bush playwrights, directors, designers, technicians and actors, and to play an active role in influencing the future development of the theatre and its programme. 2009 saw the launch of our new social networking and online publishing website www.bushgreen.org. The site is a great new forum for playwrights and theatre people to meet, share experiences and collaborate. Through this pioneering work, the Bush will reach and connect with new writers and new audiences, and find new plays to stage.

Sixty-Six Books will open the doors of the new Bush Theatre. The lease we just have signed on our new home will create the Bush Theatre on this site for 125 years. We felt it was in the spirit of the Bush to open our new home with as many artists as we could draw together. The 66 writers, 130 actors, 23 directors and the huge team that inspire and support will write the newest chapter of the Bush's story. They will be the first to cross its new stage, drink in its new bar and sit in its new cafe. Either as reader, audience, or hopefully both, I hope that you will join with us in sharing this big moment of our small but significant history.

Josie Rourke, Artistic Director

CONTENTS

CONTENTS

THE BOOKS OF THE NEW TESTAMENT

FOREWORD

Christopher Haydon,
Rachel Holmes and Josie Rourke

Four hundred years ago King James the First commissioned a new translation of the Bible. The King James Version, KJV as it is often known, was a text written to be spoken, accessible to broad audiences. The KJV was a multi-authored and collective production – in order to perfect it in its final form, its many editors gathered together and spoke the whole thing aloud to one another. It's been described as the only artistic masterpiece to be created by a committee.

Today, the KJV is acknowledged and celebrated as a major document and foundation stone of the English language, manifold in its influence on how the language is written, spoken and performed. Pulpit to print; stage to page; mediated through many forms oral and written, the KJV has, since its inception, been a fundamental part of the living English language. This is a work that has travelled to every continent of the globe. It has been shared as a melodic instrument of inspiration, illumination and mutual understanding; and it has also been wielded as a tool of colonial oppression.

Our interpretation of the KJV for the new millennium, *Sixty-Six Books* celebrates and challenges the traditions and achievements of this great work on the occasion of its 400th anniversary. As a collective of editors passionate about the living English language and committed to commissioning and producing a collaborative work, we have sought to track the KJV and its influence as far as possible on its remarkably far-reaching four-century journey around the world. We have followed the book wherever it went and reflected together on what it did. Questioning 'Little England' versions of British cultural heritage and the influence of the KJV, we've identified and commissioned great emerging and established writers to explore and reflect the broad and integrated cultural empires of diversity into which the KJV has evolved as a living text.

A significant part of our intention in commissioning this new collective work has been to attempt to chart a corrective and twenty-first century course through its problematic colonial history. The voices of *Sixty-Six Books* are polyphonic. They innovate, transmute, transpose, reinvent and talk back to four hundred years of history.

We have aimed to expose the KJV to new and innovative forms of artistic expression. As the invention of print propelled the original KJV into a book known across the globe, *Sixty-Six Books* is a project commissioned and produced at the practical and spiritual heart of the new technological revolution. Some of our writers have produced works that are digital in aesthetic form as well as in content. Alongside this are works that are experimental expressions of the new twenty-first century revival and reinvention of spoken word and live performance arts.

The genesis of *Sixty-Six Books* lies in a chance encounter between two theatre directors: one a very lapsed Catholic and the other son of one of England's first female priests. In 2008, Josie Rourke and Christopher Haydon met at a seminar on the KJV held in Stratford by the Royal Shakespeare Company to discuss how the theatre world might respond to the 400th anniversary. Finding themselves on the same train home together, both were struck by the idea that, as a text that was written to be spoken, the KJV had an intrinsic theatricality.

'Wouldn't it be great' said Josie, 'if we could commission sixty-six writers to respond to the sixty-six books of the Old and New Testaments?' Christopher agreed: and so began *Sixty-Six Books*.

With vital financial support and encouragement provided by the King James Bible Trust, the duo launched into a marathon series of meetings with prospective partner individuals and organizations.

Given the epic and some might say ludicrous scale of the project, the first question that they asked prospective partners in each meeting was, 'Are we mad?' Two individuals who did not respond with a raised eyebrow and a sharp intake of breath were Rachel Holmes at the Southbank Centre and Ben Power at the National Theatre.

The four of us formed the commissioning team and began drawing up wishlists of our favourite living writers. They came from all disciplines – including playwrights, poets, novelists, songwriters. The only restrictions were that they had to write in English and they had to be able to create something that would be performed. We developed a simple but rigorous set of criteria to guide our selection of writers: we would to the best of our ability ensure equality of representation across: gender; age; ethnicity; sexual orientation; faith and literary form.

As a result *Sixty-Six Books* is made up of writers from across five continents. Our youngest is nineteen and our oldest in their seventies. Every nation of the United Kingdom is represented. Yet of all our criteria, tellingly, religion proved to be the hardest to define. How to cope with the fluidity of religious belief and experience when wanting to be representative? All categories of identity are of course provisional and qualified. But because the religion into which a person is born does not line up with any other definition of cultural identity, it was the hardest to negotiate and curate.

It is not evident from a writer's work whether they have faith or not. Indeed many writers might not be sure of this, or remotely care about it, themselves. Equally, some writers are radically and vehemently opposed to any identification – cultural or philosophical – with any and all religions. Equally, for those for whom faith does play a role, the problems were equally contested. A religiously observant Muslim has much more in common with a religiously observant Jew or Christian than with people who are culturally Muslim, Jewish, or Christian but secular in outlook.

However individual identity might be defined or undefined, our commitment to the notion of multi-authorship had primacy in all our considerations. The Bible is contradictory and paradoxical because it was authored by a diversity of voices producing a collective repository of shared stories, experience, knowledge and ideas. Like the KJV, *Sixty-Six Books* offers an imagined democracy of shared humanity, not in concordance of agreement, but in a collective equality of shared, respectful diverse humanity.

Each writer in the cycle was commissioned to produce a concise response to one book of the KJV. We were very clear that their contribution did not need to be an adaptation nor did it need to be a re-telling of any Bible story. We emphasized the freewheeling and interpretative openness of the brief, offering an open vista for untrammeled inventiveness of the imagination. The only non-negotiable point was that whatever writers created had to be written to be spoken.

We chose every writer, fledgling or fully formed, because we collectively agreed they had both produced great work in their field and had something absolutely unique to bring to the project. As the commissions began to come in, we were surprised and delighted at how many writers had chosen to write in a form different to the one they most commonly practice. It was fascinating to observe that when tasked to reach out to the widest and most democratic audience, writers would often choose a form other than the one with which they were usually most comfortable or familiar. As editors, we'd like to ask agents, publishers and programmers of the writers of *Sixty-Six Books* to take note of the previously unrealized talents of some of their writers. In troubled publishing and media markets combined with an artistic environment in which writers need to be adaptable to new forms, technologies and distributions, innovative and flexible fields of work are vital to the survival of both emerging and established writers.

Some of these responses to the books of the KJV are sacred to the text and some secular. Some are reverent; others breach the boundaries of blasphemy. If you encounter the whole of *Sixty-Six Books*, you are very likely to be offended. In this respect also, we have been true to tradition of the KJV. As anyone knows who has properly read the Bible, it's full of really dirty and offensive stuff. Not to mention contradictions and paradoxes. There is something in the Bible that every Christian should find offensive and there is something that every atheist should find inspirational. If not, they haven't read it carefully enough. *Sixty-Six Books* knows this, and shows that whilst what is sacred to one is blasphemy to another, we all share the same stories and common humanity.

This event comes at a particular time in the life of the Bush Theatre. Founded in 1972 as a theatre for new writing in a non-elite environment, the Bush maintains a resolutely independent and democratic tradition committed to the accessible and the contemporary. It is therefore highly appropriate that *Sixty-Six Books* is the show that now reopens the Bush Theatre in its new home in the Old Shepherds Bush Library. Alongside our 66 writers, *Sixty-Six Books* will bring together over 30 directors, composers and designers, with over 130 performers and a huge team of technicians, producers and administrators to create a unique celebration of an ancient text in a distinctly contemporary environment.

Our world is fraught by religious conflict and cultural sectarianism. *Sixty-Six Books* has been created out of a constant and observant practice of tolerance, collaboration and cooperation between people of vastly different perspectives, opinions, backgrounds and contexts. We therefore offer it as a contribution towards the mutual curiosity, tolerance, and force of collective enterprise and shared humanity that characterizes the international and ancient arts of writing and spoken performance.

Jeanette Winterson

GODBLOG

God Here: People ask me how I came to be a global brand. I'd like to share some of my stories with you; the laughter and tears, the sacrifices.

In the beginning there was no social network site. Not even a Wi-Fi café. Only Dust and Space-Time. I saw an opportunity.

To create a worldwide brand you need a world. Planet Earth. My Big Idea. Start with a Bang.

God, (that's me) said 'Let there be Light'. And there was Light. See? I was incandescent with joy.

When I started out I had only 2 clients: Adam and Eve. Now Earth.com has billions of users. But I've had my ups and downs.

1 Hell down there. Heaven up here. Earth in the middle. Who knew that my simple 3-tier system would be rebranded as Class Struggle?
Follow me on Twitter for a chapter by chapter account of Earth.com – the early years.

2 Adam and Eve made from Dust. 1st Eve hates dusting. Went native somewhere in the Garden. Adam lonely.
Adam here: A dog is not enough! I need a wife!

God Here: OK OK Quit kvetching. Go to sleep and Daddy'll fix it. Quick op on Adam. 2nd Eve=Spare Rib. Millennia later men still love a barbecue.

3 New Eve dusting Eden when Snake shows up with Apple iPhone iPod iPad and free Apps. Tempting eh?

I arrive in the Garden after work hoping to relax and find Adam and Eve downloading designer fig leaves from Net-a-Porter. Fig leaves! Jesus.

4 First eviction! Adam and Eve out. Jews homeless till 1948. God-followers down the ages can now land-grab with a clear conscience.

Eve has twins Cain/Abel. Cain fads as veggie. Beads, sandals etc. Controlling type. Kills brother just because I prefer meat to veg.

SMS from Cain. 'Am I my brother's keeper?' Oy Vey! Only 4 people on Earth.com and already we have social unrest and homicide.

5 Happy Birthday Noah! Age 500 he has become a Dad. Even later than Elton John. I send iPod nano + top tunes: Fiddler on the Roof, Carpenters etc.

People are living too long. Pensions. Healthcare. Who is going to pay for all this life? Satan tables hostile takeover bid for Earth.com

6 Decide to liquidate Earth.com as tax loss. Flood plan leaks out. Noah launches Smartboat start-up. OK OK. Tip: Take 2 of everything.

7 Noah here: Oy Gevalt! 40 days of rain. Boat stinks. Ganzer Gdunga! Eaten all the chocolate. God has gone too far.

7 God Here: Note to Self: Quit with the rain.

8 Ark grounded on Mount Ararat. Awesome! Did some Photoshop but nothing like Vogue/Kate Moss. Have left fossil record for Creationists.

9 RED AND YELLOW AND PINK AND GREEN PURPLE AND ORANGE AND BLUE. I CAN SING A RAINBOW SING A RAINBOW SING A RAINBOW TOO.

9 Satan lied about mankind's WMDs. They could not launch a missile attack on heaven in 45mins. No more Shock and Awe. Covenant Time. See rainbow.

CHAPTER 10 'And the whole earth was of one language and of one speech.'

11   Tower. Twin. Trump. Eiffel. Blackpool. Gherkin. Leaning. Babel! The bastards are building a stairway to Heaven.

11   'And the Lord came down to see the tower which the children of men builded.'

11   No planning permission! Whose Earth.com do they think this is? I'm God for God's sake! Nuke 'em.

11   Note to Self: Remember the rainbow? No nuking! OK. Nuke the language. 2 years free cable TV.

12   Now nobody's talking to me. Thinking of starting a Social Network site. Had a visit from the Winklevoss twins.

13   Meet Abraham. My new friend. We have nothing in common but he's on my Facebook page.

14   Sodom. This is the 1st book of the Bible and I've had to deal with Feminism (Eve1) Environmental disaster (flood) illegal hi-rise (Babel) and now homosexuality.

15   At least Abraham is loyal. He is sleeping with his wife's Mexican maid. What a Schwarzenegger!

16   Mazeltov! It's a boy! Well done Abramovitch! Call him Ishmael after his father's Moby Dick. Book the bris.

17   'and ye shall circumcise the flesh of your foreskin and it shall be a token of the covenant betwixt me and you.'

17   Covenant count: Rainbow:1 Foreskin:1

18   Promised Abram's vrot OAP wife Sarah a baby. She laughed at me. Hey! U laughin at GOD? 'No I didn't'. 'Yes you did!' Women! Who knew?

18   Two rounds of IVF no problem. It will stop her kvetching about the maid and I am a family man.

19   Welcome to Sodom. Twinned with San Francisco. If I had wanted leather bars toy dogs and pink wallpaper I would have created them.

19   Abraham reminds me that his brother Lot lives in Sodom. Is he a swinger or what? Get him out quick is my advice. And don't look back.

19   Fire and Brimstone! So much for Adam and Steve. (ha ha). I am moving to Texas as soon as it is discovered.

19   Shame about Lot's wife. She looked back. I turned her into a pillar of salt. Sometimes I wonder about Myself.

20   Shortage of males, gay or straight, after Sodom situation. Lot's 3 girls slept with their own Dad. Murdoch denies phone-hacking victims.

21   Breaking News! World's first IVF successful. Sarah has a son. We're calling him Isaac Wayne William Kate.

21   Sarah had kicked out the Mexican maid and Abram's love-child Ishmael. So much for sisterhood.

22   'take thine only son Isaac and offer him for a burnt offering.' Yes, I REALLY said that to them. Tough love.

22   He did it! Bound and gagged the lad. Got the knife out. At the last second I said – 'no it was a joke'. We all laughed.

23   RIP Sarah kvetchy Wife of Abraham. She was the Joan Collins of the Old Testament.

24   Sixty-seven verses later Abraham is married again. I love a Hollywood happy ending.

25   Spoke too soon. 8 verses later Abraham dead. It comes to us all. Except me of course.

25   Cain/Abel. Ishmael/Isaac. Now Jacob/Esau. Why do I keep writing pairs of hostile brothers? Is it because of Satan/me? Should I talk to someone about this?

26　　The redhead idiot Esau just sold his birthright to Jacob for a bowl of soup. Soup! Jacob is clever. Soon he will own Marks and Spencer.

27　　Now Jacob sews a goatskin schmatter and cons half-blind Isaac into Blessing him instead of hairy Esau. Jacob is a smooth operator.

28　　Hey Goyim! Wondering what all the fuss is about the Blessing? Here. This is the best of me. More Life Into A Time Without Boundaries.

28　　Tweet it again: More Life Into A Time Without Boundaries.

29　　Jacob has offered to give me 10% of any deal. No wonder the Jews are the Chosen People.

29　　The Winklevoss twins are suing me.

30　　I am discovering my feminine side. Still disturbing hostile pairs but now Rachel and Leah – and Jacob has married them both.

31　　Yes Jacob has 2 wives+maids/concubines. This is the research stage of family values. What does it mean to be faithful? Is sex only for married couples?

32　　The religious RIGHT keeps saying that marriage means one man one woman. They haven't read the Bible.

32　　Jacob wrestles the Angel. A poetic and mysterious text. Put a little birdhouse in your Soul.

33　　Jacob and Esau make friends. One day there will be peace in Palestine.

34　　Problems with Strange Gods.com. New website for Delusionists. George W. Bush. Tony Blair. M Gadaffi. Mugabe. Sarah Palin. Warning: Acting like God affects mental health.

35　　Strange Gods are all wearing earrings. Jacob confiscates. He's a good boy.

36　　Quiz question: Do you believe in God? (OK, coming from me it's not neutral, I know.)

37   Jacob gives his son Joseph a Coat of Many Colours and lands him the lead role in a West End musical.

38   Rest of the family insanely jealous. TV vote rigged so that Joseph is voted off X Factor and exiled to Egypt.

38   New sin: Onanism. (nothing to do with Joseph. X Factor is a family show. Warning: It makes you go blind.)

39   Egyptian hot totty lusts after Joseph. As she's married to his new boss Joseph says no means no. This could be on HBO.

39   Joseph accused of rape! DSK sends Scotch.

40   Joseph gets free by interpreting a dream. DSK lawyers say attractive chambermaid must have wanted hurried sex with fat old sweaty Frenchman.

41   Joseph introduces Supply and Demand to Egypt. Dream=7fat years followed by 7lean years. Nile-nebbishers stash the corn. Famine comes! Pocket the profit.

42   I just want to say that Capitalism was not my idea.

43   Give me a bit of time and I will send Marx to Manchester. (Author's note: Marx does not have a brother called Spencer.)

44   Joseph operates Earth.com's first Cash and Carry. He gets the cash. They do the carrying.

45   Schmaltzy reunion between Joseph and his envious family. Film rights sold for undisclosed sum. Brad Pitt to play Joseph.

46   Tedious family tree stuff again. I blame Ancestry.com.

47   A beginning a middle and an end is the proper way to tell a story but I have difficulty with that method.

48   Moses here: God dictated this to me. You don't believe me? I'll blow your head off.

49   Time for Joseph to die. I would like a son of my own but when I type in Virgin I get an airline.

50   And this is just the beginning of the Earth. Com. Who knew?

Anne Michaels

THE CROSSING

Before you are chosen, you must choose.

You must be willing to drown,
to sleep with death outside your door,
to witness darkness so profound it can be touched.
To heed pestilence. To glean the meaning
of locusts, lice, frogs and hail,
blood and boils.

You must be willing to carry everything on your back,
and leave everything behind.

*

This is the story of a crossing.
From the loneliness of the visible world,
of mortal gods, prestidigitation, the glamour of sorcery;
to the infinite, to the
invisible. Not to choose one god
over another, but to choose
one God.
In order to reach the shore of another world,
in order to be turned inside out,
the invisible requires miracles, signs and wonders,
a divine footprint no one can forget.
Water-mountains.
An entire sea lifted in order for us to notice
a drop of light,
the weight of a mound of dates in the hand,
ordinary darkness.

*

A story is a covenant. Come close.
Let us hold together through enslavement,
humiliation, surrender, betrayal, redemption.
From the building of Pharoah's monuments
to the building of the ark, enclosing no less than
sacredness.
Let us say
when *we* were delivered from Egypt.

This story has been read from a book exhumed
from Weissensee cemetery in Berlin
after the war, it has been read from books
hand-written in the camps of Gurs and Drancy.
In Terezin, Westerbork and Bergen-Belsen.
It has been told for the sake of the dead,
for the sake of children, as a eulogy,
as a prayer. In hospitals and in hiding places.

Come close.

Even if your back is bent to the ground
you can still see a bit of sky reflected in the water.

Thus the mother of Moses surrendered her basket
to the river, hoping her son would be spared.
Pharoah's daughter fished him out:
I parted the reeds and drew him out of the water.

*

To be spared is an exile,
a doubleness: one truth behind another,
death and life in the same small
basket. Looking down from the palace
to the slaves hewing stone
he was both Egyptian
and Hebrew.
Who am I to speak?
Who am I, if I don't speak.

And even if it troubles the theologian,
the storyteller knows a man can't be
two men; Moses must denounce, strike down
part of himself. And so,
reckless with justice, defending a stranger,
Moses overcame the Egyptian slavedriver
and left that part of himself
in the sand.

He fled to Midian: the second exile,
where he defended the right of the women
to draw from the well.
In the desert, water is always rescue.
In turn, the women rescued him,
welcomed him, gave him shelter.
And from this family of the well,
Moses chose
his wife:
I drew her out of the water.

He tended the flock. He became a father.
He remained
a stranger: for he heard their cries
even in the peaceful hills of Midian
rising from a depth into the bright air
and sinking,
and he stopped again
and again, for he could not tell
where he stood: on the path
or the mistaken path.

Come close.

Moses turned toward the voice.
An unpronounceable call, formless
yet whole. Inchoate
and complete. A call from his own throat
even as he heard his name aloud
across the sand.
As the cry rose into his eyes and into

his burning mind – this moment of
turning – the bush caught fire
as if ignited by his sight.
The leaves were aflame, drawing fire instead of water
from the dry ground: the hunger of everything alive
to draw from the deepest place.
Not the way the earth takes the colour of the setting sun, but fire
from within,
a fire that did not need air to breathe, as if light could
sing. And he knelt with joy and
fear, his kneeling was a rising up,
and he knew for the first time
we can be cracked open,
crushed like an almond shell,
to feel the soul released, open and transfixed
with purpose. Every soul
has a task.
His very doubt –
I cannot speak well enough, choose another,
must it be me who speaks –
was faith. And God named himself
so that man might give sound to both
the burning,
and the light.
An open vowel, a name
for both question
and answer.
A cry
and a reply.
Moses, borne twice by water
and now, by fire.

*

He returned to Egypt and saw again
what it is to weep
for fresh water, for a single fig
pressed open to its sweetness, for a cistern,
for a sheet to bind the newly born or

newly dead, for shelter, for sleep. Let alone
rights and sanctity.

The plagues answered the plagues
of slavery: the pestilence
of corruption, oppression, bent backs,
the infestation of poverty,
the blackness of erasure and severance.
And what was delivered unto Pharoah
was delivered unto every Egyptian.
The river turned to blood,
the symbol of life become the symbol of death.
Frogs stank, heaped and rotting like falsehood, in every bed.
Crops grew molten with lice and swarming insects, feeding their
own devastation.
Where handfuls of ash fell, there grew boils
except for Goshen where the slaves lived
Hail-fire. Locusts turning the fields into
a writhing mass, every last grain and grass devoured.
A darkness that dissolved body into soul.

Yet Pharoah would not relent
Who is your God that I should obey you
and let your people go?

Come close.

Until at last –
from the one who sits on his throne
to the one behind the millstone
even unto the cattle –

the slaying of the first-born.

*

The sea roared up, a liquid flame
scouring the air. A sound that seemed to
scorch silence forever from the earth.
All beheld the climbing rage of water, a range of
watermountains, foaming, hissing, yanked upward like a fistful of

hair, the mist
dank with fish and brine – the smell
of salvation.

Who could have guessed the smell of a miracle
would not be the smell of burning but
of the sea?

The water parted, flesh drawn back to reveal
the parched bone.

Moses, borne by water, and then by fire,
and now by earth.

Higher than the pyramids rose the steep, rushing
terror, a torrent falling up:
for that is the miraculous: always
against the mortal force of the world and the weight
of fate. Suspended force.
To walk forward into vertigo, more – to
carry their children there,
into that still point of unceasing
incomprehension.

The way behind closing forever.

Thus was a people born, at the bottom of the sea.

The wheels of the chariots froze,
and sank.

The Hebrews scrambled up the steep bank,
a pillar of cloud marking the way,
a pillar of fire closing the way behind them.

Thus the world and the way of
seeing the world, was overturned.

*

I will come to you in a thick cloud, in order that the people
hear when I speak with you and so trust you ever after.
Build a tabernacle, that I may dwell among you.
A covenant of wood like a covenant of words:

to enclose – as words enclose.
20 planks, 6 planks, 30 cubits long
no other gods before me, no graven image
50 loops, 50 copper clasps
do not take the name of the Lord in vain
gold, silver, copper, a curtain of
twisted linen, embroidered linen
blue for the most sacred, then purple, then crimson
goat hair, dugong skin
Remember the Sabbath, to keep it holy
lamp oil, oil for anointing
an ark of acacia wood
2 and a half cubits long, 1 and a half cubits wide
1 and a half cubits high
Six days shall you labour
6 branches, 3 on each side
overlaid with gold, inside and out
4 cups shaped like almond blossoms
But the seventh day is the Sabbath
a single hammered piece of pure gold
and you shall not work, nor your son, nor your daughter, nor
servants, nor cattle, nor any stranger within your gates
clasps, mouldings, rings
loops of blue wool
for in six days the Lord made heaven and earth, the sea, and all
that is in them
each length of cloth 28 cubits
Honour your father and your mother
each width of cloth 4 cubits
You shall not kill
a lampstand of hammered work,
You shall not commit adultery, you shall not steal
cups, calyxes, petals
nor bear false witness, nor covet
10 strips of linen woven with cherubim
28 cubits by 4 cubits wide
50 loops of blue wool, 50 gold clasps
The laws were burned right through,

the tablets legible from both sides of the stone,
each letter facing both ways at once,
to be read from a place of humility
or of shame, mended or
rended, rendered or
sundered
3 degrees of workmanship, according to their sacredness

*

Come close.
We think we will rise to the occasion,
do the right thing
when suddenly our hand is reached for.
But it's not true.
Morality is a muscle.
It must be exercised.
How many times each day can we open our hands?

*

Moses took off his sandals on sacred ground.
He climbed the mountain and returned, radiant.
He bent his knees from awe and not from oppression.
He heard the word of God.

And still
he shattered the tablets.
Just as we, gorged with manna and the miracle
of the Red Sea
cried out in yearning
for the golden calf.
The right anger, the wrong hunger.

Moses remained in exile, forever on Mt Nebo
looking out upon his banishment.
So the place would not be worshipped,
he was not even allowed a grave.
Moses, borne by water, fire,
earth, and now
air.

*

When you are at sea, remember the miracle
that smelled of fish.

Make your heart a gimbal, a compass forever level, even when the
ship is tilting.

How many times each day we can open our hands.

*

The chasm of disbelief that opens in us
in error, in terror, in shame,
in the perversity of going against one's own soul,
the right anger, the wrong hunger,
the wrong anger, the right hunger,
errors of pity and of judgment,
of so desperately leaping to avoid our fate
that instead it rushes to meet us,
of crashing into that wall at high speed;
each time we forget to let our children
love us, each time we turn away
in selfishness, in longing for the moment to pass
or to be elsewhere, of ignoring
another's fear or hope because
the clock is ticking, the meter is running,
the batteries are low; for the colossal unforgivable action
and the innumerable small forgivable ones,
all the choices made against being loved,
or loving – there is nothing it seems
we will not do for ourselves
or against ourselves, forgetting those we love
even when they are an inch away,
abandoning all in an instant,
rationalizing our actions the rest of our lives;
we can hang from a rope in the shocking cold light
of the crevasse, we can witness
earth-moving, life-altering miracles –
the plagues, the parting of the sea – and

stand in the presence of God
forty days and nights on a mountain
and witness by God's own hand the burning into the stone
of the commandments, and still
and still –
and still – shatter the tablets.

One of the great truths of this story
is that there is no attempt to explain
these moments of passionate
refusal, this forgetting,
these ingratitudes.

Sometimes we forgive, sometimes we are forgiven,
sometimes
forgiveness is impossible.
No one can forgive on behalf of the dead.
Sometimes we stand forever on the peak of Mt Nebo
overlooking our banishment,
sometimes we find ourselves
in the wrong bed.
Sometimes home finds us despite our actions.
Sometimes we are mended before we even knew we were
wounded.
Every soul has a task.

Cleft to the heart of this story of miraculous
salvation, is the opposite story.
The tearing and mending and tearing and mending of the same
wound.
Who has not known this, or will not know this?
To stand within sight
of all you have lost.

*

Exodus is a story of spectacular redemption
and spectacular retribution, the rescue of children
and the slaying of children.
Of heeding the most difficult inner voice,

and of willfully ignoring that voice.
Of tablets written
and re-written.
And so it is a story told in the darkest places
and in the places of greatest safety.
When we are sharing food and when we are starving.

Where there is certainty there is
doubt, where there is love
there is the always loss or the fear of loss,
where there is one thing, there is always its opposite.
Everything under the sun has its shadow.
What do we make of this?
How many times each day do we have a chance
to do the right thing?
One thing we know:
the story of water and the story of fire
and the story of earth and the story of air
is the same story.
That 'to cleave' is both to separate and to
hold close. That the phrase
'with outstretched hand'
can mean both hope and despair.
Always the deepest questions
are both question and answer,
both cry
and reply:

what binds us
what binds us
what binds us

Caroline Bird

THE FOUNDATION

I was bloodline and most people who are bloodline never escape. I would move houses, move to another place, only for some deep-level alter to pick up the phone and say 'this is my new address, come and get me,' and they would. My mind was full of rules that I obeyed without thinking, which feels a lot like free will. In fact, it feels exactly the same as free will. All human beings are programmed to think in a particular way and accept certain things as normal. We look at someone speaking and we see their mouths moving and shaping words and we hear the sound of those words and we connect them with the shapes being made by the mouth and we experience communication. This doesn't freak us out because our brains have taught themselves to register this experience as a whole. But it's strange when you think about it. A hole in someone's face is forming different shapes in quick succession whilst simultaneously channelling sound waves of various frequencies that our brains have been trained to recognize and associate to certain meanings. Most of us are trained to think the same way. We all have trigger words – words that, when we hear them, make us recoil or shudder or smile or laugh or sweat or blush or get aroused or twitch without meaning to; well up. Because they push a button somewhere inside us. They switch something on. There was a doctor called Dr Green. The therapist said, 'was there a doctor with a name like a colour?' and I said, 'how do you know about Mr Green?' The therapist shouldn't have been asking those questions. He was going to get us all killed. Then he said, 'do you know anything about the word Delta? Does anything happen when I say, Theta?' And I said 'yes.' And he said, 'what?' And I said 'psychic.' And he said, 'psychic?' And I said 'psychic killers.' Psychic killers. They had fed me a drug called Demerol and programmed my brain to respond to the code words. The code words were the same for all of us: the letters of the Greek alphabet. Omega was the word that told me to hurt myself.

But that's all over now. I don't worry about that sort of thing anymore. Sometimes on the bus, when I thought something I didn't want to think, what I did was this finger exercise where I would touch my thumb with each finger on the same hand but touch the thumb twice with my index and little finger, this worked surprisingly well as it was rather difficult and it took my full concentration to do, but then of course something went wrong again and I ended up becoming a master of this technique which meant I could do it without thinking about it, and the method was useless to me then. I had to find something else to concentrate on. It's amazing how much you can do without thinking about it. People drive home and find themselves in their garages and realize they've been lost in a deep, deep daydream since they left the office. And they're totally safe and sound. Safe and sound. Didn't crash into the back of a bus. Didn't swerve off the road. They followed the Highway Code to the letter, just on autopilot. Obeyed the rules subconsciously, while they were dreaming. Sartre said 'we are condemned to be free.' What an idiot. They would attach electrodes to me, four on my head and one inside my vagina, and then they would say 'if you say anything bad about us, you will hurt yourself' and I would say 'no I won't' and they would shock me, and then tell me again, and I would say 'okay' and they would say 'we don't believe you' and shock me again. Eventually you'll believe anything. That's what shocked into submission means, in a very literal sense. *I will break the power of your pride.* Say boo to a goose enough times and the goose will start roaming round the countryside, ripping the heads off children. *And ye shall eat the flesh of your sons, and the flesh of your daughters ye shall eat.* There's a lot of freaky shit going on in the world, just under your noses. They would say: And if you tell on us, we won't have to kill you, because you'll do that for us. There are four particular numbers that you will see everywhere, especially on clocks. The worst of the bunch is 13 followed by 26 and 46. To a lesser extent also the number 66. On Sundays you will see 13 every hour, for example 1:13, 2:13 etc. You will sometimes think you have escaped a 13 and look up to see 15, only to go and look at your computer screen or your television and see a 13. Have a pre-wash with a hose in the bath so you are clean to go into the bath, then four hours in the bath. Replace the mattress with an airbed, as dust mites can't get inside that. If you go to the toilet, there will naturally be poop and urine and blood bacteria carried around with you for the rest of the day, contaminating everywhere you have been. *Whatsoever she sitteth upon shall be unclean, as the uncleanness of her separation.* Sometimes I have the day off from going to the toilet. Plan ahead. This is the kind of stuff I tell myself now, to replace the old rules with new, milder ones. No one wants to hose him or herself for an hour in cold water before they have a bath so that the bath doesn't get dirty, but then that's a better rule than cutting yourself with a knife every time you want to express a secret. I have so many secrets now; they don't feel like secrets anymore. They're just me. They've absorbed into who I am. I'm made of secrets. *(Smile.)*

Sometimes the sessions might go on half an hour; sometimes they might go on for three hours. They'd put an I.V. in my arm and there'd be a pulsing red light. Then I'd feel a pain in my right ear and these weird disorientated sounds. Who knows the things people said to my inner core…? *And I shall make your cities waste, and bring your sanctuaries unto desolation.* There's a place right in the centre of your brain that remembers everything and has heard things you couldn't even imagine. We were trained to do specific things with specific code words. The Betas were programmed for sexual behaviours like prostitution, or making pornography of an illegal sort. The Deltas were killers trained for ceremonial killing, assassination. I was a Theta. They called us the psychic killers. They made me believe I had the power to psychically communicate with 'mother', that I could psychically cause somebody to develop a brain aneurysm and die. Omega has to do with self-destruct programming. The therapist was careful about saying that to me.

I was one of twelve disciples. Each of us was ingrained with a different segment of the philosophy, like 'be good to those who hurt you, hate those who are kind to you.' We were grains inside an hourglass. When the last grain falls, we will die and the sleeping giant will awaken. The therapist told me to look for a robot inside my head and then look around inside the head of the robot, look at the back of the head, look for any wires or switches and turn the switches off. Then he told me to unscrew and open the control system wherein I found several children. He told me to imagine a laser gun and vaporise the robot with it, then free the children. I told him he was going to get all of us killed but he didn't listen. He didn't realize I was being monitored. They would say to me, alpha-alpha-zero-nine and I would say 'I told them about grains of sand falling' and they would shock me. The next time, in my therapy session, I would say 'I am one of twelve disciples. I am one of twelve disciples. Theta. Delta. Omega' and I would lift my fingernails to my eyeballs. We are the unchosen generation. We are expendable. When the last grain of sand falls, the sleeping giant will awaken. Have you ever seen *Trancers* or *Trancers II*? It's like that. Except we win. In real life, we win. Because those who know the most about the human brain and how to control it, these people are the rulers of the world. Just ask your local anorexic.

The prophets told me I couldn't give myself over even if I wanted to. They said the therapist was a prophet too and he was asking me questions to test me, and if I told him the truth, he would report back to them and I would be hurt very badly for my disloyalty. Loyalty is something I know all and nothing about. Until quite recently, if a husband sent his wife to a therapist, the therapist would call up the husband after the session and tell him what she'd been saying, because women weren't allowed to have pain that was sacred to them, it was there to be poked and pondered on and tutted at and drugged with smelling salts and liquor and big sloppy man tongues. I don't sleep with people. I don't want people beside me when I'm sleeping, listening. I'm vigilant when I sleep. 'The price of freedom is eternal vigilance' – Thomas Jefferson said that, the third president of the United States, head writer of the Declaration of Independence and a founding father. He called America 'The Empire of Liberty.' The word Empire is a powerful word. Empire. Let's build an empire out of The Liberated. Round them up. The therapist said 'is there something inside you known as The Foundation?' I said 'No.' He kept pushing. He said, 'you know you were really only a child-part, who's playing a role but you had no choice then and now you do have a choice. You've played your part very, very well, but they don't have to continue to play with you because you're safe here.' I told him, 'no one's been playing anything.' He said, 'if you help me, then I can help you.' I said, 'if this were really a safe place, you wouldn't need any help from me. You would not have so many gaps in your knowledge. You are not safe and you are not capable of keeping me safe, you are just a human being and human beings think they know how to operate on other human beings but they don't, otherwise they wouldn't have to strap us down. We would just lie down for them because they knew what was best. Then we would say thank you. Thank you for the pain, sir. Omega.'

Have you ever listened to people having sex through a wall? On the other side of the wall: weird private noises, pleasure rising in sound from their guts, buttons being pressed. Imagine there's a wall right down the middle of your brain and one side is normal and the other side is not normal. Now imagine sitting inside the normal half of your brain, doing something normal, eating pasta, reading, but you hear something happening through the wall. Muffled sounds. A right old racket. And they don't know how loud they are being because they're just caught in the moment and their own vices and lusts and needs, and you know there's a girl there and she's having something pushed inside her and the hole in her face is making shapes and every time she feels the shock, her brain sends a signal to her mouth and tells it to scream and so she does and the sound that she makes when she likes it is the same sound that she makes when she doesn't. Anyway, it's not a real girl. It's not even a hallucination. It's just an image protesting as it fades away in the back of your mind. As it dies and I become rid of it. As the walls come falling down. Imagine that. *But the houses of the villages which have no walls around them…they may be redeemed.* The Ancient Greeks didn't use notes when they recited their long speeches; instead they trained themselves in the art of memory. They built big mansions in their brains, with many rooms behind many doors, and filled them up with furniture and statues and urns. Then they associated each room, say, with a different topic like 'Philosophy' and then when they wandered down the hallways of their brains and opened the Philosophy door, there would be a statue in there, and that statue would be associated with the writings of Socrates that they had memorized years ago, and then they would recite from that memory. You can get as intricate and detailed as you like: through a door, then a trapdoor, then a drawer within a drawer within a drawer that contains a Russian doll and each layer of the doll is connected with a different fear, and then the smallest doll is the deepest fear, like the centre of an atom: break that open and you're dead. I told him he was going to get us all killed. *And upon them that are left alive of you I will send a faintness into their hearts and the sound of a shaken leaf will chase them.* People talk about locking things away in little boxes inside their minds. This isn't a metaphor, you know. It's real. The prophets just want the doctors to think it's a metaphor because then they won't bother to guide you through the mansion and help you gently unlock the box, not breaking anything, help you to understand what's inside. No. They'll just give you a piece of paper and some crayons and tell you to express yourself, and then your alters will draw lots of pictures and the doctors will think they've gotten through to you – 'oh look, they've drawn a heart with an arrow in it and an angel with a frowny face' – but you didn't express a single thing. You didn't even move your own hand.

A lot of the inpatients might as well have been outpatients. One girl was reporting everything back to her mother over the telephone: her mother was sixth generation and she was seventh. Loyalty is like planting a recording device inside you. Loyalty is like a chip inside your head that other people can detect with computers. They can see the faith in your eyes. Like a hunger for approval.

When I was four years old, she used to put a mousetrap on my fingers and leave the room. I would scream and scream, but she would only come back in to help me after I'd stopped screaming. She did this every day. This is how those walls were built inside my brain. I learnt to be silent when I needed help. I learnt that screaming makes your loved ones deaf. The problem is, of course, it's not entirely a lie. My mother loved me when I was quiet. She loves me so much. There is love all over the world. And loyalty. There are people who are trained to party. And there are people who are trained to fight. There are people who are trained to be bored. To be dumb. To be irresponsible, responsible, drunk all the time, rampantly fertile, obsessed with money, fluent in desire: Aristotle said the soul of an axe was cutting, and the soul of a hammer was hammering. To hammer. What's the difference if the soul of me was to kill with my mind? Theta. Theta. What's the soul of you? You're wrong if you think your soul is more than one thing. Your soul is an action. A rule that you live by, and it's got nothing to do with values or courage or kindness or stamina. If your action is 'destroying', then you'll destroy. Or you'll spend your life trying not to destroy. It doesn't matter which. Your soul revolves around the same action. Full stop. Live. Die. Go. Stop. Start. Shut down.

But I don't worry about that stuff anymore. There's not a word you could say that would trigger me to do anything. I don't believe that I could look at you and cause a small tumour to form in your trachea that would grow and grow until it spread to your lungs and overtook you. *Whosoever toucheth any creeping thing...* I don't believe that humans can do that kind of evil to each other just by the power of their minds. I don't believe it because I'm cured. The therapist cured me. He said, take the gun, the imaginary gun and vaporize the robots and release the children. Release the child locked in the room in the back of your mind. The child who thought she was gone. Can you imagine what that feels like? When you are a grown woman with nothing inside you and suddenly your childhood is jumping around in the front of your mind, crying and crying with these hot tears falling on your coldness. No you can't imagine. They say they are going to release you by helping you understand what has happened to you, but then you are alone, because they don't know what that understanding feels like – that makes your whole life a lie. Someone filled me up and then someone else emptied me out. A fresh start. Good. Omega. Thank you. Thank you. Omega. Thank you. Can I stop now? Or is there anything else you want to know?

Neil Bartlett

THE OPENING
OF THE MOUTH

The piece should be delivered by one performer, but in two voices. The first voice is one in which the adult voice of the performer can be heard channelling the slightly forced, projected, 'elevated' voice of a thirteen year old reading the Old Testament lesson on a Sunday morning; and the second is the natural voice of the performer, given free reign. The difference between the two voices can be as marked or as elusive as the performer deems fit. Sometimes the change between the two voices should be marked by a clear break; sometimes the shift should be more of a slide. The first of these voices is indicated in the text **thus, by being printed in bold.**

The performer should be in the middle of life.

The word 'fourth' – the second word of the text – may need replacing. If the text is the fourth piece on the bill (which it might well be, since the Book of Numbers is the fourth book of the Bible), then it can stand. But if the piece is the first on the bill, then the word should be first; if it is eighth, the word should be eighth, and so on.

This piece was written by a gay man, but can be performed by anyone who can persuade the audience that they are speaking the words of someone speaking in the first person. It will certainly help if the performer has some evident reason to be interested in the perspective of the ass, rather than being naturally and exclusively one of life's riders.

At the indication * in the text, the performer should gesture quite naturally with her or his hands, opening first one then the other with palms towards the audience, just above hip height. The physical action need not be hieratic or solemn, but for those who recognise it, it will be informed by a memory of the gesture the Vicar made and indeed makes at the altar when he presented and presents the wafers to the congregation just before giving Communion. First the right hand, then the left.

It is crucial to the intention and effect of the piece that the performer should approach whatever stage the piece is performed on from a seat amongst the audience, not from the wings; this is because the person who reads the lesson in an Anglican service approaches the lectern from the congregation, not from the vestry. The first phrase printed **in bold**, in case you're not familiar with it, is what you say when you announce the Old Testament reading to the congregation. I first did this when I was thirteen.

A pause, in which the audience should gradually become aware that one of their number is moving to the stage.

A Bible, with the Book of Numbers marked at Chapter Twenty-two, ready for the reading.

Eventually, after a moment's looking at and reflecting on this extraordinary object, the reader opens the Bible, and begins.

The fourth lesson is taken from The Book of Numbers, beginning when I was thirteen.

What do I remember?

So far, this; the book being there, up there, ready; the getting up; the walking up in front of everybody; the opening the book; the opening of the mouth. The opening of the mouth to speak. Beginning **at the twenty-second chapter, and the third verse.**

Balaam the prophet rose up in the morning, and saddled his ass, and went with the princes of Moab.

And God's anger was kindled because he went: and the angel of the LORD stood in the way for an adversary against him. Now he was riding upon his ass, and his two servants were with him.

And the ass saw the angel of the LORD standing in the way, and his sword drawn in his hand: and the ass turned aside out of the way, and went into the field, –

'…went into the field'; not *a* field, but into *the* field – meaning, well, you know – *the* field – the field we walk the dog in; the field across from Grandma's; the field we cross to reach this place – or the field I walk alone in now, the high field, with the view – so that with the one word, that word, exact, the exact, single word *the*, the story isn't *then*, or *there*, but here, and now, on this or rather that exact Sunday morning, in that building, across that field, in that and now perhaps again this particular and very exactly remembered April light and temperature, with those, and now these, faces gathered together. Gathered together, in…

Where was I?

Who was I? Whose mouth opened?

...And the ass saw the angel of the LORD standing in the way... and turned aside out of the way and went into the field: and Balaam smote the ass, to turn her into the way.

No questions, so far. No wondering what it might be like to jog on the back of an ass, because just as the field in question is the field, familiar, an ass is a seaside donkey; the gait, the smell, the surprising heat; the bristles between the pressed thighs; all exactly familiar.

So no questions. No questions of entitlement in the voice. As yet.

And no questioning that an ass might indeed see the true nature of things better than her rider. Better, though burdened. Though bridled. Dumb. And lurching now for a second time to a hot, bristling, stubborn and stinking halt, because **the angel of the LORD stood then in a path of the vineyards, a wall being on this side, and a wall on that side –**

A wall on *this side**; and a wall on *that**.

So that we're there;

This*; that*. Simple.

Here*;

Now.*...

Then*;

Now*...

There*; here*.

Now.

And when the ass saw the angel of the LORD, she thrust herself unto the wall, and crushed Balaam's foot against the wall, which can bloody hurt, coming off your bike, **and he smote her again.**

No questions still in this pause, because the ear knows that *two* must always be followed by *three*, *twice*, by a third and final. Every reading tells a story. Every story tells a picture. Every picture has a message. This is it;

And the angel of the LORD went further, and stood in a narrow place, where there was no way to turn either to the right hand or

to the left – without stopping, as if I already knew then what I do indeed know now, which is that the narrow place is real, very real, and reached frequently, as in some dream of a downhill car between narrowing rock walls, expecting every moment the grinding grab of rock on the metal, and it's a hired car too – and no less physical and immediate the sensation now when there is no dream, no rocks and no car, no vineyard heat, but nonetheless the journey reaches a narrow and narrowing place, and there is indeed no way to turn **either to the right hand or to the left. And when the ass saw the angel of the LORD, she fell down under Balaam; and Balaam's anger was kindled, and he smote the ass with a staff.**

Breath. Picture; Message.

No one taught me these things; the words did.

And the LORD opened the mouth of the ass,

So that she could speak. Walk up; open the book, open the mouth, and speak. Of course.

and she said unto Balaam, what have I done unto thee, that thou hast smitten me these three times.

What have I done? What have I done to deserve this? When did I ever deserve to speak another's voice, to hear (most magical; most necessary) my own...as another's.

There. Then.

Here. Again.

And Balaam said unto the ass, because thou hast mocked me; I would there were a sword in mine hand, for now would I kill thee. 'Now.' **And the ass said unto Balaam,** am not I myself here, now – **am not I thine ass, upon which thou hast ridden ever since I was thine unto this day? Was I ever wont to do so unto thee? And he said,** hearing this voice of the dumb beast, so called, **he said –**

(A pause.)

O magical, o *necessary* realisation of the riding man, seeing the world for once from a different point of view!;

He said,

(A pause.)

Nay.

(A silence as long as is necessary, both before and after that word, for Balaam's thought, and his realisation that he has done wrong.)

Then the LORD opened the Eyes of Balaam – but I knew then and I know now that they were opened by his unaccustomed *thought; allowed* by this thought, by the magical and necessary realisation of the riding man in the middle of his life that the ridden, bridled life between his pressed thighs, dumb so-called, sees the world also – but from a different perspective; sees, Everything; sees (even) More Than The Rider Sees; and now, the third time it is smitten, Speaks; speaks for all that is not said,

for all that is not spoken,

not spoken yet, anyway,

and so that there, Then, and again, Here, Now, **Balaam saw the angel of the LORD standing in the way, and the sword drawn in his hand** – nice touch that I always thought, it makes me smile, appeals to me unaccountably that matching sword in the angel's hand, so that he should think twice next time he talked about swords so easily, this weighty, middle-aged, riding man – **and he bowed down his head, and fell flat on his face.**

(A softening; a relaxation.)

'…he fell flat on his face.' O, yes. That, then, I didn't know; but I know now. Those words I have in my mouth, now, and that sensation in my life… 'Oh god, with that one did we not fall flat on our faces? Cheers!!' As one might say, in the middle of one's life.

(Back to the reading.)

fell flat on his face.

And the angel of the LORD said unto him, wherefore hast thou smitten thine ass these three times? Behold, I went out to withstand thee because thy way is perverse before me: and the ass saw me, and turned from me these three times: unless she had turned from me, surely now also I had slain thee, and saved her alive.

Take *that*, I think (and say) here, now; but also then. Take *that*, from the angel of the LORD. I imagined, exactly, that voice; imagined, because spoke. Exactly; necessarily; magically.

But Balaam said unto the angel of the LORD, I have sinned; for I knew not that thou stoodest in the way against me: now, therefore, if it displease thee, I will get me back again.

Oh, I can hear him. Oh, I am him, now. Making the excuses – I didn't know, I wasn't aware, I didn't see the sign officer but of course I'll go back, I'll be glad to, just don't – **and the angel of the Lord said unto Balaam, Go –**

(A pause, before the catch in the Angel's offer.)

But only the word that I shall speak unto thee, that shalt thou speak.

Yes of course officer.

I'd be glad to.

Whatever you say…

But

A beat;

But that part of the message is not what I remember.

What I remember is; the book being ready, the getting up, the walking up, the exact temperature and April light, and the starting to speak; the opening of the mouth to speak…and once the mouth of the ass is opened, it is opened.

Then. And now.

Is it not? *(In a voice we haven't heard before; confrontational.)* Why was it, did you say, that thou hast smitten me?

Speak up.

Speak up please.

Speak up.

Now.

Maha Khan Philips

THE RULES

Alright, look. I know I did something wrong.

But do I really deserve to be here of all places? Buried under the dry terracotta earth, bones splitting and crackling from the heat, spirit hovering overhead but never settling?

They're all talking about me, you know. I can hear them, even though the flesh around my ears has already played host to an insects' picnic. It was good flesh, while it lasted. It served me well, people always admired it, some even too much.

Still, I welcome the insects. At least they are honest in what they want from me. Look how quickly they do their work, devouring me, isn't that amazing? Let them have their nibbles, while I listen without earlobes.

In the village where I used to live, they call me the Evildoer. The Misguided One. The one who couldn't accept that rules are *rules*. What did she have to go and do that for, they whispered. Her life was *fine*. She had a roof above her head, didn't she? And plenty to stuff her face with? No disease had taken her loved ones away. And what had she known of the drought, of the way stalks of wheat just shrivelled into black confetti and left children crying with hunger, she was gone long before that. Wanting more, always, that one. The rest of us, well, we are really suffering.

When I lived amongst them, the people told me: the law will decide your fate, for our judges are charged to hear the causes between our brethren, and judge righteously between every man and his brother, and the stranger that is with him.

Every man. And his brother. *And* strangers. Those bloody self-righteous do-gooders. I was not a man, or a brother, or a stranger. I was a mere woman. And so I was condemned.

But hang on, hang on, I know what you're thinking. I deserved it right? I did kick him in the balls, which is definitely a no no, it says so in the rules. In black and white, underlined, with visual aids, because half the village is illiterate. He didn't even report it, though he fell on his knees at once and blew out of his nostrils in short bursts, his face plum coloured and sweaty.

On his knees. Sweating buckets, I tell you. The memory brings me joy, and why shouldn't it? Men and their nether regions, on display to the world, vulnerable for the kicking. Is it any wonder then, that men make rules to protect themselves?

No, he didn't say anything. It was his way of acknowledging everything he had taken from me. He did hit me in the face though. Funny, how much his fist could bring pain, because he was a slight man, for a farmer. Slight, and full of smells that made me want to vomit. Of the animals, and unwashed body and rotten eggs. Of dampness.

It was how he smelt that first time. The day we met, the day he sealed my fate.

But I'm getting ahead of myself, aren't I? Because after the kicking of the balls incident, and the punching in the face affair, I made a decision. I wish I could say it was difficult, but it wasn't.

I slit his throat while he slept.

It felt good, I admit it, okay? I took solace from the fact that his blood warmed my hands, that his eyes jerked open briefly, looking stunned. And then glazed over, so fast, faster than I could have imagined. I gripped his hunting knife tightly, because my hands were slippery with bits of his throat on them, and continued to saw through bone, even after I knew he was dead. I think I whistled a tune, something the mothers sing to their babes to get them to sleep. I don't completely remember.

I've just realised something.

Where is my tormentor now? Shouldn't he be here too? In this place?

Is this hell?

Please don't tell me his soul went to heaven, that really wouldn't be fair.

I know what you're thinking, I can almost see it. *I killed him.* Of course I deserve to go to hell. Of course he should be in heaven, the poor man. But you haven't heard my side of the story yet, so don't judge. Let he who is without sin cast the first stone...oh wait, that already happened, didn't it? I'm messing up the timeline.

It's confusing when your body is one place, and your mind is somewhere else. They stoned me already, little nicks and slices, while I bled and pleaded for mercy.

So here's what happened. I was made of beautiful flesh, as the insects have already established, and I was blessed to have a kind father. I fell in love with a good man, a man from the city. In love. How does that even happen? He was a lawyer. He had thick locks of brown hair and beautiful, soulful eyes and thick eyelashes. He smelt of the stars and...

What? You think I'm romanticising? Don't roll your eyes. But this was love, I keep telling you. He was everything to me. He gave me books, he wanted me to become as knowledgeable as he was. He wanted me to see the world through his eyes. He told me about great cities, all the places we would go. The villagers said I was getting high and mighty.

Well, excuse me for wanting a life.

In any case, that life never happened, because our marriage never happened.

I sent him on his way to talk to my father, who was already preparing to embrace him as son. I left him and went to sit in the fields, amongst the lilac flowers and the small grass of baby wheat. I watched the butterflies lazily go about their business, I listened to the hum of crickets and felt the sun on my face. I thought, soon I will be married, and away from this place. I should enjoy it, while I can. And so I slept.

When I woke, he was there. No, not my love, but my future husband. He already had his shoes off, he was fumbling with his belt. And soon his pants were down too. And then? Well then there was pain.

Rules are rules. And here is what our rules, black and white and underlined and graphically illustrated state: if a man finds a damsel that is a virgin, which is not betrothed, and lay hold on her, and lie with her, and they be found, then the man that lay with her shall give unto the damsel's father 50 shekels of silver, and she shall be his wife. In our village, this rule is listed on a tablet, with a picture of a stick man, on top of a stick woman. Both of them are smiling, and the woman has some blood around her stick nether regions, to make it clear that she is a virgin. Not much imagination in our village, I'm afraid.

Of course, as with all rules, there are technicalities. Did the man I love reach my father and gain his consent before the beast ploughed into me? If he did, then we were betrothed, and the beast would be killed for his crimes. But if I did not belong to another man, then, it suited everyone concerned to tie up loose ends. Everyone except me, that was.

As it happens, my father was drinking tea with an old friend. The man I was to marry, the lawyer, had not yet had a chance to declare his intentions. And afterwards, when my rapist had not the 50 shekels to claim me, my lawyer, my own love, gave him the money. He got all pompous about it too. What has happened cannot be undone, he said. I cannot marry nor support you now. Better this wastrel live, and atone for his sins by keeping you, than die, and leave you all alone to fend for yourself.

What were my sins, I asked, to receive such a cruel punishment?

Oh please, he said. You are spoiled for me now. Let's just accept our fate. For what nation is there so great, that had statutes and judgements so righteous as the law given to them by God?

I spat in his face, and he called me a whore. Others called me that too. And the beast? Well, he couldn't believe his luck.

So here I am, an insects' picnic.

Now there is a drought, nothing is left of the wheat field stained with my blood except dust. And look how the villagers wail and complain that God is punishing them, because of the evil I did. If I could, I would lift myself out of the ground, insects and all, and laugh in their faces. If I could, my spirit would stop hovering and come down, so I could pinch their bodies while they sleep and leave sinister looking bruises.

Sadly, I cannot. Because even here, wherever here is, rules are rules.

And we all know that rules just can't be broken.

Daisy Hasan

SOLE FIDE – BY FAITH ALONE

This story is set in Mizoram, one of the eight states of the region known as 'North-East India'. Christianity is the dominant religion of the state but in recent years a section of the populace has converted to Judaism claiming that the Mizos are one of the lost tribes of Israel. The story responds to the Book of Joshua by detailing this modern-day quest to find the 'Promised Land' and in so doing also reflects the impact of Christianity in this remote part of the world.

Joshua Ringa Vanlal used to be a Christian before he became an insurgent after which he was a rocker much before he'd been a biker, long after he'd been clean – but he'd put all of that behind him for now he was a Jew – a friend to the Bnei Menashe – one of the lost tribes of Israel.

In Mizoram, steeped in Christian piety and Bible-philia, a loner among the Christian brotherhood with a mind of his own is a sign of a second coming. In fact they had seen Joshua coming ever since, in a humble hamlet in the forests of North-East India in the 1950s, a Christian revival party had gone out of control believing it was the lost tribe of Israel and had awaited a messiah to take it back to the lost land.

Joshua had found himself pledged to this enterprise, thriving in the twenty-first century, by his father, Babe – once an appropriately named cherubic infant, now a corpulent business man.

The story of how Babe had adopted Joshua is part of Mizo folklore. A Nepali boy who worked in Babe's bamboo warehouses and who usually got drunk in the few illicit liquor stores that operated by night in Aizawl, the capital of Mizoram, had rushed into work declaring he had seen a huge crowd gathered around an abandoned child whose feet were tattooed, declaring they were,

On the way to the Promised Land.

Babe, then a devout Presbyterian who commanded much clout in the community, had rushed out to investigate this story. When he saw the green-inked claim on the baby's feet and squinted in the ancient wisdom that radiated from the baby's face, he had felt compelled to take the baby home. There was no dearth of women who could look after the child.

'Surely something great is among us', people said when they saw the boy's feet and this encouraged Babe to prophetically name the child 'Joshua'. His mind had begun to wander and he would often look distracted from the diurnal routines of moneymaking and Christian piety.

'Joshua – Son of None!' said the women in whose care he had delivered his new-found baby but others around the mystery boy were more charitable. 'He's bound for glory, that boy is...', they often gossiped convinced that Babe was grooming the boy 'for divine pastures.'

Joshua grew rapidly but the tattoo on his foot faded with time as did questions and rumours about who had abandoned the boy.

Babe had started seriously thinking that the Mizo tribe were physically related to the children of Abraham and when Joshua turned eighteen he thought the time had come to test his beliefs.

'Can it be possible?' he asked Reverend Rema with whom he worshipped at the local Presbyterian Church.

The Reverend was sceptical but said, 'Some groups do believe they are physically related to the Children of Abraham.'

'Perhaps spiritually related?' Babe proffered hopefully.

'Perhaps,' said the Reverend in a non-committal way.

***

Joshua was excited. He had turned out to be a beautiful boy with a solemn face which seemed to be aware that a weighty future lay ahead of him.

'You've tried doing a lot of things haven't you,' his friend Andy said to him when he told him about his involvement with the Bnei Menashe.

'You've played some deadly instruments,' Andy grinned. They had both been part of the armed struggle against the Indian government for more freedom.

Andy had dipped his finger in several pies too, but the skinny, long-haired boy had a lightness of manner that appealed to Joshua's gravity.

Joshua's unconventional beginnings had gradually made him realize that he could lead any group and he usually attracted more followers than detractors.

'Anything you do is mostly alright with me,' Andy relented even though the enterprises they had both undertaken so far had usually failed because of one mishap or another.

Joshua was not without doubts but said, 'Perhaps this will be an act of faith that succeeds.'

'Perhaps,' said Andy in a loyal way.

***

Babe had started holding public meetings where he presented Joshua confidently calling him 'Sword – The Leader. I stake my right to future power on a new Mizo identity,' he declared.

He had recently founded the Chhinlung-Israel Peoples Convention and was campaigning across the state to change the name of the Mizo tribe to Chhinlung-Israel.

Joshua was sensing a turn in his chaotic life. Andy nervously accompanied him but kept looking around to make sure none of the Christian cops were lurking around.

'The Mizos' Jewish connection is more than a thousand years old and can be traced to a cave in China where the remains of the lost tribe of Menashe were hidden.' Babe's voice rose in confidence as he addressed the crowd.

'They called themselves Chhinlung, named after the cave,' he said, 'and over the years they made their way south, settling for good in our own Lushai hills.'

Reverend Rema passed by. 'You guys stick together – God bless...,' he mumbled and Babe said, 'Thank you so much Reverend – we wish you were with us.'

Reverend Rema was on his way to keep vigil. The Church condemned every trespass as it continued to bless everyone – even the rats that had been the cause of the worst insurgency the state had ever seen. They had triggered a pestilence, then a famine then a full-blown civil war. Babe was convinced that the people needed a new religion. He paid heed to the rumours that many people had the AIDS virus. He was convinced that the boys who banged metal so hard were condemned for having deafened God's ears all the way up in heaven.

As they walked home, Joshua caught a glimpse of a purple sun dissolving behind them and felt he was about to discover a planet lost to history in the outermost reaches of the universe spinning further and further away through deep time.

***

A few days later, Babe drove Joshua and Andy to the haunt of the Menashe man – a secluded, numinous Jewish shaman – for a better sense of direction.

'The time is now...,' the Menashe man looked at the clock on the wall of his bare room.

'3.30,' Andy's eyes darted to the clock but that wasn't the sort of time this man was after. He threw on a prayer shawl and began chanting in Hebrew.

Once the chants died down he began hugging Joshua and telling him in a rush, 'I fought against the Indian Army ten years ago, but now I am a Jew... I'm the chazan, the elder, of this Sephardic synagogue.'

'Was this an icon or an idiot,' Andy wondered as he surveyed the man's quivering face and bright eyes.

So far, Andy himself had been a devout Christian. Now he felt what he was doing was controversial in the extreme. Yet he resented the way in which his Church laid down strict rules on the details of his daily life and made God inaccessible to ordinary mortals.

'I want you to follow in the footsteps of the believers who set off for the Promised Land,' continued the shaman. 'Some went North; they saw a train for the first time in their lives and reached as far out as Assam. Others went to the north-east and hit Nagaland. Yet no one reached Israel. But you will for you have been named after he who was appointed to fill the shoes of one of the greatest men in biblical history.'

'Where should we start?' Babe quaked sensing that this man had corroborated his dreams of a divine destiny for his son.

'Perhaps in Awarza,' he suggested himself for he knew that the people who lived on the Bethlehem hillside fought with those on the hillside of Salem in that town.

'Yes go there and meet with Thela. His relatives are in touch with an Orthodox rabbi whose Amishav organization searches all over the world for descendants of the lost tribes.'

He began detailing the similarities between Mizos and Jews –

'The building of altars, animal sacrifice, burying the dead, marriage and divorce, belief in an all-powerful deity, and...,' he concluded ecstatically, 'the number seven!'

A Star of David dangled from a thin gold chain around his neck.

***

'I pray that you will find your brothers,' Babe said to Joshua as they drove down the hill back into Aizawl city. They went into a garage and Andy came out with his brother, Ralt, the mechanic, who would drive them to Awarza by truck and then some way by jeep and they would reach the town in one very long day.

The profound rituals of the Menashe man which Joshua hadn't quite understood nor listened to very keenly had nevertheless inspired him. He collapsed in the back seat of the jeep and shut his eyes.

Ralt was describing to Babe how he had moved from one Christian organization to another all his life.

'We have organizations for the youth, organizations for the middle-aged, and organizations for the old. There are religious organizations and semi-religious organizations and it is assumed that one belongs to all kinds of organizations from the time one is born.'

Andy agreed with his brother. 'Life is quite simply a pre-arranged journey from one organization to the next,' he said.

'It just means there's no one here who can construct a life of their own,' Joshua offered from his slumped position feeling uncertain about everything again.

They drove through hills covered with thick tropical vegetation, bamboo forests, creepers and cane.

An Indian army soldier flagged down the jeep. He got into the back seat without being asked.

Joshua sat up. But the man was unarmed and seemed only after a lift to the next village.

Babe started questioning him about his beliefs.

'Christian not,' said the man in broken English.

'Why not?' Babe tried genially.

'Wife Christian...'

'She is our sister.'

Babe was beginning to remember how he had proselytized among the mainland Hindu soldiers as a young boy. He had lived in Champai at the time and had been part of the Gospel Post, taking the word of God to the Indo-Burma border.

He shut his eyes and imagined he was on a very big ship which was slowly approaching an Egyptian shore. He could see people bent over in fields. He imagined the ship was entering the Red Sea with Egypt on one side and Arabia on the other and he was transported to the time of the Bible – the Pharaohs, Joseph, the Exodus and the Israelites' forty years trek through the wilderness.

***

They reached the small town of Awarza to the south of Aizawl city in the dead of the night. Joshua was wide awake now and got off the jeep feeling the 'Great Day' had arrived. Everything seemed hushed and secretive in the dark as if a war was on.

There were very few lights from the shacks in the square where they had been dropped off.

Joshua caught sight of a girl standing in the doorway of a ridged iron shack sticking from the side of a deep gorge. She was chewing *kuva* and giving him the eye.

It turned out to be Thela's roadside tea stall. Thela was the chazan of the town's older Ashkenazi synagogue. He was leading a congregation of worshippers in prayers. A netted curtain separated the men from the women.

Thela, who used to pray at the Presbyterian Church but had converted to the Jewish faith in 1972, had run this roadside tea stall for several years.

'Have you come for tomorrow's revival meeting?' he asked when he emerged from the prayers. They learnt that a Christian revival meeting would take place in the morning in the hilly grounds above the town square.

Babe immediately asked him if it would be possible to address the meeting.

'I do believe we are the descendants of a legendary lost tribe of Israel,' Thela said thoughtfully. 'The Christians might also believe this. Yet they will remain one hundred percent Presbyterian.'

'Why?' Babe asked astonished.

'Because they believe in Jesus Christ. For many people it is difficult to go back to the thoughts of our ancestors.'

***

The next day Joshua awoke to the buzzing of a fly and an aching body. He hadn't realized when he must have dozed off on the wooden benches of the tea stall.

The shop was empty. He walked out in the bright daylight and stood uncertainly at Israel Point – the main intersection in the town. He saw Babe waving at him from under Zion Tailors pointing in the direction of the hill. Despite Thela's doubts about whether he would gain any converts, Babe still intended to proselytize among the revivalists.

Joshua could see hundreds of kids in jeans wandering around. The girls were dressed to look like movie stars. He spied Andy among them. Andy seemed on the verge of calling the whole thing off – saying 'you bastards,' – and going off to enjoy himself.

The whole place seemed out on some kind of carnivalesque religious frenzy. Sharply dressed men in suits were making their way to the grounds.

Joshua forgot why he was here and got lost in the great sounds as the dolled up girls rushed around with brooms and kettles, cleaning and wiping, filling and fetching in preparation for the day's events.

The revival was taking place in the grounds outside the town chapel which stood on the hill. As Joshua followed the crowd up the hill, he could hear the beating of the *khuang*. The drum beats grew louder as they approached the grounds.

'The *khuang* is a big part of our traditional and present culture,' said Thela falling in line with Joshua as he walked up the steep road. 'Without it there may have been fewer Christian converts,' he laughed.

They reached the chapel grounds which were milling with people. In the centre of the ground a place had been marked out for those who might wish to dance. The beaten earth was very dry and the dust rose to burn Joshua's eyes.

He thought he spied the girl he had seen the night earlier. Other girls were scattering water from their bamboo water carriers to dispel the dust for the dancers.

People had started singing hymns with great fervour and as the drumming heightened, men and women started gathering in the centre and moving as if in a trance.

'They are being filled with the Holy Spirit and dancing for joy,' said Thela but he refrained from taking part in the proceedings.

People were speaking in tongues but there was no interpretation. Some felt the need to pass on the Holy Spirit to others and made scattering motions with their hands and unexpected noises from their throats.

Babe approached Joshua looking a little diminished in the surrounding frenzy.

'Where's Andy?' he asked. There was no sign of the boy and the drums had now started to drown their voices.

***

The revival continued for several days and Babe had met with little success in taking the town by storm for the cause of the Chhinlung-Israel state.

Andy did not return for several nights and when Joshua finally caught up with him, he saw that the girl, who he now knew was called Pui, was with him.

The dust raised by the revival had cast a ghostly haze on the town. Andy looked like a changed man. Joshua asked –

'You've been very quiet. Do you need to come clean? Are you ashamed of something, Andy?'

'No,' Andy said, 'I'm not ashamed of anything.'

Babe tried to cajole him – 'Don't you think it's a little of our concern, Andy?' he asked slyly. 'You are our family...your offspring will be my grandchild.'

Andy said nothing in response but Pui spoke up. 'Why should you deny him some pleasure? Wouldn't he be better off...if he had some? What harm can it do?'

Joshua was intrigued.

She had approached him with no reverence and he was happy that she seemed to know nothing about his reputation.

'Anyway she won't be here very long.' Andy spoke up for the first time.

'What do you mean?' asked Joshua.

He was trying to keep some secret but it was too slippery.

He saw how beautiful Pui was. But he also knew that this kind of beauty was too wonderful to be without reprisal.

That night he tried to find out more about the girl. No one was willing to reveal much but eventually Thela gave in to his persistent questioning.

'She is dying,' he said. 'Her CD4 count is dipping quickly.' Mizoram had been on the brink of an unacknowledged AIDS crisis and Pui was its latest casualty.

'She has struggled hard to overcome the discrimination. We have isolated her and people like her.' Thela appeared indifferent.

'Pui's mother had the disease and passed it on to her,' he continued. People say she had a son too. But no one knows what became of the boy.'

Joshua shivered weakly and felt a goose walk over his grave.

***

They stayed in the village for another week.

One evening as Joshua was heading into the town square he came face to face with Pui again. He noticed how this dying girl's hands looked, how narrow her hips were yet how straight her legs stood.

This time he was determined to follow her. He fell in step with her and she didn't shoo him away.

She was making her way to the chapel grounds. They went up together and surveyed the surrounding blue hills. She drew a circle around his feet where his tattoo used to be with tapering sensitive fingers. He drew closer to her. He told her why he was here.

She seemed to know nothing about the dislike of the town dwellers. She was splendidly happy. Her life was unreal. 'She is content to sit in the sun,' Joshua thought, 'content to dip her feet in the brook. If she has no good reputation, at least she doesn't have anywhere to go that requires a good reputation.'

***

Things had calmed down considerably since the revival and Babe was beginning to get a small audience in the chapel grounds. He was trying to raise donations for Joshua's trip to Israel.

Joshua sat on the crackling dry leaves at the foot of a maple tree. The hoarse laughing of the men and the shrill cries of gregarious women came to him faintly through his own thoughts. He looked at Pui and felt puzzled and worried.

With a few suggestive words Pui had managed to make his life so far illusory. Her own life seemed much separated from the highly purposeful lives around him. He deeply envied her.

He watched Babe roll his sleeves higher up on his thick red arms.

'A man ought to see everything he can...' started Babe. 'That's experience. I, Friends, have experience. And from this perspective I tell you – we are the chosen...'

Pui, who had been listening intently, turned to Joshua and said, 'Moses descended on the unsuspecting revellers in the valley, armed with a set of commandments – that must have seemed illogically severe to the astounded Israelites. Yet the Israelites obeyed...just like the Mizos obey...we never question...we never speak out...you can't change that...how will your going to Israel change anything here? Will we speak more freely? Acknowledge the problems we have here, which no one wants to talk about?'

Her outburst had tired her and she seemed slight and ragged. 'Yet something was in her,' he thought, 'which I have spent all my life searching for.'

Perhaps it was her loss of purity, her contracting the illness...the great freedom this gave her from needing to belong to any kind of organization or of delivering any kind of vision. She seemed no judge of consequences. His throat constricted, his feet grew restless. There was a great brilliance in her and he felt it growing bigger than the world around him.

He looked up and felt a chill shiver down his spine. He could see that a group of men from the Vigilance Squad had caught hold of Andy. Some kids in jeans were helping the men hold him down.

A young priest with a rosy face took the loudspeaker from Babe and spoke out. 'This church, which, built of mud, has withstood earthquakes...bears witness...that we give a chance at repentance to this poor boy who, by the cover of darkness, has mingled with those that heaven has shunned...'

'Cannibals!' Pui spat out and turned to walk away.

Babe seemed unperturbed. Perhaps this was the chance he was waiting for.

Joshua felt his confidence diminishing and his spirit was nearly gone. He saw Babe approaching him, saying 'where have you been Joshua? I want you to address the crowds.'

Dusk was coming down over the hill.

A way of thinking alien to him came to Joshua. The unfamiliar thoughts that struck him astonished him for their courage and simplicity. The joy of rebellion gushed up in him.

'Why should I go up and speak,' he said. 'I don't have to go there if I don't want to.'

He felt like a boy who had bunked classes to swim in a deep and invigorating sea. If he had been born for a heroic destiny then it was here and now.

He turned to Babe.

'Would it make any difference to you if I pulled out?'

Babe stared at him. 'Why I thought *you* wanted to go...what's happened?' he asked.

'You'll think I'm pretty soft I guess if I tell you. The fact is I've been thinking over what Pui has said...'

Babe started to protest but Joshua continued.

'You never realize that everybody doesn't see things the way you do...and,' he added, 'they don't have to.' For the first time he looked at Babe directly. Babe dodged his eye and looked away.

'I'm telling you, you don't think things like that,' he cried angrily. 'You have no right to come here with me and talk like that.'

Joshua said in a calm voice – 'No need to get mad. I'm just telling you I don't want to go. If you had any imagination you'd see for yourself and you wouldn't have stood there doing nothing to free Andy.'

Babe's face was filled with dismayed excitement. 'Do not back out little Saviour. Listen to your father in God and do not back out. I found you out in the wilderness and saved you from the devils, your relatives. Thou art a little brother of Jesus now. Go not back to thine own people. Listen to an old man.'

Joshua stared hard at the ground and said, 'I am not like the others. I know that. I must help her and then find my own way.'

Babe stepped back and held up crossed fingers. 'Go back to the devil your father then. I am not going to fight this evil. But I make the sign against you and against your entire race.' He got into the parked jeep and taking the wheel himself drove furiously down the long road.

Pui had returned to see what the altercation was about. She stood next to Joshua and they gazed into the distance as Babe's jeep became a pinpoint on the horizon. The night was clear and sweet with stars.

'Help me free Andy...,' he said. She looked at him and nodded.

They could hear the faint, mysterious sounds of the hills.

'The one who inspires you is not the spirit of Moses...but the spirit of God,' she said.

***

References:

In addition to the Book of Joshua in the Bible, this story draws on the following texts:

1. Gwen Rees Roberts, *Memories of Mizoram: Recollections and Reflections* (2001), The Mission Board, Presbyterian Church of Wales.

2. Mona Zote, 'Heaven in Hell: A Paradox', in *Where the Sun Rises, When Shadows Fall: The North-East* (2006), edited by Geeti Sen, Oxford University Press.

3. Subir Bhaumik and Eric Silver, 'Lost Tribe of Israel?' (Monday, 6th September, 1999), in *Time World* http://www.time.com/time/world/article/0,8599,2054640,00.html (Date accessed 25th August 2011).

Tom Wells

BEARDY

SAM.

Big and strong and sweet.

Two hours to go till showtime and Sheila Beef. Is. Livid.

Don't know why cos it won't help and it's, it's frightening actually.
She's got her whip and she's just, cracking it cracking it cracking it.
At me, Debbie, the Spangles, Trapezey Pete. Debbie's not fussed, she's
miles away. Looking vague, stroking her beard. I go like: *(Whispers.)*
'Debbie,' but Sheila Beef hasn't noticed. Which is lucky. Just standing
in front of the empty cage and she's sort of, well she's, she's bellowing
really:

'Where is it then?' she goes. 'My lion? Where's my bastard lion?'

Nobody knows.

I mean I do but. Not sure if now's a good time.

Big Spangle says we should look for it. Sheila Beef seems quite keen
on the idea. Medium Spangle says he'll get the gun. That's a mistake.
'I've got four hundred people coming to see that bastard lion', Sheila
Beef's shouting. 'Paying to see it. Alive. You bring it back in one piece
alright? Or you'll end up like Sad Jimmy.'

Medium Spangle says he will bring it back alive, promises he will.
Looks dead worried though.

Still. Divvy up into pairs. I get Debbie which is ace cos, dunno. Just,
like spending time together and that. Just enjoy each other's company
really.

The others set off into Withernsea looking but. Me and Debbie stay back for a bit. It's sunny out, September sunny, but breezy too. The sides of the Big Tent are flapping. We duck inside. Poles are creaky. Little trickles of dust come down, from the woodworm. Settle on me and Debbie like mucky frost.

'Come on then,' she says, 'what's up with you?'

Don't know what to say really. Pull a face.

'I've done something stupid.'

'You won't've done,' she says.

But I have.

*

Takes about twenty minutes to get there, me and Debbie, walking away from town. It's one of those places, seasidey places that are a bit, dunno. Not really on the way to anywhere. Sort of a dead end. But we're moving on tomorrow so. Pass a few houses, tumbledown sheds, couple of old fridges and then just, away, into the fields. It's better here. Dead flat and there's all barley growing. You can see the sea an' all. Smell it. Debbie's stretching right up on her tiptoes taking these big deep breaths. Proper lungfuls. Reckons she'd like to live by the sea one day, live here. Just in a little bungalow. Maybe be a mobile hairdresser, get a Renault Clio and that.

She's off to do a BTEC, Debbie. It's a secret. Hair and beauty.

She doesn't need a BTEC to be beautiful.

We get to this big fence and Debbie's struggling a bit. I just lift her over, one-handed. Plonk her down. Really annoys her when I do that. But we've made it anyway. I point in the ditch and Debbie breathes out like:

Breathes out.

Both sit down. Grass is tickly. And we look, and we look, and we look.

'Um. It's dead,' I tell her.

Debbie nods.

'Sheila Beef will not like this.'

Shake my head. 'No.'

'What happened?'

And I just have to sort of... 'I killed it.' Cos, um. Cos I did.

Tell her about Sheila Beef on the phone, going on how this lion'll save the circus, it's the best thing we've got, only thing we've got really, no one gives a shit about the freaks and that. And then afterwards I went out and it was just sitting there, looking at me. Smug. With its, with its mane. Like it knew.

'So yeah,' I tell her. 'I just sort of...'

SAM mimes catching it.

'you know, and then...'

Wrestling it, pinning it down.

'and then just...'

Breaking its neck.

'Yeah.'

Sometimes, being strong and that, it isn't that good. What it is: I get into scrapes.

'Dragged it here so she wouldn't... But it's not an easy thing to hide really. In Withernsea.'

Debbie's thinking.

I ask her 'What shall I do?'

But she just looks confused.

'Can you hear buzzing?'

'Oh,' I say, 'I forgot.'

Get a stick and sort of lift up the side of the lion. There's this gash, this hinge of flesh down his ribcage just. Prop it open. Lay on our fronts, peer inside.

It's, honestly. It's another world.

A world that is full of bees.

And the sun's getting low now, shines through the dead lion's skin, shines through all this honeycomb like little lightbulbs, little hexagons, tiny. And the bees, they're crawling all over it, just doing bee stuff. They don't know it's odd. But it is though. It's quite an odd thing to be doing inside a lion. Most of all though, there's honey, all this honey dripping down and welling up and just, everywhere just. Sweetness.

And Debbie's laughing.

'What?'

'You're such a weirdo,' she says.

And I think: 'we both are.' Don't say it though. Not to Debbie.

Just, reach inside the lion, break a bit off. Honeycomb.

'Sam!'

'What?'

'The bees.'

'It's alright', I say. Cos they don't want to sting you really. It kills them to sting you.

Give half to Debbie. We eat some, lick it off our fingers, dripping everywhere. It's mega. Like sipping candlelight or. Or brandy or. Or a bit of a comet. Glides down your throat and. Yeah.

Debbie's got some stuck in her beard. It's looking well lush this afternoon, Debbie's beard. Glossy and, and soft and that. I lick my thumb, reach across, wipe the honeycomb off. Smile. Her lip's wobbling a bit. She gives me this look but I just, I dunno. Get the little bit of honeycomb, pop it on the tip of my tongue. Like a crumb or. Or a question.

But she can't even look at me. Looks at her hands. Pulls up a few bits of grass.

'Better go,' she says.

I'm worried now.

'You won't tell her?' I say. 'You won't tell Sheila Beef?'

She promises. Looks a bit shifty.

'Long as you don't tell her I've got this.'

And she gets this hanky out her pocket. Undoes the corners dead carefully, like petals. Shows me what's inside.

'Debbie!'

She's not allowed near anything that cuts.

'Found it in Sad Jimmy's stuff.'

And I want to take it off her, stop her doing it but. Hear this voice, dead near, all 'bastard this, bastard that.' There isn't time.

Tell Debbie: 'leg it.'

And she does.

*

Sheila Beef's answer to not having a lion is to dress me up as a lion. Lock me in the cage. Hide me round the back of the Big Tent.

'Ready for the finale,' she says. Rubbing her hands.

I'm not that into it as a plan.

Try telling her I'm here to be big and, and strong. Got to put my little shorts on, do some heavy lifting but she just, dunno. Picks her whip up. Disappears.

I can hear the crowd going in. They're well rowdy. Cos it's the last night and everything. Debbie's getting the worst of it. She's in the ticket booth, there's all these pissed-up lads asking to tug her face. Hear them shouting: 'give us a kiss then,' wolf whistling and that. Women won't go near her in case they catch a beard. Kids just look at her, burst into tears.

And the Big Tent's filling up, creaking and groaning, sagging, on its last legs sort of thing but Sheila Beef's not fussed cos: showtime. She's

got the Spangles warming up, chucking the Little One backwards
and forwards, spinning him, bouncing him and that. Trapezey Pete's
having a wee. There's a little gap in the line where Sad Jimmy would've
stood. Sheila Beef's inside, whipping the crowd up. Cheering,
clapping, stamping. It's a bit much, to be honest, all this noise. Start
to panic a bit. Cos I don't mind doing the strong man stuff but this
is all, this is a bit new. And Debbie must know I'm worried cos she
comes to see me.

'You alright?'

Make a face like 'not really' but she's a bit distracted to be honest. I
think it's one of those times when she's not really wanting to know
if I'm alright or not. Sometimes it's just something you say. And
Debbie's all edgy and that, looking over her shoulder, breathing fast.

'I need you to do me a favour', she says.

And I'm like: 'course.'

'Need you to buy me some time.'

She's got all the ticket money with her, and Sad Jimmy's razor so I can,
I sort of work it out, what's going on. And it's. Um. I dunno.

'Will you do that for me Sam?'

So, yeah. I just:

Slow, sad nod.

And she leans in through the bars, Debbie, and she kisses me. Just a
tiny kiss, like a blink really, a flutter. Feel her lovely soft beard on the
side of my face, much softer than I expected.

And she's gone.

Cos she wants to be ordinary, Debbie. More than anything.

I reckon she couldn't be ordinary if she tried. Reckon she's too
wonderful but.

But it doesn't really matter what I think.

*

I'm not that good at being a lion.

Especially since they were all expecting a real lion. I'm just a tit in a furry top.

Try to roar a bit but. Won't come out.

The crowd are getting angry now, hammering with their feet, chucking all these empty cans, full cans, rocks and that, anything they've got. They think that's alright, an alright thing to do. Think it's fair enough. And Sheila Beef's still here, whipping. Getting them all wound up. Tent's groaning like a shipwreck, splinters dropping from the ceiling. It's about done in. Just want it to stop really.

So what I do: I think about Debbie.

Think about how her life'll be better and that. Without this. No beard and, and with her bungalow and her BTEC and everything. Hope she'll manage it. Cos it's hard work really, holding a life together. If no one's shown you how. Difficult, I think.

And I think there's, there's a way I can help her, hopefully.

So I'm eyeing up the pole in the middle of the Big Tent, holds it all up. Thinking: probably as rotten as the rest. One good shove I reckon. Whole lot'll be crashing down. This lot inside and, and me in the middle.

And I don't want to do it really. But. I dunno it's. It's the best I've got.

Try to feel peaceful. Strong.

And I push, and I push, and I push.

Stella Duffy

THE BOOK OF RUTH (AND NAOMI)

Two women sit beside each other. They are different in race and/or accent. There is at least a fifteen year age gap between them.

They speak to us, perhaps look at each other occasionally for reassurance, to confirm the story, to nod, but generally they speak out.

NAOMI: When Elimelech died...it wasn't easy, we were in Moab, I wasn't with my own people. Grief's hard enough, but when you're not at home...

RUTH nods, supporting, encouraging.

NAOMI: And I'd never known any different, from my father's house to his, I wasn't used to being alone, looking after myself, and I had the boys...

RUTH: Mahlon and Chilion. Ephrathites, from Bethlehem-Judah.

NAOMI: Like me. And Elimelech.

RUTH: I'm Moabite.

NAOMI: Yes.

RUTH: Yes.

They smile at each other.

NAOMI: So the first thing to do was find wives for the boys. We'd already met Orpah...

RUTH: Not Oprah. Common mistake.

NAOMI: Lovely girl.

RUTH: As long as you don't get her name wrong.

NAOMI: She made Chilion happy.

RUTH: She did.

NAOMI: My baby...

           RUTH waits, letting NAOMI remember.

RUTH: And then Mahlon and I...

NAOMI: My firstborn. You were a good match.

           RUTH doesn't say anything but we understand she's not sure.

NAOMI: You were, you'd have had lovely children...

           Both women wait, remember, the children that didn't come. They may have different feelings about this.

RUTH: The Lord giveth...

NAOMI: Yes.

           Pause.

NAOMI: First Elimelech, then both my sons. Both. Husband and sons. I'd left my home for them, it's what we do, I had no one.

RUTH: You had us.

NAOMI: I told the girls they should go back to their own people. They were still young, it wasn't as if I'd have more sons for them to marry.

RUTH: Or that new sons would have wanted wives twenty years older than them.

NAOMI: No.

RUTH: We tend to have our girls marry old men, not the other way round.

NAOMI: Orpah left...

RUTH: I stayed.

NAOMI: You did. And we came back.

RUTH: To Bethlehem. It was all new to me.

NAOMI: You were new for them.

RUTH: I was. Star attraction, come see the Moabitess!

NAOMI: They weren't that bad, were they?

RUTH: Maybe not. As you said, grief, it's hard when you're away from home. And I was grieving Mahlon still.

NAOMI: Of course you were. It was the beginning of barley time, I suggested Ruth go and help out with the harvest –

RUTH: It was more, 'That Boaz, he's a relative, see if you can't get him to notice you.'

NAOMI: A nice boy.

RUTH: Hardly a boy, he was your age if he was a day.

NAOMI: We needed somewhere to stay, an income, sometimes you just have to use what you've got.

           RUTH smiles at NAOMI, it's a 'using what you've got' smile; NAOMI shakes her head and laughs.

NAOMI: Exactly. And this way, if he liked her, Ruth would stay in the family.

RUTH: Stay with you.

NAOMI: Yes.

RUTH: Boaz was all right, he said I could glean in his fields, told his girls to give me a hand –

NAOMI: She knew nothing about harvesting barley.

RUTH: Why would I? He ordered his young men to keep away. That was helpful.

NAOMI: It was.

RUTH: I asked him, 'Why are you being so kind?' and he said...

NAOMI: I'd told him what a lovely daughter-in-law you were!

          They both burst out laughing.

RUTH: Lovely!

NAOMI: Lovely!

RUTH: He asked that the land would bless me. You have to
          understand, everyone else was treating me like a foreigner,
          Boaz said the Lord approved of me even though I wasn't...

NAOMI: An Israelite. Very broad-minded, Elimelech's family.

RUTH: He invited me over...

NAOMI: We knew it was working then.

RUTH: Bread and vinegar, they dip bread in vinegar – not my idea of a
          good supper – and he ate some of the corn I brought. That was
          it.

NAOMI: You don't eat a girl's parched corn if you don't fancy her.

RUTH: Weird customs this lot.

NAOMI: Maybe, but he sent his lads back with an ephah of barley for
          us.

RUTH: That's about a bushel.

NAOMI: Four pecks. Eight gallons.

RUTH: Twenty-one point seven seven two four kilos. Quite a few bags
          of sugar.

NAOMI: Barley.

RUTH: Yes. After that, she was all 'Get washed and anointed and
          dressed up, go and show yourself when he's spent the night
          eating and drinking.' Said I should go in when he's lying
          down, and uncover his feet – his feet!

NAOMI: I know what Elimelech's family are like.

RUTH: She said he'd tell me what to do. So I did.

NAOMI: And he did.

RUTH: Eventually. Took a while. First of all he was freaked by me coming into his room; half-pissed, who wouldn't be? So I whispered...what's that phrase you like?

NAOMI: Spread your skirt over thy handmaid.

RUTH: Handmaid. Yes. Anyway, Boaz was all about praising the Lord because I'd gone to him and not one of the younger or richer blokes, but then he got worried and said there were other men who were more closely related...

NAOMI: To Mahlon.

RUTH: Yes, and that I should lie down until morning in case one of them wanted to come in.

NAOMI: And if not, then he would –

RUTH: Sleep with me –

NAOMI: If no one else did. Come in.

RUTH: That bit wasn't so great. Lying there, not knowing.

NAOMI: Sorry.

RUTH: Not your fault. We needed to make it safe...

Pause.

RUTH: And that did, make it safe. In the morning, Boaz measured my veil against six lengths of barley and gave me the lot.

NAOMI: I could have wished him further for that. There's only so many barley loaves you can eat, we had barley for weeks after. Rissoles, risotto, barley-stuffed artichokes, barley frittata...

RUTH: *(Interrupting.)* I thought this meant we were together, Boaz and I. I'd be able to stay, take care of Naomi, it would all be fine...

NAOMI: It was.

RUTH: But not right away. Boaz insisted on all this protocol, told his kinsmen there was a parcel of land that belonged to Elimelech and asked if any of them wanted it. He meant me. I was the parcel of land.

NAOMI: Over-fond of analogies, that one.

RUTH: When one of them said yes, they'd take the parcel of land, Boaz said he'd have to buy it from me...

NAOMI: I believe he called you the Moabitess?

RUTH: Exactly, buy it from the Moabitess. Then that kinsman –

NAOMI: We never did get his name.

RUTH – said he was worried about his 'inheritance', sullying his name with a Moabitess, so he took off his shoe, gave it to Boaz, and that meant the deal was done. Boaz accepted the man's shoe to confirm he'd bought us. The two of us.

NAOMI: The two of us.

RUTH: Elimelech and Chilion and Mahlon's leftovers.

NAOMI: My boys.

RUTH: Boaz and I were officially together then, because of the shoe swapping. I got pregnant fairly quickly, and everyone was all over Naomi, because there was a grandson, and Boaz didn't last much longer, and then it was just the two of us. Again.

NAOMI: With Obed.

RUTH: My son.

NAOMI: My grandson; the father of Jesse, the father of David.

RUTH: My great-grandson David.

NAOMI: So we did all right, in the end. It was hard – sending her off, Ruth, to be with Boaz – but it wasn't for long, and we got the baby out of it.

RUTH: Our boy.

NAOMI: And it meant she could stay.

RUTH: I could stay.

Pause.

NAOMI: I'd always known I think, that there was something else, I got on well with Orpah, I wasn't a bad mother-in-law –

RUTH: You were great.

NAOMI: But it was different with Ruth, from the first day they
           brought her to meet Mahlon, there was something... So when
           Elimelech died, then both the boys...and she –

RUTH: Lay down at your feet. Spread my skirt.

NAOMI: Yes. It wasn't strange, not at all.

RUTH: Yet you told me to leave.

NAOMI: I thought it would be better for you. Start a new life.

RUTH: I didn't want a new life. *(Quietly.)* Wife. Intreat me not to
           leave thee, or to return from following after thee: for whither
           thou goest, I will go; and where thou lodgest, I will lodge: thy
           people shall be my people, and thy God my God: Where thou
           diest, will I die, and there will I be buried: the Lord do so to
           me, and more also, if ought but death part thee and me.

NAOMI: What could I say to that?

           Pause.

NAOMI: I brought her back. Now they all say I'm the most fortunate
           of women, 'thy daughter-in-law, which loveth thee, which is
           better to thee than seven sons'.

RUTH: Much better.

NAOMI: Yes.

           They smile, at us, at each other, and kiss, lightly.

RUTH: Ought but death.

NAOMI: Ought but death.

           Then they hold hands, looking out again, to us.

           The End.

Andrew Motion

DAVID AND GOLIATH

No one not even the king knew where I came from.
Everyone knew what lay ahead in the deep valley
between two mountains. Six cubits and a span high.

Brass helmet. Coat of mail and the weight of the coat
was five thousand shekels of brass. Greaves of brass
on his legs and a target of brass between his shoulders.

The grip of his spear was thick as a weaver's beam.
Its head alone weighed six hundred shekels of iron.
and one bearing a shield went before him. *Choose*

you a man for you and let him come down to me.
That was his message. My message was a question:
Is there not a cause? I took up my staff in one hand,

my sling in the other, and picked five smooth stones
from the brook. I looked at the stones and they looked
back at me. The stones knew all there was of history.

Generously supported by the Marquess of Salisbury

Wole Soyinka

THUS SPAKE ORUNMILA...

In the name of Olodumare, Deity Supreme, who sits not in judgement, but presides in ambidextrous equity, right and left, over the affairs of humanity, and to whom notions such as infidel, unbeliever or pagan are for ever anathema. **A-a-ase.**

Opening bars of 'How are the Mighty Fallen'. Fade out as Reading begins.

How are the mighty fallen!

Are there stars still glistening in the firmament of kings?

There is no tragedy in the overthrow of kings, be they consigned to dungeons, banished, garroted or guillotined, thrown over their royal parapets or impaled on their own palace spikes; the real tragedy of our time is lodged in the walking, strutting two-legged *things* that would be kings, tongues of cant that promise liberation but fashion new forms of enslavement, harbingers of an era of enlightenment, in truth tawdry, inglorious mimics even of the flawed majesties of nation builders and sometimes – wreckers.

Kingship has ever carried its own seeds of destruction, albeit slow in germination. Even language has taken its toll. 'Scandal' has displaced 'royal dalliance'. Scions of ancient dynasties affect 'the common touch' but only as the lowest social mores. Bribery stains the family escutcheon, pollutes the founts of moral peerage, scorns service as pedigree. These are not even intermediaries of business interests seeking the ears of governments, but ermine dragged in seamy deals through royal corridors, bordellos, and racetracks. Where reduced in stature by the jackboots of the military, they grovel for contract leftovers, scramble to serve 'the government of the day'.

Are these the monarchs whom the griots rhapsodised? Shaka of the amaZulu? Asantehene of the Golden Stool? Richard Plantagenet and his chivalrous rival Emperor Saladin? No, nothing but cruelties of today's tinsel crowns endure.

Their ears are no longer tuned to the lyrical strings of Sundiata's balafon, the love offerings of Suleiman or the limpid cadences of King David's harp and psalms. Their portion is the raucous immediacy of Jimmy Cliff's electric guitar and lyrics, fervid, turbid, and subversive.

Up: Jimmy Cliff's 'The Harder They Come'.

> *The harder they come*
> *The harder they fall, one and all,*

Fade out.

The crash of the mighty generates not a whiff of purifying lament. No bard wraps them in lyric shrouds, not even as one king in tribute to another. When they die, the people turn their heads away, spit or dance on their graves. For the poets – and all that is of redeeming grace – have been wasted, tortured, buried alive in prison cells or hounded into exile. The survivors are objects of public scorn for there is only one route their trade permits – turn court jesters, or forever hold their tongues.

We shall not glamorize the past. Let it therefore be acknowledged that, in the arena of cruelty and violence, the honours remain even, ancient and modern are evenly matched. Some, like the Magnificent Suleiman, much given to reflection, acknowledged their own entrapment…

What men call sovereignty is worldly strife and constant war.

These ancient Kings, now cloaked in the soothing patina of antiquity and elevated to epic magnitude, rode into history on steeds of violence, often steeped in superstition, prey to dreams and auguries but then, were they not just as fearful and cruel as the people over whom they reigned?

Put two thousand prisoners to the sword did King Richard Plantagenet, to the applause of his Christian followers! 'Give us seven men from the House of Saul that we may hang them,' thus bring an end to the cycle of blood-debt that had brought famine on the land. King David obliged, and hanged indeed were the offering. And it is told that the Lord of Hosts approved the act, for Nature was appeased, and the wind of famine dropped. How quaint they would have found the symbolic Rites of Restitution even of pre-literate times, or a Truth and Reconciliation Commission of the reign of that great Avatar of Peace, Nelson Mandela and his prophet, a man of great visionary valour, Desmond Tutu.

In truth now, how much has changed? In two thousand years and more, how far up the ladder of evolution has humanity clambered? Is the blood-lust withered in the veins of the species? Figures of myth only reflect human tendencies, sometimes histories, else visionary aspirations, often all inextricably tangled. Was Gilgamesh history or myth? He built cities, enacted laws, was not spared his share of brutalities. Or King Thor, at once god of fertility and destruction. His Yoruba sibling bears the name Sango, another handyman with the hammer of thunder, destroyer yet administrator of justice. All were kings and gods in the same body and essence. King David was Ogun in mortal visitation, Ogun, god of war, custodian of the sacred oath, Muse of the poets, breath at the blacksmith's bellows, cultivator, pioneer of the sciences. And the mortal tendencies that bind both, and many more – a love of women, wine, and strife. Nation builders both but – inevitably – people destroyers. Nonetheless, theirs were realms where poetry wore the robes of grace, and catharsis…

Faintly in the background: 'Dead March in Saul'.

> *How are the mighty fallen,*
> *Tell it not in Gath, publish it not in the streets of Ashkelon…*
> *Ye mountains of Gilboa, let there be no dew,*
> *Neither let there be rain upon you, nor fields of offering…*

That was – once upon a time. The prophet's voice today is of Jimmy Cliff and it is not the voice of catharsis, but of pending anomie and just deserts, the voice of the new prophets, not tuned to patience, deaf to the sermonizers of self-denial, dismissive of divine apportionment, aroused to the primordial cry of instant equity.

> *So as sure as the sun will shine*
> *I'm gonna get my share now, what's mine*
> *And then the harder they come,*
> *The harder they fall, one and all*
> *O-oh the harder they come*
> *The harder they fall, one and all*

The warnings of the new poets were not heeded. The crash of the mighty narrates the history of mankind, though it takes its toll in human loss. It comes in waves, echoing upheavals of Nature and evoking notions of prophetic empathy, for has the season of convulsions not been felt in frequency and magnitude of floods, earthquakes, firestorms and Tsunamis, stretching from the Atlantic to the Pacific?

How have the mighty fallen? With a thunderous crash, like the statue of Saddam, and with pitiable inelegance. Tsunamis do not grow in deserts but castles built on sands heave and collapse just as surely as sand dunes lift and shift shapes between night and dawn, bury encampments of the complacent desert lords. *They that play the king?* Unasked, unsought, uninvited, one and all, they force wind-filled heads into the royal diadem. It is decreed, *he that plays at king* ends *as flies to wanton gods*. Most shall prove merely fortunate to escape the fate of Saul – beheaded, dismembered and plastered to his palace walls, but not before that broken monarch had witnessed the deaths of his own sons, as has his modern progeny, pinned to the city walls of Tripoli.

Strains of 'The Harder They Fall' in the background.

The bell tolled first in Tunisia, the king was put to rout, still the warnings of Prophet Jimmy went unheeded. Tunisia's commoner, at the bitter end of his tether, sets himself on fire, and the act consumes self-anointed kings across the Maghreb, its flames leap across seas and deserts into arena of ancient and yet unfinished conflicts where once King David, his tribes, armies and adversaries lived, strove, thrived, perished and regrouped. History continues its remorseless turn of the wheel but – without the poetry, no, the poetry has fled, and the language of power is at the mercy of jackdaws, crows, and vultures, augmenting the screech of torturers. And killers. Their lips are ever glued to the name of god. To him is greatness, his greatness extolled even as youth is hanged in the dank secrecy of the prisons of Iran for daring sanctimonious priest-kings, for humming refrains to the gospel of Jimmy Cliff.

Fallen indeed are the mighty civilizations of the race of Persia, of ancient Babylon, dried the fountains of the arts of literacy, collapsed the archways over the valleys of the Tigris, even as the Hanging Gardens of Babylon fore-echoed the gallows destiny of a tyrant, the counterfeiting Suleiman of his age, King Saddam Hussein.

What a stiff-necked breed these king players of modern times! Whatever gods King Qaddafi worshipped, he of the many splendored Bedouin tent with a harem to shield his body, those gods had taken leave of him, as he of his senses, beyond recovery even from the ministrations of King David's harp, or the healing balafon of Sundiata. Once, so long ago, Muammar of the king's palace guard overthrew a dynasty of parasites, but only that the janissary could himself set up a dynasty of one, to whom all bow in fear and homage. But the circle of karma closes on the dissolute rich as on the richly deserving. The arc of restitution distends, then draws ever tighter on thrones of the alienated.

Egypt followed swiftly upon Tunisia, and tremors were felt in Morocco, an earthquake of uncharted dimensions. The kings of Saudi heard, took heed, sent out town criers to spread news of great reform: the price of bread was lowered and other palliatives in tow to douse the flickering flames from Tunisia. But the chant of the populace continues – *Too late, and too little.* And Yemen followed suit, where the king's men dispensed pellets of lead for pallets of bread, the Leaven of Life without which even Freedom is an empty word.

Syria, ancient Arma, buckled at first, then the heart of King al-Assad grew rigid as the Obelisk of Axum. His ears turned away from the warnings of the singing prophet of Jah, he came down ever harder on his people. Syria, a calloused finger of the secret fist of power named Ba'ath, drenched her streets with the blood of commoners. King Muammar, reviled in the Occident as the Madman of Libya took heart and followed suit, donned the iron gauntlet. True, it was indeed madness as of Saul that plagued King Qaddafi but there was also a perpetual high, No one truly knew the substance of his addiction but it answers the same name – alienation. Helicopter gunships spewing fire on human waves, King Muammar no longer sees the teeming servants of Allah – to Muammar, all are vermin, and the nation overdue for cleansing.

Shall we hear the lamentation of a David chanted over their biers? No, their destiny was prefigured in the end of Master-Sergeant King Doe of Liberia, his mouth forced open to serve as a urinal for one of the multitude of children he had orphaned, often in a manner worthy of the ancients. And his ears that were fashioned after the saying '*Ears have they but they hear not*' were sliced off by his captors, for he clearly had no use for them. Thus messily do the mighty fall in a once mighty continent!

Yet again and again, others before them have impaled themselves on the signpost of precedence, visible to all but the blind, deaf and incorrigible. Among the parade of forerunners, let us recall Macías 'Ki'NGuema' of Malabo who had long preceded Saddam to the hangman's noose. To do him final honours, hangmen journeyed forth from distant Morocco, for Macías was a man much famed for his dark powers, more potent than the Witch of Endor, powers that many feared could reach beyond the grave and drag his judges down to his abode in hell.

And in the land of Zimbabwe, *how are the mighty fallen?* Like ruins of the ancient fort of Zimbabwe, landmark of a vanished civilization that multitudes flock to see from the ends of the earth. For Mugabe was a man much beloved of a continent in thrall, a hero of deliverance from marauding tribes, bleached skin and flaxen hair, who crossed the ocean, seeking land, plunder, and slaves. How shall such wreckage of reversals be remembered? No, not through the songs or lamentations of a king-poet. Behold now the false monarchs, who pulled down the edifice raised by multitudes, an edifice named Freedom, leaving nothing of themselves but the shards of fallen idols. Their deaths will leave no imprints but the panegyrics of beneficiaries, for, living, they proved mere shadows flitting past the murals of true kings. *The harder they come, the harder they fall...*

> *Well they tell me of a pie up in the sky*
> *Waiting for me when I die...*
> *So as sure as the sun will shine*
> *I'm going to get my share now, what's mine...*

'What's mine,' is the gospel beamed across the globe by the true owners of Zimbabwe, Ivory Coast, Congo, Libya, Morocco, fanning out from the western tip of North Africa to the furthermost ends of decadent, sanguinary Iran. 'What's mine?' Only that born-with attribute called Freedom. It sustained the slaves from Africa in the Americas. Freedom untrammelled. Ineluctable. Freedom as the unfolding mat of history, as the seizure of humanity in the here and now, freedom as the rotor and rails of vision, freedom in the material and in essence, freedom as the breath of air after rain, fresh and enlivening, as the food of sustenance and the wine of astonishment, intangible yet palpable, freedom as the quarry of the hunt since the time of the earliest human primogenitor, as the diamond-hard crystals settled in sediments of the seer's divination bowl.

The line of Samuel is ended. The priesthood voice is broken, for far too many of the tribe of priests would play the king. The sages are tenured, their counsel cast aside except they fawn upon, and parrot their paymasters. Temple, church, synagogue, mosque and shrine offer less wisdom than will be found in the proverbial mouths of babes. The ancient prophets whose piety made them guarantors of equity are no more, their successors are not sought after but locked in frenzied contest for followers, in contests promoted on television's market shows whose miracles would shame mountebanks, miracles that entrap the feeble-minded or the desperate, to whom no straw is too flimsy to clutch in hope of material salvation. Few, all too few remain of the anointed keepers of books of pieties that shed illumination, for many are rivals in the power stakes of mimic kings and emperors, trapped as flies in the web of recognition. They scream *Submission! Submission!* Yes, but submission to whom? Of whom are they intercessors? To whom do they carry the articles of human surrender, these leeches on human fear?

So where now is wisdom to be found?

Among the needful scavengers of the market after closing hours, the derelicts and touts of motor parks whose scriptures are encrypted on rickety conveyances, bearing goods and jostling humanity – there we find the unfiltered magma from which the lyrics of Prophet Jimmy take form, for indeed the haunts and habitations of the wretched of the earth yield more truths than the homilies of these upstarts, self-seeking rationalists of the *status quo*, dispensers of disempowering platitudes. The immediacy and permanence of truths are plain on the mastheads and panels of ramshackle, dust-gathering chariots that trundle through the roads of Africa, bearing goods and resilient humanity. And what is written there?

No telephone line to heaven. Beware the pie-in-the-sky salesmen, beware the hypocrites who chant – *Power (and all else) comes only from God.* Ask them why they jostle and scramble, train, empower and grant the brainwashed advance absolution to kill and maim. The pie-in-the-sky gospelers gorge like famished crows on the rotting pie of power and domination on earth, yes, even though millions perish at their bequest. These are clerics who would be king, and claim first-name acquaintance with the Almighty. Let us swap places, chants the Prophet – theirs the pie in the sky, mine the sustaining crust on this hard earth.

And it is also written there: *The Beautyful Ones Are Not Yet Born*. It is this lament that scales the snowcaps of Ruwenzori Mountains, cascades down Kabwelume Falls, skims surfaces of lakes of the Rift Valley and roil from steeple to minaret, peak to heartbreak peaks of Rwanda. *The Beautyful Ones Are Not Yet Born*, and the Mighty, despite the industry of the tailors of King Qaddafi and cohorts, of Mugabe patron of Bespoke House, remain as beautiful as the cartoon figures of Mickey Mouse. The fall of all is foretold, barring only the few that number no more than the fingers of one hand. Their monuments will not be found. Can they not read:

No condition is permanent? Even as a slingshot felled mighty Goliath, so today a flying ember from the bonfire of a self-immolator ignites fires across walls of separation and contempt.

The Fall of Man began with the rise of kings. Were not the people warned? *You want a king over you? So be it.* And their Lord placed a king over them, even though – thus attests Prophet Samuel – he was mightily displeased. Yet, to the devil his due – those also reigned who, no less cruel, at least united peoples, established nations, enacted laws, patronized the arts. Kings are best remembered as myths, like Gilgamesh the Sumerian, like Thor of the Vikings or King Oduduwa, myth, king and deity. When they acquire flesh and sceptre, they tear the heart out of humanity and shape it to their heads for crown. Their inventiveness is without limit – tyrant, benevolent despot, emperor, monarch, sultan, dictator, maximum leader, führer, living Guide, divine intercessor, shah, emir, oba, obi, priest-king and prelate, bearers of the Ultimate Word, secular or divine, called Ideology or Scriptures. We know their chequered lineage from ancient times, but how deep into antiquity shall we voyage...?

Strains from the chorale 'How are the Mighty Fallen'.

Shall we begin with Killer King Pharaoh who would not 'let my people go'? No, let one who, from fear of a prophesied new age, plunged households into mourning with a rage of infanticide, serve as the enabling Progenitor. From the Herodian mould sprang the dynasties of King Hitler, and his twin brother, Joseph Stalin...

And Stalin begat many issues, among them Nicolae Ceauşescu who, with his queen, ended at the stake, perforated through his granite heart. His soulmate was Enver Hoxha, known as the prince of darkness, for therein he kept his people, and forbade them even moderate enlightenment. Stalin scattered his seed far and wide across continents, but his truest heir was Pol Pot of Cambodia of whom it is said: Stalin slew his millions, but Pol Pot has slaughtered his tens of millions. Straining to trump the magnitude of Pol Pot in his swathe of land cleansing came King Mariam Mengistu of Ethiopia who truncated the line of Emperor Haile Selassie, King of Kings and Lion of Judah. Rivalry of the Stalinist and the Hitlerite remains the world's legacy, unabaiting, as fierce as the internal rivalries within each House, each newly whelped striving to outdo siblings in deeds of horror and fidelity to the Holy Text, from which all blessings flow. Haile Selassie earned fame for mowing down unarmed students in their place of learning – they had demanded bread for the people, for Haile Selassie's incontinence, year after year, oversaw the Great Famine Treks of Tigre, Wollo and Haraghe, trails marked to this day with signposts of bleached skeletons. Mariam Mengistu eradicated feudal dread, replaced it with radical terror. Seven years of leanness proved prelude to seven more years of famine, for King Mengistu merely collectivised famine as mandated by his Book of Books, uprooted ancient tribes and corralled them in new settlements where they perished in their hundreds of thousands. King Mariam brought death home to urban dwellers, piled high as the lamps on lampposts, to instruct the citizens of a new Age of Reason that had come upon them, for he was the anointed Guardian to the Ultimate Word, inflexible.

The line of Adolf Hitler, though often mongrelized, rendered inseparable from the House of Stalin, since both are united at the tabernacle of Power, had its own illustrious descendants. Prominent of these was King Ayatollah Khomeini, only let this be added: Khomeini was the implacable sword of God whose motto was, 'my predecessor Shah Pahlavi flogged you with whips, I shall scourge you with scorpions', a prelate who sought to extend his dominion all over the world of believers and non-believers alike with the pronouncement: 'Kill the blaspheming poet wherever he may be found, and whatever the laws of his own nation'. Among others are numbered on the continent of Ham, Idi Amin Dada, self-crowned King of Scotland, caterer of human delicatessen to the crocodiles of the Nile. And Macías Nguema whose history we have narrated, in tandem with King Papa Doc Duvalier and his army of zombies and Ton-ton Macoutes, seasoned practitioners of the cult of resurrection. Surpassing even the wealth of King Croesus was reckoned Mobutu Sese Seko Nkuku Ngbendu wa Za Banga, whose irreverent rendition was 'The All-Powerful Cockerel of Inflexible Will who goes from Conquest to Conquest leaving a trail of Cuckolds behind him' – whispered behind his back by his loving subjects. Closely following in inordinate accumulation was Jean-Bédel Bokassa also of lowly sergeant stock. He crowned himself emperor in resplendent extravagance that beggared the coronation of King Selassie and Napoleon Bonaparte combined. Bokassa's meat and drink was stamping school pupils to death in prison cells. On Robert Mugabe, the Lord continued to smile his inscrutable smile, for his dream of a state funeral comes ever closer. Let us not pass over Omar Al-Bashir the Terror of the black race of Sudan, whose fanged locusts known as the Janjaweed have eaten up the land of the Fur in West Sudan. Al-Assad of Syria, the macadam of whose streets is no longer black but red of the congealed blood of his citizens leads in the Guinness Book of Records in notches on the guns of state snipers in strategic placement. Muammar Qaddafi, he that would be philosopher-king, millions of copies of his Greenhorn Book of revolutionary precepts lie mouldering in warehouses of Tripoli...and so unto King Osama bin Laden the abstemious warrior who felled three thousand in one fell swoop and has spread his spores of hate around the globe, locked in ecstasy of a virtual empire to his deity, for which all humanity is a hindrance that must be pulverized. Playing God, Osama forgot his own mortality...one and all they compete in the stakes for the bizarre, the extreme reaches of solipsism, locked in the doctrine of the Divine Right of Kings, sleeping the deep sleep of Rip Van Winkle, for whom the time of awaking is over, the time departed when king-poets rhapsodized their enemies and made generations think kindly of them, look more benignly on their flaws, their foibles, their lecheries, and cruelties.

We do not fast, rend our clothes or pour ashes on our heads but are nonetheless touched by the very mortality of the few that redeem this breed of visionaries and reprobates, and can dirge with them, be they David the reluctant shepherd king, poet and lover, or Suleiman, lawgiver, builder, lover and poet, be they named Saladin who taught the arts of chivalry even in war, or Ptolemy the Second, lover of scholarship, designer and builder...all the way to their mythic figurations that foretell the tragic and triumphant passages of remarkable beings, memorialized in monuments, the Arts of poesy, the sublimity of architecture and symphonic grandeur...

Up: Chorale 'How are the Mighty Fallen' (Handel).

Roy Williams

THE SULEMAN

SCENE ONE

ABISHA follows DONI into the living room.

ABISHA: Right, so what was that?

DONI: It was nuttin.

ABISHA: I know it was nuttin. Any one would think you don't like gals no more.

DONI: What you saying?

ABISHA: You like boys now Doni? Joke!

DONI: I just, didn't feel like it, alright?

ABISHA: Well you changed. Every single night, you felt like it, whenever you saw me, in fact, you felt like it, remember?

DONI: I remember.

ABISHA: The way you used to walk up to me, whisper in my ear, right in front of David sometimes, saying how badly you wanted me, so badly your balls were burning, blatant! I go to Nicole, who is this dawg! And a fine one at that.

DONI: Alright, man.

SIMOME: What?

DONI: You have to talk nasty, 24/7? You tell yer friends everything?

ABISHA: I tell them what I want them to hear. You coming back, now?

DONI: In a minute.

ABISHA: Don't go all pussy on me now Doni.

DONI: I'm not.

ABISHA: You gotta gimme summin. *(Grabs his crotch.)*

DONI: Abisha, don't…

ABISHA: *(Annoyed.)* Oh man! What is up wid you? You sure you don't want man.

> *DONI glares at her.*

ABISHA: So what?

DONI: Just gimme time.

ABISHA: It's bin weeks.

DONI: I aint some toy, you just wind up you nuh?

ABISHA: You barking at me?

DONI: Sorry, I didn't mean.

ABISHA: So, you turn man, good. I thought yer brother was going to finish you off, you know he offered me dough.

DONI: What?

ABISHA: For me to dash you.

DONI: My brother?

ABISHA: Scout's honour.

DONI: I don't believe this.

ABISHA: Don't pull your face like that. At least he loves you.

DONI: Even so, that's no excuse. So what, cos he's running tings now, he thinks that gives him the right…

ABISHA: Will you stop worrying about Sol please, I can handle him.

DONI: Abisha, don't, don't even try.

ABISHA: Don't tell me what I can't do Doni. Ever. Course I'm not going to do it. I was never going to do it, but he doesn't know that and he don't need to know, not for a long time. Brother or not, don't go flapping your gums to him Doni. Let me have my fun. Know what, I shoulda taken it, take it, run off, and then laugh! Like it would make any difference. You would come back. Every brer that have a taste of Abisha always come back.

ABISHA holds his crotch again.

ABISHA: Oh come on.

DONI: Just leave it.

ABISHA: I'm trying to sex you wid some sweet lyrics, and I'm getting nuttin in return, I'm doing all the work here.

DONI: Look, it aint gonna happen tonight, so just leave it, yeah?

ABISHA: One more go.

DONI: Please!

ABISHA: What is up wid you?

DONI: You really wanna know?

ABISHA: I'm asking?

DONI: You won't get it, Abisha.

ABISHA: You calling me stupid?

DONI: No.

ABISHA: Well then?

DONI: You bring David here?

ABISHA: You know I did, it's my yard.

DONI: Did you love him?

ABISHA: He was alright, not as good as you though. David would have to do it to me, six times a day, and twice on Sunday to keep up wid you.

DONI: That's not what I meant Abisha.

ABISHA: What den?

DONI: Did you love him!

ABISHA: Well, seeing as you and I were sexing each other every chance
            we had behind his back, then no, I didn't love him, happy
            now?

DONI: I think he knew about us. The way he looked at me, chatting
            to me before he died like he knew. I bet that's why, I got
            dashed, passed over for Sol, has to be.

ABISHA: So, what you telling me, are we done now?

DONI: I felt like a bastard.

ABISHA: Are we? Ca I plenty of oder man to chase.

DONI: You don't know what it is that moves me about you, haven't a
            clue.

ABISHA: So tell me then, daze Doni, what do you want from me? I tried
            making it right wid yer mum, but she didn't want to know, she
            dashed me, what you want?

DONI: I felt like a bastard, cos even when David was chatting to me,
            I found myself thinking of you, whilst he was lying there, I
            found myself thinking of you. At his funeral, all the time I
            was looking after my mum I found myself thinking of you.
            Coming here tonight, no stiffy. *(ABISHA laughs.)* I found
            myself thinking of you. Ca I love you, girl. Not Abisha, the
            sket, not Abisha wit the big mouth, who loves to flap her gums
            about people's business all day, just Abisha, who I know would
            lay down in traffic for me. I loved you from the first time I
            laid eyes. Bare men wanted to rush you, David couldn't stop
            bragging about how good you are, but not me, nuh, I thought;
            yer too good for that. Still are. There's more to it, than just
            sexing each other, deh has to be, yeah? I'm sorry, but I had to
            tell you, you need to know.

ABISHA: Say that again.

DONI: What bit?

ABISHA: The whole bit. All of it. David. Never said he loved me. Not
            once. He never sexed me.

DONI: You lie!

ABISHA: On my life.

DONI: How come?

ABISHA: I don't know, maybe he like man too.

DONI: Hey, I am not…

ABISHA: I know yer not. Take a breath, will you please? I was just
            something he used to prove to himself. You're the first,
            congratulations. *(Kisses his forehead.)* Boy, you are the craziest
            brudda I know. Look at me. Smile for me. Come back to bed.

DONI: Abisha, I told you, I don't think I can…

ABISHA: And now I'm telling you, it doesn't matter.

            ABISHA takes his hand; they go back to the bedroom.

SCENE TWO

SOL is in his office on the phone.

SOL: Well I don't want to hear that, do I? No, Ryan, Ryan, I don't
            want to hear that blud!

            SOL motions DONI who is hovering by the door to come in.

SOL: Just remind him for me yeah, remind them all, that it is me
            who is running tings now. The king is dead. Long live the king!
            Ryan are you deaf or something? Aright, alright, I am listening
            to you. I am listening to you. Yeah. Yeah.

            SOL puts the phone down; he goes over to hug his brother.
            SOL comes back, picks up the phone and carries on the phone
            conversation to RYAN like he had never left.

            Yeah? Yeah?

SOL invites DONI to have a drink.

SOL: Yeah. Yeah.

SOL opens his mouth, pats like lips to indicate to DONI that he is bored with this conversation.

SOL: Yeah. Yeah.

SOL places the receiver on his crotch several times. He and DONI laugh.

SOL: Yeah. Yeah. Yeah, look, this is all interesting Ryan, but the fact still remains I'm the king now, not you, not any one. Get it done for me.

SOL hangs up.

SOL: Finally!

DONI: You know Ryan already. He loves to chat.

SOL: Brother, you are not wrong. So?

DONI: So?

SOL: What do you think?

DONI: You look good bruv.

SOL: Mad. It is mad, Doni.

DONI: Am I supposed, you know, kiss your hand or something?

SOL: Do you want to?

DONI takes his brother's hand; he is about to kiss it when SOL pulls it away.

SOL: Get out! Behave yourself, will yer! Yer my brer, yer my blood.

DONI: Good to hear.

SOL: Why?

DONI: I thought there might be.

SOL: Well there won't be. As long as you agree, the best man won.

DONI: I suppose I will have to.

SOL: For as long I live and breathe Doni, you have always got that way about saying things.

DONI: What do you mean?

SOL: There is a hidden meaning, a threat.

DONI: No.

SOL: No?

DONI: No threat.

SOL: No offence bruv. But you shoulda waited till David keeled over before you started running off your mouth.

DONI: I'll know better next time.

SOL: Yer doing it again.

DONI: What now?

SOL: There will not be a next time, are we clear on that?

DONI: Crystal. Wrong choice of words, my liege.

SOL: Say what?

DONI: King. The kingdom is all yours.

SOL: Nice, I always like it when I hear the truth from you. Sit.

DONI: Is that my shirt you are wearing?

SOL: You don't mind.

DONI: Buy your own clothes you cheapskate.

SOL: You weren't wearing it.

DONI: Not the point.

SOL: It's all about image Doni. If they see me fleecing you, my own brother, they know I will not think twice about fleecing them. Get me?

DONI: I'm beginning to. So, does that mean I won't be getting it
          back?

SOL: You will be getting it back.

DONI: Wash it first; I don't want your BO all over it.

SOL: See? This is why I want you around man, my big brother,
          keeping me real, keeping me safe.

DONI: I'm yours blood.

SOL: Well I know that. But thanks.

DONI: Sweet.

SOL: So, what you up to tonight?

DONI: Nothing much.

SOL: Good, you can blaze it with me.

DONI: I just want a night in.

SOL: A night in?

DONI: I've been out every night this week. I am tired.

SOL: D, you're twenty, not forty.

DONI: I want to lie on my sofa, watch a movie, play FIFA.

SOL: That's a shame; I thought we could go underground tonight.

DONI: I thought it was shut down.

SOL: Reopened last month, catch up.

DONI: Sorry, not feeling it.

SOL: Yer supposed to be with me, D.

DONI: I am with you.

SOL: So, what's the problem?

DONI: There isn't one, I'm just tired.

SOL: You know I could order you.

DONI: Yes, you could.

SOL: What would you do?

DONI: Order me and find out.

SOL: It sounds like you are threatening me again.

DONI: That is in your head.

SOL: David always used to say, jus because you're paranoid, it doesn't mean they are not out to get you.

DONI: Sol, I will come if you order me to, but I hope you won't have to do that.

SOL: Big D, so serious. I don't have to order you, I don't want to order you, you'll come.

DONI: I can't.

SOL: I got chatting to a couple of honeys there last week. Buff aint the word.

DONI: So have them both.

SOL: You know me, I share the love.

DONI: Thanks yeah, but no.

SOL: I order you.

DONI: You said you wouldn't.

SOL: I said I didn't want to.

DONI: Very well, Your Majesty.

            SOL laughs.

SOL: Just messing. You don't want to go, don't go. Who are you on with it now?

DONI: No one.

SOL: Lie bad.

DONI: For truth.

SOL:	No way are you passing up two rounds of the finest pussy for FIFA. You don't love yer footie that much D. I ask again, who are you on with?
DONI:	No one you know.
SOL:	Wanna bet?
DONI:	Sol?
SOL:	My merc is on the table. Here are my keys. What you have?
DONI:	I don't have anything.
SOL:	I know that.
DONI:	(Sighs.) How long have you known?
SOL:	Not long. Ryan saw you both.
DONI:	Are you going to tell me?
SOL:	That you are out of your fucking mind, no D, I don't need to tell you that at all. Is she that good, at freeing it up?
DONI:	I need to know, what you are going to do?
SOL:	Nothing, cos you are giving her up, right? Right?
DONI:	I don't know if I can do that.
SOL:	David used to say, don't know…
DONI:	Was made to know. I'm not David.
SOL:	You're lucky it isn't him who's standing here, trying to drum some sense into your head, cos he woulda merked you by now.
DONI:	I know that.
SOL:	No explanation, done deal. Do you have any idea how many brers she's had, how many have flinged her down, dug her out. Ask her, I bet she's lost count the skank. Last one was David he had her, have you no shame?
DONI:	David never touched her.
SOL:	He did more than touch.

DONI: She says different.

SOL: She would.

DONI: She says he couldn't.

SOL: What does that mean? She calling him queer? The Man who
           love us like we were his own? And you low dat? He weren't like
           that, I can't even believe that you would even think that.

DONI: My apologies Your Majesty, may I be excused?

SOL: No you may not. You are coming with me to the underground,
           we're going to find those honeys, and we are going to work
           them, just like we used to, and yer gonna love it. That is an
           order. I aint joking D, I command you.

DONI: Well then you know what I am going to say.

SOL: For your sake, it had better be yes.

DONI: I'm sorry.

SOL: You want a sket, I will buy you a sket, I will buy you a whole
           heap of skets. Why this one?

DONI: If you stopped watching porn on your iPhone long enough,
           you would know why.

SOL: You are doing this to get back at me.

DONI: No I'm not.

SOL: Get over it, D.

DONI: I am over it,

SOL: So, drop the skank.

DONI: I love her.

SOL: I can't have you undermining me.

DONI: I'm not doing that.

SOL: I can't have everybody think I am weak already.

DONI: I don't have anything. I will go, far from here. Banish me.

SOL: Banish?

DONI: Yes.

SOL: You think I aint capable?

DONI: I love her, bruv.

SOL: I have to show strength. I was born to rule. I have to show them.

DONI: By killing your own brother?

SOL: I never said.

DONI: No, but you will.

SOL: Not if you...

DONI: Drop the skank. Could you at least say her name for me?

SOL: I don't care what she says, David had her, you know where, over there, against the wall. He had her there all night, I saw him do it. Shoulda heard her scream, couldn't get enough.

DONI: You're king and you know it. Just don't even think of touching her, yeah?

SOL: Sounds like another threat to me.

DONI: Good, cos it is.

SOL: Foolish boy, D.

DONI: Hear me, I am not turning her loose.

SOL: So, be it.

DONI: Sol? Sol, come on. This aint you.

SOL: So be it. And it is Your Majesty.

DONI: Very well, Your Majesty.

SOL: I don't just want to be a good king D, I intend to be a great king, the greatest. The most powerful. What could be more powerful than killing my own brother. You brought this.

DONI: May I be excused?

SOL: D?

DONI: Your Majesty?

SOL: Some boys are waiting for you outside.

DONI: Ryan's boys?

SOL: If you come out alone, it means you said no.

DONI: So, I get taken for a drive?

SOL: It's not too late. I can't be weak.

DONI: Tell my mum for me.

SOL: That you are a prized ejut?

DONI: Yeah.

SOL: You are so mad.

DONI: Your Majesty!

        DONI leaves. SOL is alone on stage.

SOL: D? D? D? D? *(Screams.)* DONI! Why are you so mad?

Sam Burns

TWO BEARS

Characters

KING

QUEEN CONSORT

MOTHER

CHILD

FORTY-AND-TWO YOUTHS

The 'crowd' can be played by the audience or can remain unseen.

Quotation from 'The Children's "Don't"', in *Ruthless Rhymes for Heartless Homes* by Harry Graham (1898).

SCENE

2 Kings 2: 23-25

23 And he went up from thence unto Bethel: and as he was going up by the way, there came forth little children out of the city, and mocked him, and said unto him, Go up, thou bald head; go up, thou bald head.

24 And he turned back, and looked on them, and cursed them in the name of the LORD. And there came forth two she bears out of the wood, and tare forty and two children of them.

25 And he went from thence to mount Carmel, and from thence he returned to Samaria.

Outside a cheese factory.

Amid general applause, FORTY-AND-TWO YOUTHS (Off) call out as many synonyms for 'baldy' as presently exist. They have childlike voices.

The KING and the QUEEN CONSORT exit their car. They wave to the assembled crowd.

KING: Croup begat asthma and asthma begat the whooping cough, and whooping cough begat pleurisy and pleurisy begat gout.

QUEEN CONSORT: Yes, dear.

KING: And gout begat ingrowing toenails, and ingrowing toenails begat conjunctivitis. Conjunctivitis begat lumbago, and lumbago begat cystitis.

QUEEN CONSORT: It's *not* cystitis. I've told you. You just drink too much tea of a morning.

KING: Cystitis begat haemorrhoids.

The QUEEN CONSORT is mildly revolted.

Which in turn begat astigmatism. Astigmatism begat gumboil. The gumboil begat the classic migraine.

The FORTY-AND-TWO YOUTHS take advantage of a lull in the cheers to abuse the KING's naked scalp at top volume.

The classic migraine begat male pattern baldness.

The QUEEN CONSORT looks firmly at the KING.

QUEEN CONSORT: They're children.

KING: Children?

The QUEEN CONSORT smiles fondly at the KING's balding pate.

QUEEN CONSORT: 'Tis years of sorrow and of care
Have made his head come through his hair.'

The KING runs his hand over his head.

Darling. Don't. Attrition.

KING: Sorry.

She links arms with him. He waves to the crowd to distract his free hand.

QUEEN CONSORT: Well, it's not too shabby a turnout. For a Monday.

KING: Not if you count the abusers, certainly.

QUEEN CONSORT: And in all this drizzle. Aren't your people hardy?

KING: Truly we're very magnetic.

Beat.

QUEEN CONSORT: That can't really be it.

KING: No.

QUEEN CONSORT: The factory. They must be giving away free shortbread.

KING: It's a cheese factory.

QUEEN CONSORT: Cheese? Is it really? Are you certain?

KING: Indisputably.

QUEEN CONSORT: Not shortbread?

KING: Shortbread's tomorrow.

QUEEN CONSORT: Oh bother.

KING: Or possibly Thursday. *(Beat.)* No. Hold on a moment. When's the fish meal place?

QUEEN CONSORT: I successfully tried to forget. *(Beat.)* Oh, what a shame though. I was rather looking forward to shortbread.

The KING and the QUEEN CONSORT amble their way towards the cheese factory doors, shaking hands with the non-taunting sections of the crowd and accepting flowers en route.

KING: We should take more care. Poor cheese people. They like to think we care, you know. They very much appreciate a smear of background knowledge.

QUEEN CONSORT: Like saying 'Bore da' of a morning in Wales.

KING: Precisely.

QUEEN CONSORT: Which I always do.

KING: But what do you know about cheese?

QUEEN CONSORT: Nothing.

KING: Well then.

QUEEN CONSORT: I thought I'd copy off you. I'm sure you know masses about cheese.

The KING runs his hand over his head again. The QUEEN CONSORT shakes the hand of someone in the crowd.

Thank you so much for coming.

KING:	I do know a bit.
QUEEN CONSORT:	Then dazzle me, dearest.
KING:	Well…it kicks off with milk.
QUEEN CONSORT:	I know *that* much.
KING:	This particular concern uses milk from a dozen nearby farms.
QUEEN CONSORT:	You *have* done your homework.
KING:	The milk is heated to 72 degrees to see off harmful pathogens.
QUEEN CONSORT:	Such a relief.
KING:	Then it's pumped into the vats where a starter culture –
QUEEN CONSORT:	No…just…
KING:	What?
QUEEN CONSORT:	Just tell me about the samples.
KING:	Oh.
QUEEN CONSORT:	I need to prepare my taste buds.
KING:	Well, it's three as a rule. *(To the crowd.)* Smile? Well. I can try.

A camera flash.

	(To the QUEEN CONSORT.) Three different kinds of cheese.
QUEEN CONSORT:	*(To the crowd.)* I do hope you don't get too soggy.
KING:	They'll have some sort of…pleasure, thank you …some sort of local speciality.
QUEEN CONSORT:	Ah. The house cheese.
KING:	If you like.
QUEEN CONSORT:	*(To the crowd.)* Thrilling to be here. Absolutely thrilling.

KING: And something blended.

QUEEN CONSORT: What does that mean?

KING: Something laced with garlic, you know. Or cranberries.

QUEEN CONSORT: How ghastly.

The QUEEN CONSORT accepts a bunch of flowers.

                        How charming.

KING: And then a Red Leicester to finish.

A contemplative pause.

QUEEN CONSORT: We're nowhere near…

KING: They always make one.

QUEEN CONSORT: Why?

KING: For the colour.

QUEEN CONSORT: Oh. Of course.

KING: 'He's seen his share of yellow cheese.'

QUEEN CONSORT: Do you fear one day they'll offer you a blue?

KING: They're politely requested not to.

QUEEN CONSORT: Ah. Such power.

The FORTY-AND-TWO YOUTHS kick off again. The KING is agitated.

                        They're *children.*

KING: Why aren't they at work?

QUEEN CONSORT: Ignore them, my love. Rise manfully above it. *(Beat.)* Oh look. That wall has an award from the Concrete Society.

She manoeuvres him away from the crowd to admire the little plaque.

Look. Awarded in...darling.

The KING continues to nurse his head.

Stop it. I mean. What does it matter? You lack hair. It's true. It's a solid observation.

KING: Oh, thank you. Yes. That's buoyed me up no end.

QUEEN CONSORT: But what does it matter?

KING: If it were you though. Imagine. How do you think *you'd* feel?

QUEEN CONSORT: I'm sure I'd bear it with grace.

KING: I'm sure you'd do nothing of the sort.

QUEEN CONSORT: But what does it prove? That your father was bald and you wore tight hats in your youth. Where's the shame in that?

KING: If only I'd a shapely head.

QUEEN CONSORT: It's not *vastly* abnormal.

KING: It's just...it's not very me.

The QUEEN CONSORT briefly appraises her husband's head.

QUEEN CONSORT: I don't know. I think it suits you rather well.

They tire of the Concrete Society award and wander back towards the crowd.

Sign of wisdom, you know.

KING: Ha.

QUEEN CONSORT: Good living.

KING: And virility.

QUEEN CONSORT: Well. That too.

KING: I've heard all the myths. *(To the crowd.)* Morning. Morning. Lovely to be here.

QUEEN CONSORT: *I've* heard it's a sign of a higher than average intellect.

KING: It means I'm getting old. That's all it means.

QUEEN CONSORT: Oh rot. You were bald at twenty-five.

A MOTHER and her CHILD weave their way to the front of the crowd. The QUEEN CONSORT moves away to talk to somebody else.

The MOTHER bobs. The KING smiles.

KING: Hello. Thank you so much for coming. Who's this young man?

MOTHER: My son.

KING: How do you do?

The MOTHER nudges the CHILD.

MOTHER: Shake the King's hand.

The CHILD holds his hand out. The KING shakes it. The CHILD sneezes.

KING: Bless you.

The MOTHER gazes at the KING.

What?

MOTHER: And he went up and lay upon the child, and put his mouth upon his mouth, and his eyes upon his eyes, and his hands upon his hands: and he stretched himself upon the child; and the flesh of the child waxed warm.

KING: I'm sorry?

The MOTHER bends and touches the KING's feet with her fingers.

Oh…now. I really wouldn't. Security bods all around, you know. Armed. They're like hawks.

> They'll think…well, I really don't know what
> they'll think. Now…please. It's for your own…

The MOTHER rises. She smiles.

> Ah.

MOTHER: Be all right now.

The MOTHER takes the CHILD by the hand and turns away.

KING: Right.

*The MOTHER and the CHILD melt back into the crowd. The
KING stares after them.*

FORTY-AND-TWO YOUTHS: Hey! Baldy! Heal my scrofula!

*The QUEEN CONSORT wanders over, also watching the
departure of the MOTHER and CHILD. She hands the KING a
bunch of flowers.*

QUEEN CONSORT: Dahlias.

The KING inhales the dahlias.

> I was handed a baby once in Driffield. Do you
> remember?

KING: Vaguely.

QUEEN CONSORT: February. *Freezing.* Only looked a few days old
and in no sense fit to be out. *(Beat.)* She had a
tube in her nose.

KING: I remember.

QUEEN CONSORT: I don't know what they thought *I* could do. Does
one marry into the royal touch?

The KING scrutinises the crowd.

KING: They *look* quite healthy.

QUEEN CONSORT: No. That's just how they arrange them. All the
fresh ones towards the front. It's for the local
news.

KING: Oh.

The KING inhales the dahlias again.

QUEEN CONSORT: Lovely, aren't they?

KING: Are you sure they're real?

QUEEN CONSORT: I'm sure they are.

KING: They don't have much of a scent.

QUEEN CONSORT: I don't think dahlias do. *(Beat.)* What's wrong with the little boy?

KING: I don't know. She didn't say.

The KING emerges from the dahlias. He shakes a hand.

        Thank you so much for coming out.

The QUEEN CONSORT shakes a hand.

QUEEN CONSORT: *(To the crowd.)* In this terrible weather.

KING: *(To the QUEEN CONSORT.)* He sneezed a bit. But he had a full head of hair.

QUEEN CONSORT: A wig?

KING: He had his own eyebrows.

QUEEN CONSORT: Well. There are other things.

    Pause.

KING: I hate this.

QUEEN CONSORT: Yes. I know you do. *(Beat.)* Queen Anne healed Samuel Johnson. In 1712.

KING: Did she really?

QUEEN CONSORT: *I* don't know.

KING: I suppose if it makes her *feel* better.

QUEEN CONSORT: Well, of course. That's the point, isn't it.

KING: Hm.

QUEEN CONSORT: Provided she still takes him to the doctor.

KING: Good God.

QUEEN CONSORT: And I'm sure she will.

The KING is rubbing his head with his hand. The QUEEN CONSORT stares.

Please stop nursing your head. They'll think you have lice.

The FORTY-AND-TWO YOUTHS kick off again with their variations on the theme of 'baldy'. Some of the voices the KING hears are older now.

KING: They are *not* children.

QUEEN CONSORT: *(To the crowd.)* He doesn't have lice.

The KING stares hard into the crowd.

KING: *(To the crowd.)* They're not children.

Pause.

I've a cousin, you know. Full head of hair and well into his sixties, but he was hellish miffed to find a single strand of grey at twenty-seven. Over-privileged little freak. Me? I found a tuppence-sized circle of scalp on my twenty-fifth birthday.

QUEEN CONSORT: *(To the crowd.)* Yes…I'd heard some rumour that rosemary oil was the thing. Some such tincture.

KING: *(To the crowd.)* On my crown.

QUEEN CONSORT: *(To the crowd.)* I shall pass on your suggestion. Anything for a quiet life.

KING: *(To the crowd.)* I have to use sunblock now. Lest it blisters.

QUEEN CONSORT: *(To the crowd.)* Yes, he's terribly sensitive.

KING: *(To the crowd.)* And I don't even fancy cheese today.

QUEEN CONSORT: *(To the crowd.)* I've an umbrella just like that.

KING: *(To the crowd.)* When I was a child I could stay out all day in the August sun. Climbing trees. Fording streams. I'm sure as a gun I didn't burn.

QUEEN CONSORT: Can you tell that for certain? In black and white?

KING: *(To the crowd.)* That was the Highlands. Admittedly there was a great deal of fog. *(Beat.)* Bare arms though, of a summer. Fishing. Polo.

QUEEN CONSORT: Nanny hovering in the wings with a parasol.

KING: *(To the crowd.)* And I took two dozen falls that should've killed me. Two dozen times I remounted.

QUEEN CONSORT: *(To the crowd.)* When I was a child I had to look around before I sat. One isn't meant to, these days. One's supposed to trust there'll be a chair. I still *do* look, of course. Every single time. I'm not an idiot. And I do the looking for him.

KING: *(To the crowd.)* My hair was like Christopher Robin's. Ambassadors invariably would tousle it.

QUEEN CONSORT: *(To the crowd.)* It was! I've seen the pictures. He was absolutely precious. *(To the KING.)* Did your bathrobe have a hood?

KING: No.

QUEEN CONSORT: Did the other boys recite that poem of an evening? In the dorm?

KING: Not that I heard.

QUEEN CONSORT: Oh. Well. *(To the crowd.)* And are you all fond of cheese?

The FORTY-AND-TWO YOUTHS hold threateningly forth.

KING: *(To the crowd.)* And I'm frightened now. I'm terribly, terribly frightened.

QUEEN CONSORT: *(To the crowd.)* I adore cheese, yes. Cheese and shortbread. And fish meal. All my favourite things.

The KING looks over his shoulder, then back into the crowd.

KING: *(To the crowd.)* Do you see the constables?

QUEEN CONSORT: *(To the crowd.)* My favourite *brand*? Well, I'm awfully fond of those little square slices. You know. In the polythene wrappers.

KING: *(To the crowd.)* The pair of them there. In the doorway. In the stab vests. With the batons.

QUEEN CONSORT: *(To the crowd.)* I'm joking, of course. It's that Serbian one. Made from donkeys' milk. *(Pause.)* *Is* it expensive? I didn't know.

KING: *(To the crowd.)* With the claws and the teeth.

QUEEN CONSORT: And I am a little partial to the triangles. In the foil.

KING: *(To the crowd.)* See what happens when I look them in the eye.

The KING looks over his shoulder again. He nods.

To a background of sirens and batons on riot shields and similarly upsetting noises, FORTY-AND-TWO YOUTHS are escorted from the premises.

The noise dies back.

The KING studies his hands, then runs one over his head. He smiles at the nearest bystander...benignly shakes their hand.

Be all right now.

The KING turns to the QUEEN CONSORT.

QUEEN CONSORT: There's some sort of oil, she was saying.

KING: Who was?

QUEEN CONSORT:	A very pleasant lady in the crowd.
KING:	Oh.
QUEEN CONSORT:	Massage, she said. With some sort of oil. Her husband was with her. Or her son or something. *He* had a full head of hair.
KING:	We'll have to try it.

He smiles and offers his arm.

Shall we?

Together they turn and walk towards the factory doors.

QUEEN CONSORT:	Oh goodness.
KING:	What?
QUEEN CONSORT:	I suppose we'll need to wear a silly hat as well. If it's cheese.
KING:	Oh yes!
QUEEN CONSORT:	One of those little blue…you know.
KING:	Yes. A little blue hat.

The End.

Salena Godden

THE CHRONICLE

In the beginning was the story, it was the first story, and the story was spoken and the story was heard and the story was remembered and then sometimes forgotten. When pieces of the story were forgotten, these pieces went missing and the holes in the stories, the gaps, they were filled with pieces of other new stories.

In the beginning was the story. The first story was the story of love – the life of love, the love of the life, the living love and the loving life and this love was the root of all stories; this one love, the life, this life, our life, our time here, from our birth and to our death, from creation to destruction, this was the root of the story and all stories told ever after.

And soon the story, the first story, was fragmented, the first story was many stories and it was all stories, and all of these stories had holes too, pieces from the first story and pieces of their own invention, all of these stories, grew fat and filled with other pieces of stories and pieces of other stories. The first story begat stories begat stories begat stories begat stories.

Then there came the first writer and the first writer was the one who said: *hang on a minute, that's good, let me get a stick and get that down.* And with that, the first story was taken from the mouth, plucked from the air and scribbled with a stick in the dust. That first story, it was written in blood and tears and sweat and it was stained on walls with the juice of berries.

That first story was written, it came from the heart to the mind to the mouth to the ear to the hand and to the eye, it came from the root of the first story, the story was told and the story was heard and now the story was seen. And the root of that first story is love, the story of love, the life of love, the love of life, the living love and loving life.

The one love in this one life on this one earth under this one sky.

Love with the face of joy and love with the face of loss, how the heart fills and how the heart empties. And how alive is the life of love. The story was the story of the good and the story of the bad, the story of the light and the story of the dark. And since time began the story was shared and the story continued to grow and grow and spread and swell and spill. Story begat story begat story as the story was drawn and the story was written and the story was sang and spoken in verse, the story was heard with the beat of a heart and the skin of a drum.

The story became many stories, story begat story, as it travelled on the wind and through time. The story was told with different tongues and language, but always under the same stars and under the same silver moon and the same golden sun. Even though the stories changed and altered, the sky was always the same sky above, and the earth was always below the feet, this would never change. The life of love, the life of being alive would always be the story. The story spread like wildfire around the camps and cooking pots, these stories were shared around the dancing flame and whispered into the ears of sleeping babes.

The story, the holes, the holes in the story, the story, the holes and the holes in the story, how they were always filled with other pieces of another story, this same story, the story of love, now split into a million stories which danced in firelight and flame, making shapes on the walls and in the shadows, but always under the same planets, for the universe was always there, the space was above us and the dust and the dead, always hard below our feet. Always the same sky above, always and forever.

And we learned the names of some of the storykeepers and the storytellers, we learned and remembered them as Homer and as Sophocles and as Euripides, Sappho and Cattullus and Tu Fu, Ovid and Virgil and Sheikh Musharrif ud-din Sadi and Omar Khayyám.

There were stories that washed away with the tides in the sand, that watered and filtered through rocks and time. And then there were stories that were recorded, printed with ink so the holes could not be seen to be filled anymore. Some stories were set in stone and sealed.

Some stories would never change but always be.

Time slipped by with the ever flowing river, with the ebbs and tides of the oceans, the wax and wane of the moon, as the stories travelled through time and the stories begat Rumi begat Dante begat Chaucer begat Spencer begat Marlowe begat Cervantes. The stories spread and by now there were some stories that came with pictures and others that came with song and with rhythm. There were stories that were illustrated, stories with puppets and stories played out upon the stage with costume and theatre and dance.

Then came the year 1564 and that was the year that the story begat William Shakespeare.

And then time fed the story that begat Donne begat Milton begat Voltaire begat Defoe begat Goethe. Then came the stories of Wordsworth and Coleridge, Jane Austen, the story begat Blake begat Robert Burns and Byron, begat Keats begat Mary Shelley begat Leopardi and the year 1799 was when the story begat both Pushkin and Balzac.

The new century was born and with it the ink did run and flow with stories and then begat Victor Hugo. In 1809 the story begat both Edgar Allan Poe and Gogol. Then came Dickens, Turgenev and Brontë. Melville and Whitman and that same decade was blessed as it did begat Baudelaire, Ibsen, Lear, Hans Christian Anderson, Emily Dickinson, Lewis Carroll and Strindberg. Stories begat Flaubert begat Rimbaud, begat George Bernard Shaw begat Joseph Conrad, begat Chekhov begat Charlotte Perkins Gilman, begat Yeats begat Proust, and Oscar Wilde begat Somerset Maugham and Rudyard Kipling then came Gertrude Stein. That time carried the story on and saw the births of the stories of Rilke, Thomas Mann and Hesse, Dostoevsky, EM Forster, Joyce and Woolf. William Carlos Williams and Kafka, the story then begat Pound begat DH Lawrence, then begat Céline begat Sassoon.

These decades were rich and fertile and the year was 1888 and that time did begat Pessoa, Raymond Chandler, TS Eliot and Eugene O'Neill, Cocteau then came Agatha Christie, Henry Miller, Tolkien. The story begat Mayakovsky, Rossetti, Dorothy Parker, Knut Hamsun,

HG Wells, Tolstoy, Wilfred Owen, Aldous Huxley and Joseph Roth.
F. Scott Fitzgerald and William Faulkner, the story begat Enid Blyton
begat Robert Frost begat Lorca begat Brecht begat Nabokov, Arthur
Conan Doyle, EE Cummings, Georges Bataille, Charlie Chaplin and
Mae West and as that great century ended the year 1899 guided the
story to begat both Noël Coward and Ernest Hemmingway.

But then came the twentieth century and during this century the
stories could not only be heard on the wind and read on the papery
page or seen acted with costume and dance and ballet and opera but
stories were now broadcast through the airwaves, through pictures
in boxes and from needles in hard-pressed vinyl, it was now a time
of gramophone and wireless. And the story was blossoming, and the
story did thrive, the story of love, the root of all stories was the essence
of love, the life of love, the love of life, the living and the dying, the
one love. Now stories were bought and sold and recorded and printed
and published, there were stories that were depicted on moving
images, theatres and cinemas, radios and televisions.

And we can never forget how the story was feared by some and
sometimes it is still kept locked away. Over time the story has been
censored and banned completely, but the story still continues to
be. We must remember that some writers went to war for the story,
how so many have fought to have the story heard, some have been
imprisoned, lost their freedom and their lives, others went mad trying
to tell the story their way – but the story still spread, how it grew and
grew, always under the same sky and with the same earth beneath our
feet.

The twentieth century began with the birth of Langston Hughes,
with Steinbeck and with Orwell. Stories begat Neruda begat Graham
Greene begat Canetti. The first decade of the twentieth century was
when stories begat John O'Hara, Daphne du Maurier, Evelyn Waugh,
Sartre, Ayn Rand and HE Bates, Beckett, Auden and Mark Twain, Ian
Fleming, Jean Genet and Tennessee Willams, stories begat MacLaren-
Ross begat John Fante, Camus begat Cortázar begat William S
Burroughs begat Dylan Thomas begat Laurie Lee begat Billie Holiday
begat Saul Bellow begat Ivor Cutler and Arthur Miller begat Roald
Dahl begat Serge Gainsbourg.

And then there came a surge of the births of great women in that time, who were all born together the stories named them Elizabeth Smart, Carson McCullers, Edna O'Brien, Diana Athill, Muriel Spark, Iris Murdoch and Doris Lessing. Then came the stories of JD Salinger and Bukowski then Patricia Highsmith and Philip Larkin and Kerouac and Frank O'Connor.

In the 1920s the story begat Maya Angelou and Philip K Dick and Saramago, Kurt Vonnegut begat Calvino begat Hubert Selby Jr begat Capote begat Tony Hancock begat Ginsberg begat Jacques Brel begat García Márquez begat John Osborne begat Milan Kundera.

And time was steady, the stories always flowing and always moving the story along for the 1930s begat the story in the lyrics of Nina Simone and Ray Charles and Johnny Cash. This was the time for the birth of Ted Hughes and Walcott and 1930 begat Pinter. Then came Toni Morrison, William Wantling, Woody Allen, Umberto Eco, Beryl Bainbridge and Sylvia Plath and then came the birth of Leonard Cohen. Story begat DM Thomas begat Perec begat Hunter S Thompson, begat Raymond Carver begat Atwood begat Heaney.

Then came the 1940s and this decade begat the birth of stories in lyrical song from Lennon and McCartney, Joplin, Morrison, Dylan, Simon, Richards and Jagger and Bob Marley. And the 1940s were fruitful seeing the births of great voices of the storytelling through lyric and fiction and verse and we remember their names as Ian McEwan, Brian Patten, Richard Brautigan and Paul Auster. Alice Walker, Ian Dury, Elfreide Jelenik, John Martyn, Julian Barnes, Stephen King, Paulo Coelho and Murakami, Debbie Harry, Neil Young, Patti Smith, Bowie and Hendrix, Nick Drake. And as that decade closed and this chronicle ends in 1949 the year that begat the story of Tom Waits, John Cooper Clarke, Gil Scott-Heron and John Hegley.

Together we will remember these names and we will make sure that the story survives, that their stories continue. One cannot write a chronicle, portray history without betraying oneself. Here lies my potted, poetic history, a lyrical history. This is the history of the first story, one story, the story of love, the love of the life, the life of the love of the story.

For in the name of the love of the story we have built houses for the story and called them libraries. We must keep these archives sacred, ensure these temples are open for all to find the story forever. These houses, these libraries, are the home of the first story and the next story. There cannot be a last story, we all know, the story will only grow and last, as long it is shared.

And here is the good news chronicle – We are all the caretakers and we are all keepers of the story. We are all prophets as we coninue to read the story, hear the story and share the story faithfully. When we go back to the first story and find love, we can discover we are all royalty, we have a kingdom and it's the world within us. In the centre of each and every one of us is the temple of the story. We are all vessels, we are all the inventor of the story and that story is the story of love of this record of our living life. We will be in exile no longer, as long as we all have the first story and this is the key. We all have a place in the kingdom of the story, the first story, the story that was whispered as we slept as children is the same story we will whisper to our own kin and their kin afterwards just as the story begats story begats story.

We are kings and we are queens in the kingdom of the story. Together we are the temple where the story dwells and thrives and continues. Our citizenship is here and there, we hold a passport from here to there, a journey that takes us from the first word daubed in berry juice upon a cave wall to the next book we read. We are all gypsies and we are all carriers, taking versions of the story and remembering it in our own beautiful and unique way. Here we are now, side by side, and between us all, we are the home of the story, we are the temple of the story and the story, the root of that our first story is the story of love, the story of the life of love with its heart filled and its heart emptied, this living, this loving, this life to be told a million times always under the same planets, the space opening above us and the dust and the earth always below our feet.

Tim Rice

FROM SOLOMON
TO CYRUS THE GREAT

Music by Stuart Brayson

The second book of Chronicles explains
From Solomon to Cyrus what went wrong
In Judah for no less than nineteen reigns
A sorry tale as subject for a song
Yet bards must never from their duty shirk
To bring true stories to the world at large
Not every king of Judah was a jerk
But quite enough were hopeless when in charge
Yet everything seemed perfect at the start
King Solomon had wisdom, wealth and peace
And furthermore the Queen of Sheba's heart
His summer surely had an endless lease
He built the temple, housed the ark with pride
And most important, God was on his side

The second book of Chronicles reveals
The sad post-Solomon decline and fall
How sinners, weaklings, psychopaths and heels
Drove what was left of Israel to the wall
There were some worthy kings against all odds –
Jehoshaphat, Josiah, Hezekiah –
But others turned to false and easy gods
And perished in the one true Yahweh's fire
Jerusalem destroyed – the Jewish fate
Her temple, city, nation, turned to sand
Till Cyrus King of Persia, truly Great
Returned the exiles to their promised land
Thus Chronically Persians saved the Jews
Ironically not what they'd now choose

Naomi Foyle

THE STRANGE WIFE

Ezra 10: 10-11

10   And Ezra the priest stood up, and said unto them, Ye have transgressed, and have taken strange wives, to increase the trespass of Israel.

11   Now therefore make confession unto the LORD God of your fathers, and do his pleasure: and separate yourselves from the people of the land, and from the strange wives.

EZRA: Palestinian witch.
I know her village ways.

She brewed up rabbits' blood
and menstrual filth,

told him it was unguent,
smeared it on her wrists, her breasts –

cast her foul spell.

MARIAM: I didn't have to come here.
Didn't have to bring fruit
across this threshold.
No one made me enter his room.
No one forced me to stand mute.

YONATAN: In the garden where I used to play
crimson roses, ripe grapes
bleed their duty-free bouquet.

Sprinklers hiss across the lawn.
Sunlight ignites the droplets;
a rainbow glistens in the spray.

Grass so green it hurts my eyes.
You'd never guess there was a water shortage
in this land that calls night day.

EZRA: I'm not blind.
              I'm not deaf.
              I'm not losing my mind.

YONATAN: Beyond the wall he never let me climb,
              a synagogue, a school, market stalls.

              There's a man selling avocados from a cart
              Is he Jewish or Arab? Who can tell?

              Behind him, Jerusalem rises
              like a whale in the waves of the hills.

              There, Givat Shaul Bet swallows Deir Yassin.
              But I still hear Ben-Gurion's guns and grenades.

              Blowing up houses, shooting, for hours –
              children, parents, old people, the ill:

              just so much krill in the leviathan's way.
              We killed thirty babies that day.

MARIAM: I said I wanted to see him
              with my own eyes.

              To feel part of this family,
              have a memory,
              a story.

              But perhaps I just wanted
              him to see me.

EZRA: I see you. I see you.
              Don't think I don't know who you are!
              I remember each hair on your head.
              I remember every lousy word you ever said.

YONATAN: Deir Yassin's old village school
is now a Jewish mental health centre.
In the East, we're building
a 'Museum of Tolerance'
on a bulldozed burial ground.
Why can't we see it?
Can the linguists explain
why we still have no words for their pain?

Above the city, our National Forests   MARIAM: Deir Yassin
are rooted in ruins and graves. But despite   'Ayn al-Zaytun
the dank shadows our history casts,   Dishon
figs, almonds and cacti still flower –   Jura
our park maps call their terraces 'biblical';   Beit Mamzil
the vines that bind them 'wild'.   Biddu
I've seen hacked olive trees sprout   Beit Surik
decades later, split the trunks of our pines.   Sabbarin

EZRA: Like animals they treated us.   MARIAM: Saris
Worse than animals. Vermin.   'Ayn Karim
Rats to be flushed from their nests –   Sataf
tortured, slaughtered,   Zuba
our homes burnt like haystacks –   Qaddita
my parents fled from the pogroms   'Alma
with nothing but the rags on their backs.   'Amqa

YONATAN: And we, *Saba* Ezra? Who were driven ourselves
across continents, oceans, out through the gates of the world?
Above the black forest, flashes of sapphire –
swimming pools, sparkling with water
pumped from Palestinian wells.

MARIAM: Our catastrophe
The *Nakba*.
The hell they built
in an everyday heaven:
a place, not perfect, but human.

EZRA

YONATAN: Cheerful as roosters, the red roofs of the settlements
crest the parched ridges in garrisoned tiers. Look
closer – brown fountains – the settlers' raw sewage
stains stolen hillsides,
gushes down onto Palestinian fields.

MARIAM: Plan D
they called it:
de-Arabization.
Operation Broom.
Operation Scissors.
Operation Cleansing the Leaven.

EZRA:

G-D GAVE US A HAVEN.
The Arabs attacked us.
War is war. Babies die. People flee.
We won. They lost.
They should shut up already!

But no, they hijack planes,
murder athletes,
train their kids to be suicide bombers.
Ach, what's a little shit
compared to Qassam rockets?

From *my* window, Yonatan
I see the light of the Promised Land.
We, the Chosen People,
came here from the camps
bled for every grain of sand.

We brought civilization with us;
watered, dug the sod,
grew cucumbers, peppers, melons
invented cherry tomatoes! –

We made Israel
worthy of G-d.

YONATAN:

WE INVADED *THEM*
if we want to live in peace
– at home –
we have to ask forgiveness
for our crimes.

Ethnic cleansing.
Segregation.
Occupation.
Endless war?
That's not our culture, *Saba*
not God's will on earth.

Our hatred is a worm, a sickness,
our ancestors contracted
on the desert, the Steppes,
harboured in their guts.

As long as symphonies & salad
mean more to us than justice,
trust me, *Saba* Ezra –
the Palestinians will resist us.

MARIAM: We met on a demonstration
against a house demolition.
He was holding a sign in Hebrew,
wearing his *yarmulke*.
Jews in cars shouted 'traitor'.
I poked him in the chest.

Do you feel better now? I asked.
Now you've taken an hour out of your busy day
to massage your conscience
down here in Anata?

He replied in Arabic. Very bad Arabic –
but I could understand.

I won't feel better, he said,
until there's a just peace in this land.

EZRA: For years, my father wrote to his brother
until his fingers were black with ink –
please Ira, come, come to London,
there's work here, we'll house you,
the baby can sleep in the sink –

                 but no:
Ziva's family needs me in Warsaw;
this Hitler with his ridiculous moustache
how long can he last?

Ira, Ziva, their children, her brothers, her sister, her parents:
starved and tattooed,
herded into that chamber,
gassed with a *pesticide* –
heaped in a hole, buried like *pigs*.

The letter shook in my father's hands.
A white leaf in a howling storm.
No matter how warm the fire
he never stopped shaking –
except when he clutched my arm

so hard, I still bear the marks of his nails.
Oh *Abba*, I did as I promised –
brought Hannah and Sarah to safety.
But for what, Yonatan?
For what?

Your own father died
in the Yom Kippur War –
and *you* ask forgiveness of *terrorists*?

YONATAN: My father was a photo on a dresser,
a news-clipping framed on your wall.
You told me he was a hero
every Shabbat when I was small.

I'd stare at my father's slender face
and wonder who he was.
Did he really want to fight the Arabs?
And if we kill them, won't they kill us?

I know my father was brave.
But that answer was never enough.
One question led to another until
I had de-Zionized myself.

MARIAM: My father has the key now
to my grandmother's house.

She couldn't speak of that time
without weeping.

Her father was shot.
Her brother died in a work camp.

She and her mother escaped.
Women in the village were raped.

The house is still standing, at least.
Jews live there, of course.

Artists, they are. From Australia.
I've only been once.

The key is safe in a wooden box.
One day he'll give it to me.

EZRA: I thought your court case
          was the worst day of my life.
          My grandson, a pacifist.
          What did I do to deserve this?
          Everyone at the synagogue knew.

          The Rabbi said it wasn't my fault:
          your mother had spoiled you,
          let you read all those books.

YONATAN: You made her destroy them.
          Forced her to cut my books into bits.
          You forbade her to visit me,
          even write to me – but she did.

EZRA: But going to jail wasn't sufficient.
          You had to punish my prayers:
          you married that Arab *shiksa*.
          Not just me you defied now, no.
          Not just your family you shamed.
          Not just your country you betrayed.
          Now you blasphemed the very graves of the Shoah.

YONATAN: Blasphemed the – ?
          On my wedding day you locked
          my mother in her house.

EZRA: She kept your old room like a shrine.

YONATAN: You made her watch
          as you ripped my sheets into shreds.

EZRA: I bought them – they were mine.

YONATAN: She was terrified, *Saba*.

EZRA: I CRIED, Yonatan. I cried –

YONATAN: Then you made her kneel
          as you recited the burial Kaddish
          for her only child, on his wedding day.

EZRA: YES. Yes I did.
          You are dead to me, Yonatan. Deader than dead.

EZRA   123

Your mother may think she still loves you –
women are soft in the head.
But she is my daughter
and this is my home.
Miriam, show him the door.

YONATAN: Mariam, *Saba*. It's Mariam,

my wife.

Miriam died, *Saba* Ezra. Remember?
The Rabbi came and told you.
Mariam and I promised Miriam
we'd take care of you now.
Saba, I know you're angry with me,
but please don't shout near Mariam –
she's carrying our child.

MARIAM: She gave me a name that means 'bitter, uncertain'
Because my land and her song were bitter, uncertain.

The sweet kiss of youth meant nothing to me;
in my school, the young were bitter, uncertain.

We refused to take candy from enemy soldiers.
We knew we were stronger bitter, uncertain.

She watched and she waited for a man to adore me.
But my heart was a stranger, bitter, uncertain.

And when I fell hard for the one I should not have
I came home to harangue her, bitter, uncertain.

She made couscous, falafel, pita bread, *za'atar*:
I fed on my hunger, bitter, uncertain.

At last she said *Daughter, if you must then you must* –
I knew the words she had strung were bitter, uncertain.

Eighteen months later, her voice lost its power.
I bent down to sponge her, bitter, uncertain.

Bless him, she whispered, *your husband, my son*:
Mariam, you're no longer bitter, uncertain.

EZRA: I'm not blind.

I'm not deaf.
I'm not losing my mind.

She's wearing Miriam's clothes.
She's plundered her drawers,
stolen your dead mother's shawl.

But that's her people all over –
thieves, murderers, whores.

YONATAN: Hush, *Saba*, hush.
Mariam's wearing
her own mother's shawl.
Miriam liked it,
so Mariam gave it to her –
that's Arab hospitality, *Saba.*
And when Miriam fell ill
she said Mariam must
have it back, of course.

EZRA: I remember how she trapped you
– teasing, tempting
dancing, denying –
I know all her Jezebel games!

Coughs.

MARIAM: *Ya Allah!*

YONATAN: Shh. Shh. You're not well.
Here, let me cool you.
Today is your birthday
One hundred years old…
I'm sorry. I'm sorry.
I shouldn't have said –
It's all in the past –
Mariam warned me:
don't get upset.
Please, don't get upset.
We're here to look after you now.

MARIAM: When the second Intifada began
I hated myself for loving a Jew.
Time after time I pushed him away,
as if what Allah ordains, we can undo.

Then, one day on a demo, I saw him
moving toward a line of soldiers
armed with tear gas, a water cannon,
sound bombs, rubber bullets.

Palestinians, a few Jews, Internationals –
the first canister heaved through the air,
clanged to the ground, struck sparks from a rock
the marchers shouted, scattered and ducked.

But Yonatan smiled, pressed a cloth to his nose –
and kept walking on, with an easy rhythm,
as if he were strolling toward the sea
to plunge in for a swim.

EZRA: You're a fool, Yonatan, a fool.
Ach, how did I spawn such a clod?

YONATAN: Perhaps I'm a fool to come here,
But I'm still your grandson, *Saba*.

MARIAM: My eyes stung and streamed.
People crouched, coughed.
But running and stumbling, I knew:

Yonatan is a miracle,
a mystery I never want to solve.
Look at him now. Wiping your brow.

I think he even believes you can change.

EZRA: Ira, Ziva, Mordecai,
Hannah, Rachel, Sarah,
Isaac, Miriam…Yonatan

YONATAN:

In the world which will be renewed   Ira, Ziva, Mordecai
and where He will give life to the dead   Hannah, Rachel, Sarah
and raise them to eternal life   Isaac, Miriam, Falastine
    Mohammed, Omar

MARIAM: I look at these hills   YONATAN: Saffiyeh
            and my heart hits the Wall   Fatima

            like a sparrow   Mahmoud
            flying hard into glass.   Abdul.

            I shriek, yes
            sometimes I shriek at him.

            But that day, in the fog of the gas,
            the concrete inside me cracked.

            And I knew I would marry Yonatan
            even if I lost my own family.

            Even if I had to leave him
            every time the IDF drop their bombs.

            Leave my husband to cook for himself,
            sleep by himself, talk to himself,

            every time his people massacre mine.

            What a strange daughter, strange sister,
            strange wife I am.

EZRA: *and rebuild the city of Jerusalem*
            and complete His temple there
            and uproot foreign worship from the earth

YONATAN: How do I know
            I won't fail my child?
            How do I know
            I don't still need you?
            Like God, like the dead,
            you move through me
            in ways and to where
            I can't know.

MARIAM: *Insha'allah,* my own years shall be long.
            Insha'allah, I shall see my people freed.
            Insha'allah, when I am old,
            as we mop up his spittle and sweat,

my children will wash me
with a cool cloth dipped in the water
of the *wadi* that flows through what was
once my grandmother's village.

EZRA*:* Ira, Ziva, Mordecai,
Hannah, Rachel, Sarah,
Isaac, Miriam, Yonatan.

YONATAN: In her eyes, I am worthy.
In her body, I am rooted.
In her struggle, I am tested.
In her love, I raise my tent.

MARIAM: One hundred years old
your hands.

Gnarled as the stumps of olive trees
and forever at my throat.

Otherwise, so like his:
elegant fingers;

palms creased soft as vellum;
lines, praise Allah, he rewrote.

EZRA: Gone. All gone.
G-d in his wisdom has taken them.
G-d wants me to spend my last years
worshipping Him alone.

YONATAN: *Saba, Saba.* You're not alone.
We're here to take care of you,
We've come to pay our respects.
You're a hundred years old today –
like a prophet.
God has blessed you, *Saba* Ezra
with long life, a great-grandchild.

MARIAM: Small as an olive inside me.

YONATAN: *Mazal tov. Mazal tov.*

MARIAM: I'm sorry for your losses, *Saba* Ezra.
            Insha'allah, may your last years
            bring peace to your heart,
            and justice to our land.
            Salaam, Saba Ezra. *Shalom.*

EZRA: Like a prophet, he says.
            A prophet?
            The prophets had descendants.
            I HAVE NO ONE.

            The End.

Notes

Saba – 'grandfather' in Hebrew.

shiksa – a derogatory term for a non-Jewish woman.

za'atar – a mixture of herbs, sesame seeds and salt, popular throughout the Middle East.

Ya Allah – 'Oh God' in Arabic.

'Alma, 'Amqa, 'Ayn al-Zaytun, 'Ayn Karim, Beit Mazmil, Beit Surik, Biddu, Deir Yassin, Dishon, Jura, Qaddita, Sabbarin, Saris, Sataf, and Zuba are fifteen of over 500 villages, towns and cities depopulated or destroyed in the well-documented 1947-9 Zionist campaign to clear the Holy Land of Arabs. [Source: Ilan Pappe (2007), *The Ethnic Cleansing of Palestine*, Oneworld Publications.]

Ezra's two verses beginning 'In the world that shall be renewed' are from the burial Kaddish, also known as the Jewish Prayer for the Dead.

Mandla Langa

WHEN HE HAD BEEN LOVED...

Almon Goba sat in the back of the pick-up listening to the rain lashing the tarpaulin cover, the torrent conspiring with the wind to produce a continuous roar. He was comfortable with the noise. It made conversation impossible. Not that he was unsociable; no, he just wanted to think, to think. He wanted to remember the crossing in June 1976, on a Saturday night like this, from South Africa – or, to be more exact, Zeerust in the former Western Transvaal – into Botswana, into freedom. He recalled the hush as the van rushed into the night, going against the wind, the tyres crunching and spitting out the gravel before his two guides left him at the banks of the river. Swollen by unseasonal downpours the river was scary. Holding a small suitcase containing a change of clothes, a toothbrush and a book above his head, he forded the river and came out the other side, in Botswana – and walked.

Eleven o'clock on Sunday, he was still walking, seeing his new host country for the first time, feeling the sun bearing down on him, the dust rising to paste itself on his wet garments. There was nothing remarkable about the new land; it looked like some of the places he knew, the farms where he had worked when on school vacation or other fenced-off acreages owned by white people, where he had started to suspect that something was wrong in the land. Here, the bleakness was in the bleached stones, the scattered huts fashioned out of straw and cast-off things, the hills, a dull, tawny desert leavened by scrub dominated by thorny mimosas. A serviceable white van, seeming to emerge out of the savannah woodland, came up the stony path and pulled alongside Goba. The driver, a middle-aged white priest appraised him with incurious blue eyes. 'Are you a refugee?' he asked, before correcting the rudeness of interrogating someone before introducing himself. 'I'm Father Columbine,' he said.

'Yes,' Goba admitted. 'I'm a refugee.'

'You look a real sight,' Father Columbine said.

'Yes. The water. The river.'

'Get in.'

Although the priest was alone, Goba clambered into the back. He was self-conscious about his appearance. It was a bumpy ride on the corrugated road from Pitsane to Lobatse. They stopped in several villages where Father Columbine conducted Mass. He would return from the service accompanied mostly by elderly men in hats and greatcoats that needed a lift and these would join Goba in the back. With every addition, the small, canopied van was filled with the feral odour of poverty. Knowing very little Setswana, Goba feigned speech impairment although, he knew, he wasn't fooling anyone. He couldn't quite pull off the sign language and his denim suit and shoes caked with reddish earth were a dead giveaway he'd just recently crossed the River Pitsane.

In the late afternoon, the pick-up rolled into Lobatse, a bustling town no bigger than Zeerust, where Goba was to take a train to Gaborone. He thanked Father Columbine. The old men smiled, probably amused at how quickly he had recovered from his disability. It was late at night when he reached Gaborone where he was picked up at the station by two Movement representatives, one, a stocky man his own age and the other, Absalom Gumede, quiet, amiable and eternally curious, who'd be Goba's friend and comrade for almost forty years. It was to his funeral that Almon Goba was now heading, once again reluctant to socialise as he travelled at the back of a pick-up.

His unwillingness to engage with the fellow passengers also came from not wanting to hear their stories. Knowledge would impose an obligation on him to take action. And he was a little tired today. He had heard it murmured at the beginning of the journey that there would be trouble. With Goba were two families, a middle-aged woman dressed from head to toe in the white robes of the worshippers of the Church of the Nazareth with her husband and their fourteen-year-old daughter. The second family was a much older man, his wife and two grown-up sons, twins by the look of it, in late adolescence. To the religious parents' discomfort, the two young men kept shooting sharp glances at the young woman, whose beauty stammered in the silent gloom of the covered transport. And on the rare occasion that she raised her eyes to return their furtive gaze, they quickly looked away as if what they had encountered in those depthless eyes foreshadowed their doom.

Fearing to look at the people too closely, Goba pretended to be asleep and, eyes closed, he thought back to the first evening in Gaborone, to the two men taking him for a meal at the President Hotel, realising that he was in a hotel for the first time in his life, and that he was twenty years old. Absalom Gumede told him that tomorrow he'd have to report at the police station, and rehearsed him on what he'd have to say. 'The people here,' he said, 'don't like inconsistency.'

And so, the following morning after a night where he'd just collapsed, Gumede accompanied Goba to the Central Police Station adjacent to the hotel where they'd had dinner. Sleek cars, including a white E-type Jaguar, and all bearing South African plates, were parked within a fenced-off enclosure guarded by an unarmed khaki-clad cop who seemed ridiculously young. 'These are hot cars confiscated from the lumpen,' Gumede explained. His face clouded. 'These people give the Special Branch an excuse to come here. And they'll do more than hunt for car thieves.'

Goba didn't say anything. Gumede looked at him. 'You're not much of a talker, are you?'

'No. I listen a lot.'

'Can you sing?'

The question caught him by surprise. 'Not really,' Goba said. 'Used to sing in the school choir but had to leave it.'

'Why?'

'The choirmaster would stick two of his nicotine stained fingers to force our mouths open to form a perfect O.'

'I suppose he also instructed you on voice modulation,' Gumede said. He shook his head. 'What an ass.'

There was no time to further indulge in chitchat because they were already at the reception desk of the police station; having stated their business to the desk sergeant, they were taken upstairs where Almon Goba, now separated from his guardian, faced foreign officialdom on his own. He signed a statement taken by an officer with terrible handwriting. At the end, his interviewer asked him: 'And so, what do you intend doing?' To which Goba gave the answer he had spent half the night rehearsing. 'On escaping the oppression of South African apartheid, I decided to make Botswana my second home.' The statement taker, obviously having heard this formulation many times before, gave a slight shiver as if straining against rolling his eyes or giving a Setswana version of 'yeah, right.'

Later, instead of returning Goba to the residence where there were eight other new arrivals that were either busying themselves with the workings of the liberation movement or were bored out of their minds, Gumede took him on a guided tour of Gaborone, where he was shown the wall that stretched for blocks on end around the State House and which enclosed the official residence of Sir Seretse Khama, Botswana's first president. Apart from the posts and telecommunications building standing not far from Radio Botswana, the African Mall, there wasn't much to see. Pointing at the squat though imposing American Embassy building – the only building with a generator, which kicked in as soon as there was a power failure – Gumede said that he'd soon be applying for a visa to go and study overseas under the auspices of the African-American Institute. 'What would you like to do?' he asked Goba.

'I'd like to go and fight,' Goba said. 'Learn how to use a gun and go back home.'

'And then?'

Goba found the questioning irritating as if he were being put to a test. He'd just finished dealing with a Motswana policeman and wasn't craving another third degree, no matter how skilfully clothed it was in solicitude. He wanted to tell Gumede, who might have missed this little fact, that he, Goba, had barely escaped being shot in Soweto as part of the student contingent that stood up to the police, armed with stones and dustbin lids while the police fired live ammunition. He had seen what the head of a student looked like after being hit by a fully jacketed metal slug; his nostrils still held the smell of death. What did Gumede want him to say? He shrugged in lieu of an answer.

They were at the front of a school, Marua Pula, which catered for the moneyed of the land and expatriates who had foreign currency. The school children, scrubbed and seemingly well-fed in beige and blue colours, reminded Goba of the white schools in the country he had just left, to which they were bussed to engage in debates on topics aimed at stimulating young minds. Well, the young minds if not the glands of the black visitors simply slavered at the opulence of the schools they visited, the labs with the latest equipment, a language lab complete with recording gizmos, twelve-track mixing tables, processors, monitors, a studio. 'We were in this school,' he told Gumede, 'which had all these things. Stuff we'd only seen in magazines. Computers, tape recorders, microphones, all sorts of accessories. And the thought that hit me was, if white kids have all this, how do we ever catch up with them?' He shook his head. 'An idea that immediately came to mind was, well, if we can't have access to these learning aids, then surely it's only fair that no one does.'

'You'd smash them,' Gumede suggested.

'Yes. I thought we'd break into the place once everyone's gone and set it on fire.'

'But you know that the only person who'd get affected is the night watchman, who'd be blamed and then sacked for sleeping on the job while you heroic guerrillas provided the pyrotechnics. And he'd be someone's father, brother or uncle – in your township.' Gumede spat out the last word like a curse. 'And the white students would have something for spicing up the dinner conversations and the insurance company would pay up and upgrade the labs and everyone would go home and have a beer. Just another day in Africa.'

He waved and beckoned over a group of boys and girls in grades eleven and twelve, who all seemed excited at seeing him. Monitoring their approach as they peeled themselves off a larger group of students milling around the tuck-shop, Gumede was smiling. It was as if Goba was seeing him for the first time. Gumede, at ease, balanced against railings in a pair of tan chinos, a khaki shirt and scuffed veldskoene, the tough bush shoes that seemed to be much in favour among both Batswana and South Africans. He still had on his head the soft khaki hat called a 'Sportie,' whose brim he'd now and then tug as if to reassure himself that it was still in place. It was in the company of young people that Almon realised how shy Gumede was. Today, when he introduced Almon Goba, one of the more coquettish of the young women, Tsidi, said: 'Ah, now you've brought us someone more handsome than you…how are we going to manage?' And they all laughed and Gumede blushed, his chocolate-brown shade turning indigo under the unforgiving Botswana sun.

In the late afternoon when the smoke from cooking fires hovered over the dwellings, the Movement residence in the suburb of Tlokweng rang with the voices of a group of sixteen or seventeen mainly young people who'd been joined by a few of the South African refugees. The small choir, conducted and taken through its paces by Absalom Gumede, was aided by a young student who set the key with a mellifluous blast of his mouth organ. Earlier, Gumede had given a short lecture on the basics of interpreting the flies and inverted ampersands and golf clubs, numerical notations, into music that made sense to the ear. Even though he had heard it before in the sun-drenched classroom where about ten Standard VIII pupils, mostly hard cases under punishment, had to take a class in Music, which they all hated, Almon Goba had to admit that Gumede had a way of making it sound interesting, almost fun. 'These sheets of paper,' he said, 'stuck to the wall with tape, thumb tacks or even chewing gum are your licence out of boredom and preoccupation with your personal troubles. The songs here,' he gestured with a ruler, 'tell a story of how it all began, a story about our lives and which our country needs to hear.'

Absalom Gumede was driven by his own personal philosophy. After a few weeks, in mid-August, he was having difficulty sleeping. 'Hey, AG?' he called from his bunk above. 'You asleep?'

Goba considered ignoring him, but thought better of it. 'I was dreaming when you called me.'

'Well,' Gumede said, 'I probably saved you from a nightmare.'

'What is it?'

It was past midnight; the other men were snoring and muttering in their sleep. 'I've a confession to make.'

'I don't like to hear confessions,' Almon Goba said. 'People's stories have a way of becoming your problem.'

'Then why are you here,' Gumede asked, 'if not to carry other people's burdens?'

'I'm here for my own stuff,' Goba said. 'We might be united in our hatred of apartheid and what the racists have done but – at the end of the day – we're lone hunters.'

'Well,' Gumede said, 'I'll make a recommendation you should go for training so that you're recruited into special ops.'

'Special ops?'

'Special operations units are highly trained,' Gumede said. 'Some form suicide squads, real daredevils infiltrated inside the country to carry out acts of sabotage. Sometimes assassinations.' He paused. 'You'd like that, I suppose?'

'It's what I joined the struggle for.' Almon Goba craved a cigarette, but on crossing the river into Botswana, he'd told himself he was breaking some habits. And smoking was one of them. 'And you? What's your story?'

'I thought you didn't want to hear confessions?'

'I know you'll tell me anyway.'

In 1975, while the war was raging in Angola, Absalom Gumede was one of the youngest members of the Che Guevara detachment that was set up once ANC President Oliver Tambo and Angolan President Dr Agostinho Neto decided to open military training facilities for the Movement. It was a dangerous time with people dying left, right and centre, casualties of covert operations mounted by UNITA and the South Africans in collusion with the CIA. At that time, Gumede and Zenzo, another young trainee from Johannesburg, were rivals for the attention of a beautiful Angolan woman whose mother ran a tavern in Caculama in the Malange province.

Orlanda de Almeida was a languid poem of dimples and hair and a flawless caramel skin; conjuring up her image even after such a long time was like evoking a spell, reliving a series of feverish moments. But Gumede knew that he was being unrealistic in this tussle with Zenzo. Proficient in Portuguese, which he spoke with a flourish like a streetwise Angolano, Zenzo had an edge over Gumede. And, when reduced to a figure of fun, when Zenzo wangled an increasing number of permits to be out with the truck, where on return he cited chapter and verse what he and the delectable Orlanda did – how their bodies sang! – Gumede prayed. He pleaded with the shadows in whose honour his grandmother had burnt incense and herbs to bring luck and thwart the enemy.

When Zenzo next went out of the camp, this time driving an East German IFA truck, he probably never heard the detonation of the TM-46 anti-tank mine that flung the truck into the air and turned it into scrap. 'Whatever joy I might have felt,' Gumede said, 'was soon destroyed by news from home that my parents, Ma and Pa, were killed in a car accident. It all happened almost in the same week of Zenzo's death.'

'A coincidence.' Almon Goba wondered why he was trying to reassure him.

'Possibly.' Gumede was unconvinced. 'To me, though, one thing was clear. When you make a covenant with the shadows – and these could be God, Jesus Christ, Buddha, Allah, Yahweh or what the AA people call the higher power – it must be underpinned by goodness, a purity of heart. Anything less unleashes terror.'

'So,' Goba asked, wondering why he was picked as a confessor, 'you what? You got converted by the experience?'

'You would, too, if you believed you'd had a hand in your parents' death.' He paused for such a long time that Goba thought he'd mercifully gone back to sleep. Then: 'Orlanda disappeared. Possibly went up north into Brazzaville, I don't know. I heard she was pregnant. I requested the camp commissar to get me a Bible. I'd already read it, in my father's house and, as you know, it's your only reading matter under detention. I don't know, perhaps I wanted to kill myself, put the muzzle of the AK-47 under my chin and pull the trigger. But I read on. And I was filled with humility when I realised how people in ancient times could totally dedicate themselves to service. Like Nehemiah who was charged with reconstructing the temple in Jerusalem, which had been destroyed by war, I also wanted to contribute to something, to building a monument, even something that might lead to my own humiliation.' He returned to Luanda the following day.

A few years later when in Angola, Goba sought to look at the world through Gumede's eyes. Sometimes he scanned the Caculama bush as he ran at a trot during *fisico*, the exacting tactics class where recruits were trained in endurance. On these occasions, he'd wonder if any of the villagers crowding doorways and bearing witness to his platoon's noisy manoeuvres were related to Orlanda de Almeida. If she'd been pregnant, as Gumede had supposed, would hers be among these naked, stick-legged and pot-bellied toddlers sucking their thumbs? Because he hadn't met her, he named every attractive young woman Orlanda, popularising the name among the choristers of the Amandla Cultural Ensemble, where he had been one of the conductors substituting Jonas Gwangwa, the famous trombonist responsible for shaping guerrillas into polished performers, whenever he was out of town. During one of Gwangwa's prolonged absences, this one occasioned by a car accident that had him out of commission for months on end, Gumede's term in ACE was judged as most productive by the nascent department of arts and culture.

As soon as he was made an officer, Absalom Gumede moved from the trainees' barracks to a room in the officers' block, which formed the base of the letter U, the other arms made up of elongated one-storey barracks that were part of a camp bequeathed to the Movement by the Cubans. Although it was a one-room residence, with a trapdoor leading to the fortified dwelling underground, he had turned the place into a bedroom/study, some of his law books still on the rough bookshelf when Almon Goba arrived. The room was sunny, with a view on the courtyard where the company assembled for roll call at 0500 every morning; at the back the window opened on a wide swath of viridian, the Angolan bush, which stretched into the misty hills.

'What did he do during the day?' Almon Goba had asked one of the commissars from the recording department. These were actually doing highly secretive security work and were feared, people who wielded anonymous power. But Almon felt he needed to know; he was also surprised that the officer seemed ill at ease. He was unused to being the subject of an interview.

'We would see him standing framed against the window,' the young man said, 'usually minutes before the assembly, which, as you'll know, was characterised by singing and chanting – and slogans of affirmation.' He paused.

'One had an impression he wanted to join in the singing, from his attentive stance. But then he was already an officer.'

'Was that all he did?'

'As regular as clockwork,' the commissar said, 'he'd listen to chamber music and swing his arms as if conducting a choir. After breakfast, he'd go on a five-kilometre walk. Most of the time, when he came back, we'd be engaged in our programme.'

'What did people call him?' Suddenly to know what Absalom had been called was important. 'His MK name?'

'They called him Comrade Nehemiah.'

'Why?' Almon Goba remembered their last conversation in Botswana.

'When he was not with the Amandla people, he'd be poring over his books, a whole stack of legal stuff he got via the Print Shop in Luanda. People liked him because he'd been in the camps and had left and came back. Not many people did that. Most people, when they left and tasted the life outside, you wouldn't catch them dead in the military. I had a feeling he was doing some personal service, like those religious people that get attached to some order.'

Every 28 October, the Movement in the camps of Angola would commemorate the day of the heroic guerrilla, *el día del guerrillero heroico*, a practice borrowed from the Cubans. It stemmed from the disappearance over the ocean during a night flight from Camagüey to Havana, of Father Camilo Cienfuegos, who was one of Fidel Castro's guerrillas and a hero of the Cuban revolution, on October 28, 1959. On this day, which also celebrated the birthday of ANC president Oliver Tambo, the camp routine changed. From morning to nightfall cadres debated legal matters, strategy and tactics; everyone, from the president to the lowliest recruit enjoyed equal status. There was no camp commander, no rookie. People were encouraged to raise any points they felt strongly about. They discussed, for instance, how to attract white people to the ANC, to MK. It was here that Absalom Gumede spoke about service and the need for comrades to dedicate themselves to building lasting monuments. For him, law was the cornerstone of establishing a new democratic order. It was here that Gumede stressed the importance of setting up professional bodies where none existed and strengthening those that were in place. He spoke of an independent judiciary, revolutionary student movements, civic associations, religious structures, and the women's movement – all these institutions would transform and build a new and democratic South Africa. 'What he said made a lot of sense,' the commissar said, 'but he'd also shoot himself in the foot.'

'How so?'

'For one, the ANC is a secular movement but he'd quote some holy writ to anyone inclined to give him an audience. I think that's where the name Nehemiah started. I don't know if he knew that name. But he'd always tell people they had to carve a stone to build a temple.' He snorted derisively. 'We were here to fight against the racist regime; we were not stonemasons.'

'But that's how he put it? People had to build?'

'Yes. Like Nehemiah.'

'You think he was…unstable?'

'All of us were unstable,' the commissar replied, quickly. 'He was all right.'

'This is *not* right,' said the middle-aged woman in the white robes of believers. Almon Goba who had begun to doze, was startled into wakefulness. He looked around him and saw that save for the indignant woman all his fellow passengers were fast asleep. 'It is not right,' she said again, this time making no pretence she was addressing anyone else. The rain had let up somewhat, reducing its earlier onslaught into a slight drizzle. In the shadowed interior of the pick-up Goba saw the woman shaking her head, her eyes glowing like a cat's.

'Were you saying something, Mama?' Goba asked. He parted the tarpaulin flap to get his bearings. Released from something that had fastened it on the roof, a corner of the canvass slapped Goba across the face, a blow that stung and blinded him for a moment. They'd just passed the Mooi River Toll Plaza, 146 kilometres to Durban; how many hours would that be? Two hours, perhaps. If he were driving, he'd eat up the tar and make it in a little less than 90 minutes, but then KwaZulu Natal traffic cops were big on making examples out of speedsters with Johannesburg or Gauteng Province plates. The woman coughed. 'Are you all right, son?'

'I'm fine,' he said, rubbing the side of his face. He had an impression his fingers had traced a swelling. 'You were saying? Earlier?'

'We're carrying a heavy matter,' she said. 'My husband and I and Teresa.'

'Teresa's the little girl?'

'Yes,' the woman said. 'She's not so little anymore, someone's made sure of that.'

'What happened?'

'My husband will be very unhappy that I'm speaking to you about this,' she said. 'But you look like a sensible man.' She peered into the dark, removing with her eyes whatever invisible layer covered the other passengers, concentrating on the huddled outlines of bodies of the other couple and their twin sons. Her husband snored on and, at one point, gave a percussive fart. Almon Goba had a feeling that the young woman, Teresa, was not really asleep.

'My name is Lydia Zungu,' she said, in a voice of trombone timbre, perfected in hundreds of vigils, 'and my husband is Benjamin and we are of the Church of the Holy Nazarene. We are a God-fearing people. We pay our dues every Sunday and we bring up our children – Teresa here and her brothers – we bring them up with values which will make them better people. We aim to harm no one. That is why this thing that happened is simply not right.'

'What happened?'

'We'd gone on pilgrimage in the North-West,' Lydia Zungu said, 'and we left the boys at home with a relative, but we took Teresa along, a big mistake in the light of what happened.' She swallowed, scanning the dark. 'We'd all gone for morning ablutions and left Teresa, she's only fourteen, left her among her age-mates, other girls and a few boys who seemed harmless. I now believe there's no such thing as a harmless being as long as it has a penis. These boys, together with bigger ones, dragged the girls to a field. The others escaped but by the time they raised a hue and cry, Teresa had been beaten up and raped.'

The boys were caught and there was a trial. 'We've just come back from there, now. And we thought we'd get justice.' Lydia Zungu shook her head as if dispelling an offending memory. 'The boys, sons of the more well off in our church, were let off on a technicality. What is a technicality, you tell me, when a child's womanhood has been ripped apart? What's technical about our pain? We supported the new government when it came to power and we also lost relatives who donated their lives to the struggle. For peace and justice. But this justice everyone trumpets, we haven't seen it. Maybe this justice wears the robes that make it invisible to the poor.'

Almon Goba believed himself incapable of eloquence. 'My tongue,' he said, 'does not have the words to tell you how sorry I am to hear what happened to your family. There are people who did try to get this country on an even keel. What I'm saying will not restore Teresa's virginity, but it might give her comfort in hours of despair. I learnt so much from a man I met a long time ago.'

When Nelson Mandela was released on 11 February 1990, Absalom Gumede, who'd been admitted to the Bar, was in London in discussions with the British Anti-Apartheid Movement. Standing in front of South Africa House, watching the release unfolding on the television screen, watching

Mandela, thinner and greyer, coming out accompanied by Winnie Mandela, tears rolled down his cheeks. Later, he was part of the legal team working with CODESA, the Convention for a Democratic South Africa, which would negotiate terms for a new South Africa. The negotiating parties would investigate the establishment of the new constitution, setting up the interim government, the future of the homeland system, which had taken citizenship from millions of black South Africans and, much more importantly, setting up the electoral system.

By the time of the elections in 1994, Absalom Gumede was one of the most sought-after legal minds, appearing mainly for people that the transition period was leaving behind; the groupings fighting landlords; women at the heel of male oppression. He was there at the hearings of the Truth and Reconciliation Commission, TRC, which was where his troubles started. He felt that there was something obscene about creating an analogy between the crimes of the apartheid regime and the human rights violations of the liberation movement. Possibly driven by a passion which few understood, he became a thorn in the side of certain clerics, government ministers or political party bosses he regarded as limp minded. 'These people,' he'd thunder, 'would have us believe that reconciliation can be achieved through an act of parliament. True reconciliation could only follow a thorough re-examination of the past, which is irreversibly intertwined with the future we're trying to create.'

At first, when a mere advocate, an attorney, someone whose utterances could be dismissed as a tactic to increase his cachet in a commercial world, it was possible to ignore him. In any event, the new and democratic South Africa was trying to find its feet and this exploration manifested itself in various forms. The legal system, once a cornerstone of policy that had oppressed black people for more than three centuries, had now thrown up various interpreters and advocates of a new jurisprudence.

But his challenges to the government reached a higher level of stridency. It was different from the time when his outbursts could be seen as a symptom of the general confusing euphoria of the times, bearing in mind that freedom was still in its infancy. People were engaged in a series of experiments. Then, Gumede wrote an open letter to President Nelson Mandela, where, while praising the establishment of the TRC, he cautioned against a crisis of expectation such a commission would unleash. 'Our people,' he wrote, 'have been at the receiving end of injustice for so long that to give them hope that their oppressors will one day face retribution could be iniquitous.'

His warning was informed by a case of two young men who had refused to incriminate themselves in the killing of two policemen. According to the rules of the TRC, applicants were required to make full disclosure, and these men were then regarded by the panellists as recalcitrant and thus beyond the pale. Ironically, the ones who admitted to the killing were later released, amnestied; their culpability codified as justifiable behaviour during an insane period of war. Advocate Gumede, then, campaigned unsuccessfully for the men to be released. 'The truth,' he said, 'obviously shall not make you free – in the New South Africa.'

The second case, which turned him into an outcast, was his refusal to be on the defence team for a minister who was accused of corruption. Since the minister was very popular – and a hero of the struggle – many of his supporters felt that condemning him was giving grist to the mill of sceptics and racists who saw corruption as second nature to black people in power. Thus, any black person that strayed from the fellowship of patriotic cheerleaders was excommunicated. 'We cannot,' Absalom Gumede said, 'stand here and pretend that it is correct for us to go against the code of conduct and rule of law that made our constitution the envy of the international community. The minister must just resign and show us all that he is a man of integrity.'

'Where is he, now?' Lydia Zungu asked. 'This man.'

'He died two weeks ago,' Almon Goba said. 'I'm off to his funeral.'

'It's a pity.'

'He had done what he had to do,' Goba said.

'Welcome to Durban.'

Other than for two or three in-and-out conferences in air-conditioned rooms, Almon Goba had managed to avoid Durban for almost sixteen years. Having lived in Johannesburg since returning from exile, Durban and its humidity reminded him of the camp in Angola, the swampy, malarial existence of arrivals and departures. Even though he had spent a lot of time in Johannesburg before going into exile, Durban was his birthplace, where his umbilical cord was buried and, more importantly, where his mother and father were buried six feet under twin graves topped with concrete and granite headstones that bore uplifting inscriptions.

Here he was, at the end of March, studying the faces of more than a hundred mourners in the Red Hill cemetery, the thirteen-inch handmade teardrop conductor's baton with a white shaft nestling in its case. He looked up at the treetops. The sky seemed bluer than usual, an impression created by the streaky stratus clouds that were edged with an orange tint from the sun. He smelled the air, gauging its intention. The rain had stopped and it was getting warm. Many of the mourners, especially the women, had armed themselves with umbrellas, which would serve as shelter from the rain or shade from the sun. This duality of things, the fact that every experience was accompanied by its shadow, left and right, good and evil, had been the philosophy of the man lying in the casket today.

Looking remarkably alive as he lay inside the coffin, Absalom Gumede, would never know that he had inspired hot debates in shebeens. Many dinner conversations invariably touched on his courage – or foolhardiness – that came from a belief in his own personal version of the New Jerusalem. Here, under a windless sky, Goba listened as a young man, possibly a relative, recited lines from a poem by Margaret Walker.

Let the martial songs be written, let the dirges disappear.

Let a race of men now rise and take control.

The master of ceremonies, a priest, kept peering into the middle distance, echoing the anxiety that Almon Goba was feeling. Where was the choir? Where were the paralegals, clerks, attorneys and even one or two judges that had taken part in the choir that Absalom Gumede had organised, in the years when he had been loved?

And then the busses arrived, unloading throngs of men and women in legal robes, some holding onto their hats, rushing, skirting other graves and mourners in Red Hill, already beginning to sing the songs that celebrated the man lying in the box. Almon Goba took out the conductor's baton and readied himself to take over from Comrade Nehemiah.

Jackie Kay

HADASSAH

Mordecai bring me up like I is his own and in a way I is his own. He call me Hadassah. It mean morning star. He say there is a song about the morning star; he say Hadassah shine a light where no light shine. My parents die when I am little, and that's how Mordecai come. He is not uncle nor cousin to me, more like a father, more like father and mother. Days gone, I smile on my face when we stand by the river. I know my smile is same as Mordecai as he smile back. Look at us in the river, Mordecai say. The river know us. Then I imagine they have another life, the two people in the river; I imagine we leave them there. And when the men take us, and I lose Mordecai, it is there I go in my head – the time by the river. I like to think of a big reef basket carrying Mordecai and me down the dark river beside the river rushes and the lizards, the crocodiles and the logs that look like crocodiles, the white egrets on our tail, and white blossom on the trees.

Mordecai tell me I am around fifteen years of age when I am taken away, far away, to another land, a land of milk and honey. When I gets here a man who promise me food and shelter come and meet me. I don't like the man who name is *the King*. On the day I arrive, the King is angry with a woman, name of Vashti. The King is angry with Vashti because she will not do as he say. He ask her to come to this big do where he say he has forked out good money for the food, and he wants to show her off to the men, name of Pimps. One girl, Nell, tells me Vashti say, 'I will not eat with men who treat me like I am a piece of meat.' And that the King gets rid of her; he slices off her head as if she is an egg, Nell say. He can do what he likes, Lily say, the police never come. Nobody care about us. We are scum. Then Lily starts dancing round our room singing at the top of her voice, 'We are scum, we are scum, we are scum!' Until Agnes quiet her and say she is going to get trouble with all her silliness.

When Vashti leave, or has her head chop off like an egg, the King send for me! I tremble in his pad – white and green and blue hangings; tied round his purple curtain – silver rings. He say let me show you my pad. His pad is in the same building as the place we sleep, but it is different from our dump. We never go there unless he comes and take us there or send for us. 'I work hard for this,' the King say. And he take me to his kitchen: grey marble top and cupboard and mixer tap. Then we go into his bedroom and I am embarrass. On the King's bed is a cover of gold and silver. On his bedroom floor is a thick red carpet and smaller rugs, blue and white and black rugs. A wardrobe and drawers in dark wood. 'See, the furniture is all matching,' he say. In his living room: leather sofas and big lights and black and white walls with tall marble columns at the side of the room. The King wear a long quilted dressing gown, a dark purple. From time to time, it fall open and I see red Y-fronts.

He say, 'You're going to be *The One* now. Do you know what it means to be *The One*?' I don't know, but I nod because I don't want to be like Vashti and have my head slice like an egg. He say, 'you will be my eyes and ears. Any talk of running off, you come to the King, have you got that into your pretty head, you give the King the nod and the wink?' I nod and he say, speak up. 'You are learning the lingo, aren't you? You know please and thank you?' I say, please and thank you. He laugh; but I don't know what is so funny. He say, 'You never come to me unless you got something to report. Get it? You never come to ask for anything for yourself. Girls that do that get punished. Sort yourself out. I don't want to hear nothing about your problems, got it? You got your periods then get one of the girls to get you tampons or whatever. Understood?' I blush, my cheeks hot. I say please and thank you again. He say, 'I'm trying my best to keep you safe from the Pigs; if you girls don't earn the bacon, how am I supposed to feed you?' I don't understand, so I just say Thank you with no please, and he likes that and say 'You're a fast learner, aren't you, Hadassah?' And he pull my curly black head toward him. And he teach me a new word. After the new word finish, I say, Thank you, again and then I leave the Pad quick, back to my dump where we girls, black and brown and white girls lays in a bed – four or five girls on one mattress on the floor. I lie down on the bed and keep my eyes open, wide as I can.

The floorboards are bare and there is the smell of fear in the room mix with the smell of sweat mix with some horrible smell and nobody trust anybody. I learn the King's English fast so that I can do as the King ask. I learn words I don't want to know the meaning of; I learn words I wish I did not; so many words for the same thing.

Whenever I think the girls are whispering something the King want to know, I lie quiet and listen. I always been a girl who can listen long time and keep still. Quite a few plans, I tell him, and every time I do he give me a gold coin. Know what this is? This is a two-quid coin. I collect my gold coins in a tin. I find a good place to hide them under the wooden floorboards on a low shelf. I am careful nobody is watching when I put a new coin in my tin. I like doing that. I like to count them.

One night, when I am asleep in a huddle with the other girls in our dirty dump, I hear a knocking at the window. I open it and see Mordecai standing on the balcony! Mordecai! He say our people are in trouble; they holding them in Immigration. I never know what asylum means then. I still not sure. I know if you go mad you sent to asylum. Mordecai told me the King is a good man, who has his faults and is with the wrong people, but has a heart of gold because he is the one who is help people like us get asylum. At night, I lie awake thinking about this and thinking about the King who help send the women mad. At night in that one room you hear the sound of girls and young women cry, and sometimes pray and sometimes cry and pray together.

I don't think Mordecai really know the kind of man the King is or the kind of things he want girls to do. I tell Mordecai that I learn words I wish I didn't. Mordecai don't understand what I say. He say he has no influence over the King and that I am close, that word on the street say I am as close to the King as anybody. I tell Mordecai, the King say you can't trouble him for nothing or else he will have your head. On day one, he tell me: ask for nothing. Mordecai say, 'did I bring you up to care about yourself? No, remember our time by the river back in our own country? Remember how you were happy then. You have to be brave and go to the man they call the King and speak up for your people.'

There is eight of us who come from our country. Eight of us who is with Mordecai and me, hidden first as cargo on the boat, and then in a lorry, inside boxes, where we can't breathe, where we think we are going to die, no air, no water, just the dark. We arrive, and a man who is a friend of the King's take me and Mordecai and we never see the rest of our people. 'They were stopped. They didn't make it through.' Mordecai tell me now. 'They have been kept in a holding place.' 'I have not been out,' I whisper to him. 'I have not felt the air on my face. I am prisoner here.'

'You have to talk to the King and get him to help. They need help to fill in the questionnaires.' I shake my head. I can't. I can't. I will get into trouble. Mordecai say 'Hadassah, remember what I used to tell you when you were a girl, how you shine a light where no one else can shine?' I remember, I say, but in this godforsaken country, it is each man for hisself. Mordecai look astonish, maybe surprise at my big word. I hear somebody say *godforsaken* the other day and I like the sound of it. I been waiting for a chance to say *godforsaken*. 'Don't you see Hadassah if they get them, they will get us. We'll be sent back home where they will find us and kill us.' Mordecai's eyes looked sad and small and black, not like the eyes of the man he is when we stand by the river. Mordecai plead one more time, see what you can do. And Mordecai climb down the drain pipe and vanish into the dark.

The next morning I still don't feel brave and leave my bowl of cereal uneaten on my lap. At lunchtime, when our soup come, I leave that too. And at dinner time, when pasta is there, I leave that. One of the girls, Chiamake from Nigeria, notice. She say eat your food, girl, or you will starve. Another girl, Betty from Glasgow say, Are you no wanting this? I'll have it then. And she wolf down my pasta. Next day, I do the same. And Betty wolf my food. Third day – the same, the same. Betty can't believe it! All I have each day is a lemon squeeze into a glass and hot water. Each day I sip my lemon and hot water slow, slow. By then, the hunger gone, and I feel light-head but also concentrate, and I am frighten no more. Not eating make me strong, make me see clearly. Strange it is – nothing in my belly but my thoughts see-through.

And then I ask Clara, who is the one who do the shopping, who is allow out because the King know a girl will not run away because no one has any place to go and even when someone do run away the traffickers find you and sometime Nell say they chop your body into pieces and throw it in the river. They do that even with the small children. Even when they are put in Children Home, they wait and they find them and they steal them away. I tell Clara to use the money in my special tin, my two-quid coins I been saving for *my rainy day*, a rainy day I imagine will change to sunshine when Mordecai come and take me to another place in England; when Mordecai take me where people wear funny hats and push long sticks in the river. I see a picture like that in a mag in the King's Pad.

I give her the coins and I say, buy food for a party. What do you want? She ask me. So I tell her to get rice so I can make jollof rice, and plantain, and cassava, and chicken legs and cabbage and carrot and onion, pumpkin and black-eyed peas. I say we can get all those in England? And she say *yeah yeah yeah, course*. You can get anything in England: you can make what you like. You want moyin-moyin, cassava, coconut, curry goat, ackee, green plantain, paw paw, prickly pear, egusi soup, collard greens, sweet potato, cocoyam, garri, akara? What you want? Say the word, Clara say, egusi? Just say the word. What in particular you want for the big party? She got so carry away she forgot I tell her already! So I tell her again. I say get me some rice so I can make jollof rice and some chicken so I can make fried chicken and some plantain and some collard greens and some cabbage and carrot and onion and salad cream so I can make coleslaw and some black-eyed peas so I can make moyin-moyin. Get me some banana leaf. I like to make moyin-moyin for Mordecai but he is gone now with disappointment. He does not know what my plan is. Clara leave the house with my gold coins to get the food for the feast. 'You're crazy?' Lily say, 'Using up all your money like that! It's a waste, girl. What about your rainy day?' But I do not have another rainy day and I have to think how to save my bacon.

The King is out and is coming back with new girls. Out a good few hours. I always feel sorry when the new girls arrive and I see the fear in their eyes and I know the words they are going to learn and what they are going to do with them.

Clara arrive back with all the ingredients she buy from a fab shop in Finsbury Park. Usually Clara come back I like ask her question about Finsbury Park: can you see ducks? Are there children on swing? Can you see big bird? Lots of tree? Did you see yourself in pond? A picture of Mordecai and me by the river jump into my mind and I like that. But today, I ask Clara nothing about the park. I am focus because I fast.

I ask three girls to help prepare the food – Nell and Lily and Chiamake. I say follow me to the King's kitchen. At first they scare because we never go there. He never even lock the door he know we too scare. But I tell them the King say it is ok and they believe me. 'You sure about this?' Chiamake say. 'I'm sure.' Anyway, hunger come first! We pound the onion and the chilli and add paprika and magi cubes and rub on the chicken wing and thigh and leg, then fry, then roast; we fluff the jollof rice, and we fry the plantain and chop the cabbage and carrot fine-fine for the coleslaw. We steam the collard greens. I am happy when I see black-eyed peas. We wrap the moyin-moyin in banana leaves and steam for pudding.

We lay the table with red napkins and silver cutlery. I am hungry and just the smell of the food feel like eating. While the chicken roast – before the return of the King and the Pimps and the new girls – I go into the King bathroom and pour bath. I pour myrrh in the bath, lavender oil, sprinkle sea salts – my, how the King like pamper hisself! – and I wash my hands and feet and hair and then I dry in the most soft towel I ever feel. I don't feel worry anymore. The fasting make me brave. I pour bath for Nell and she pour one for Lily and Lily pour one for Chiamake. It like they are all under my spell. Chiamake say 'if anything bad happen to us it is worth it to feel clean like this.' Nell say, if the King comes back early and is angry that we have taken a bath to clean ourselves for the feast, so be it. I nod and smile. It is the most happiest feeling I have all the time I am in England. If he is furious and want to hit me; my body can take it. It is strong; it has been without food for three days. Inside my head I am the girl of the morning star.

After the bath, I dress in clean clothes that I find in the King's wardrobe, women's clothes that I am surprise to find. And I dress the girls too. We are all ready in our red and purple and black dress, in our silk stocking. We have no shoes, no nice shoes, so we just remain in our stocking soles. We are all waiting. I go into the kitchen and open a bottle of red wine. I find a big jug and pour the wine into the big jug like I see the King do. Then I tell the rest of the women to come and sit round the table and enjoy the feast. They also frighten at first, but the smell of the food change their minds! All the women sit down: Betty sit down first, then Lily, Ruth, Chiamake, Ivy, Clara and Nell and Abigail; Elisabeth and Mary and Hannah and Phoebe and Joanna and Judith; Eunice, Hannah and Anna and the other Anna. All of them gather around the big King table, eyes wide at the feast. All the women, the white, and the brown and the black women in the big dining room with the oval shape table and the wall hanging and the rude picture of girls on the wall.

They all look astonish but too hungry to argue. All the women now sitting round the table, all the women from the House of Disrepute. I hear it call that and I repeat it. I say to the women, Let us raise a glass at the table in the House of Disrepute! And everyone laugh and say Thank You. Some say Cheers. Some say Chin Chin. Betty shout Slanjiva! I say, this is a *godforsaken* place, and everyone roar again. Nell say, Hadassah you have some sense of humour. I pour the women some more wine. It is the month of Adar. When the King come back I will make him save our people and I will have revenge for what the Pimps have done, the words they make us say every day. I am strong in my head, and I will not forget the words we are force to say and the things we have to do with them. Steady on, Eunice says. We got to remember which side our bread is buttered on, Ruth says. We don't have to remember, I say, and the deep anger in my voice even surprise me. We don't have to remember what the King tell us to remember. We are our own people.

When the King come into his Pad, he is going to have a big surprise, a big surprise. Perhaps even he will astonish. When Mordecai come back and the King been to Immigration to answer the question and our people leave the Holding, I get us out. I make a plan with the women, a plan to get the men who hurt us. They take their life in their hand when they ask for something, you see. I wait to see what the women say. Perhaps it is the wine but suddenly there is roaring round the table, roaring and cheering. Hannah bite her chicken leg; Eunice bite her chicken leg. Everyone laugh. Joanna can't stop laughing till she splutter her wine out on the table. Chiamake say 'Hadassah, you are a brilliant cook.' Thank you, I say. I wait till everyone has her share, and then I say, Lily, please pass me the rice and I spoon a single spoon of jollof rice, a chicken thigh, a small spoon of coleslaw. Today, I tell the girls, today I break my fast. 'You have no breakfast so you break your fast,' Nell say because she like word like me, not the kind of word the King teach, but other word, a whole world of other word. Yes, I say, smiling to Nell with some *elegance* (another word I learn and like, *elegance*) my head held high. Today I break my fast. I am Hadassah. My name mean morning star.

Neil LaBute

IN THE LAND OF UZ

Job 1:1

In the land of Uz there lived a man whose name was Job.

Neil Finn

Smiling as the shit comes down, you can tell a man from what he has to say.

Silence. Darkness.

And then a series of lights, coming up slowly but turning stunningly bright. Each one revealing a person on their knees.

Maybe ten in all. Ten glowing figures. They speak.

ALL:	...our Father, who art in Heaven...hallowed be thy name...
PERSON 1:	...dear God...high above me...
PERSON 2:	...all-powerful and so, so merciful...
PERSON 3:	...hear these, my humble words...
PERSON 4:	...bless me...I beg of you...
PERSON 5:	...oh Heavenly father...see me now...
PERSON 6:	...I kneel before you, your servant...
PERSON 7:	...I pray to you, oh God...
PERSON 8:	...here on my knees and at your mercy...
PERSON 9:	...wrestling as I do with my soul...

PERSON 10:   ...trying to understand, to *comprehend* your infinite wisdom and your plan...

PERSON 2:   ...and above all, my sweet Lord...

PERSON 4:   ...beyond all else, I thank you...

PERSON 8:   ...yes, Father, yes, I'm thankful to you for what you have done...

PERSON 5:   ...for having set out before me so many challenges...

PERSON 7:   ...and struggles, such great struggles...

PERSON 3:   ...for this I thank you...I thank you...

PERSON 9:   ...for your wisdom, Dear God, your wisdom and guidance that you've shared with me, by placing these tests on my character...

PERSON 1:   ...thanks be to you, merciful God...

PERSON 10:   ...confronting me as you do, my Father on high...I thank you for all...

PERSON 6:   ...as I bow down before your everlasting glory, dear God... your beacon of light...

ALL: ...Master of all, forever, I thank you...

PERSON 2:   ...for the niggers, oh God, for all the niggers and chinks and spics that you've created...I thank you...for that asshole Allah and that fat little Buddha and all those other mother fuckers I despise, who reject you and your son, Jesus Christ...

PERSON 7:   ...and the boys, the little boys whom I teach each day and watch...on the recess grounds as they run and play and stare up at me with their searching little eyes...I thank you for this, dear Lord...for the children you place in front of me...

PERSON 9:   ...the money...the money you rain down on me, shower over me each day...that I find impossible not to take and ferret away in my own accounts – off-shore are best – and for this I am grateful and give myself to you, knowing that this is *my* trial and *my* test and that you have chosen me alone to toss upon these rocky shoals...

PERSON 5: ...the feel of my wife's face beneath my hand...the snap of my fist against her...it comforts me to know her blood is the blood you've asked me to spill...that I am merely a messenger of God...

PERSON 10: ...each time he fucks me, Father, each time my neighbour puts his cock into me...I know that his thrusts are your thrusts, his groans of pleasure come from you and yet they challenge me...beg me to stop and return to my husband and children...

PERSON 4: ...for confronting me with this, oh my dear God, I thank you even with my tears and curses of your name...in my heart I know that you are great and powerful...that you alone placed me in that car at night, drunk and unafraid of what might lie ahead...

PERSON 3: ...watching my daughter sleep...standing in her room at night and seeing her there in her blankets...I thank you for this...

PERSON 1: ...each time I curse you I praise you, my God, each time I scream out your name in vain is me heralding your greatness...my giving over to the joy and beauty of your salvation...no matter what they say about my girlfriend, no matter that you make no offer of redemption for a woman like me... condemn the kind of love I share and feel and yet it is in my blood, it is the way I was born...you placed it there and so for this I praise you...

PERSON 6: ...having made me a murderer...the basest of all your creatures...one who crawls on all fours where others walk... watching...waiting...to kill again...I thank you....

PERSON 8: ...worse than a killer, some have said...to protect those who do, who kill or lie or steal...for this I do rejoice...you challenge me with everything and all...with nothing but power and excess...

PERSON 9:   ...and when I fail, when I keep it as you knew I would, I trust it to be a part of your infinite plan and it comforts me, oh God, it does so comfort me...knowing each loss is my gain...each stolen note is my crown of thorns...thank you, Lord...

PERSON 3:   ...innocent and without sin and placed there by you, Heavenly Father, conceived and born and placed on that path for me to stumble upon...to touch if I choose to...to devour if I wish it to be...

PERSON 4:   ...you put that young woman into my path as a trial... placed her there as surely as you placed me in my car and all that alcohol in my blood and my phone in my hand...all of it was you, dear God, and for that I thank you...

PERSON 7:   ...to taste a boy...to know that feeling, the taste of him, in your mouth...penis, ass, limbs...not yet a man...it is you who has done this to me, while others pine and court and fall in love, like figures in a storybook...this is the road I travel...filled with desire and fear and dread...and I thank you...

PERSON 10:   ...further and further and then further still...I thank you for this...for testing me and for taking me back each time. Each time I weep into my pillow and say 'enough!' you know that it is a lie and know that I will fail them again... and still you love me...

PERSON 2:   ...for all the arabs and the faggots who you, in your infinite wisdom, sweet Lord, have gathered to spread into my life and into my state and even my town and local school, yes, and to go so far as even in my own neighbourhood so as to help drive down the housing market, to rub elbows with at the store, to be sickened while they eat their curries and veggies and chop sueys, slurping away and chattering in their foreign tongues, I herald you...

PERSON 1:   ...'Goddamn you! Goddamn you!!' I sing...

PERSON 6:   ...to kill is a crime...an obscenity...a sin against mankind...

but the thought of it, the idea of doing it was not mine but your own...for every thought I have had you've had before me...every action one that you have imagined before I or anyone else was ever born...you have made it all possible... given me the right...

PERSON 5: ...each time the neighbours call us in and the police arrive... each time she looks over at me and murmurs 'I fell,' how can this not be your love?...how can this not be a sign from you on high telling me to march on with your will...every broken tooth and bruised eyelid attests to your kingdom that awaits me...

PERSON 8: ...'first kill all the lawyers' they joke since Shakespeare wrote it...worse than the criminals themselves, they say... but you love me, don't you, Lord? You say you do, you promise me this...and so I sleep each night...bathed in your love and your divinity...

PERSON 7: ...the shape of his ass...

PERSON 5: ...the snap of her nose...

PERSON 8: ...the sanctity of an acquittal...

PERSON 2: ...the stench of a Muslim...

PERSON 10: ...the stain of his cum on my lips...on my lips...

PERSON 4: ...the scream of her body being hurled through the air...

PERSON 1: ...the slit of love between her legs...

PERSON 9: ...the sobs of loss...of fortunes lost...

PERSON 6: ...the surge of electricity that will run through my body...

PERSON 3: ...the sweet pop of her hymen beneath me as it breaks...

PERSON 4: ...did someone die out on that road if no one saw it happen? Did I really drive off and leave her there? Did I? Tell me, dear God, I humbly ask you now...tell me what I've done...why you test me so...

PERSON 9: ...filthy lucre, dear God...wipe it on my face and hands...

dirty money, sweet Lord, plunge my head beneath its surface...may it never end...may the torment and tests of my lifestyle never ever end...

PERSON 10: ...his prick washes me anew...each time, each time...bathed and cleansed in what we do...what you, dear God of love, has made possible...you dangle his fruit in front of me and know I cannot walk away from it...and yet I remain your child...

PERSON 6: ...caught and tried and humiliated...this is the child you see before you now...you made me want to kill and now they want to kill me...an eye for an eye...'why don't you kill yourself?' they scream at me...but I know that I live because you wish it so, will it to be...I am your son...

PERSON 7: ...to shatter innocence...to steal youth and trust...this is your gift to me...

PERSON 2: ...covered in sores could be no worse, I know that to be true...rather a leper in the street than watch my son swim in the same pool with a Jew or a black...we are all your children you tell me...but even children hate each other... you made that emotion possible and I bathe in it...

PERSON 1: ...and yet the promise that you will now and always forgive this transgression and all my others...that you'll love a sinner like myself if I will return to dwell by your side... reject all carnal embrace...how can I choose? 'How?' I ask myself...'her pussy or a seat at the foot of my throne,' you demand and still I cannot...

PERSON 8: ...those husbands whom I help win their divorces...the daughter who I knew had cheated her mother...no longer aware of right and wrong but just the letter of the law... man's laws...but given life due only to you...God on high... maker of all our laws...created for me, just for me, for me to fail...to serve money and ego and pride...why would this be, if it be not your will?...

PERSON 5: ...only when I kill her will it ever be enough...only then will my journey be at its end...only then...

PERSON 3: ...to want and desire and long for...to wait for her to shower and walk in on...to hide in her room and watch her change, cowering in her closet and waiting, fearing all that might be if I'm discovered. I embrace this as my life, my plight, my road to Golgotha...and this cross I gladly bear...

PERSON 6: ...life is a miracle...

ALL: ...it is not ours to question...

PERSON 8: ...anguish is a miracle...

ALL: ...it is not ours to question...

PERSON 4: ...ugliness is a miracle...

ALL: ...it is not ours to question...

PERSON 7: ...beauty is a miracle...

ALL: ...it is not ours to question...

PERSON 1: ...joy is a miracle...

ALL: ...it is not ours to question...

PERSON 5: ...death is a miracle...

ALL: ...it is not ours to question...

PERSON 9: ...hate is a miracle...

ALL: ...it is not ours to question...

PERSON 3: ...love is a miracle...

ALL: ...it is not ours to question...

PERSON 10: ...for us to be tested each day, every breath, by everything around us and to the ends of our limits is absolutely and without question the work of God...

ALL: ...for thine is the kingdom...and the power...and the glory forever...

PERSON 2:   ...everything we don't understand is a miracle...Job himself
               had nothing on us...*excess* is the devil and the devil is God's
               boogeyman...for God he giveth, yes, but surely he also
               taketh away...

ALL: ...forever...and ever...and ever more... amen.

Silence. Darkness.

Kwame Kwei-Armah

WHEN WE PRAISE

When I was asked for a response to the Book of Psalms I began to think, as you would expect from a dramatist, to toy with notions of character and plot. Who could represent the essence of these chants and poems to 'the most high'? How would I articulate in words the emotion, the hopes and the of-times desperation that must have filled the heart of the psalm sayer? Each time I sat to write, I struggled. Each time I thought I had it, I'd wake in the morning and know that I hadn't.

It suddenly dawned on me that maybe I was having problems because my personal relationship with the Book of Psalms, my major interaction with those lamentations and celebrations has been through the prism of song. Specifically through the lens of the modern African American gospel artists who have so deeply personalised their experience of faith and new world pain, that it ultimately makes manifest a shout, a wail, a joyful scream pushing that most expressive of instruments – the human voice – to higher and higher ground. So, my response to the Book of Psalms is to present you with those voices, those heartfelt spiritual articulations, those soul meanderings that have used the King James adaptation of the ancient Hebrew text as a jumping-off point by which to praise, to heal and to access the hidden places of the human soul.

Playlist

1. 'When Jesus Sings', Various Artists, from
Fred Hammond Presents: In Case You Missed It...And Then Some.

2. 'He Reigns', Kirk Franklin from *The Gospel Soundtrack.*

3. 'When You Praise', Fred Hammond & Radical for Christ, from *Purpose By Design.*

4. 'Psalms 23', Buju Banton Featuring Gramps of Morgan Heritage, from *Reggae Gold 2000.*

5. 'Praise On the Inside', J Moss, from *V2 (The J Moss Project).*

6. 'When The Spirit Of The Lord', Fred Hammond & Radical for Christ.

7. 'No Weapon', Fred Hammond & Radical for Christ.

8. 'Again I Say Rejoice #2', Israel & New Breed, from *Alive In South Africa.*

9. 'I Love to Praise Him', Donnie McClurkin, from *Psalms, Hymns & Spiritual Songs.*

Toby Litt

NOTES FOR A YOUNG GENTLEMAN

Characters

MAN ABOUT TOWN (or TOWN for short)
– A Young Gentleman dressed in top hat and tails, aged 20

COUNTRY GENT (or COUNTRY for short)
– A Young Gentleman dressed in hunting pink, aged 20

The two actors should be identical-looking, twins if possible, and proper posh rather than putting it on.

The two Young Gentlemen enter simultaneously – MAN ABOUT TOWN stage left, COUNTRY GENT stage right. Both carry an identical hardback book titled in an old-fashioned font – 'Notes for a Young Gentleman'.

They bow to one another, pass one another in the middle of the stage, find their places centre stage right and left, bow to one another again, open the books and commence to read.

They should each read as if the advice were both for the audience and for the other Young Gentleman. Their identical delivery should be extremely measured and should overlap with neither one another nor with any audience reaction or unsettledness. The words should be spoken into a decent silence.

MAN ABOUT TOWN: A gentleman should arrive at his destination, after however arduous a journey, quite as if he had just taken a turn around the rose garden.

COUNTRY GENT: A gentleman should never acknowledge a mere fact.

TOWN: A gentleman should behave no differently in a prison than in a palace – to be affected by place shows lack of character.

COUNTRY: A gentleman should never confuse superiority with nobility.

TOWN: A gentleman – English – should reassure foreigners of his *bona fides* by appearing to be nothing more than a parody of an English gentleman; this is particularly important with Americans.

COUNTRY: A gentleman should never be heard to say anything other gentlemen have not said before.

TOWN: A gentleman should greet physical agony much as if he were greeting his old Latin master.

COUNTRY: A gentleman should never pass comment on his latest meal, no more than he would upon his latest evacuation.

TOWN: A gentleman should smoke, if not for pleasure then to set his companions at their ease.

COUNTRY: A gentleman should never condescend to condescend.

TOWN: A gentleman should, when he is in the country, kill something larger than a squirrel at least once a day.

COUNTRY: A gentleman should never evince surprise, except whilst opening Christmas presents from his children.

TOWN: A gentleman should seem to lack nothing.

The two Young Gentlemen bow to one another, slowly swap places, passing one another centre stage, bow to one another again, and start reading again.

TOWN: A gentleman should never appear utterly entranced by anything other than a horse or his fiancée on the day their engagement is announced.

COUNTRY: A gentleman should greet with genuine warmth only the following persons – his sister's daughters, his maternal aunts and his mortal enemies.

TOWN: A gentleman should never be seen to handle money, except in a brothel or a casino.

COUNTRY: A gentleman should have as deep a familiarity with the great religious texts of the world as is commensurate with not having read them.

TOWN: A gentleman should never keep a diary – to pay attention to one's own affairs suggests one may wish to profit thereby.

COUNTRY: A gentleman should take domestic politics slightly less seriously than backgammon.

TOWN: A gentleman should never go beneath ground-level except when, once a year, inspecting the wine cellars.

COUNTRY: A gentleman should be as fluent in the little language of love as in *le passé composé*.

TOWN: A gentleman should never run, except towards certain death.

COUNTRY: A gentleman should walk as if he were being carried and – if ever the circumstance arises – be carried as if he were walking.

TOWN: A gentleman should quote no one but his nanny, and then only back at her, with fondness, just before she dies.

The two Young Gentlemen should close their books and speak their final words straight to the audience.

COUNTRY: A gentleman himself should die with an air of mild curiosity.

TOWN: A gentleman, having once departed, should never return.

The two Young Gentlemen bow to the audience, to one another, and depart – MAN ABOUT TOWN stage right, COUNTRY GENT stage left.

The End.

Nancy Kricorian

THE PREACHER, OR HOW ECCLESIASTES CHANGED MY LIFE

Ecclesiastes 1: 18

For in much wisdom *is* much grief: and he that increaseth knowledge increaseth sorrow.

*

Sunday, I sat between my father and my mother, in the third pew from the back, drawing flowers on the back of the collection envelope with a tiny yellow pencil. Black-clad aunties in the front sang 'Onward Christian Soldiers' in a minor key, their hats bobbing to the swells of the electric organ. When the Pastor spoke about Jesus' great sacrifice on our behalf, Mr Arakelian wept for what unspoken transgression or injury I didn't know. If she found me after the service, my grandmother's friend Auntie Alice would bite the skin of my inner forearm and show me the garden that her teeth had left. I hid behind the pillar near the church door where the Pastor shook each person's hand just the way Jesus might have done. Our Pastor was a Southern Baptist who could have been the twin brother of TV evangelist Billy Graham. The Watertown church was Armenian Evangelical, a legacy of New England missionaries who converted Ottoman Armenians from their national Apostolic Church to various Protestant sects. Our congregation was filled with Genocide survivors, their children and grandchildren.

*

Sunday School was held in the church basement. First they showed us filmstrips about lost lambs and prideful squirrels that repented and found their way back to God. Then we were separated by age into classrooms inscribed with moveable blackboard partitions. The Pastor's blue-eyed, bird-thin wife was our teacher. She sat on the piano bench with her back to the keys while our small circle of dark-eyed eight-year-olds submitted to her ministrations. She told us that when she was our age, she had accepted Jesus as her Lord and Savior. 'And children,' she said, 'When Jesus came into my heart, I was filled with love for everyone. The sky was bluer, the grass was greener, and the whole world was lit with God's grace.' I bowed my head, closed my eyes and made a chapel of my hands, silently asking Jesus to forgive my sins and to take up residence in the hotel of my heart. When I opened my eyes, the Pastor's wife smiled at me expectantly. But the floorboards were still a dull brown, the dropped ceiling was grayed and stained, and I still didn't like the sly face of the girl sitting next to me.

*

At the Pastor's wife's recommendation, my parents sent me to an all-girls Christian summer camp in Maine as the previous summer I had brought home a song from the local day camp with the rollicking refrain, 'Roll me over in the clover, roll me over lay me down and do it again.' So off to Bible camp I went where in the green hills, among meadows, pine groves, and rocky trails, we prayed out loud before meals, we prayed before flag raising, we prayed during Bible Exploration, we prayed at the sundown service and we prayed again in our cabins before bed. After meals we sang an assortment of Christian hymns and songs with titles like 'Jesus is a Way Maker' and 'God Loves A Cheerful Giver.' During Morning Watch, I sat on a rock on the hill holding in my lap a red leather-bound Bible with my name embossed in gold on the cover, a tenth birthday gift from my aunt. I turned the thin, brittle pages as I read through the begats in Genesis, one of my favorite passages. At the end of the week at evening campfire in the darkened Rec Hall, the Camp Director called girls to the Lord. As she spoke, girls would trickle forward to be counted among the saved. We also swam in the lake, did arts and crafts, learned archery – the usual.

*

I used to lie awake at night imagining what Hell was like, with molten lava spilling across the cavernous floor as bright flames shot up from boiling cauldrons. Satan himself was there looking just like the one on the sign at the Underwood Devilled Ham Factory at the far end of our street. He was a bearded red creature with a scarlet arrowhead at the end of his tail and a pitchfork that he brandished in one hand as he jumped up and down, laughing with delight at the misery he caused. My school friends who attended the wrong churches – not Evangelical but Catholic or Armenian Apostolic – were all there among the damned. Their faces were blackened with soot, smoke rose from their singed hair, and they wept into scorched hands. When they saw me on the right side of the Inferno Gate, they called out to me, 'Why didn't you tell us about your Jesus?'

*

Year after year, I went back to camp, learning how to dive headlong from the pier and how to cook a tin-foil dinner in the coals of an open fire. I felt at home in the landscape, from the broad mown hill to the paths that threaded through the forest, and most of all along the edges of the lake. At school, I was anxious and self-conscious, but at Bible camp I was breezy and popular. The summer that I was sixteen, I met Ruth, who was a year older than I and had just been made a Junior Counselor. Sturdy and tall with short blond hair, she wore a jaunty red felt hat and carried a Swiss Army knife that bristled with blades and tools. She knew how to tie all the knots, she pointed out the constellations by name, and when she prayed out loud, her voice was so calm and assured that even the fidgety young campers hushed to listen. She was much smarter, funnier and easier to talk to than the boy I was dating, who wrote me stilted letters with smiley faces in the place of punctuation. Ruth persuaded me to enroll in the counselor-training program so I could stay at camp an extra fortnight. Her specialties were sailing and riflery, so I chose those as mine and was assigned to be her assistant. We spent our free hours sailing the lake, and in the late afternoon, we went to the leafy rifle range where we talked as she scored targets. As a vegetarian and an admirer of Gandhian non-violence, for me shooting was an odd pastime, but Ruth was my best friend so I loaded the gun and aimed for the bulls-eye.

*

The Camp Director and the Nurse were in charge of counselor training. The Director, who had a sharp, sun-reddened nose, a honking voice, and a goose-like waddle, supervised our progress towards passing the practical requirements – surviving a four-night camp-out, lighting a one-match fire, tying five knots, memorizing an assortment of nature lore and the like. The Camp Nurse, who doled out pills in the infirmary, monitored our spiritual education. She schooled us in calling girls to Jesus, for we would be responsible not only for the physical well being of the campers in our charge, but also for saving their immortal souls. The Nurse's round, pasty face, her cropped, copper-colored hair, and the gray-tinted glasses she wore to protect her eyes made me think of nothing more than the larva I had found when turning up stepping stones in our back garden. She wasn't fond of me either, especially after the conversion role-play exercises she had us do. I volunteered to be the non-believer, and rallied the Grand Inquisitor, Jean-Paul Sartre and the wiles of Satan himself in my arguments against the narrow path to Heaven that was proffered. I guess I was a little too convincing. Ruth confided to me that the Nurse and the Camp Director had pulled her aside to warn her that I was a bad influence.

*

One night Ruth and I met on the hill after we had tucked our respective campers into their beds. I was a Junior Counselor by then, although on probation because of suspicions about my 'spiritual development.' Ruth and I lay on our backs in the grass that thrummed with crickets and stared up at the net of bright stars hung across the black sky while we talked about predestination. Had God chosen us for heaven or did we have the right to choose for ourselves? Ruth explained, 'There's a gate you pass through entering heaven. On the outer arch you see, "Those who will shall enter." Once inside, you turn to read the inner arch, where it says, "Those whom God hath chosen."' Her voice was mesmerizing, and the paradox she described echoed in my mind, but I doubted that my name was written in the Book at Heaven's door. A few nights before, I had dreamed that Ruth and I were in the Nature Cabin, surrounded by dusty bird nests, snake skins, and rock collections, and that she had kissed me. When I woke up with my heart pounding, I prayed for forgiveness.

*

Each morning my alarm clock went off in the dark cabin, and I'd leave the sleeping girls to climb the dew-damp hill, sometimes crossing paths with a skunk that was ambling home. Ruth and I sat on stacked wooden boards near the boiler under the dining hall, a dark, uncomfortable spot lit by a single hanging bulb. The Camp Director and the Nurse, who watched us warily, had made sure our schedules barely overlapped, so we had taken to meeting before dawn to read the Bible and pray together. We had chosen Ecclesiastes for our study. To me, there was no part of the Bible more exquisite or more despairing. The Preacher, whom I thought of as the original Existentialist, understood the hard travail of the human soul. In his book, there was no Hell and only God was in heaven; vanity, vexation of spirit and evil alternated with the goodness of industry and human communion. Each morning after praying for guidance and understanding, we read the incantatory prose out loud a few lines at a time, discussing possible interpretations. 'So I returned and considered all the oppressions that were done under the sun; and behold the tears of such as were oppressed, and they had no comforter; and on the side of their oppressors there was power; but they had no comforter.' We were smitten by the words, and I with her.

*

One night towards the end of that last summer, Ruth and I left our cabins and met in the pine grove. From there I followed her down the steep path to the beach. We were breaking camp rules by being on the waterfront that late, and then we broke more rules, hefting one of the silver canoes from the rack and pulling out two wooden paddles. I climbed into the bow, Ruth taking the stern, and she pushed off, with the sound of metal scraping against sand. Our paddles dipping in unison, we glided across the lake. Tall pine trees lining the far shore, dappled moonlight and shadows played alongside the boat and across our wake. When we reached the middle of the lake, we stowed our paddles and surveyed the scene in perfect stillness. I remembered the Preacher's words: 'Two are better than one, because they have a good reward for their labour.' We were the happiest of God's creatures.

*

I started my first year at college, and Ruth returned to the Bible school in the Midwest where she was in her second year. Right before I left camp, one of the other counselors, all of whom attended Christian colleges, told me that whatever I studied at the godless institution I had chosen, I should not take any classes in Religion or Philosophy because those professors would attempt to destroy my faith. But she didn't predict that an Introduction to Women's Studies would have the same effect. When I went home for the holidays, the Pastor's Sunday homily was taken from Saint Paul the Misogynist. As I sat in the pew, I felt like a hot air balloon that had been tethered to the ground by dozens of ropes that had been loosened slowly one by one, until there was just one last rope holding the balloon and its basket to the earth. When the Pastor quoted, 'Let your women keep silence in the churches; for it is not permitted unto them to speak,' I heard the snap of that final cord. Up and up I rose, drifting across the landscape, exhilarated and terrified, not knowing where the wind would take me.

*

A couple years later Ruth and I met for lunch at a café in the Harvard Square. With another semester of college to go, I was living with my boyfriend – and despite my atavistic fears, having sex before marriage had not resulted in my being run over by a car or struck down by lightning. Ruth had recently graduated from Bible college and been hired as the assistant to the new Camp Director, a job which would prove to be Ruth's stepping stone to eventually running the camp herself. The old Director, it turned out, had been hastily removed when it was discovered that she and the Nurse were lovers who had spent their days off together in a cheap motel room not far from camp. The Nurse went to Africa where she worked as a missionary. No one knew what became of the Camp Director.

*

I had a dream about returning to camp. It was nighttime in the clearing along the far bank of the lake. I found myself with Ruth and a circle of familiar faces sitting around the stone pit. We sang the old songs and watched sparks leap from the crackling fire. My hair and my clothes filled with the comforting smell of wood smoke, and I was happy that there were no more watchful, suspicious eyes. But even in the dream, I felt that I didn't belong any more. It was Ruth's camp now, and I, and the Director, and the Nurse, would have to know, to search, and to seek wisdom somewhere else.

Carol Ann Duffy

THE BEAUTY OF THE CHURCH

Look, you are beautiful, beloved;
your eyes, framed by your hair,
are birds in the leaves of a tree,
doves in the Cedar of Lebanon;
your hair shines, a stream in sunlight
tumbling from the mountain; you are fair,
loved; your mouth, entrance; your kiss, key;
your lips, soft scarlet, opening;
your tongue, wine-sweet; your teeth, new lambs
in the pastures; your voice is for psalm, song.

I see your face; I say your face
is the garden where I sought love;
my head filled with dew; my hands
sweet with myrrh; my naked feet
in wet grasses; my mouth honey-smeared.
Your voice called at the door of my heart.

I am sick with love.
Turn away your eyes from mine,
they have overcome me.
You have ravished my heart with your eyes.
You have kissed me with the kisses of your mouth
in our green bed, under the beams of cedar,
the rafters of fir.
You are altogether lovely.
Your cheeks, spices and sweet flowers;
your breath, camphire and spikenard;
saffron; calamus and cinammon;

frankincense and aloes;
your throat is for pearls;
your two breasts are honey and milk;
your left hand should be under my head,
your right hand embracing me.
Just to look at your hand,
I am sick with love.

You are the apple tree among the trees of the forest.
I lie under your shadow
and your fruit is sweet to my taste.
You are a cluster of camphire in the vineyards;
an orchard of ripe figs, pomegranates.
I am yours and you are mine,
until the day breaks and shadows fade.
No river to quench love, no sea to drown it.

I was in your eyes and I found favour.
I was all you desired and I gave you my loves.

I say the roof of your mouth is the best wine;
you are rose, lily, a cluster of grapes.
I looked for you at night on my bed.
I rose and walked the city streets,
searching for you for whom my soul yearned.
I found you. I held you
and would not let you go,
until I had brought you to the field,
where we lay,
circled by the roes and hinds of the meadows.
I rose up to open to you
and your hands smelled of myrrh.
Your navel, a goblet which needed no wine.
How beautiful your feet.
The joints of your thighs were jewels.
Your knees were apples.

I sleep, but my heart wakes to your whisper.
You have brought me to this bed
and your banner over me is love.
Set me as a seal, beloved,
for love is strong as death,
set me as a seal upon your heart.

Ian McHugh

ALL THE TREES
OF THE FIELD

A restaurant; an anteroom off from the kitchen.

CRAIG comes in and closes the door behind him. He wears an apron. He's tense, in a heightened state.

ASH is absolutely calm. There's a fresh red wine stain on her blouse.

CRAIG: Your shirt.

ASH: It's a blouse. Don't worry about it.

CRAIG: Let me get a cloth –

ASH: No, leave it.

CRAIG: It'll be ruined.

ASH: Collateral.

CRAIG: ?

ASH: It's just a blouse, Craig.

CRAIG: Okay. Okay. Are you...? Has something happened?

ASH: It's fancy here. I like it. I feel underdressed.

CRAIG: Is everything –

ASH: I'm fine.

CRAIG: You are?

            Beat.

CRAIG: Good.

Beat.

CRAIG: Good.

ASH: *(Laughs.)* Good!

CRAIG: Look, I've only got a few minutes. They'll miss me.

ASH: You're important.

CRAIG: ?

ASH: They need you.

CRAIG: We're very busy. They need everyone.

Pause.

ASH: It's good to see you.

CRAIG: You too.

ASH: You mean it?

CRAIG: Yes!

ASH: You're busy.

CRAIG: But it is good to see you. Really.

ASH: Come here.

CRAIG hugs ASH.

ASH: You're shaking.

CRAIG: No.

ASH: Oh, you thought something had... An accident, or –

CRAIG: No, I'm just... I'm just...

CRAIG hugs ASH again, harder, a little longer.

ASH: I went to where you live.

CRAIG: Yeah?

ASH: It's a dump.

CRAIG: Ha!

ASH: What do you want to live there for?

CRAIG: Who did you meet? Was it Alex? Simone?

Beat.

CRAIG: Red hair? Pretty?

ASH: And who's Jack?

CRAIG: Oh, *(Laughs.)* I am.

ASH: No you're not.

CRAIG: No, it's my middle name. Thought I'd, you know –

ASH: Your middle name's John.

CRAIG: Yeah, well.

Beat.

CRAIG: Did Alex tell you I was here?

ASH says nothing.

CRAIG gives her a circumspect look.

ASH: I said I wanted to write you a letter.

Beat.

CRAIG: Yeah.

ASH: I was...I...I thought you might have told her...not /

CRAIG: No, I wouldn't /

ASH: to tell me /

CRAIG: No.

Beat.

ASH: No. She'd have asked why.

CRAIG: I didn't think you'd –

ASH: You could've made up a story, maybe.

CRAIG: I just thought –

ASH: You could've said we were 'lovers'.

CRAIG: I just thought –

ASH: Said I'd ditched you. Broken your heart.

CRAIG: I thought –

ASH: That I'd leave you be?

           Beat.

CRAIG: No...

ASH: I've not come to wind you up. I wanted to see you. Say hello.

CRAIG: No. I mean, I'm glad.

ASH: She misses you.

CRAIG: Your shirt. Blouse. I am sorry.

ASH: We'll pretend it's blood.

CRAIG: ?

ASH: I'll say you came at me with a knife.

           Beat.

CRAIG: Ha.

ASH: *(Impatient smile.)* You look tired.

CRAIG: Do I?

ASH: Late night.

CRAIG: Uh, yeah.

ASH: Yeah? *(Laughs.)* How late?

CRAIG: Went to a party.

ASH: Very nice.

CRAIG: Not really, it was in Romford.

ASH: Romford?

CRAIG: Very late.

Beat.

CRAIG gives a sheepish shrug.

ASH: Don't be coy.

CRAIG: She's Irish.

ASH: I don't need the sordid –

CRAIG: Ha ha! Not sordid.

ASH: No?

CRAIG: Couldn't believe my luck. Her name's Charlie.

ASH: I don't need to know –

CRAIG: And yourself?

ASH: ?

CRAIG: You always had an eye for the boys.

ASH: Just an eye, mind. Was a time holding hands with Janey
            Saunders at the back of the bus was enough for you.

CRAIG: Do you still see Janey?

ASH: Ha! You player!

CRAIG: No, I –

ASH laughs.

Pause.

ASH: You look so tired though.

CRAIG: Yes. Well we're –

ASH: You look drawn.

CRAIG: Where are you staying? You can stay at mine.

ISAIAH   179

ASH: No, I couldn't, really.

CRAIG: I'll meet you in the pub later. I get off in... *(Looks at watch.)*

ASH: I'm not staying. I'm off later.

Beat.

ASH: You look disappointed.

CRAIG: *(Almost surprise.)* Yeah. I –

ASH: How much do you make here?

CRAIG: *(Off guard.)* What?

ASH: Is it like, temping, casual, or are you –

CRAIG: Oh, you know...enough.

ASH: That bloke with the face. Seems like a total arsehole.

CRAIG: He's just... We're busy, you know. *(Looks at watch.)* In fact I should –

ASH: Why do you let him talk to you like that?

CRAIG: He's my boss.

ASH: I wouldn't let anyone talk to me like that.

CRAIG: He's my boss.

ASH: What do you do? What do you do here?

CRAIG: Whatever they tell me.

ASH: ...?

CRAIG: Uh, clean tables, mop up, chop veg if they need me to, take the food out. Sometimes they let me pour the wine.

ASH: Not any more. So you're a waiter.

CRAIG: No, I don't take the orders.

ASH: It can't be that hard.

CRAIG: No, I mean, they have enough waiters.

Beat.

ASH: I think you should leave.

CRAIG: ?

ASH: Quit.

CRAIG: Yes, I know what you —

ASH: Now. You should do it now.

            Beat.

CRAIG: No. Why would I? This is my job. I like it.

ASH: No you don't.

CRAIG: It's the best job I could get.

ASH: Come on. I'll do it for you.

CRAIG: You'll...what?

ASH: I'll tell him where he can stick his job.

            She makes to leave; CRAIG grabs hold of her.

CRAIG: No! Wait —

ASH: I heard them talking, while I was waiting for you, saying you
            were slacking, saying you —

CRAIG: Heard who?

ASH: Him. And the blonde one. The girl.

CRAIG: I don't think so.

ASH: God's honest. That girl. Say the word, I'll smack her.

CRAIG: I'm not leaving. I'm not just going to —

ASH: You've gone soft.

CRAIG: No, I need the money.

ASH: Come with me. Now. Come on. Do it.

CRAIG smiles and shakes his head in exasperation.

CRAIG: Look. Meet me in the pub in an hour. Pub at the end of the road. I get off in an hour. Hour and a half, tops. You'll wait, yeah?

ASH: Yeah?

CRAIG: And stay. Please. I want to catch up properly. I'm sorry. I'm sorry I haven't...you know...

ASH: Craig –

CRAIG: And if you're around tomorrow, Alex makes this amazing goulash. And you can meet Charlie.

ASH: Who?

CRAIG: Charlie. The girl I'm seeing.

ASH: So you're seeing her now?

CRAIG: Well...

ASH: I thought you'd just met her.

CRAIG: I'd, you know...seen her around.

ASH: You fell in love from afar.

CRAIG: Not in love. I like her.

ASH: How many poor girls have you slept with since you ran away?

CRAIG: I didn't run away.

ASH: She's just a girl, Craig. Flesh, not spirit.

CRAIG: *(Impatient.)* You'll like her. She's a teacher.

ASH: Oh my.

CRAIG: *(Stubborn perseverance.)* She teaches history.

ASH: Amazing. Does she know you're using her?

CRAIG simmers.

ASH: No?

Pause.

ASH: Have I made you mad?

CRAIG: No.

ASH: *(Smiles.)* I have, haven't I? I've made you mad.

CRAIG: No. You haven't.

ASH: You're steaming mad, aren't you?

Beat.

ASH: Come on, do your war cry.

CRAIG: ...What?

ASH: I'll do mine.

CRAIG: Don't!

ASH: You know how loud I can scream.

CRAIG: I do.

CRAIG hangs his head in despair.

ASH: I can get you out of here.

CRAIG looks up at ASH; almost surrender.

Pause.

ASH lifts CRAIG's hand and holds it.

ASH: You've stopped shaking.

CRAIG: I wasn't shaking –

ASH: The wind has dropped.

Beat.

ASH: Just a breeze.

CRAIG: Just a breeze.

He shivers.

ASH assumes control.

ASH: It's late afternoon. Still light.

He nods.

ASH: The ground is still warm.

Beat.

ASH: And the air is cool. Dry.

CRAIG is enveloped in the vision.

ASH: The trees... There's a line of trees.

CRAIG: A line on each side.

Pause; she has him in the palm of her hand.

ASH: What kind of trees?

Beat.

CRAIG: Cedar.

Beat.

The sun...the highest branches...the light...

ASH: There's nothing else.

CRAIG: The leaves...

ASH: There's nothing else.

CRAIG: The noise...

Long pause.

CRAIG is held still in space and time, without thought.

Suddenly:

CRAIG: You made me give my books away. You made me stop being
            friends with Andrew Elliott.

ASH: I didn't make you do anything.

CRAIG: No, I didn't mind. I didn't mind.

Pause.

ASH sees he's wavering.

ASH: Come with me. Come with me now.

CRAIG: You know I can't.

ASH: You don't want to.

CRAIG: It doesn't matter.

ASH: So you do.

Pause.

ASH: What?

CRAIG: I understand things a bit better now.

ASH: You do? What do you understand?

Beat; he's tentative, as if afraid of saying something hurtful.

CRAIG: *(Almost dismissive.)* Things about myself.

ASH: What do you understand about yourself?

CRAIG: Just that... I want to get out a bit. See things. Meet people.

ASH: People.

CRAIG: *(Hesitant.)* Yes. People. Other people.

ASH: Oh I see, *other* people.

CRAIG: Yes.

ASH: Craig, there are no other people.

He looks away. She looks at him intently, until he has to look back. She holds his gaze.

ASH: You hate it here. You live in a hole, you make no money.

Beat.

ASH: How are you going to find your way out?

He looks away.

ASH: I made you for something better than this.

CRAIG: *(Incredulous.)* You made me?

ASH: We're bound to each other /

CRAIG: No. I /

ASH: protected.

CRAIG: *(Frustration.)* I need to think for myself.

ASH: I can think for both of us.

CRAIG: Don't joke. I need to be able to think for myself.

Pause.

CRAIG: I could barely speak to anyone that wasn't you. My mum thought I was mad. I couldn't even look at her.

ASH: Craig –

CRAIG: I didn't want her to worry. I wanted to explain, to try to...

Beat.

CRAIG: I couldn't open my mouth. I miss it, but I –

ASH: What do you miss?

CRAIG: *(Laughs.)* Everything.

ASH: Yeah?

CRAIG: Yeah. You can't pull it apart, can you? It's all bound up
            together.

She looks at him, needing more of an answer.

CRAIG: I don't know... *(Thinks.)* Waking up at the river, covered in
            mud, freezing. Laughing. Having a clear head. Having nothing
            but you in mind. In all of me. You know? The world bending
            around us. And everything just...smelled better, tasted better. I
            know it's ridiculous but...strawberries, chocolate...cornflakes...

ASH: And?

Beat.

CRAIG: And... And it felt like I could see further. Things were clearer,
            sharper...

ASH: And...?

CRAIG: And... *(He's lost in thought.)*

Pause.

ASH: Let's go outside. I bet you haven't been outside all day.

Beat.

ASH: It's cold. Colder than you'd think. You just want to open your
            mouth and breathe it in.

Beat.

ASH: We'll take a walk. Stretch our legs. The streets are packed. It
            makes your head spin.

Beat.

ASH: Craig...

CRAIG: The light... The sun... The way your clothes smelled...smoke...
            that sound...

ASH: We'll walk till we're out of town.

CRAIG: The noise...

                He hears the noise: the wind through trees.

ASH: We won't stop till we're in the fields.

CRAIG: And nothing mattered. Nothing at all.

                Beat.

ASH: Don't you want that again?

Luke Kennard

A LOST EXPRESSION

Man in his thirties, professional. Shirt and jacket, tie.

Let's say I already know this is going to fail. Say I'm preparing a meal. Do we have any amateur chefs here tonight? No, start again. Say I'm site manager on a building project. We're building a utopian housing solution. An anti-tower block. Anti- everything the tower block has come to represent. It's only three stories high. It covers a square mile. There are parks and ponds within its walls; they're covered and heated, because, you know, the weather in this country. Our message to the people who're gonna live there: We love you. You're worth all of this land.

But here's the thing: my boys, my team, they don't do any work. The foundations are down, the scaffolding's up, but my team have started, what do the Americans call it? 'Goofing off'. That's right. They're goofing off. Nothing is getting built. Nothing. I expect a little horseplay. I expect euphemisms coarser and more offensive than the terms they substitute. That means you simultaneously say the thing you were going to say, you say it in a more grotesque manner while paying sarcastic lip-service to the oversensitivity of your audience. I expect euphemisms coarser and more offensive than the terms they substitute. And I expect that to map onto their behaviour more generally. Did you know euphemism used to mean 'keeping a holy silence'? To speak well by not speaking. I don't expect a holy silence.

But this has got nasty. They have a 25 gallon plastic waterbutt – they've sawed it in half. It contains ice and cans of lager. They call it 'Matilda'. I don't know why. They've made hammocks out of the chrome struts and ropes.

They climb to the top of the scaffolding and drop breeze-blocks on each other's heads: nobody's died yet, but we've had some bad concussions. They laugh at each other's concussions. They say, 'Duhhh! Look at Steve! Buhhhh! He's *drooling!*' They have league tables of successful concussions.

They chase one another with drills. They play chicken with the forklifts. I am trying to account for the writing-off or serious damage to three forklifts.

They play Russian roulette with pornography on their smartphones. Six of them stand in a circle and... No, actually it's too unpleasant. 'Never tell someone something you wouldn't tell me.' That's what my mum used to tell me.

Also, there are three rival contractors working on the same building and I'm supposed to be overseeing all of them, although there's been a mistake and they all think they have responsibility for the same process.

But my company have had this idea. There are big speakers arranged all up and down the scaffolding and I have a contact mic attached to my tie. Whatever I say, they have to listen, they have no choice. Whenever I try to speak into the mic: squawks of feedback. It's loud. Feels like it physically touches your brain. That's all I can do – cause them to momentarily stop whatever they're doing and writhe in agony for a few seconds.

This has made me unpopular.

And anyway, it's being built on a flood plane, the utopian housing solution. And being a low-riser, it's at high risk. And anyway, my father, who owns the construction firm's umbrella company, is about to pull the plug on the project. Umbrellas, plugs. What is it with me and water?

And anyway, my grandfather, who used to run the country, is about to start a civil war. So basically my utopian housing solution is going to be knee deep in septic water. And there will be bodies floating in it. That's if it ever reaches completion. Which it won't. I tell them I wish I'd never been born. It comes out as ear-piercing feedback.

(*Irritated.*) No, start again. Say I'm preparing a meal.

    Lights down. Up again.

Let's say you're on a sinking car ferry. You're stuck in your car – the doors are jammed and the boat's going under. They've only just given up trying to cut you out, they've thrown up their hands. Only one of them could make eye-contact with you. He grimaced. Mouthed, 'I'm sorry.' They've staggered away. Smell of oil, petrol, salt. The car rolls into the ferry's back wall. A half-finished roll of extra-strong mints strikes you on the forehead. Your daughter's star-shaped plastic sunglasses strike you on the forehead. Your mobile starts ringing, it's me, and I say, 'Bad news…'

Lights down. Up again.

Let's say I take my trousers off. I'm not going to take my trousers off. Let's say that I do, though. I take them off and I walk through the office I work in and nobody says anything. I leave the office by the revolving doors. I wait for the person coming in to push the door. I let them do the work. I take the trousers and I go to an alleyway, a dirty alleyway at the side of the office, and I stuff the trousers into the gutter. Nobody sees me do it. The next week I go back and I retrieve the trousers. They're ruined. I try to… No, they're good for nothing.

Some people see me doing this. I tell them it's a symbolic act. They're just like *(Rolls eyes.)* 'Yeah, okay.'

'If you are well brought up,' I tell them, 'you don't roll your eyes at anyone. You don't question why somebody does something. If you see someone with no trousers talking about symbolic acts, you put your arm around them. You offer them your trousers. Your first thought is always, how can I help this poor, poor man? That's what I mean by well brought up,' I tell them.

Lights down. Up again.

Let's say I tell you a story about our last business conference. Hey, come back! It's a good story. I set the scene: We're in a modern room panelled-up to look like a traditional pub. There's a fake open fire. Me, Richard and several of my senior colleagues are sitting on leather sofas around a table by the fake open fire. I'm drinking this whiskey called Mortloch, which I guess means *the lake of death*. Death *is* like a lake, I tell him. Do you not just want to try it? I say. It's amazing! It's the best whiskey ever! It tastes like train sets and old books! We are at a business conference and I know full well that Richard is a recovering alcoholic. His smile of forbearance is *just* starting to slip. Just one little sip! I tell him. Our colleagues stare at me in horror. Samantha mutters that I'm just trying to get attention, and whether she's right or not, it appears to have worked. I have your attention. You're in there too. You haven't worked for the company long. You're pretty. I haven't noticed it. Others have. I take you aside. I tell you that you have to remember my purposes in telling you this story may be quite different to the reasons I had for doing it in the first place. *(Pause.)* Let's say I'm preparing a meal, but… No.

Lights down. Up again.

Let's say I've just started laughing out loud in the middle of your friend's funeral. Loud, fake laughter. And what offends you is not the laughter *per se*, but its disingenuousness. *(Pause.)* Are not all my words fire and a hammer that shatters rock?

Lights down. Up again.

Let's say I'm at a party and I'm talking to you. You can't work out if I'm nice or slightly creepy. I tell you that the English have a figure of speech. The English have a lot of figures of speech, I tell you. But this is one of them. We say, it's second nature to him now. Maybe rock-climbing, water skiing. It's become second nature to him. But that's a misappropriation, I tell you. You're eating a pretzel. That's not the point. We had a first nature, I tell you. *We had a first nature* is the point. You take another pretzel. You are deciding that I am creepy. I don't want to sound preachy or anything, I tell you.

Lights down. Up again.

The other prophets were insane; that was the feeling among the prophets. Which is to say each prophet thought as much about his fellow prophets who bit their own fingers when they ate, if they ate at all, and whose struggles, which were real enough, seemed at best a delusion, at worst affectation. You were on your way to the supermarket to buy coriander for the soup you were making. You were thinking about picking the kids up after school. In the morning you had argued with your significant other and you still felt kind of bruised from that. We were a pretty off-putting bunch, all told.

Lights down. Up again.

Let's say I've invited you to an open-mic poetry event in a warzone.
You don't want to offend me, so you agree to come along. I'm on
8th. First I drop a clay pot on the stage and it smashes. Then I insult
the poets who read before me. I say they were a bit 'performancey'. I
say they were dull. I say they clearly don't know the first thing about
poetry. I say the problem is we have started to derive sexual pleasure
from one another's suffering. That this was the inevitable end-result of
our cruelty, our gluttony, our profligacy, and that this is the only real
problem, that we derive sexual pleasure from one another's suffering.
That any poetry which fails to address this central question of our
time is worse than useless. Outside: airstrikes.

    Lights down. Up again.

Let's say I tell you about my dad's friend who was in a car accident.
It was winter, icy, a cloud had settled low on the city. He piled into
a tree. He lost blood. He almost died. He talks about it as if it were
the best thing that ever happened to him. He had this vision that
everything around him had burst into flower. He cries when he
tells you. He can't tell you the story without breaking down. The
bare branches, the scrubby liminal spaces. Let's say I'm explaining
that to you through the squawks of feedback coming from the
scaffold-mounted speakers. You have a handful of dry cement. A lost
expression.

Let's say that.

Paul Muldoon

HALTER-NECK

Music by Michael Bruce

AMERICAN EXPRESS CHARGES ZERO COMMISSION
BUT AN EXORBITANT RATE OF EXCHANGE
COULD IT BE I'LL STILL GET SOMETHING FOR NOTHING
DESPITE YOUR BEING OUT OF MY RANGE
EVER SINCE WE MET I'VE BEEN FULL OF APPREHENSION
FEARFUL THAT OUR FIRST DATE WOULD BE PROROGUED
GOD KNOWS WHY WHEN SO MUCH IS OUT OF FASHION
HALTER-NECKS ARE SOMEHOW BACK IN VOGUE
ISRAEL'S STILL FAR FROM SORROW-FREE
JERUSALEM'S STILL IN HER MOURNING GOWN
BUT IT'S YOUR HALTER-NECK DRESS THAT WEIGHS ON ME
IT'S YOUR HALTER-NECK THAT DRAGS ME DOWN

IN CASE IT MIGHT HELP YOU ARRIVE AT A DECISION
JUST ALLOW ME ONE CHANCE TO INTERPOSE
KINDA LIKE THE SCENE BACK THERE IN EPSOM
LIKE MY HORSE LOSING JUST BY A NOSE
MY LOSING A RACE IS NO CAUSE FOR LAMENTATION
NOT ONLY NOSES ARE PUT OUT OF JOINT
OF TOPICS THAT MIGHT BE UP FOR DISCUSSION
PERHAPS WE'LL BE ABLE TO PINPOINT

QUITE WHEN I MYSELF WOULD THROW OFF THE YOKE
RAW SHOULDERS SMELLING OF SWEAT AND SMOKE
SAMSON UNBOUND
QUITE WHEN THE TEMPLE WOULD BE BURNED
RAZED BY THE BABYLONIANS WHO THEREBY EARNED
SOME QUESTIONABLE RENOWN
SO MANY EGYPTIANS DROWNED IN THE GLASS-WALLED SEA
THROUGH WHICH WE THOUGHT WE'D REACHED SOLID GROUND
YET IT'S YOUR HALTER-NECK DRESS THAT WEIGHS ON ME
IT'S YOUR HALTER-NECK THAT DRAGS ME DOWN

SO MANY WILL SEE THIS AS MY COMPLETE SUBMISSION
TO ONE TO WHOM I'M ALREADY IN THRALL
UNDER WHOSE SPELL I'LL SIP COSMOPOLITANS
VINEGAR-SPONGES WORMWOOD AND GALL
WORMWOOD AND GALL HAVE LONGSINCE BEEN MY DAILY PORTION
X MARKING THE SPOT ON YOUR TWIN-ROE BREAST
YOU MIGHT OFFER ME STILL AS SOME CONSOLATION
WERE ZERO NOT THE CHARGE AT AMERICAN EXPRESS
AND ZERO THE CHANCE OF MY HORSE WHEEE-HEEE
BREAKING THROUGH TO WIN THE TRIPLE CROWN
WHILE YOUR HALTER-NECK DRESS STILL WEIGHS ON ME
WHILE YOUR HALTER-NECK STILL DRAGS ME DOWN

Owen Sheers

THE FAIR

&

TENDER

Characters

THE LORD
Male late fifties/early sixties. A powerful, handsome patriarch.

JERUSALEM
Female mid twenties. A beautiful young woman.

SAMARIA
Female late twenties/early thirties. JERUSALEM's older sister, also beautiful.

S'DAM
Female early twenties. JERUSALEM's younger sister, also beautiful.

EXT: A STREET CORNER IN A CITY – NIGHT

Three young women stand beneath a street lamp. They are dressed provocatively and appear to be waiting. As they wait, they hum a tune, barely audible. There is movement in the shadows. The shape of a man appears, indistinct.

When the women see the man they stop humming. They look towards him expectantly. He doesn't move.

JERUSALEM: Can we help you honey?

The man still doesn't move.

SAMARIA: He's a shy one. It's alright love, we won't bite.

S'DAM: Much.

The women laugh. The man steps out of the shadows, cutting them dead.
They shrink away from him against the wall.
He is tall, elegantly dressed, his expression caught between rage and dismay.

THE LORD: Don't you know your own father when you see him?

JERUSALEM: I know you. But I don't see my father here.

THE LORD: Have you really forgotten so much?

JERUSALEM: Not enough. What say you sisters? Who do you see?

SAMARIA: A man.

S'DAM: Another man.

SAMARIA: Nothing more.

S'DAM: Nothing less.

THE LORD: You've turned them against me.

JERUSALEM laughs.

JERUSALEM: They needed no help from me!

THE LORD: You have forgotten the days of your youth.

JERUSALEM: No. That's the problem. I haven't.

S'DAM: I wish I had.

SAMARIA: I wish I could.

THE LORD: Perhaps you can't forget because there were some you never knew. You were too young. When I found you.

JERUSALEM: Ah, the story!

THE LORD: Yes, the story. Because it is true! And you have forgotten.

JERUSALEM: What makes you so sure?

THE LORD: Why else would you do this to me?

Beat.

THE LORD: *(To JERUSALEM.)* They hadn't even cut your cord. When I found you. What need to unmoor you into this world if they'd already decided to let you die? That's how they left you – still tied to your mother's womb, slick with her blood and your own, naked. In a field. Abandoned like a rotten harvest. Others walked past, but I didn't. I bent to you and I picked you up. I washed you, anointed you with oils, swaddled you in my coat. And that's when I made my promise. From that day on you would be mine.

JERUSALEM: Yours?

THE LORD: Yes. Mine. And when you asked me to save your sisters, I found them and brought them to me too. And I treasured all of you like my own.

SAMARIA: Treasure, that's about right.

S'DAM: You lock up treasure don't you?

SAMARIA: Oh yes. You keep it safe. Keep it close.

THE LORD: Did you ever lack for anything?

JERUSALEM: No. You gave us everything.

SAMARIA: Everything.

THE LORD: *(To JERUSALEM.)* You grew like a sapling. You ate bread made from the best flour, honey from the sweetest hives. I gave you oils, clothed you in fine linens and silks. I put bracelets on your hands, a silver chain about your neck.

JERUSALEM: Yes, you put me in chains.

THE LORD: I put jewels on your forehead and rubies in your ears. And you were beautiful. You were beautiful.

JERUSALEM: I was.

SAMARIA: We were.

S'DAM: Beautiful.

Beat.

JERUSALEM: And? Please, don't stop now. Where were we? Oh yes, our beauty. Our beauty that you saved, then made.

THE LORD: You dare to mock me? After all I did for you, and after what you've done to me in return? I shouldn't have bothered coming.

JERUSALEM: But you did.

THE LORD: Yes. Because when I found you in that field, when I found you polluted in your own blood, I made a promise. And I will keep that promise.

JERUSALEM: Whether I want it kept or not?

THE LORD: Yes.

JERUSALEM: You still don't understand do you? What happened.

THE LORD: Oh I understand. You fell in love with your own beauty. Knowing it wasn't enough for you. You had to *feel* it. You had to see it, reflected in the eyes of other men. So many other men. As you spread your legs for them and they took you. As they bruised your breasts, as they devoured your gifts, as they fed upon the honey and oils from which I had made you. As they –

JERUSALEM: No! You don't understand.

SAMARIA: Shall we tell him?

S'DAM: Shall we teach him a lesson?

THE LORD: You? You can't teach me anything. I taught you everything you know.

S'DAM: Yes, you did.

SAMARIA: But what did you learn in the teaching?

THE LORD: That those I saved would forget me. That they'd use the embroidered cloths I'd given them to deck their rooms in high places. That from there they'd make themselves available to any young captain or scurf passing in the street below. That those I had taken in, those I'd cared for, would leave me and become whores.

JERUSALEM: Whores?

He gestures to them, their clothes, the street lamp, the street corner.

THE LORD: Do you deny it?

SAMARIA: He doesn't understand.

THE LORD: What? What don't I understand?

JERUSALEM: That you made us. And then you made us again.

Beat.

JERUSALEM: You know what your problem is?

THE LORD: My problem?

JERUSALEM: Beauty. You have a problem with beauty. You create it. Oh, that's what you do. No one has an eye for it like you. But then you hate what it brings with it. You want its light, but not the shadow it throws. You want all to admire it, but only you to have it.

THE LORD: The shadow?

JERUSALEM: Inside you. Some would call it jealously, but it's darker than that isn't it? You call us whores. Perhaps we are now, but we weren't then. We were just young women who took lovers. Who wanted to explore the world they'd been given, to make our own way in it. It was you who placed us among them, those captains, those rulers. It was you who pressed those jewels to our heads, parading your works for all to admire. What did you think would happen? That we'd stay with you forever?

SAMARIA: And why might we want to leave I wonder? Why would we want another man to take us away?

S'DAM: Maybe because you gave us everything, but then you wanted everything too, didn't you?

JERUSALEM: Whether we wanted to give it or not.

THE LORD: What have you done with them? I have a right to know.

JERUSALEM: Only what you did to ours.

SAMARIA: Isn't that fair? An eye...

THE LORD: How could you? You bore them, you fed them.

JERUSALEM: We did. But they weren't ours.

SAMARIA: They were yours.

JERUSALEM: Tell me, how much vengeance does salvation buy you?

THE LORD: It was punishment. For your disloyalty.

JERUSALEM: You turned our lovers against us.

SAMARIA: You opened our doors to those who hated us.

S'DAM: You starved us of food.

JERUSALEM: You took away our clothes.

SAMARIA: You let them rain stones upon us.

S'DAM: You burnt our children in the fires.

JERUSALEM: You made us who we are. Your worst nightmare.

S'DAM: You imagined it.

SAMARIA: And then you made it true.

JERUSALEM: You have a talent for that don't you?

Beat.

THE LORD: You had forgotten the days of your youth. I had to show
            you the way.

JERUSALEM: We should have seen it coming.

She turns to her sisters.

            You remember Tyrus?

SAMARIA: Ah, yes. Beautiful Tyrus.

S'DAM: Tyrus?

JERUSALEM: You were too young.

She turns to THE LORD.

JERUSALEM: He was one of your best wasn't he?

SAMARIA: The very best. You taught him all you knew didn't you?

JERUSALEM: Until he shone so brightly it was too bright and the shadow
            he threw became too much for you.

SAMARIA: Which was when you cast him down.

JERUSALEM: Far down, so he could never return. Until he became all
            shadow, and nothing else.

SAMARIA: We should have seen it coming.

THE LORD: It's not the same. I've come back for you.

JERUSALEM: But why?

THE LORD: Because I made my promise.

SAMARIA: Or is it so you can save us again?

JERUSALEM: Cast us low.

S'DAM: So you can lift us up again.

JERUSALEM: And we can thank you for it. Is that what you want?

S'DAM: Is that the deal?

SAMARIA: For us to declare ourselves yours again.

S'DAM: All yours.

SAMARIA: But there's no need is there?

JERUSALEM: Because we already are. Look at us.

SAMARIA: Look at what we've become.

S'DAM: And it's all thanks to you.

JERUSALEM: Yes, my Lord, all thanks to you. All thanks to you.

The three sisters begin to hum the same tune as before. As they do, they slowly advance upon THE LORD.

He backs away from them, into the shadows.

THE LORD: You have forgotten Jerusalem. You have forgotten the days of your youth.

As he retreats, the women turn their backs on him. Their humming becomes singing. As they sing they begin to cry.

Come all you fair and tender ladies
Take warning how you court young men
They're like the stars of summer morning
First they appear and then they're gone.

My father is a handsome devil,
He wears a chain that five miles long
On every link a heart does dangle
Another maid he's loved and wronged.

If I'd had known before I courted
I never would have courted none.
I'd a locked my heart in a box of golden
And fastened it up with a silver pin.

I wish I were a little sparrow
And I had wings and I could fly
I'd fly away to my own false lover
And when he's talking I'd be nigh.

But I am not a little sparrow
I have no wings nor can I fly
I'll sit down here and weep in sorrow
And try to pass my troubles by.

Fade to black.

Note

The suggested arrangement of the song, *Come All You Fair and Tender Ladies*, for
this piece is by Elizabeth LaPrelle.

DANIEL

Jack Thorne

OLIVER LEWIS

*A normal suburban kitchen-cum-dining room. A table – at which
sit ANN and STEVE. They've just eaten dinner.*

STEVE: And he said *(Yardie accent.)* 'Sir, right, how come in all like the
movies an' that they always get it in so easy.'

ANN: *(Laughing.)* With that voice?

STEVE: 'Cos, like, me and Therese yeah, it takes a squeeze, you get
me?'

ANN is laughing hard.

ANN: Therese? Have I met Therese?

STEVE: What could I say? I'd told them to be fucking open and here
he was – and he was probably just trying to show off how big
his dick is –

ANN: Poor Therese –

*The phone starts to ring. STEVE picks it up and then puts it
down again. ANN stares at it, STEVE doesn't seem to give it a
second thought.*

STEVE: Exactly! Poor cow. So I said – well, it does depend on a
number of factors Sean. How turned on she is –

ANN: Brilliant!

STEVE: The more turned on she is, the easier you'll find it. How big
her hips are is also a consideration. But it's a very good point
because these situations will not play out like a film. OK, lets
do a list shall we? Common misconceptions about sex, and top

of the list 'it's easy'.

ANN is just smiling gently at him now.

STEVE: Hilarious right?

ANN: *(Soft.)* I sometimes forget how good a teacher you must be –

The phone starts to ring again, STEVE picks it up and then puts it down again. ANN leans across the table and takes his hand.

STEVE: You think I handled him well then?

ANN: Yes.

Pause.

ANN: Did he respond?

STEVE: In places. Asked whether viagra made it better even if you don't need it.

ANN: Good question.

STEVE: I said I couldn't tell him. He asked whether that was because I needed it and so couldn't tell or because I hadn't tried it. I said he had to watch his mouth. We then got into a long discussion about contraception. It was a really good session. I told them using a femidom was like making love to a carrier bag – anyway, it got on to – we then had a pretty serious conversation about why they should all use a condom.

Pause. She's just looking at him. He looks back. And then looks away. And then looks back.

STEVE: Sorry about the car.

ANN: I enjoyed using the train.

STEVE: Well, it would have been nice to talk...

ANN: We talked on the train

STEVE: I just...I'd had a few with – I'd had a few the night before and wasn't sure I'd not be over the limit.

ANN: It was fine. Those girls made me laugh.

STEVE: Yeah. They were – pretty...uh.... Do you think they knew?

ANN: Knew what?

Beat, the phone starts ringing again. STEVE picks it up and puts it down again. ANN looks at him.

ANN: Why don't you just unplug it?

STEVE: I prefer to know.

Pause.

STEVE: Now, I've been trying to plan what we could do this week.

ANN: Well. OK... Fun things or...

STEVE: Some fun – definitely some fun.

ANN: That's good.

STEVE: Maybe the woods. Do you fancy Epping Forrest?

ANN: I've always fancied Epping Forrest.

STEVE: And also – they're, uh – people wanting an interview.

ANN: Oh.

STEVE: Sorry. Sorry. They're pretty – insistent.

ANN: Have they offered money?

STEVE: Well, they mentioned it...

ANN: Should we do that then?

STEVE: Apparently – not – for money.

ANN: Do they want to interview you too?

STEVE: Apparently it's better to say something and to say it to everyone.

ANN: Who said that?

STEVE: Well, Tom and he put me in touch with a guy called Oliver Lewis, who does some media advice for the firm every now and again. And if we want them to leave us alone. Do them all. And for nothing.

ANN: OK.

STEVE: Even. And I mean, this surprised me... Even the ones who were cruel.

          Pause. STEVE studies her face.

STEVE: Yes. They want to interview me too. 'The Father that lost a daughter but gained a murderer'. You read that one? Yeah. Oliver Lewis said it's best we come as a pair.

ANN: Did he?

STEVE: Yes.

          Pause.

ANN: Did we – have we used a femidom?

STEVE: No. I read about it online.

          Pause. The phone starts ringing again. STEVE picks it up and puts it down again. He looks at her plate.

STEVE: You've barely eaten.

ANN: What do you want to know? What does picking up the phone and putting it down again teach you?

STEVE: I'm counting.

ANN: Right. Counting what?

STEVE: How often – the phone – rings.

ANN: That must be fascinating. How interested are they in my wife? How many times will they ring? Are you going to do a barchart later...

STEVE: The trouble is as soon as you say something to one of them, the other one tries to denigrate you as much as possible.

ANN: 'The father who lost a daughter but gained a murderer.'

STEVE: No money. Together. United front. Show it hasn't broken us. Show the accusations haven't stained us. Tom too maybe. Probably be nice to include him.

ANN: He can be part of our united front too.

STEVE: Exactly.

ANN: Yeah.

He checks to see if she's taking the piss.

STEVE: Yeah.

He gets up from his seat.

STEVE: Back in a sec.

He walks out of the room quickly. She's left alone. She controls herself pretty well.

STEVE re-enters in a style he thinks heroic.

STEVE: I'll tell you one thing I'll have to get used to again. Buying more toilet roll...

ANN: What?

STEVE: You use a phenomenal amount, I think it's the female condition but it could just be you...

ANN: What?

STEVE exits again and then re-enters from another room carrying a six pack of toilet paper.

STEVE: Not for me – I just need a pee – but... Better to have it – ready.

He exits for the bathroom again.

The phone starts ringing. ANN watches it. She doesn't pick it up. She waits for it to ring out. This takes a while.

STEVE re-enters. He looks at his wife with cold eyes. The phone rings out. They both wait. She may know he's there or she may not know.

STEVE: *(There's something in his throat, he clears it.)* More wine?

ANN: Did you count that one? It was just the one. But one could have phoned while it was ringing so that could be two. It could be two.

STEVE: I just want to know.

ANN: It's better is it? To know?

STEVE: Better than being in doubt, yes.

             This question feels directed.

STEVE: Shall I clear away?

ANN: Can we have coffee first?

STEVE: Great idea.

ANN: I'll put the kettle on.

             She exits to do so. Stopping briefly to look at the wall as she does. She looks with a frown.

ANN: Didn't there used to be a picture here?

             STEVE doesn't answer immediately.

ANN: Yes. There was a —

             STEVE still doesn't answer. She realises something. She touches the wall and then exits. STEVE thinks and then thinks again.

STEVE: *(Calling to her from off.)* Mary asked if she could come round...

ANN: *(Offstage.)* Brilliant.

STEVE: Yeah?

ANN: *(Offstage.)* Well, yeah, I'd like to see her...

STEVE: I think it's worth taking things slowly...

ANN: I know.

STEVE: There's no rush after all...

            Pause. ANN re-enters.

STEVE: Um. Jerry and Brian send their best. Brian put a notice up on the staff boards about it – a newspaper clipping – *Independent* I think –

            Pause.

STEVE: I'll tell Mary to give it a week, OK?

ANN: OK

STEVE: I just think starting slowly...

ANN: OK.

            Pause. ANN exits and returns with a cafetière and two mugs on a tray.

ANN: Doubt? You're afraid of doubt –

STEVE: I'm not afraid of –

ANN: Doubt?

STEVE: I'm not afraid of it. I just don't want it. As a preference.

ANN: Is that right?

STEVE: And I just don't want you overdoing things again.

ANN: I've never overdone things.

STEVE: No.

ANN: They threw the case out...I was not guilty...

STEVE: I know you were.

ANN: I didn't overdo things.

STEVE: I know you didn't.

ANN: You want me to be where you can see me...

STEVE: No –

ANN: OK. Well. Mary's my friend. So…

STEVE: And you're my wife so…

ANN: I know what I am.

STEVE: And what I am.

ANN: You took – her picture down.

STEVE: I know what I did.

ANN: When – when did you take it down?

STEVE: That's not – that's not – that's not a good question to ask.

Pause. They're both on dangerous ground and know it. They breathe heavily – almost in unison.

Pause. The phone rings, STEVE looks at it. STEVE calmly unplugs it from the wall.

STEVE: You're right. There's nothing to know.

ANN: No.

STEVE: I'm going to get the number changed.

ANN: OK.

Pause. STEVE plunges the cafetière and pours two coffees.

STEVE: I'm just pleased to have you – home – OK?

ANN: It's the same for me.

Pause.

STEVE: Yes. I'll tell Mary to give a week. That seems a compromise.

Pause.

They both think many things.

Pause.

ANN: Seems so quiet doesn't it? The house?

STEVE: Shall I put on some music?

ANN: That wasn't...what I meant....

STEVE: What do you fancy?

ANN looks at STEVE.

ANN: Surprise me.

STEVE: There's a new band one of the kids introduced me to at school – singer – Johnny Flynn – you heard of him...?

ANN: No. No. I've not heard of him.

STEVE stands and then doesn't move.

STEVE: I'm – pleased – so pleased – you think I'm a good teacher.

ANN: Yes.

Pause.

STEVE: I'll go find the music.

ANN: OK.

Pause.

STEVE: I love you.

ANN: OK.

Blackout.

Nick Payne

FUGITIVE MOTEL

Characters

JANE

HARRY

A hotel room. It's raining. Night.

JANE: It's really chucking it down.

HARRY: Yeah.

JANE: Quite like the sound, though.

HARRY: Right.

JANE: Sound of the rain.

HARRY: Yeah.

JANE: Quite like it.

Beat.

JANE: Can I be honest with you?

HARRY: Of course, yeah.

JANE: I'm actually – Mean I'm actually feeling pretty nervous.

HARRY: Really?

JANE: Yeah, pretty much.

HARRY: Me too.

JANE: Really?

HARRY: My mouth's almost completely dry.

JANE: It's not?

HARRY: Been tryina lick it for the last ten minutes or so.

JANE: Mine too.

HARRY: Really?

JANE: Yeah I've been tryina lick it too.

HARRY: Do you mind if I have some chewing gum?

JANE: Course not.

HARRY takes some chewing gum from a trouser pocket, offers some to JANE, she takes it. HARRY takes a piece for himself and returns the packet to his pocket. Both chew.

JANE: I feel much better actually.

HARRY: Really?

JANE: Yeah, definitely actually.

HARRY: Me too.

JANE: Isn't that weird?

HARRY: Yeah.

JANE: Just saying it helps.

Beat. HARRY kisses JANE, soft, tender.

JANE: Might take my shoes off.

HARRY: Sure.

JANE removes her shoes.

HARRY: I might take my shoes off too you know.

JANE: Go for it.

HARRY unties his shoe laces and removes his shoes (he takes slightly longer than JANE).

HARRY: I might take my socks off too actually if that's alright?

JANE: Yeah, totally.

HARRY removes his socks and tucks them into his shoes.

JANE: Better?

HARRY: Yeah. I get really sweaty feet.

JANE: Really?

HARRY: Yeah, I don't know what it is.

JANE: The back of my knees always get really sweaty.

HARRY: The back of your knees, really?

JANE: Weird, right?

HARRY: I get really sweaty palms too.

JANE moves to HARRY and runs a hand over his.

JANE: They're not that bad.

HARRY: Thanks.

JANE kisses HARRY, soft, tender.

JANE: It's weird kissing with chewing gum.

HARRY: Yeah.

JANE: Makes me feel like a teenager.

HARRY: I've felt a bit like a teenager all evening.

JANE: Weird, isn't it?

HARRY: This is probably the worst thing I've ever done. I mean it's probably the best – I mean it's probably the most exciting thing that I have ever literally done. But it's definitively the worst too.

JANE: We haven't really done anything.

HARRY: No. But.

Beat.

JANE: Do you want my chewing gum?

HARRY: Okay.

JANE moves to HARRY, removes her chewing gum and places it in his mouth. HARRY chews.

JANE: I might take my tights off?

HARRY: Sure.

JANE removes her tights.

HARRY: How's that?

JANE: Yeah, better.

JANE and HARRY smile a little at one another.

JANE: I hope this doesn't sound weird. But. I wonder if it's worth just stating a few preferences?

HARRY: Preferences?

JANE: Yeah, like. Some sort of dos and don'ts.

HARRY: I see.

JANE: Do you know what I mean?

HARRY: I do, yes. Would you, would you like to start?

JANE: Okay. I'm not, I'm not really that in to blow jobs. And, I mean, I don't really enjoy the whole being cummed on thing. I mean, I don't mind it, but, in an ideal world –

HARRY: That's – I completely – That's not a –

JANE: And I just – In terms of…I'm not really a massive fan of anal.

HARRY: Good to know.

JANE: I mean I'm not, I'm not like *dead* against it, but –

HARRY: Not a problem.

JANE: Also.

HARRY: Please.

JANE: I'm not really into being tied up or blindfolded. Anything that restricts movement, really, I just find a bit weird.

HARRY: With you on that one.

JANE: Really?

HARRY: Absolutely.

JANE: You?

HARRY: Pretty easy going, really. Not a huge fan of talking, though, have to confess. You know, during. It tends to make me feel a little self-conscious.

JANE: Totally, totally fine.

HARRY: Should we talk about dos?

JANE: We should.

HARRY: We don't have to –

JANE: No, we definitely should.

JANE gestures for HARRY to start.

HARRY: Okay. Well. I quite...enjoy...I would quite enjoy, watching, you, pleasuring, yourself. As a for instance. And, although, as you say, I'm not a fan of anal, I, I do quite enjoy – position – wise – *behind*.

JANE: I...I tend to quite enjoy having my breasts, my, my nipples, touched. And kissed. Gently, though. Really, really gently. My back, too. Kissing the bottom of my back. Position-wise, I tend to enjoy a bit of on top.

Beat.

HARRY: I'm, I'm feeling fairly horny now, so. I wonder if it's worth –

JANE: You sure?

HARRY: Yeah, I think it's probably worth – I mean as long as you're sure that this is still something –

JANE: I mean, yeah, I mean definitely.

HARRY: Okay then.

JANE: Great.

HARRY: What's the best way to – How would you like to –

JANE: I think – I mean if we just get on the bed, that's probably –

HARRY: As we are or –

JANE: No, I think – Yeah, I think pretty much as we are, really.

HARRY: Okay.

JANE: Great.

***

A different hotel room. Early evening. Sunshine.

HARRY: Where would you like to go?

JANE: I don't know really.

HARRY: What are you in the mood for?

JANE: I don't know. Chinese?

HARRY: I could do Chinese.

JANE: Is there anywhere nice nearby?

HARRY: I don't really know the area.

JANE: No.

HARRY: We could get takeaway if you like? Just a thought.

JANE: Is that what you want?

HARRY: I'm easy.

JANE: *(A joke.)* 'You don't say'. *(Beat.)* Sorry. *(Beat.)* Look.

HARRY: Something the matter?

JANE: Can I ask you something?

HARRY: Of course you can.

JANE: How do you feel? About me.

HARRY: How do I feel?

JANE: Yes.

HARRY: About you?

JANE: Yes.

HARRY: Well –

JANE: What do you feel I suppose is what I'm asking.

HARRY: What do I –

JANE: When you, when you think of me, how does that make you feel?

Beat.

HARRY: Ecstatic.

JANE: I'm being serious.

HARRY: I know.

JANE: I'm not messing around.

HARRY: Neither am I.

JANE: Because I think that I might be in love with you. And, it's odd, because. You're not really my type.

HARRY: Right.

JANE: I mean not in a bad way.

HARRY: Glad to hear it.

JANE: I'm being serious. Will you listen to me. I'm trying to say something.

HARRY: I'm listening.

JANE: In spite of not being my type, you seem to be having a huge affect on me. I went home, I went back home and Stephen said how was your trip and I said fine and he said did you miss me and I said yes, I did. I thought that I'd feel guilty. Lying. But I didn't. I felt no guilt whatsoever. And that was the first time. I mean, Christ, that was just the first time. I've felt progressively less and less guilt as the months have worn on. So I'm asking you how you feel about me because –

HARRY: I feel exactly the same.

JANE: Don't just say that.

HARRY: I'm not.

JANE: Don't just say that because you're thinking I'd better say something –

HARRY: I'm not.

JANE: Better just say something to shut her up.

HARRY: I'm in love with you, too.

JANE: You better not be messing me around.

HARRY: I'm not. I promise you I'm not.

JANE: Well. Good. Because. I think this is pretty fucking magical.

            Beat.

JANE: How would you feel about making it official?

HARRY: How do you mean?

JANE: I was – A couple of nights ago, I was, in bed, with Stephen, and he was picking at one of his toes and I said what are you doing and he said nothing. And I said what do you mean nothing? And he said he didn't understand what I was asking him. What were you picking at I said. He wasn't picking at the nail and he wasn't picking at the toe. He was just idly picking. It just started me thinking. Do you see what I'm saying?

HARRY: Yes.

JANE: I think we should really try and make this something other than something on the side.

HARRY: I completely agree. I was, the night before last, I was in bed with Sarah and she, she started nibbling my ear. She always does it. Like a mouse. It's like having a mouse. And I felt myself growing uneasy. I wanted to say: stop. Please. Do the two of us a favour and just stop. But I didn't. We had sex and she nibbled my ear almost entirely throughout. Over and over and over. Once she'd cum, I got out of bed and I went into the bathroom and I sat on the toilet for about ten minutes. I told myself that I was going to tell her about you and I. I sat there rehearsing what I was going to say, mumbling. When I went back into the bedroom she was asleep. So, what I'm saying is that, yes, I completely agree with you. I think that I should tell Sarah and I think that you should tell Stephen.

JANE: Where are you free? To do it.

HARRY: Are you thinking we should do it on the same night?

JANE: I mean – Why not?

HARRY: No, I mean –

JANE: Clean break.

HARRY: Absolutely. Well.

HARRY takes out his mobile telephone – something very modern – and begins scrolling through his calendar. JANE, likewise.

HARRY: Okay. How about the...twenty-fourth?

JANE: We're at a barbeque. Sorry.

HARRY: Okay. Okay. Twenty-sixth?

JANE: Capoeira. I'm so sorry.

HARRY: Don't be silly.

JANE: No – You know what? I can just miss it.

HARRY: We're supposed to be seeing friends anyway.

JANE: Really?

HARRY: I was just thinking I could do it afterwards, but you're right. Better to do it on a free evening.

JANE: What about the twenty-seventh?

HARRY: *(Checks, then.)* Perfect.

JANE: Really?

HARRY: It's a date.

Both HARRY and JANE take a moment to update their calendars. HARRY and JANE put their mobile telephones away.

JANE: How did you meet?

HARRY: You mean Sarah?

JANE: Yeah. I mean if you'd rather not –

HARRY: No, no, of course. Well. We met at university.

JANE: Wow.

HARRY: A house party. She was outside, crying.

JANE: Oh no.

HARRY: Tears, right the way down her face.

JANE: God.

HARRY: I was fairly drunk, so I just wandered over and said are you alright.

JANE: What did she say?

HARRY: She just screamed at me. Fuck off, she screamed.

JANE: No?

HARRY: Fuck off.

JANE: What did you say?

HARRY: Nothing. I fucked off.

JANE: That was it?

HARRY: Yeah.

JANE: But – I don't understand – How did the two of you end up –

HARRY: Right, I see, sorry. I thought you wanted to know how we met? I thought you –

JANE: Yeah, no, I did, but –

HARRY: So that was how we met but we didn't actually end up together until a couple of weeks later.

JANE: She took her time to succumb to your charms.

           Beat.

JANE: Do you think she'll be upset? When you tell her. About us.

HARRY: I do. Yeah.

***

A different hotel room. Night.

HARRY: I'm sorry it took me so long to get here.

JANE: Don't worry.

HARRY: Traffic was nightmarish.

JANE: It's fine.

HARRY kisses JANE, a 'hello'.

HARRY: How are you? How have you been?

JANE: Fine. No, yeah, fine.

HARRY: Really?

JANE: Yeah, no, definitely. How are, how have things been with you?

HARRY: Good. Thank you. Good.

JANE: Yeah.

HARRY: Yes. Well. All things considered.

Beat.

HARRY: So.

JANE: Yes.

HARRY: You told him.

JANE: I did.

HARRY: And?

JANE: Why don't you sit down?

HARRY: It's that bad, is it?

JANE: It's not bad. No. But.

Beat.

JANE: I don't think I can leave him.

Beat.

HARRY: Right. I see. Right. What happened?

JANE: He fell apart.

HARRY: Really?

JANE: Completely.

HARRY: In what way?

JANE: He started crying. I mean sobbing. I mean heaving and sobbing. I thought he was going to pass out.

HARRY: He didn't though, did he?

JANE: No, God, he was fine. Well. Not fine –

HARRY: No –

JANE: But he didn't pass out.

HARRY: So. Does this mean –

JANE: I don't know. I'm sorry. I'm not. I'm not sure what it means. No. That's not true. I do know. Harry, I am so incredibly sorry –

HARRY: Please. You don't. You don't have to apologise.

Beat.

JANE: How did it go with Sarah?

HARRY: *(As in 'good'.)* Well. Surprisingly. It went surprisingly well. She agreed. She agreed that things, that the two of us, that we've, for a while at least, been drifting apart from one another. All in all, it was remarkably agreeable.

JANE: Wow.

HARRY: She, she even mentioned that she'd recently been for a drink with someone.

JANE: Really, wow.

HARRY: Only the one, but. She said that they'd really got along.

Beat.

HARRY: I did a little packing.

JANE: Packing?

HARRY: Some clothes. Books.

JANE: You've – The two of you are definitely going to –

HARRY: I think so. I think, yeah, I think that that's probably it.

Beat.

HARRY: And, so, in terms of Stephen, in terms of the two of you, you're thinking that, on reflection, you're thinking that –

JANE: I just – Seeing him, like that, in such a state, like a child, crying, like that, I just... He kept saying please don't go. Please don't go please don't go please don't go. When I tried to move away, just to give us a little distance, he started saying don't leave me. Don't leave me don't leave me don't leave me. I can forgive you he said.

HARRY: But do you want to stay with him?

JANE: I think that I probably do.

HARRY: Well either you do or you don't.

JANE: Don't be angry.

HARRY: Don't be '*angry*'?

Beat.

HARRY: Well we should think about leaving otherwise they'll charge us for the room even if we don't stay here.

JANE: Don't be like that.

HARRY: Like what?

Beat.

JANE: I didn't make you tell her.

HARRY: Well, in a way, you, you did actually.

JANE: What's that supposed to mean?

HARRY: It doesn't matter.

JANE: Course it does. Harry –

HARRY: I thought you... I thought you said that you were in love with me?

JANE: I did. I am. I was.

HARRY: Right.

JANE: I thought that he'd given up. On us. But, when we spoke, when I spoke to him, I realised that that wasn't true. He said that he just had faith, he just had faith that we would work things out. Which was why he never pushed it, why he never made an issue of it. He said he never doubted for a second that we would just work things out. I said is that true, is that true I said. Do you really mean that I said.

HARRY: And what did he say?

JANE: He didn't say anything. He just nodded. He just nodded his head.

           The End.

Yemisi Blake

I NOTICE THE SOUND FIRST

i.

Sound the alarm on the holy mountain!
It is the day of darkness and doom!
screams the Jesus man outside Oxford Circus Underground
Station.

His megaphone voice stands clear above the traffic
spluttering city smog onto the pavements.

It's the first thing the boys and me hear after getting off the train,
it sends us into a fit of laughter.

'That guy's crazy fam, seriously mental!'

There are six of us, all year 10s
blessed with the luck of an INSET day.

No uniform, Big Tees and bussing sags,
a Travelcard, and £20 in our back pockets
and nothing but shopping and spotting girls on the mind.

Sound the alarm on the holy mountain!
It is the day of darkness and doom!

His call to repent tracks us as we window shop.
I'm searching wisely for the perfect way to spend my crisp note.
Some of the guys have already dented the balance with creps and
over-priced bottles of water.

We spot a girl passing and simultaneously give her the eyes,
hoping she catches a scent of CK Be, stops and sparks a
conversation.

We snake through the high-street stores.
In TopMan, I buy a belt buckle in the shape of a lightening strike.
Joe gets a Nike Air max T-Shirt from Foot Locker.
Louie actually goes in Claire's Accessories to buy a bracelet for his
girlfriend.
Puke!

The rest of us stand outside trying to find shade,
the four o'clock sun causing sweat-marks
and that AIN'T cool!

We take a breather, sit in McD's over nuggets
Strawberry milkshakes, and jokes.

Bellies full, we leave
only forty more minutes of good shopping light left.
We are far away from the Jesus man,
but can still hear his faint warnings and prayers.

(Quieter.) Sound the alarm on the holy mountain
It is the day of darkness and doom.

(Quieter still.) Sound the alarm on the holy mountain
It is the day of darkness and doom

(Silent pause.)

ii.

I notice the sound first.
As if our tube home has erupted through the ground.
I feel glass hitting my eyelids and cheeks.
I'm on the floor, blooded palms.

Slowly I look to see what's around me.
Sunlight scattered through dust cloud and smoke.
A hand grabs my wrist before losing strength.

Muffled voices surround me,
none that I recognise. No friends around me,
no shopping bags, nothing. Not even the faint warming voice
from a megaphone in the distance.

(Whisper.) Sound the alarm on the holy mountain
It is the day of darkness and doom.

Michael Rosen

AMOS THE SHEPHERD CURSES THE RULERS OF ANCIENT ISRAEL

I say,
You have sent a whole people into exile,
You have forgotten how to be brothers to others
In your fury,
You have lost all sense of pity

You have sold innocent men for money
You have crushed the poor and the needy
You have taken their grain
So that you can build yourself fine stone houses.
You have even attacked pregnant women
So that you might make your country larger

In your palaces you store up your own violence
Just as you hoard your plunder and loot.
You lie on your marble couches,
Stretch out on your beds
Eating the lambs of the people's flocks of sheep
Eating the calves from the people's herds of cattle
Drinking basinfuls of wine
Anointing yourselves with fine oils,
Turning away the poor at your gate.

You dare to think that the instruments you sing to
Are playing the music of David
You who do not feel the pain and sorrow
Of destroying the word of Joseph.

In time
You too will go into exile
You will not even drink the wine
From the vineyards you've made,
And the great banquets you once feasted on
Will slip into the past
Just like your dreams of overweening power.

Nancy Harris

THE HOUSE NEXT DOOR

Characters

RUTH, 10

ESTHER, 8

Generously supported by Georgina Vestey

Two swings side by side in a garden.

ESTHER and RUTH sit on them. They look into the house next door.

ESTHER holds a large rock in her hand. She lifts it up as though she is going to throw it. Hesitates.

ONE

RUTH: Aim for the window.

Beat.

RUTH: That one. Aim for that window.

Beat.

ESTHER still hesitates.

RUTH: Esther.

ESTHER: I don't think I should.

ESTHER puts the rock hand down.

RUTH: She killed her husband.

ESTHER: She did not.

RUTH: Her baby too. She killed them both. She cut them up and boiled them and fed them to the cat.

ESTHER: Who says?

RUTH: Everyone.

ESTHER: They do not.

RUTH: They do too. Everyone knows. It's a fact.

ESTHER looks into the house next door.

ESTHER: Why?

RUTH: Why what?

ESTHER: Why would she kill her husband and her baby and feed them to her cat?

RUTH: Cos her husband was annoying and the baby wouldn't stop crying.

ESTHER: How do you know?

RUTH: I heard it.

ESTHER: No you didn't.

RUTH: Yes, I did. You could hear it all the way from the shops.

ESTHER: You weren't even born.

RUTH hits ESTHER on the arm.

RUTH: Neither were you.

ESTHER: Ow.

ESTHER rubs her arm, looks into the house next door.

ESTHER: All babies cry.

RUTH: Yeah but for some mums it's like a person scrawling nails down a blackboard. It gets under their skin and into their heads and sends them fucking loopy.

ESTHER: Don't say fucking.

RUTH: Fucking.

ESTHER: Mum said you're not to say fucking.

RUTH starts to swing.

RUTH: Fucking, fucking, fucking, fucking, fucking.

ESTHER stares into the house next door, then looks at the rock in her hand.

TWO

They sit on different swings.

They look into the house next door.

ESTHER still holds the rock.

ESTHER: She doesn't have a cat.

RUTH: What?

ESTHER points to the house next door.

ESTHER: Next door. *She* – doesn't have a cat.

RUTH: She does. I've seen it.

ESTHER: When?

RUTH: Lots of times.

ESTHER: Liar.

RUTH: Little black one.

ESTHER: You're lying.

RUTH smiles.

RUTH: Has a white dot just over its nose. It's always there.

ESTHER: I've never seen it.

RUTH: …she probably ate him too.

RUTH starts to swing, happily.

RUTH: Aim for that window. She's always at that window, looking in here. Looking at us. Looking out. It's the easiest one to hit.

ESTHER looks at the rock, then at the house next door.

ESTHER: She would have been arrested.

RUTH: They can't arrest you for eating a cat.

ESTHER: I meant her husband and her… If she did what you said she did – she would have been arrested.

RUTH: Not if they don't have proof. You can't arrest someone if there's no proof. That's why she fed them to the cat.

ESTHER: People would have asked.

RUTH: People don't care.

ESTHER: People would have wondered where they'd gone.

RUTH: Just throw it.

ESTHER: What about DNA?

RUTH stops swinging.

ESTHER: If she fed them to the cat, the DNA would be in the bowl. It'd be all over it. That's evidence.

RUTH thinks about this for a beat.

RUTH: They couldn't find the bowl.

She starts to swing again. ESTHER looks at the rock, then at the house next door.

THREE

They sit on different swings again.

RUTH is swinging, ESTHER is not.

ESTHER still has the rock.

ESTHER: She's an odd fish.

RUTH keeps swinging.

ESTHER: That's what mum says. She says she's an odd fish. And that she never says hello in the post office.

RUTH: Did you tell mum that she killed her husband and her baby?

ESTHER: Yes.

RUTH stops swinging.

RUTH: Did you?

ESTHER: Yes.

RUTH: Did you say I told you that?

ESTHER looks guilty.

ESTHER: No.

RUTH: Did you?

ESTHER: No.

RUTH punches her arm.

ESTHER: Ow.

RUTH: You're a fucking idiot Esther.

ESTHER: Don't say fucking.

RUTH hits her again.

RUTH: Fucking.

ESTHER: It died in its sleep.

RUTH: What?

ESTHER: The baby. And the husband left soon after.

RUTH: Did mum say that?

ESTHER: Yes.

RUTH: It died in its sleep?

ESTHER: She's not been right ever since. It's a tragedy. That's what mum said.

RUTH glances at the house next door, then back at ESTHER.

RUTH: Mum's full of it.

ESTHER: She's not.

RUTH: She just doesn't want you having nightmares and pissing all over the sheets.

OBADIAH   239

ESTHER: Mum said we should feel sorry. That she isn't right in the head.

RUTH: That's cos she's a murderer.

RUTH takes the rock from ESTHER.

RUTH: And you're a piece of chicken shit.

ESTHER: I'm not –

RUTH gets ready to throw the rock at the house next door.

RUTH: – who's afraid to throw a stone.

ESTHER: I'm was going to throw it.

RUTH: Chicken shit.

ESTHER: You didn't give me a chance.

RUTH stops. Offers ESTHER the rock. ESTHER looks at it.

RUTH: Go on then. Now's your chance. Aim for the window.

ESTHER looks at RUTH, hesitates.

RUTH: Chicken. Shit.

Slowly, ESTHER picks up the rock from RUTH's hand.

A beat.

Then she throws it.

The sound of smashing glass.

FOUR

They sit on different swings.

ESTHER swings, RUTH doesn't.

ESTHER: There was a red carpet and a brown sofa and a picture of Jesus on the wall.

RUTH: What else?

ESTHER: A big box of biscuits but they looked kind of old.

RUTH: What else?

ESTHER: She gave mum some tea and me some orange but we didn't drink them cos the cups were sticky.

RUTH: What else?

ESTHER: I said I was sorry and mum gave her the money in a little envelope. And she said she forgave me. And gave me a kiss.

RUTH: Mum?

ESTHER: No, her.

RUTH: Ugggh. What else?

ESTHER: She took out the Bible and read us a bit and mum said I should thank her. So I thanked her and she gave me another kiss.

RUTH: Uggggh.

ESTHER: Then she took out some paper and got out a pen and wrote down a line from the Bible. About eagles.

RUTH: Eagles?

ESTHER: And as you do unto others it will be done unto you. And mum said she hoped *she* wouldn't throw a rock at our bathroom window.

RUTH: Was that a joke?

ESTHER: Mum laughed. *She* didn't.

RUTH: Mum's an idiot.

ESTHER: Mum was acting sort of funny.

ESTHER stops swinging and takes the piece of paper from her pocket.

She gives it to RUTH.

ESTHER: That's what she wrote down.

RUTH: *(Reading.)* Though thou exalt thyself as the eagle, and though thou set thy nest among the stars, thence will I bring thee down, saith the LORD.

ESTHER nods, sagely.

ESTHER: Yeah.

RUTH: What does that mean?

ESTHER shrugs, starts to swing again.

RUTH looks at the paper.

RUTH: She's a freak.

ESTHER: That's what mum said too.

Beat.

ESTHER: I think she liked having visitors.

RUTH throws the paper away.

She starts to swing.

They swing a couple of times in silence. RUTH glances at the house next door.

RUTH: What does she look like up close?

ESTHER thinks.

RUTH: Ugly?

ESTHER: No.

RUTH: Evil?

ESTHER: No.

           Beat.

ESTHER: Tired.

           Beat.

ESTHER: But she has nice hair.

           Beat.

ESTHER: She doesn't have a cat.

RUTH: How do you know?

ESTHER: She said. She never had one. Can't.

RUTH: Why?

ESTHER: She's allergic. They make her sneeze.

           They swing for another beat thinking about this.

           Lights down.

Nick Laird

CETACEAN

From the first word it was obvious
I was dealing with a maniac. A demoniac
ego-, mono-, megalomaniac. No quarter asked
nor none received and he lurked in the air;
the granary; the tavern; beneath the cedar trees
where I had fled and fell and lay
depleted, huddled, panting on the sharp
carpet of its needles. I lifted one to test
its desiccated tine against my thumb
and snapped it cleanly in two pieces.

      West I headed, the gold coast,
through the low fields of einkorn and emmer.
travelling always in company,
sticking to principal thoroughfares,
and never slept until our trader had pulled anchor
and the whorehouses and white warehouses of Jaffa
had fallen off the vista.

But he was not the sort of god foxed
by a new name or a new beard,
by a new god or any sort
of barrier or border I could make
from fire or earth or air or water;

I was cuffed from my bunk
and the floor woke me up
as two blue jugs flew
from their hooks and shattered.

I had hurt my wrist and the table
came at me before the room swung
down to right itself and rose and fell and
kept on falling

                    Outside boiled and slapped.
I'd told the fat cook the thing that happened
with the Voice when we agreed my passage
but it had sounded so ridiculous
I said instead that in fact I fled
from my wife's crazy family –
I mean really *batshit* crazy –
                         but the crew knew and steamed through
grabbing me and slamming me out the hatch
into the storm. I was damned and wore the fact
upon my face like a black mask.
Outside the sky was an open gash through which
the water sluiced and tipped and three directions
of the world were solid walls of water, falling.
I was thrown and thrown over and catching nothing
hit the water.

                    The storm was cut short.
It stopped.
But even calm
I never swam
and couldn't now. I sank until the waters
compassed me about even to the soul.
I felt I had shrunk to the size of a doll

bobbing back to the absolutely flat surface,
and noticing how on the deck the sailors
stood immobile and in silence, more fearful
than relieved it seemed at such
vindictiveness and whimsy.
And down I went and I went

further, to the start of mountains,
to the living ribbons on the sea-bed
where the water-knuckles pummelled,
where the grip of liquid-fingers held my body
tight in a watery vice screwed in gradually
shut until my chest and spine must surely
snap.

           I was about ready to give up,
and breathe in, but then suddenly the pain eased,
and then ceased completely.

I appeared to be in a pleasant dream.

           But as I sank it grew beside me,
the shadow, and an eye loomed;
involved, purposeful, plate-sized,
an arrangement of grey with blues
and light and it stared, making an eye-catch,
and what flashed in the glance had none
of a cat's insolence or the dog's workable love,
none of the sadness of heifers and calves –
but what caught made it turn aside and the water
snap, so I was swung back hard by a hundred
liquid straps and entered into dark and air.

I was interred.
I lay on my side and vomited.

All my muscles in constant tremor and after
this alleviated I passed out cold.

When I woke the purging set on me,
and only some hours later was I fit
to start to demarcate – by sound, by touch –
the limits of the prison.

I was sitting in a slight depression
on a not unpleasant rough damp sponge,
a tongue. All was blackness without stars but feeling
tenderly I could discern several thin
ridges, like the struts of a shut kiln
or bread oven, and after a minute or so
I had the whole measure of the pitchblack
sorry crawlspace I can even now find myself
inside again when I wake before dawn
and raise my hand straight up to check
that there is nothing there.

                    I had no way of telling time
except that if I slept what seemed a decent stretch
I counted it a night. And I dreamt.
First night I dreamt I was being built
into a temple wall, watching seven hooded priests
lay out in very precise rows
neat bricks of river-mud, mixed with split reeds,
and watched another seven then lift those bricks
the sun had set already and closed me in,
to an inch or so in front of my nose,
to undiluted true darkness.

The mouth of a whale is not cold but in there it is
difficult to breathe. And I was mad with thirst:
for the want of fresh water, a droplet of it,
my tongue became inflamed and blistered –

but I must tell you of the song it made –
a keening, faint, before the tone would break
and I become the clapper in a bell so
   much I shook with sound,
then the creature would chirp twice like a nightjar.
Bizarre, at least to me, and what was I?
A parasite. A prize.

The second night I dreamt I was a stowaway
curled up within a massive woven basket
of clean linen for the monastery.
And then in my dream I fell asleep.

In the low sound slowed down
there might have been a pattern, the tunnel-
throated basso moan that came from somewhere
just below me, and lasted for a moment,
would often be succeeded by a softer moan, echoing,
the pair repeating in a little dialogue of self
with soul. Exquisite, to begin with,
and then monotonous.

But when he would exude a lengthy continuous sighing
ending in an upsweep or a downsweep
of some frequency so loud, and yet at the same time so deep,
and in such a scale and tone I am transported
through the sea –
                              I can feel a solid thing
opening before me, without end, and closing in
behind precisely.

Melancholy those calls were,
if calls they were. My own despair was given
voice and a shared grief bodied forth,
highly modulated.

                              Like sometimes I
would sing along and then it seemed to
answer me with little pulses in its calls –
comforting, the other presence in the room.
I never called it monster. How gentle
it appeared, how it behaved so carefully.
No two ever were as intimate as one
inside some other one. Its mouth.
I was invisible to all but him.

Sometimes I called it her.
Sometimes I called it brother.
I dug my fingernails into its doughy skull
and once punched at its cretinous resinous flesh
until my knuckles bled.
Sometimes I wept for hours
upon the apron of that tongue
or watched a darkness so complete I'd
grow convinced my eyes were shut.

I wondered if we rested on the seabed.
We must have travelled seven leagues
or seven leagues times seventy
and when it dived I felt the pressure
of the barrel roll and churn, and felt these fingers
of accumulating speed pressing into me,
the helices and whorls,
and found myself up against the side-flesh
that was like a screen of melted wax
that had recast, reset, re-sealed –

I thought how this
was now the wall I wanted through –
my palisade – my barricade –

and yet the getting through would kill me.

There was nothing beyond it.

The world was this and there were worse
things for a god to be. It was a god to me
and I had stolen something of the glory
of its godhead, and without a thought
leaned forward now into the tilt
as we banked before the dive.

On the third night I was dreaming
that I had become a whale, and carried in my mouth
a man, and in my dream I edged him out
gently on an empty beach, yellow as a prayer-mat,
when the sun was at its highest so his shadow fell
around him as just an outline on the sand,
as he lay there blinking and sobbing
and stinking of herring.

Adam Foulds

FLARE

Stage in the state left by the previous performance, curtain up or down, it doesn't matter. A director walks on. A clever, sincere, well-educated, serious young woman, she carries notes of some sort and a copy of the Bible or a smaller volume containing the Book of Micah.

DIRECTOR: Hi, hello. Apologies for this brief interruption. I've been asked to come on and talk a bit about what would've been happening next if we'd gone ahead with it. This slot was for a piece about the Book of Micah. We commissioned and received a script that was sort of okay but in the end we, I, thought that it kind of missed the mark.

Micah's this really short book, one of the Old Testament prophets you sort of forget about, unless you've read it. It comes and goes in a flash. It's very…'loud' is the word I want to use and the play didn't really get that. The Micah I'd imagine was a difficult son type, very touchy, always unpredictably going off like a flare. I wrote here *(Consults notes.)* that his sudden brightness lights up a battlefield at night his parents don't even know they are standing on. It's everything, all society: land, commerce, iniquity, sin.

Yet his anger at his parents and all of Israel is washed through with pity. It's like he knows that they are all younger than he is and weaker. But at breakfast you can picture him sitting there with them, watching his father's financial paper dripping blood on the table, and out it comes, the God turbulence, calamitous justice. Where is it? *(She reads:)*

But truly I am full of power by the spirit of the LORD, and of judgement, and of might, to declare unto Jacob his transgression, and to Israel his sin.

(Skimming through.) Stolen land, evil done with both hands, building up Jerusalem with theft which could have taken us off into a whole contemporary political thing, um, mountains collapsing, wounds, cannibals. There's some truly horrifying stuff. *(Reads:)*

Who hate the good, and love the evil – This is the rulers he's talking about; who pluck off their skin from off them, and their flesh from off their bones;
Who also eat the flesh of my people, and flay their skin from off them; and they break their bones, and chop them in pieces, as for the pot, and as flesh within the caldron.

A figure of speech so violent and prolonged you have to ask yourself whether it's Micah here doing the chopping and cooking, destroying people. But also there's this other tone of voice that comes through, the other side of justice. He uses it for this unbelievably sweet, dreamy prospectus for peace. It's the bit everybody knows:

…and they shall beat their swords into plowshares and their spears into pruning hooks…nation shall not lift up a sword against nation, neither shall they learn war any more. But they shall sit every man under his vine and under his fig tree, and no one shall make them afraid…

So that's Micah, the book we're not doing. It's not just that, between us, the script we received was, let's say, mediocre I mean fine. Actually, I started to lose faith in the possibility of rendering it at all. It occurred to me that really the ideal play about Micah would be unstageable. I pictured the second half beginning with Micah destroying the theatre and the surrounding city, probably with fire. Then in the cleared, smouldering space, he and the audience would farm together for years. The audience would be so engrossed in their hard, productive labour, their natural piety, the rhythm of days, the seasons studded with festivals, that they wouldn't remember the lives they left behind or notice when Micah disappears.

Something along those lines. Which obviously would be impossible. So. Good night.

Moira Buffini

GOD IS JEALOUS

God is jealous

The Host is slow to anger and great in power
He moves in the whirlwind and in the storm
And the clouds are the dust of his feet.
Mountains quake at him
Hills melt
His fury is poured out like fire.
With an overrunning flood
He will make an utter end

He will
Or we will

What do we imagine against the Host?

For while we are folded together as thorns
Folded, drunken
Drunken as drunkards
He will devour
He will devour us

But imagine
Dare to imagine without him
Build cities without him
Eat knowledge without him
Be not his slaves

God is jealous
Our chariots rage in the streets
Justle against each other
They seem like torches, run like lightnings

The moment comes
The Host opens the river gates
Our palaces dissolve
And still, imagine against him

Blood, lies and robbery
The noise of a whip
The rattling of wheels
We dare
We dare you, jealous God.
Our bright sword
Our glittering spear –

'Behold, I am against thee,' saith the Host

Empty, void, waste
Our hearts melt
Knees smite
Our faces gather blackness
None shall look back
Our children dashed in pieces at the top of all the streets

We draw our waters for the siege
Fortify strong holds
Go into clay
There shall his fire devour us
It shall eat us up like cankerworm

'Behold, I am against thee,' saith the Host
'Thou hast multiplied thy merchants above the stars of heaven
Thy mistress of witchcraft selleth nations through her whoredoms
Thy kings are as locusts
Thy nobles lie in dust

Thy people, scattered on the mountains.
No healing of thy wound.'

But the cankerworm spoileth and flieth away

We will manage our own destruction
And of that
God is jealous.

Trevor Griffiths

HABACCUC DREAMS

Dark space, cave-like, echoic. Shuffling movements off; approaching, a man's voice singing, nasal, eerie.

SONG

(Ralph Stanley unaccompanied version)
O Death
O Death
Won't you spare me over till another year
Well what is this that I can't see
With ice cold hands taking hold of me
Well I am Death none can excel
I'll open the door to Heaven or Hell
Whoa Death someone would pray
Could you wait to call me another day
The children prayed, the preacher preached
Time and mercy is out of your reach
I'll fix your feet till you can't walk
I'll lock your jaw till you can't talk
I'll close your eyes so you can't see
This very air come and go with me
I'm death I come to take the soul
Leave the body and leave it cold
To draw up the flesh off of the frame
Dirt and worm both have a claim…

He's arrived, song suspended, looks around him, tall, immensely old: Donatello's Habaccuc, redressed for now in mothy joggers, long tattered greatcoat, bristled head, fingers peeping from khaki mittens, life-tools hanging from upper body, pans, tin mugs, plates, kettle, spoons, knives, flatpack boxes; a man of the highways, rags a-flutter.

HABACCUC

Is it you Lord? Yahweh? God? Baal? El? As in Isra'el? And Ashera, El's wife, our woman deity long erased from the record? Here and now or dreaming from afar. One God, manynames…

(Resumes song.)

O Death

O Death

Won't you spare me over till another year…

(Bleak, remote.) In this one year – twentyten to twentyeleven – one hundred and four gravel-collectors, most of them women, half of them children, the children of Canaan, doing no harm and in their own land, were slain on the beaches of Gaza by Israelite snipers…Your people, lord. Our people. *(Loud.)* Yes, it is Habaccuc!!! The unrepentant one! The one who lives the life of the people. The one who cannot take No for an answer. Ha! Two thousand years later and more, how much longer shall I cry and thou wilt not hear, how much longer shout out to thee of violence and thou wilt not save, why show us the vicious sins committed, the deadly damage done, the monstrous grievance felt, and offer no way of ridding the world of the injustice and the terror they leave behind…

The wild anger settles. A downlight grows ahead of him; rests halfway between dim and bright; he scans it, drawn, uncertain.

Is it you, god? Or is it moonlight? Which of us ever knew? Isaiah, Ezekiel, Daniel…? Ha. Prophet as Dreamer.

He takes a medicine bottle from his greatcoat pocket, swigs from it.

Temazepam. Bliss in a bottle. Puts paid to pathological insomnia and reasserts the subject's right to dream. Taken with appropriate hallucinogens, mushroom down the ages, say, or good grass, it creates powerful transcendence modes in which dream and real can and will fuse. Mel Brooks' 2000-year-old man knew all about that... *(In Brooks' Old Man's muttery East Side voice.)* '...Certain barks made you jump in the air and sing Sweet Sue, other barks made you drowsy and you were not to get on an animal and drive...' *(Takes in audience.)* As perhaps now. As possibly here. Habaccuc Dreams.

The light strengthens a little; unnerves him.

It **is** you, isn't it. This is what you do. Every time. Always have done, millenium after millenium. If you were appearing in *Variety* and your billing were written by Spike Milligan it would read **GOD: the Sadistic Tease**. Topped only by Milligan's own bill-matter for himself: **SPIKE MILLIGAN: The Performing Man.** You still terrify me. Still. Long after belief died in my heart. Long after the vision told upon tables *(Takes out his notebook.)* crumbled to dust. Plus. I spent some seasons with Icemen, learned their ways, learned the art of throatsong, found the spirit within, the very voice of God that I remember giving me answer...back in the day. **That** may surprise ye, oh yes. Ha.

He shuffles slowly forward into the cone of light. Gazes up towards the cone's apex.

But I'm back now. And ready to speak my mind. *(Finds his page. Sniffs.)* I have been to the ends of the earth. Over twenty-five centuries. Special Envoy. Bearing the solemn promise of the One True Lord that Justice in this world and Everlasting Life thereafter will be the reward of those who believe in and obey the same one true lord etc. Lord, let me state it as clearly as I can. The people...

Met Police sirens, two blocks away; distinct for a moment; gone. He holds up a kettle, plays it with a spoon.

(Aside: another him.) Kettling. They have their ways, we have ours… *(On.)* The people are many things but they are not stupid. For at least the twenty-five hundred years you've had me tramping the world instead of going to my grave, the verdict on whether you have rewarded the faithful and punished the evildoers is already in. You did neither. You do neither. Most people born on this earth have lived, live now and will continue to live lives of rank misery and serial injustice at the hands of the rich and powerful, whatever the system of governance and moral code in place. And not only does it not get better, it gets worse. As they see it, as we see it, you get our faith, we get nothing, the rich and powerful own the world and suck on its goodness. You see it, generation after generation, century on century, light year on light year, and you do nothing. 'Woe to him that buildeth a town with blood and 'stablisheth a city by iniquity,' you had me write. Ha! Woe? Don't make us laugh, Lord. The pain's too great to bear…

Shouts, confused cries, people being chased, slap of running feet on roadway under Victorian vaulted bridge, a clue perhaps to the scene's actual location. He listens. It fades.

The years spent schlepping the world have taught me much. This is some world. These are some people. It wouldn't take a lot. It wouldn't take a lot. *(He rubs a mittened hand across his bristled head, tired suddenly. Eases down to the floor.)* I was going to say something else, about Babylon, culture, science, maths, well before the Greeks, not a mention in the good book… And something quite trivial, about me being allegedly conveyed to Daniel's lion's den prison in Babylon to take him a lunchbox as a sign that the Lord would protect him. An angel picked me up by the hair of my head and flew me to Babylon, 600 miles away. Stood by presumably. Brought me back. Didn't happen. *(Shows it.)* This is my hair. *(Grabs it. Too short.)* Always. Donatello knew it. Why didn't God? *(Looks around him.)* Because he was never there. Like now? He's not here. Maybe he never was. We just filled in the silence. But no, wait, I think, I know his voice, I know it, it is part of me. But then the seasons with the Icemen, where shamen teach the sacred art of throatsong, which Tuvans call the Voice of God.

Levers himself to his feet. Resumes his place in the cone of light. Finds his place in the notebook.

In the days before the fall of Jerusalem you spoke with me in the Cave of Eli, I had asked you to spare the lives of the children of Bet Heim from the bloody spears of Babylon. After a long silence you answered. *(Shows notebook.)* I wrote it down in my table, 'I find it in my heart to care...', I took it you meant they would be spared. They weren't. What did it mean? God Lies – Hold The Front Page!? I read the line out loud several times, trying to recall tone and rhythm, and suddenly I was in throatsong. Only I couldn't say that line, the line I'd written in my tables, the voice wouldn't say that line. The line it said, over and over, was not *I find it in my heart to care* but *(He draws exaggerated breath, sucks the lungs full. Reaches chill deep within.) I find it in me... (Drone.) hard to care... (Sniffs.)* This you'll remember in response to a plea to spare the lives of the children of Bet Heim. *I find it hard to care...* The Voice of God.

He turns, begins to move off, picks up the song. Smoke wanders through the downlight.

O Death
O Death
Won't you spare me over till another year
Won't you spare me over till another year
Won't you spare me over till another year

End.

Helen Edmundson

IN THE NIGHT, A PROMISE

A room where children sleep. Bunk beds. Cot-bed. A night light that throws patterns on the walls. Semi-darkness.
A woman sets up a video camera. She turns it on. She sits on the end of one of the beds, and records the following words.

I will throw the children from the windows.
Waking or sleeping, they will go.
There will be screaming, from every corner of the house,
And you will think – they must be playing. Surely?
But they will not be.

You, I will burn. I will burn you in your bed,
The bed where you cried out another's name,
And begged for other ecstasies than mine.
There will you melt, evaporate in flame,
And know too late the fire of my jealousy.
There is no innocence here. Better to start again.

I will destroy the matter of our home.
The doors and bannisters, the skirting boards and frames,
A pile of dereliction on the ground.
The cupboards of our every day,
The drawers where secret things were stored,
The baby clothes we could not bear to give away,
The china and the photographs,
All wrecked and smashed upon the floor,
And salt and herbs all trodden in with glass.

And water will flow from the sockets.
And pipes, exposed, will fill the air with gas.
And I will drown the telephone you pressed against your mouth,
On damp nights on the terrace,
Turning your face away.

The trees, I will fell,
And bring down all the fences and the gates.
And every flower and shrub I will unplant,
And leave the fruit to rot upon the grass.
It will become a feeding ground for foxes.
This place of sin.
This blasphemy.
And people who pass near will suck their teeth and flinch,
To see the hawks upon the stacks,
To hear the bitterns crying in the eaves,
And they will hold their breath and rush away,
As from an open grave.

One child, one daughter, I will keep.
Perhaps the one who speaks my name.
Perhaps the one who does not cry,
But falls upon her knees.
I'll lift her up. I'll take her far away,
The remnant of our promise.
We'll settle somewhere by the sea,
Sterilised by salty waves,
And I will love her, fiercely.

And all the world shall learn her worth,
And all the world shall learn my name.
And I will sing and hold her safe,
And she shall know no other thought but joy,
And she shall know no fear,
And all that passed, I will forgive,
And we shall live, and know no other love,
For all eternity.

She stays still for several moments, staring into the camera. Then she stands and turns it off. She takes out the tape and puts it in her pocket. She picks up the camera. She stops, to look at the sleeping forms of the children. Then leaves.

Suheir Hammad

IT IS HAVING FALLEN OUT OF GRACE

it is everything one touches turning to dust.

it is a fall from grace, descent into eviction, path leading to missing, impossible mission of rebuilding something from memory that never was.

there is a room of solitude required to hear god's voices echo and reverb in one's head. this room becomes a mansion becomes a prison becomes a bunker from all other voices, including reason, also sense. compassion. such fine difference in tenor between god's voices and those of the opposite. how loud the din in this head, how rare the clarity.

dear god i have seen people i love go search for your temple, and get lost in a maze of mind.

i see this also in the mirror.

dear god, may i worship you instead by a tree?

before you know it, you've created a life of surviving. you look down at what you have built and it crumbles beneath you. the saints, those who survive the deepest sadness, say this is a purification, the utter basement of depression. the singed soul does not make joyful noise, the beat down eventually stops looking up. what was promised, also history, even the future ahead, all of it must be given away, sold, flipped, left out on the stoop, in order to start over.

it is to walk the world without a set of keys to some space, some things, that belong with you. those who call this freedom, do not know.

it is to want human touch, company, so sharply, you cut yourself off and stop wanting. in the eye of a perfect storm, one will look up and see blind light. maybe hear voices. there are such floods in the seasons of a life. people weather them in the streets of new york city for years, lives, at a time. when these elements gather, there is no comfort. there just isn't.

this is the time when what was sweet soured. what i grew, died. the ceiling fell on my head, while demolition was painted construction. i drove away what i loved and was abandoned by it. i do not believe in much of anything. i am not comforted by faith, i doubt even the mustard seed.

dear god, may i please offer you my prayers by a river?

i am sitting in an emptying room, having very much fallen.

the desert the mystics write of. the night of the soul, an exodus swinging within a life, out a mind. if there were someone here to communicate with, i imagine i'd open my mouth to a keen, that's all.

this season of learning the hard. i am sitting between boxes, in a ghost house haunted by all i did wrong, all the decisions that got me here. packing up the excuses that no longer work, the loves not manifest. the mess i've made.

have you ever counted the stairs leading to your door? if one begins to count the steps, and the weight and the years, one's back braces, knees unbuckle. all the stuff done carried up those steps, shoulders rounded with the weight. it all comes down.

women and poets are not prophets.

i have no memory of any temple. i barely have this mustard seed.

dear god, am i the stone the mason forgot, or refused, to include in the foundation?

Elinor Cook

THE END OF THE ALPHABET

Characters

ALLIE (f)

ZACH (m)

NB. As far as possible, the play should be staged very intimately, with only a very small audience.

A toilet cubicle.

ALLIE is leaning over the toilet, on her knees.

She has been sick but not for a while.

ZACH has his hand on her back.

He is on the phone.

He listens.

ZACH: Uh huh.
Uh huh.

He listens.

Yes she's been sick, I don't know, six –

ALLIE: Seven –

ZACH: Maybe seven times.
Right.

He listens.

OK.

He listens.

I see.

He listens.

Has she banged her head?
Um.
Allie.
Have you banged your head?

ALLIE: What?
No.
That's a stupid question.
We would have said that right at the beginning, wouldn't we?

ZACH: No she hasn't banged her head.

He listens.

Uh huh.
Right.
OK.
They want to know if you're sure.

ALLIE: Of course I'm sure.
I'd know if I'd banged my head wouldn't I?
Are these people idiots?

He listens.

ZACH: They say a lot of people say that.
They say you might have done it in your sleep.

ALLIE: I haven't, I haven't –

ZACH: She hasn't.

ALLIE: Tell them about the shakes, Zach.
The black spots.
The numbness in my fingers and toes –

ZACH: Yes feverish and febrile.
Uncharacteristically hostile.
That's right.

He listens.

ZACH: They want to know if you have a rash.

ALLIE: A rash?
I don't know.
You tell me.
You're the one looking at me.
Do you see a rash?

ZACH: OK.
I see.
Apparently we need a glass.
Apparently we need to press the glass over the rash.

ALLIE: But I don't have a rash.
I don't have a rash.
Do I?

She starts examining herself for rashes.

ZACH: If it disappears once I've lifted up the glass then that's good.
What, it's bad?
Hang on a minute I'm a bit confused.
Is it bad or good?
What?

ALLIE: But I don't have a rash.

ZACH: Does it hurt when you look into the light?
Look into the light Allie.
(I'm just asking her.
I'm asking her to look into the light and she's doing it.)
Can you tell me if it hurts?

She squints into the light.

ALLIE: I –
I don't know.
Maybe?

ZACH: An intense, searing pain?

ALLIE: No?
Yes?
I don't know?

ZACH: She isn't sure.

ALLIE: Oh God I'm going to be sick again.

ZACH: Ah.
She's about to be sick again.
Does that make a difference?

ALLIE: Am I?
I don't know…
I don't know maybe I'm not.

ZACH: She's not sure.

ALLIE: It might be passing.

ZACH: It could go either way.

ALLIE: OK I'm not.

ZACH: She's not.

          She breathes deeply.

ZACH: OK right.
          Yes.
          No.
          Yes.
          No.
          Yes thank you very much.
          You've been very helpful.
          Thank you very much indeed.

          He hangs up.

ALLIE: What did you hang up for?
          We hadn't finished.
          Had we?

ZACH: Right.
          A nurse is going to phone us back within 30 to 55 minutes.
          Possibly an hour.

ALLIE: But do they know what it is?

ZACH: They don't know what it is.

ALLIE: They don't?

ZACH: They don't.

ALLIE: Well.
          Well that's just great.

          She breathes.

          He comes and sits beside her.

          Silence.

ALLIE: Zach?

ZACH: Yes.

ALLIE: I'm –

	I'm a bit – Worried.
	Beat.
ALLIE:	I'm a bit worried that I might be sort of – Dying.
	Beat.
ZACH:	You're not dying.
ALLIE:	You hesitated.
ZACH:	No I didn't.
ALLIE:	You did.
ZACH:	I, I just didn't have enough breath to speak. At that moment.
ALLIE:	What?
ZACH:	You're going to be fine.
ALLIE:	Are you sure?
ZACH:	Of course I'm sure.
ALLIE:	But you're not a doctor.
ZACH:	No I know but –
ALLIE:	So you can't be sure.
ZACH:	You're going to be fine.
ALLIE:	But I feel terrible.
ZACH:	But you're going to be fine.
	Silence.
ALLIE:	My hands are numb. They've gone all yellow, look.
ZACH:	That's – That's normal.
ALLIE:	Normal for what?

ZACH:	It always happens.
ALLIE:	What do you mean? Zach? When does it always happen?
ZACH:	When you, you know. It's just normal, I heard it somewhere. Everyone knows it.
ALLIE:	I don't know it.
ZACH:	It's normal. I'm sure it's normal.

Silence.

ALLIE:	Well can you look it up on the internet?
ZACH:	No, Allie.
ALLIE:	Why not?
ZACH:	Because I – I – Just no.
ALLIE:	It's because you're scared of what it's going to say, isn't it? You think it's going to say I'm dying.
ZACH:	No –
ALLIE:	Then why won't you look it up?
ZACH:	Because I – I don't know. The internet it's – You know. There's always so many options and you never know which one to click and then you just get overwhelmed by all this information and you don't know what to believe anymore.
ALLIE:	It's because you think I'm dying.
ZACH:	No that's not it.

ALLIE: I'm dying.

ZACH: You're not.

ALLIE: I'm dying.

ZACH: You're not.

            Silence.

            He strokes her hair.

ZACH: You're not.

            He strokes her hair.

            Silence.

ZACH: How are you feeling?

ALLIE: I don't know.
            Bad.

ZACH: You'll feel better soon.

ALLIE: I don't know.

ZACH: Of course you will.

ALLIE: I feel really, really bad.

ZACH: I know.

ALLIE: All sort of –
            Weak.

ZACH: Yes.

ALLIE: And wrong.

ZACH: I know.

ALLIE: It's scary.

ZACH: I know.

ALLIE: But I'm going to be alright.

ZACH: Of course you are.

ALLIE: If you say so then I will be.

ZECHARIAH

And you say so.
Don't you?

ZACH: I say so.

Silence.

She puts her head in his lap.

ALLIE: How long have we been here?

ZACH: A while.

ALLIE: What time is it?

ZACH: I don't know.

ALLIE: Do you think it's still night?
Or is it morning now?

ZACH: Morning.
I think it's morning.

ALLIE: Is that good or bad?

ZACH: It's good.
It will start to get light soon.
That's good.

ALLIE: Yes I suppose that's good.
I hate the dark.

ZACH: I know.

ALLIE: I just want to close my eyes.
Do you think that's alright?

ZACH: That's alright.

ALLIE: I'm so tired.

ZACH: So go to sleep.

ALLIE: No I can't close my eyes.

ZACH: Why not?

ALLIE: I don't know.
My head hurts.

ZACH: I know.

ALLIE: My knees hurt.

ZACH: Yes.

ALLIE: My eyelashes hurt.

ZACH: I know.
          I know.

          Beat.

ALLIE: This isn't very comfortable.

ZACH: Do you want to go to bed?

ALLIE: I don't think I could get there.

ZACH: I'll carry you.

ALLIE: No.
          No let's just stay here.

ZACH: Are you sure.

ALLIE: Yes.

          Here is fine.

          For now.

          Here is good.

          Beat.

ALLIE: Will you stay with me?
          You don't mind?

ZACH: Of course not.
          I'm not going anywhere.

ALLIE: You'll stay here?

ZACH: Yes.

ALLIE: And make sure I don't die?

ZACH: Yes.

ALLIE: Well.
If you're sure.
Thank you Zach.

Silence.

ALLIE: Zach…

Silence.

ALLIE: Did your parents ever tell you why they called you that?

ZACH: I don't think I ever asked them.

ALLIE: Didn't you?
Why not?

ZACH: It just never occurred to me, I suppose.
I might ask them now.

ALLIE: You should.
And tell me.
I'd be interested.

Silence.

ALLIE: It always made me think about this book I read when I was little.
It was called *Z for Zachariah*.

Beat.

ALLIE: Did you ever read it?

ZACH: No.
What's it about?

ALLIE: It's terrifying.

ZACH: Is it?

ALLIE: But it's brilliant.

ZACH: OK.

ALLIE: It's about the end of the world.
Or nearly the end of the world.
There's this girl, in this valley, and she's all on her own.

Her family go off in a cart with tarpaulin over the top.
I never knew what tarpaulin was.
I still don't really.
They go off to try and find help because everything outside the valley is dying.
All this scorched, dead earth.
Dead bodies.
Dead birds.
But for some reason –
In the valley –
They were safe.

Pause.

ALLIE: So they go off, her parents, her brothers.

They say, we'll be back in a few days, and then –
They never come back.
She's just left there.
She's the only one left, in the whole valley.
And so she just gets on with things.
She goes to the store and gets provisions.
She wears a plaid shirt which is really for men.
She rolls the sleeves up.
She cooks and cleans and grows vegetables and she has chickens and a dog.
It's a lovely dog.
I think if she didn't have the dog I wouldn't have been able to read it because it would have just been too unbearable.

ZACH: But she has the dog.

ALLIE: She does.
She did.
Then –
Then Loomis comes.
Loomis is the man who arrives in the boiler suit.
A red boiler suit with a mask and it makes his breath come out all raspy and Darth Vader-like.
She watches him for ages.

	With the dog. She hides in a cave and spies on him. She watches him take off the suit and he's pale and naked underneath, with long gingery hair. He swims in the river and she watches him. She doesn't know if he's friend or foe.
ZACH:	Which is he?
ALLIE:	Well then eventually – I can't remember how but. She meets him. They meet. And he's a scientist. He's looking for civilisation. She's the first person he's seen in months. And she likes him. She really likes him. She's sixteen. She's coming-of-age. She decides she's going to marry him. She imagines a wedding in a bower with flowers in her hair and bare feet and a long hippy dress instead of a man's plaid shirt. They're going to get married and have babies, lots of babies, they're going to repopulate the earth. But then he – This is the bit that's so – He – God it's horrible.
ZACH:	What happens?
ALLIE:	He – He rapes her. He rapes her.
	Beat.
ALLIE:	I was nine when I first read it. I didn't really understand that bit.

It was only when I read it again.
That I realised quite how –
How horrible it was.
I read it again.
And again.
And again.
I don't know how many times I read it.
And so when you told me your name was Zach.
I thought of *Z for Zachariah*.
I still do.

Silence.

ZACH: Why is it called that?

ALLIE: Oh.
It's because she has this Alphabet book.
Or maybe it's something they learn in Sunday school, one or
the other.
A is for Apple.
B is for Ball.
Z is for Zachariah.
The end of all things.

Silence.

ALLIE: It's OK though because it's sort of a happy ending.
Sort of.
She tricks him.
She might even kill him I can't remember.
She steals his boiler suit.
She pulls the mask down over her face and now it's her who's
breathing like Darth Vader.
She climbs to the top of the hill, she looks down at the valley,
so lush and green and full of hope.
And then she turns and looks at the world outside, which
is the opposite, it's brown and black and burned and there's
nothing living, no one, nowhere.
But she believes she'll find someone.
Someone out there.
Someone who can help.
Maybe in the cities.

ZECHARIAH   279

Maybe in another country.
But there has to be someone, somewhere.
Someone searching, just like her.
So she sets off.
Plodding over the hill in his heavy red boiler suit with the raspy mask.
Alone again.
And you turn the page because you hope, you hope –
But that's it.
You never know if she finds anyone.
Or if she just keeps walking.
Walking and walking and walking.
Forever and ever.
Amen.

Silence.

ZACH: How are you feeling?

ALLIE: A bit better I think.
           I'm not sure.

ZACH: You should get some sleep.

ALLIE: I think I feel better.

She closes her eyes.

Silence.

She opens her eyes.

ALLIE: You don't think the world is ending do you?
           Just outside.
           Without us knowing about it.

ZACH: No.
           Not yet.

ALLIE: What if it was just us.
           The only two people left.
           What if that happened?

ZACH: Well.

I think we'd probably be alright.

ALLIE: Yes.
Yes I think so too.

She closes her eyes.

She sleeps.

He looks at her.

He holds her a bit closer.

She sleeps.

The End.

Molly Naylor

WHEN YOU LEFT I THOUGHT I'D DIE BUT NOW I'M FINE

I – GARETH

After talking for an hour, we leave the party separately, obviously. At no point in the night do I imagine that we'll go home together. The fact that we are in the same room, the coincidence of it all, the hundred, thousand, million-to-one chance of us meeting again twenty-five years from when we last saw each other leaves me breathless. So the kiss on the cheek and the number in the mobile is enough. It changes my whole weekend, which otherwise would have been spent with a good deal of uneasy pottering but now seems luxurious. I go to a gallery and cook a steak. I treat myself to a bit of TV, or try to, but every programme I find seems to consist of a bunch of attractive twenty-somethings being impenetrably ironic. It's a weird sort of irony, seemingly devoid of humour and influenced by the cadences of Middle American speech patterns. I watch a film instead. I have a feeling that if I try and find a programme aimed at my demographic I'll end up having to watch *Gardener's World* or something.

Even when you know in the pit of your stomach that something is probably going to become something, a relationship, maybe love; even if you really feel like you know that's at least a possibility if not inevitable; you have to pretend you're, you know, just going to see what happens. Unless things have changed dramatically since I last went on a date, ten years ago. Unless you are delusional though, or an arsehole; you do generally tend to know almost immediately whether or not it's going to work. In the short-term. Could I sit and have dinner with you. Could I go to the pub with you. Sleep with you. If it's yes, then you do sort of know. The long-term is more difficult to predict.

I call her on Monday and we make plans for Wednesday evening and all I have to do now is live for a few days. We text. An activity I'd assumed was mainly the pursuit of thirteen-year-olds. We text in full sentences.

On Tuesday I see a show I have to review. I hate reviewing plays. If it's bad I have to be honest about this and if it's a hard-working young company, I feel awful. This isn't a play, *per se*. It's a one-man show. There are some okay parts, and it's not entirely without humour. The audience like it, which makes me like it less. This, and the fact that there is a buzz around it. He must have good PR, because I've never heard of him and he hasn't been on TV. He's called Tim Eagle, I assume, because the show is called *Tim Eagle Is A Hopeless Romantic*. And maybe he is, but I'm not sure I care. *That's quite a good line*, I think, jotting it down. I can probably open the review with that. I imagine what sycophantic critics will write – this show is brave, revealing and observational. But it's too revealing, and the observations don't pertain to me and the word 'brave' is bandied about loads in theatre these days. It's lost all meaning. The unpolished nature of the show annoys me. He's bumbling, he forgets his words and makes mistakes. And when you've seen as many shows as I have, you can't help but look at this as failure on some level.

Afterwards I have a couple of drinks. I wouldn't usually, on my own, but she sent me a message during the show and I quite like the idea of sitting in the bar and exchanging texts for a while.

As I wander to the tube station later I'm still texting. I am almost tired of the feeling of excitement that's been in my stomach for the last few days. It's buggered my appetite completely. I'm almost at Holborn when I realise I've left my notebook in the bar. I think about leaving it, then I remember that aside from tonight's notes there's an interview with the Iranian sculptor that I need to file on Monday. I go back, and someone's sat where I was, reading it. I realise slowly that it's Tim Eagle. Bollocks. He looks up and sees me. Holds the book up. Raises an eyebrow and goes *looking for this*? As if he's a detective and I'm a criminal returning to the scene of the crime, having left my dagger. I give him an embarrassed smile and expect him to hand me my notebook so we can go our separate ways and never speak of it again like nice, socially awkward Englishmen, but instead he starts to read passages from it. *Hapless? Hapless? What the fuck does that even mean? Indulgent? How is it indulgent? It's not about me, it's about love, it's outward looking, I can't believe you didn't get that.*

I said that it could be construed as indulgent.

And what about this – not as brave as he thinks it is. How the fuck would you know how brave I think it is? Perhaps I don't think it's brave at all. Perhaps it's just a show I made that many people really like and you just didn't get. And why have you written failure in capitals, what does that even mean?

I want to tell him that I'm actually getting tired of doing reviews, and that out of context the comments sound worse than they are. I don't say any of this as it sounds weak and besides, I did write those things, there's no point pretending otherwise. He pockets the notebook and walks away.

At home, later, I sink into a bath. I'm annoyed that I even feel guilty. Tim's not a bad writer. He could write for radio, or get a job on that TV show, the one with all the teenagers getting off with each other all the time. That's supposed to be where all the young, trendy writers go. One thing's for certain though, he can't keep stealing critic's notebooks. I imagine his bookshelf. A depressing row of cleverly crafted put-downs and self-aggrandising analysis. He could colour code it. Or arrange it according to severity.

The next few days have had their shine smudged slightly, but the texts keep coming and adrenaline levels remain stable until Wednesday. We have dinner in a pub by the river. We're nervous. She tells me about her teaching job, and I imagine how much her students must like her. I tell her about the Tim Eagle review. She gets excited as she's seen the show. I talk about how shambolic it was, how unpolished. She gets passionate about it, saying that it's supposed to be shambolic; it's about shyness, and awkwardness, vulnerability. The form reflects the content. I change the subject.

We arrange to meet on Friday and kiss lightly at the tube station before she gets onto a District Line train. I stare into the tunnel after it, watching the shrinking squares of light.

On Thursday I work on the interview with the sculptor, sort of making it up as I go along, trying to remember what he said and using Google to help me with the rest. It's going to be an awful piece of hack journalism. At midday, the administrator tells me my nephew is in the foyer. Morris lives in Berlin. What an earth is he doing here? In the lobby I'm greeted, not by my nephew, but by Tim Eagle. Holding my notebook. Looking out of place and slightly wild-eyed. I break the silence. *You could have said you were my son.* We both cringe and then laugh slightly at the over-familiarity of this comment.

I did consider it. But I thought the people you work with would have met your son. If you have one.

Which I don't, I tell him, a little too quickly. He hands me my notebook. I thank him. He nods, but doesn't leave. I sigh. *Look. I'm going to go and get some lunch. Do you want a pint?*

In real life, Tim Eagle is funny, which is refreshing. In my experience, comedians are an incredibly un-funny bunch off stage. We get into the age-old debate about the point of critics. And I agree that yes, we are all dickheads. But I get the publicity for his show up on my phone. Four stars, *The Telegraph*. Four stars, *Metro*. Five stars, *Time Out*. *Who do you think gives you stars Tim? And where do you think you'd be without them? There is a huge audience out there who makes its decisions after reading reviews.* He tells me that what frustrates him is that critics never give you permission to fail and that's what you need, in order to take risks. Because without risk how can artforms progress and evolve?

I end up buying three rounds. We discuss the show and he tells me about the girl who left him: the reason he wrote it. And even though she left, he still believes in love. I ask him if he's ever listened to Art Brut. He says he's been meaning to check them out actually and I'm pleased by his look of approval. I quote 'people in love' from their first album: *people in love lie around and get fat. I didn't want us to end up like that…what becomes of the broken hearted? Get drunk for a few weeks then back where they started.* He calls me a cynic. Suggests I haven't met the right woman. Maybe that's why I didn't get married. I correct him. *I have been married.* And the whole bloody story comes out. About how we were very young. It was the done thing. To please our parents. It only lasted for two years before we got divorced. He asks if I've seen her since and I wince because I know he'll love this. *Actually, weirdly; I bumped into her at a party last week. Complete coincidence. And we went out last night. And I'm seeing her again this Friday.*

He smiles. He loves it. Of course he does. Because Tim Eagle is a hopeless romantic.

On Friday we meet in a pub in Bloomsbury and this feels more like a date than Wednesday. But it's not perfect. There are pauses in conversations that feel very conspicuous. As if they should be full of something. There's the obvious question of whether we talk about the past twenty-five years, fill each other in on what's been happening, or whether we act like we've just met. Which is actually what it feels like, but beneath this feeling is the truth – that we've already slept together, met each other's families, argued, fallen out of love… already gotten divorced.

I wonder what Tim Eagle would make of it, with all his romance and hope. And I try to feel hopeful. It feels silly, as if I'm trying to get away with wearing Bermuda shorts, or an earring. The only hope I find is minimal and logical. It's in the fact that things are different now. And the difference between now and then is that then, I never questioned whether it would work or not and I thought I had all the answers. And now, all I have are questions. No answers.

On Sunday I start on the Eagle review. It takes me ages. I struggle with the last paragraph, everything sounds hackneyed. Finally I give up. Go with what I've got, even thought it's corny. Sod it.

With his first solo show, Tim Eagle asks us for permission to fail, and fail he does, but spectacularly, with charm, courage and hope. This is a show for anyone who believes in the promise of love.

*

II – SALLY

I think about Googling 'how to get divorced' but decide to go for a walk instead. Norwich looks brilliant today. Everywhere looks good in the sunshine, but I take extra pleasure when Norwich looks good because it's one of those places that people assume is shit.

It's been a week. I wonder how I'm supposed to feel. I suppose I'm in shock. Jackie explained to me the processes you go through when your husband leaves you. First, shock. Then panic. Then sadness. Then anger. Which is good, Jackie says, the anger is galvanizing, you should really embrace that anger (Jackie's a holistic therapist, you learn to tune her out when she talks like this) because after the anger comes peace and acceptance. You're looking at eighteen months, minimum for the whole process.

I did think about selling the flat. But Jackie pointed out that I should wait, as there's a large chance that Graham will come back. This sort of thing is typical at his age, she says, it happens to most couples at some point and you can get through it with a bit of patience and understanding.

So. I suppose I must be in shock, I think as I wander through town. Which means panic is next. I wonder what that's going to be like. I am ready. I am in the brace position. I notice a deal at the florist. Three bunches of daffs for a pound. I stop. Inhale the sweetness and buy six.

At the weekend, Jackie invites me to go to the seaside for the day with her family. They pick me up early. Jackie's kids used to be lovely, I'm sure of it, but now they seem so…impressed with themselves. And obviously I'm no expert on parenting, but it seems odd that Jackie and Matt give credence to every single whiny moany bullshitty thing that comes out of their mouths as if it's genius. As if it deserves to be written down and archived, rather than relegated in favour of a pint and a packet of crisps. I have to sit in the middle. Jackie keeps giving me little looks of pity from over her shoulder, checking to see if I've collapsed into tears.

After fish and chips in the drizzle, Jackie takes Becky to the loo and Matt takes Tom, and I'm left on the seafront alone. This rare moment of solitude hits me like a wave and gives me an inexplicably tingly feeling until they return.

I somehow get into a routine of having lunch with Jackie and Claire every Friday. I'm not sure how this has happened, it feels very decadent. But as I work from home I can't find an excuse not to go. This Friday we find ourselves in Nandos. The tapas place is closed and I can see us all pretending we're disappointed with having to squeeze into a booth and order spicy chicken. We talk about how I'm doing. There's a clarity when someone leaves you for someone else, a sort of finality that is maybe easier to deal with than an open-ended break up. But Jackie says that of course this is open-ended, he is coming back, he's just getting it out of his system. I try and picture him apologising, begging me to take him back. Jackie and Claire refer to the other woman as 'the slut', which doesn't make me feel better because in my mind she now looks like one of The Saturdays. But aside from this stomach-churning ego blow, I still haven't felt the full force of stage one – shock. Claire tells me how she felt before she met Pete. Hopeless. Desperate. Like she'd be alone forever. I go and order. Chicken salads for them. For me, chicken burger and two sides. Jackie says I should keep my strength up. Funny though, I haven't actually lost my appetite at all. Which, Claire pointed out, is a happy by-product of stage one. No such luck for me. My mouth is already watering at the idea of the extra-hot sauce.

Jackie and Claire are being very kind. This fact feels like it's written in capitals. VERY KIND INDEED. They are trying to help me fill my days with things. But there are a million things I've been putting off for years that I suddenly, with great urgency, want to achieve. Claire discovers I'm reading the new Jonathan Coe book. She tells me that her reading group is discussing it this week and that I should come. The coincidence is too much for her and she won't take no for an answer. Claire says that although Graham is definitely going to come back, it wouldn't be a bad thing to meet some people in the meantime, get my confidence up, maybe even have a fling. But when I turn up I promptly forget everyone's name, and for the first half hour I don't say a thing. I am acutely aware of the fact that I haven't said a thing. I have nothing to say about the book. I liked it. It was funny and a bit sad like all his books. They're slating him for the pop-cultural references and the unconvincing framing device. Which I totally bought. I can't say why I bought it, I just did. It was a good story. And the fact that this isn't a clever enough thing to say makes me hate the book group. I stealth-check my phone. Nothing. Graham's funny five minutes has lasted for a month so far.

On Sunday evening I suddenly feel like shit. I panic a bit. Maybe this is my heart breaking. There's too much adrenaline in my body. Being in the flat doesn't feel right. Jackie and Claire encouraged me not to get rid of anything, to hold on, because it'll make it easier if and when we get back together. But all Graham's stuff is a problem for me. The stuff that we bought together that is, actually, all his taste. I start to move everything I can out in the hall and decide to sell it. Get rid of it and buy some things that are to my taste. And I cry. Not out of loss, but because it occurs to me that I am thirty, and I'm not even sure what my taste is.

Thursday night is Salsa. I am very busy for someone whose life is newly empty. I'm not dreading it though, as I've spent the day writing copy for a zoo brochure and I'm keen to stretch my legs. If only to justify the long bath and glass of single malt I'm going to have when I get home. I've recently taken to bringing my laptop into the bathroom and watching TV on it while I soak. But first: organized fun and unsolicited human contact in a community centre in Halesworth.

I see pretty soon that I've been set up. Jackie and Claire introduce me to a Spanish bloke called Paco who they have obviously told I'm single and up for it. Their smug smiles as Paco and me dance past are too much to take. I arrange my fingers into a rude gesture against Paco's back and try to manoeuvre him into a position that will allow Jackie to see I'm flipping her the Vs.

Afterwards I'm determined to leave immediately. But Paco offers me a drink and I end up sitting opposite him with a loud cocktail. I tell him straight. *I don't know what Jackie and Claire have told you, but I'm not looking for a boyfriend.* I almost giggle at the word boyfriend. Surely there's a better word for it once you're in your thirties. Paco is surprised. His English is good but he stumbles over his words as he hastens to explain that he is 'a homosexual'. We both look over at Jackie and Claire who are staring at us with unashamed eagerness. We glance back at each other and start to laugh. Paco does one of those accidental snorts and this sets us off even more. Claire and Jackie look very confused.

If I hadn't met Paco Lopez that night it would've been the last time I ever went to Salsa. But I keep going because he's a lot of fun, and we start hanging out on other nights too and going for walks at the weekends. He doesn't feel sorry for me. He is not trying to teach me how to win back or bag myself a man. We usually don't talk about men at all. We talk about our families, and our favourite things. He's blue tits. I'm buzzards. He's primroses. I'm violets. Thai Green Curry. Beef Wellington. The Stones. Bowie. And these are good conversations. Because I start to realise that I do have tastes after all.

On one of the best walks we do, over Dunwich Heath and all the way to Aldeburgh, he tells me about the first boy he ever loved. We laugh at the idea of fifteen-year-old Paco trying to turn the captain of the hockey team gay, and Paco says something in Spanish. He explains the saying means something like 'it was not to be'. And he shrugs, and there's a lovely ease to his manner that I want for myself. A lightness, a fuck-itness. And right then, I know, suddenly and for certain, that Graham is never going to come back.

We walk through some woods and see a lovely, tiny cottage that I immediately imagine living in. It's small. A one-person house. I notice there's a To Let sign in the garden and my heart starts to beat faster. I hear Jackie's voice in my head. You can't move out to the middle of nowhere. How are you going to meet any men? And what will Graham think? I take down the number on a scrap of paper. Paco tells me I shouldn't buy another house. I should embrace my freedom. Travel, do something. I'm about to get annoyed with him telling me what to do, until he says we're stupid in this country for being obsessed with the property ladder, except his broken English makes him say 'the proper ladder' instead and I laugh.

Claire and Jackie stage what must in their minds feel like some sort of intervention. They ambush me at my flat and tell me they're worried about me. The flat's messy, I'll give them that, but I've been meaning to tidy it. I've actually been meaning to sell it. They try and talk me out of it, so emphatically that I become completely confused about what to do. I sit down, completely stumped. My phone starts to ring and it's Paco. I ignore it, angry suddenly. I ask them to leave, sharply, and put my phone on silent. I walk to the corner shop, angry, buy a bottle of wine and scowl at the man who tells me to cheer up, it might never happen. I walk back to the flat, angry. I know I should calm myself down, this isn't like me, so I find a romantic comedy to watch, open the wine and a box of Maltesers. But none of this helps, it makes me worse, because I don't actually want to watch a rom-com, it's just what Jackie would tell me to do, or a magazine would tell me to do. Because rom-com coping is all about nostalgia. Making romance out of sadness. Going, look – Julia

Roberts is a bit sad, and she still ends up with a handsome and reliable man, so it can happen to me too! It's about putting on a sad song and looking out the window into the rain…and the idea of how institutionalised I have become by nostalgic narratives makes me more angry. So I switch it off. Keep drinking. Take out the scrap of paper with the phone number of the estate agents and start to think. And later, when the wine is almost finished I no longer want to break everything. But I am still not in rom-com mood, and I open my laptop and Google 'how to get divorced'.

It's just started to get properly warm when Paco falls in love with a man he met in the fish and chip shop and the sale of my flat goes through. I start to have more time to myself. Time to plan what I'm going to do with the little garden at the new house. Moments of solitude that I've stopped letting Jackie and Claire fill for me. I see Jackie briefly one Wednesday, she pops over while I'm packing. I can tell she feels sorry for me, having to deal with all this packing. A broken-hearted woman folding her life away. Moving to the country to be a spinster. People are afraid of packing. It's one of those things we are taught to feel sad about. Nostalgic. For a second the weight of it all gets to me. But I shake it off. It's just packing. With Lou Reed on the stereo. And the sun pouring in through the windows. I give her a hug when she leaves. Smile. Because everyone feels differently about moments of solitude. I carry on packing. Smiling. Enjoying the logic of boxes.

*

III – IRIS

Some days I am in love with the whole world. Every last affected, pouting, posturing one of them. Today is not one of those days. Today is the sort of day where I want everyone to just really, shut up. Especially my mum. And my friends. Who I am beginning to suspect are incapable of human emotions. What the fuck is it about teenage girls? And actually, boys too. I reckon that the behaviour of most teenagers has less in common with a normal functioning adult than it has with a psychopath.

The day starts badly because no day that starts with a heart-to-heart with the deputy head can ever be considered good. He wants to have a deep chat about the divorce and how it's affecting me. He is definitely more upset about it than I am and wonders how I'm feeling about my Options. I feel like what he wants me to say is that I don't know how I am going to finish my Spanish coursework because of the stress of it and I've been thinking about cutting myself. This would be something he could fix. I tell him the truth, that I miss my dad but I get to hang out with him without my mum there, which is good, and aside from that nothing much has changed because we never hung out the three of us anyway. He feels sorry for me. That's the worst bit. On my way out, I pause in the secretary's office to sort out my bra straps and I overhear him saying to the head, *that's the fifth one this week*. And the head makes this low, disappointed sound, and they both sigh.

Later I call dad to see if I can go round. He's still in the lab. So I watch *Britain's Next Top Model* with my mum as she eats low-fat rice cakes and applies fake tan. She critiques each girl's hair and walk. I make a joke about it being like Crufts. I go to bed early.

I'm at Alisha's a few days later when Dad calls and tells me he's moving to Boston. That of course he's not going to ask me to go with him because of my GCSEs, and mum, but I can visit in summer. I hate crying in front of Alisha but I'll miss him so fucking much and I'm probably going to turn into a fake-tanned idiot who knows nothing about anything. Alisha doesn't understand why I don't like my mum. She says my mum is well fit. Alisha is starting to reveal some dickhead tendencies. But she gives me a hug and lets me smoke a fag out her window. She likes my mum because she says things like 'defo' and 'totes' and unlike Alisha's parents she's cool with the whole lesbian thing. I don't tell Alisha that this is because in last month's *Grazia* there was a feature on 'girl crushes', and on the cool scale lezzers are 'going up' as opposed to jeggings, which are 'going down'.

At school on Tuesday Alisha has apparently gone mental and brings in a plastic bottle of tequila mixed with strawberry Ribena and forces me to drink it with her in the disabled toilet. She guilt-trips me into missing double science, which is rubbish as we're doing all this good stuff about photosynthesis and so not only am I destroying brain cells, I am actively missing out on essential information. It's doubly bad. Why couldn't she have gone mental in English instead? Who cares about Seamus bloody Heaney? Yes. The digging is a metaphor, I get that.

Alisha sits on the handrail and I sit on the toilet seat and we're like bloody poster girls for Broken Britain. I like this line, I'm about to say it to Alisha but she starts to tell me all about how her sister is jealous of her and how it's causing all these problems. Alisha is so beautiful that when we first got together I told myself she had hidden depths but I am now almost certain that she is about as deep as the toilet I'm sitting on. Which is pretty deep, now I think about it. I just didn't want to say deep as a puddle. It's a cliché. I'll leave them to Seamus! Ha. That was a bit unfair. Oh god, I think I'm pissed. Alisha smokes a cigarette and it's this that gets us caught cause the smoke drifts down to Mr Peter's office. Our parents are called. I want him to call my dad but of course he phones my mum and she has to stop producing 'I married a hotty and now she's obese' or whatever it's called and come and pick me up. I hope Alisha and me get banned from seeing each other. It'll be easier than breaking up with her.

I'm suspended for a couple of days and then I have to go to a meeting with my mum, my dad and Mr Peters. I try to explain that there's no need for everyone to get all worried, I was just being an idiot. I'm not sure if Alisha has admitted it was her idea but I'm not going to tell them it was mine. They are deeply concerned about me, Peters says. My mum is perhaps deeply concerned about how the filming is going without her, and my dad just looks confused. Peters launches into this big speech about broken homes. About how a stable upbringing leads to increased confidence and achievement levels. About how a child needs a mother and a father. About how parenting styles have lapsed. I interrupt him, which is rude but I can't help it, and say look. I'm not sad about the divorce. I'm sad about the fact that my dad is moving to Boston. Peters looks confused. *Boston, Lincolnshire,* he asks.

Boston, Massachusetts, my dad and me reply (my mum says *Boston, America).* Nobody quite knows what to do with this, least of all me. And Peters says I shouldn't go and visit over Easter because of revision and something inside me breaks, sort of falls apart because of this assumption that I am going to stay here and live with my mum. And I look at my dad, and I can tell he is thinking the same thing. And I look at my mum, who's looking at her phone. And I say *well, that's if I stay here, I could go with him.* And there's a tiny smile on my dad's face that gives me the courage to add, *which I could.* But then Peters really loses his shit, of course that's not going to happen, it's ridiculous, as a teenage girl I need a mother in my life and besides that, the school system over there is completely different and my GCSEs will be in jeopardy. My mum tries to wrap the meeting up and I feel a bit hopeless and a million miles from anything.

It rains for two weeks straight. I hang out with my dad tons, to make up for the fact that from now on I'm going to see him about once a year but at the weekend my mum suggests we go shopping together. I'm so shocked that I can't gather myself to respond properly, in the obvious way, which is to very quickly say I'm revising, sorry. Instead I say yeah, okay. We wander round Harlow together and try very hard to make conversation and I even tell her that I've split up with Alisha. I feel a bit fat and a bit ugly and a bit of a disappointment. We see another mother-daughter combo strutting past and I almost see my mum's heart skip a beat with yearning, coveting the connection, the things they have in common as two pairs of tanned legs move in harmony, handbags slapping pointy hips and straightened hair swishing like curtains against gold-orange cheeks. I feel sorry for her and for a moment wish my Converse away. I let her choose a dress for me to try on. She pulls back the changing room curtain and I'm blushing because this makes me feel about nine, but if you look past the straggly hair and bruised knees I'm sort of beautiful. And we look at each other in the mirror and she does a little nod, and for a moment we're really looking at each other. And then she hands me a gold bolero thing that will apparently make my waist look smaller and I'm a problem again.

Friday night is dull now I have no girlfriend. I log into Facebook. This does not help. The little red number thingy says I have three notifications. They are all an invite to 'Caz + Bex's Awesome Fifteenth Bday Party Woohoo!' A quick look at this and the updates from a bunch of other people only serve to reinforce my rising suspicion that everyone I know is a dickhead. I will inevitably attend 'Caz + Bex's Awesome Fifteenth Bday Party Woohoo!' and will inevitably get pissed on Malibu and coke with the dullards in my form because there will, inevitably, be fuck all else to do that night.

And that's when it hits me. That it doesn't matter. And I understand, suddenly the reason why everything has felt so temporary for the last few weeks, or even since the divorce, like I've been waiting for something. An idea starts to take shape, and I walk downstairs past my mum who's doing a face pack and watching *Ten Things I Hate About You*. I walk straight past and out the front door and I think about how if this was Alisha's family there's no way she could just walk out of the door on a Friday night. Alisha's family is trying to do an impression of perfection, but Alisha told me that her dad shagged his secretary (another cliché – ugh) and I know for a fact that her older brother sells weed. I walk down the street and it's that point in the evening when it's getting dark so the lights are on but people haven't closed their curtains yet. I peer in, nosy as anything, and I see the young couple eating pizza at number eighteen. And the old couple at number twenty-four on their sofa. At fifty-six there's a woman eating a box of Maltesers on her own. And mainly it is people on their own, watching TV or lit by the white glow of laptops. And I think about what Mr Peters would make of all this, all these single people on a Friday night, eating Maltesers and surfing the net. He would probably shake his head and make his disappointed sound. And I know he is only trying to be nice to me but there's something about him that makes me want to shout LOOK, WE ALL DIE ALONE ANYWAY. I think about my dad. And I start to run.

I run past the shop front with the broken window, past the borded-up takeaway, past the new Caffé Nero and both Greggs bakers. Down the alley next to the card shop and I'm soaking now. But I don't care. Because suddenly it's one of those days where I am in love with the whole world, and I am sorry for nothing, and don't need to smoke cigarettes. The sky is fast turning navy as it gets dark and the rain's proper, it's like being in Alisha's power shower. He opens the door. And I have an important question for him and I know he won't say no, because I know him so well. And I ask it. Say hello first. Then go – *I want to come to Boston. I want to live with you.* We hug, and my brain fast-forwards to the airport. Departures. Saying goodbye to her. Hugging her and meaning it, but then walking away. And meaning that too.

*

Laura Dockrill

A NOBODY

I mean I've always been a numbers man – I don't quite get the way
words fit together
But my discovery has left me with a story – a language I'll use
forever
Scribbled data onto the insides of my eyelids like imaginary tattoos
Makes me sound a bit of a nutter but I can't help it – it's true…

Spider lines tangled into
Web
We find
Upon time like silver spinning threads
As fine as those on our own head
Making us microscopic
In the madman politics of our prophets
The telescope glides marked in studs
Guide me through the weeping rivers of blood

What about this?
Carried over ready heads into the sea
Blurted out of a big mouth like a schoolboy error
Only to be fed folk gossip
A nobody? A no one.
A scruff of baby skin in a wonky crown
See the concern of my hourly frown
Is just to say, he never let you down.

In waters clear us
Chopping triangles like gushing ink
Spills into eyeballs

And locked the throat
Through teeth gates
I hold his hand

40 days and 40 nights
Leave like a withered leaf tumbling through the night
No test would ever divert
Or turn his pumping heart to dirt
I know where my friend belongs – with us – in herds
I sing his song and I know all the words

There was milk and honey,
And fish and meat
There was water and bread and
A bed for sleep
The soul was fed
Medicine shared
And we were all broken up, but just as quick, sewn back together
again

My feet dance a house onto wet ground now black
As shiny as a conker, as slippery as beetles back
As dark as the cylinder of squid
Builds his story brick after brick

DOUBT the bad fruit in the box
In the hen house lives a fox
The washing machine ate a sock
An arm and face fall off the clock
The whole place stinks of swine
Echoes the clawing mouth of time
In the looming palm of your eye
Tells a very frightening story
I hope that it is built on lies
And not that your mind is stormy
Swallow another drop of gold
You will never get old
Brittle bones

Howling remorse
Don't utter a mutter
Hold your horse

Touch dainty gentle as concentrated and as delicate as a raw pure egg
in the mouth of a Labrador
I'm sure I saw the seashore pour from your soul into the sore
Such light is only designed for night –
You make it alright. You make everything alright.

Its crackers in the maze of mind
Barmy answers to nutty questions he can't find
He eats bananas off of trees as long as time
He scoops marbles out of grime
Try to play his puzzle where the pieces don't match
Just please don't ask him to look back

Inside and around a circle of chalk
People will always talk
He walks like a stalk without pretence
Anything is possible in a world of nonsense

Here's a tip – never ask your shadow – *who are you*? Your shadow will
ask you back…plus you'll look like a bit of an idiot.

There is a bit about perfume and some feet here.

Our eyes like mini-rowers trusting, in tune, in pattern
We drink until we are outrageously drunk – we eat until our bellies
fatten
Your coat pockets filled with rocks
Too heavy to wander
In a sadness that wallows
And turns the hills to sand
And you are sinking
And you are the bluest you have ever felt; so blue you think you are
dying
And just at the last moment – even a thief managed to steal your

heart.
That is how kind you are.

What does your paradise look like? Is it as pink as the feather of a
flamingo?
As yellow as yolk?
Is it a poker table in the centre of a smoky basement of a den, half-full
glasses of amber juice, which does something terrific to you?
Are there oversized apricots and snow and sunshine at the same time?
Are there flowers with pollen bobbles so large they could dust your
head a peppery orange?
Is the water so clear you could find your eyes waiting for you in the
peach coral,
Under the thundering song of a melancholy whale?
You're with your mother again reading you a story before bed – and
you take in every word she says and feel as free as a ship's sail?

Do you crawl on jelly hands into a land only you understand, as
snuggled as a prawn; you lie on your side
And dream of what's inside
Into your ear climbs an angel that gives you sight to see
You are larger than the hands of a giant and defiantly *not* a nobody.

Steve Waters

CAPERNAUM

A dark room. MARK and PETER. They are both older men but MARK is younger than PETER.

MARK: So. You were at Capernaum?
You were at Capernaum when he came?

PETER: Capernaum? No – all gone. Lost.

MARK: Nothing can afford to be lost, Peter. Capernaum. Tell me.

PETER: Capernaum. Well. Father. In a bark. On Galilee. The water warm off the bow of the boat, casting the net into the green depths. Haul it up, thick with the shine of fish.

MARK: Peter, forgive me, may we set aside the fish?

PETER: Yes, throw back the catfish. Finer net for the sardines, little pieces of silver. Then row to Tarichae, to the pickler, barrels of shine and the smell. *(Sniffs.)* Drag the boat up the shingle. Good work. James, Andrew, myself.

MARK: But…Capernaum. When he came?

PETER: You ever see father's house? Finest house I ever lived in. I wonder who's in that house now. Do you have word from there – from Capernaum?

MARK: I don't know anything about it. I believe – I believe they burned some houses –

PETER: Burned? Why?

MARK: 'Why'? Would they need reasons? Tore down my family's house in Jerusalem, stone by stone, said it was 'unsound'.

PETER: Well. In that instance a reason was supplied.

MARK: Small solace for my family.

PETER: You think they burned my father's house, then?

MARK: I don't know. As I say I was never by Galilee.

PETER: Never? I thought...

MARK: Only once, in passing, once, perhaps. On the road to Galatia. But we are not here to...to speak of me.

          Pause.

PETER: Well placed it was, by father, who cleared the land, built it. Half way between the synagogue and the shore. Prayer and work to hand.

MARK: He made a good judgement. Now...

PETER: Good choice of stone.

MARK: I see. What is the stone with you there?

PETER: Basalt, the local stone, now that's a tough old stone. Dark, gathers in the heat, gives it out too, yes, we'd sit, evenings, our very bones aching with the work, we'd sit and drink and, yes, sometimes sing.

MARK: On the warm stone?

PETER: Warm dark stone, yes, the sun retreats, the stone harbours the warmth.

          PETER's lost.

MARK: Peter. Peter, if we had more time...

PETER: I don't know you I don't think. Was it Paul sent you to me?

MARK: No. Have they not spoken to you...about Paul?

PETER: No. *(Pause.)* Ah. I see. So, how did he, how did he...how did they?

MARK: Oh, the customary way.

PETER: The 'customary way'? But they have so many ways! Such rare wit in their cruelties. Such fine care. So, so they, what, they burned him?

MARK: Peter, this is not why I came and excuse me but I do not wish to think of it.

PETER: The customary way.

MARK nods.

Is it a compliment, Lord, that we should inspire such cruelties? Is it pleasing to you? Is it?

MARK: And you know they say we burned Rome now.

PETER: Rome! Would that we had!

MARK: To accuse us of this. I find it almost…funny.

PETER: This place, this stew of conniving, harlotry and trickery and lying and wanton fickle – fickle – this lying, ugly, oily, despicable…wretched – this hollow, hollow, sickening, dirty, cowardly – I mean what did we know, hey, what did we know of Rome then?

MARK: Nothing. Rome was another world.

PETER: Father always said pay their tax, avoid their gaze, our fish are bountiful and God's never even heard of them. Have you, Lord? Have you heard of them? Have you?

Pause.

The customary way.

MARK nods.

Paul.

MARK nods. A long silence. PETER is weeping.

MARK: I'm sorry. Peter, I'm sorry but we had reached, we reached the time he came to you at Capernaum.

PETER: Yes. Forgive me. Not myself.

MARK: Of course.

PETER: You can read in this dark?

MARK: I can. My eyes have grown very acute in darkness.

PETER: Yes, yes. Spend our whole lives in the dark these days. One day
that hatch'll burst open and the light will melt our eyes.

MARK: Peter. He came to your synagogue. I think your wife's mother
was unwell. Do you remember the nature of her sickness?

PETER: Her sickness. Oh. No. 's gone. A fever?

MARK: We must be more precise.

PETER: What was it? Old Ruth. Well – younger than me now. What
was it?
No, nothing, nothing. Set it down as a fever, I'm no physician.

MARK: The belief will be stronger if the facts are plainly unfolded.
Was there discolouration of the skin? Was she stricken with the
drouth? Was she lacking strength in her limbs?

PETER: I know she was hot.

MARK: Hot?

PETER: Yes, she was hot. The heat in her, water couldn't quench it, she
was that hot.

MARK: But in what part of her?

PETER: Oh, in every part of her!

MARK: But did she sweat? Was she, say, in pain? And if so, what was
the nature of the pain?

PETER: I know only she was hot, this was a lifetime ago. I do know
I found her the coolest water from the deepest quarter of the
well. Held it up before her, Ruth, look at the light weaving
about in it, like fish, this, this'll bring your health back, she was
still a young woman, Bethany, my wife, she was just a child –
you're sure we have no word of them?

MARK: No, no word, no. So she, Ruth, was afflicted with a fever.

PETER: Yes, yes, fine, fever, as I say.

MARK: But then he came to her, you brought him to her –

PETER: Oh, and I thought even then that was wrong, a mistake in actual fact.

MARK: No Peter, no you did not, no.

PETER: What?

MARK: We must not complicate it, do you see?

PETER: I did not? I did not…

MARK: You, you complicate it unduly. There must be no caveats, no variations, no digressions, no doubts, no evasions.

PETER: I see. No.

MARK: So. 'At the even, when the sun set, they brought all to him who were diseased…'.

PETER: She was there, I see her, yes, in the house.

MARK: This was your house?

PETER: Yes, I can see her there Mark. In the courtyard, in the shade there, under an olive tree, sheets all wet with her sweat –

MARK: Now this is good, this is very good.

PETER: And he, yes, he was angry at me, for bringing him there, when he had made this choice of me, to then, then to take him into my own house to serve some mere family end, oh yes, there was a deep anger there, you know I often think he resented – was impatient at – what - our needs, the needs we all had.

MARK: Hold to the events. What did he do, what did he then do at the house?

PETER: Oh. Nothing. Nothing to speak of.

MARK: Peter, Peter, what did he do?

PETER: Honest truth, nothing.

MARK: But he healed her!

PETER: He simply took up her hand. Lifted her up.

MARK: And then in so doing the fever passed from her!

MARK writes it.

THE GOSPEL ACCORDING TO ST MARK

PETER: You never saw him yourself did you?

MARK shakes his head.

Oh, there was such…ferocity – in those eyes – but the hands, the hands were always dry, cold even, but boy, you flinched at, his gaze, even when it was full of love there was such a fury in it…

MARK: But…'The fever passed from her'? Peter?

PETER: More and more I can only think of it as cruel, what we did. To them, to our kin. Like, later, at the synagogue, did we speak of this yet? – how they'd walked all those hot miles from Nazareth, his mother, brother, her head covered, sick in herself, his mother after all, out of whose very waters…and poor old James taking her weight, walking in frayed sandals on a hot day, in the full force of the sun, through the checkpoints, all the questions, of officials, all the long, bored questions, all the long waiting in the hot sun, and no mule even, on foot, so thick with the dust they looked dead already, then, at the very door of the synagogue, their tears or sweat or both scoring through the dust on their faces, and she would not set foot in there, no, not in the temple, filled to the gills with us, his followers, oh, rank with our smell, put off by some lad on the door, who shouts, 'Behold your mother and brother', James seething at his brother and even we stopped what we were about, simply to see how he would take their visitation and then, then for him to say…to simply say – in their presence, to say, of us, not them, but in their very presence, to say of us, not them, 'Behold my mother and my brethren'. Now, tell me, is that not cruelty?

MARK: Peter, I will not, I can no – I may not – Peter, when God speaks to us every consideration falls away – and I am sorry but this, all this is self-indulgent, but our people die, are dying and then dying again, yes we are weak and yes we have fallen short but these words shall set down, shall set down for ever what you were blessed – *blessed* – to witness.

Pause.

PETER: You weren't with Paul then?

MARK: What? Yes, I was with him. Once.

PETER: Once?

MARK: Once, yes.
         The truth is Paul does not – did not think well of me.
         But these are old matters.

PETER: All of this…is that. Paul did not think well of you? That's
         strange. Now I find that strange. Yet you know of his –

MARK: Oh, I revere him. I think of him, as I do of you, as one of
         the greatest men alive, well who lived, I think of you as the
         men who make God possible, yes…I think of you…and that,
         the fact that I could not earn his respect…makes me quite –
         disgusted – with myself – now, may we return to the task here?

PETER: You see what it is was that we had the kindness burned out
         of us. Quick to judge, quick to suspect, well, we were always
         in danger, we measured men by their conviction and little
         else and yet we were the bringers of kindness, is that not the
         strangest aspect of it? You said before you were in Galatia –

MARK: Did I?

PETER: Yes.

MARK: It seems your memory is stronger than you say.

PETER: Oh my memory is bottomless – but it can be wilful. You were
         with Paul in Galatia?

MARK: Yes, yes, I was.

PETER: Well that's something, isn't it?

MARK: Yes. Yes, I was with Paul at Seleucia, at Pergamus and Ephesus;
         I was with Paul at Caesarea, Laodicea and Philadelphia; I was
         with Paul at Lystra, Iconium and Deroe, even when he was
         sick, I was with him, even as we drank from pools covered
         in flies or burned in the rock gullies or were spat on with
         the spittle of children and the old even then I was with him,
         but then, but then, that one time, it was in Pamphylia – in

Galatia. And I – well, I – I was not strong enough. I knew, I knew there, no, I am not an apostle, not an evangelist, no. I was actually…nothing. Stool of dung, tare in furrow, I was nothing, am nothing much at all, no.

PETER: Now, that's not right.

MARK: You don't know me, as you said so how can you say that, now that you know that I – now that you know what I am.

PETER: Especially now. You've courage. You've come to Rome to be with us. And look, there, you are a scribe.

MARK: I am. Yes, and even that simple simple task, even that –

PETER: John Mark – stop all this, stop it. John Mark, yes, you are a scribe. So you may set things down. Yes? You set things down. Am I right?

Pause.

MARK: Yes. Yes, I may set things down, yes.

PETER: So – alright. Set this down.

MARK looks at PETER.

MARK: Yes. I will set this down and leave no trace of myself in it. I will set this down as sure as your father built his house.

PETER: Words stronger than stones.

MARK: Yes – words that hold heat after the sun has gone.

PETER: Words to outlive us.

MARK: But only, only if they are told rightly, in words of stone, set one upon the other.

Pause.

So. Again. Capernaum.

Billy Bragg

DO UNTO OTHERS

In the Bible we are told
God gave Moses in the days of old
Ten great commandments
For his people to hold true
But the greatest commandment of all
Is in the Book of Luke as I recall:
Do unto others as you would have them do to you

It may be you don't believe
In the story of Adam and Eve
And call upon science
To prove it's all untrue
But in the cold light of the day
These simple words still point the way
Do unto others as you would have them do to you

So just lift up your eyes
Don't pass by on the other side
Don't be bound by what you think others may do
A little bit of faith
That's all it really takes
Do unto others as you would have them do to you

Now the way the world is run
Too many people looking out for number one
Don't seem to notice
The damage that they do
Though its not widely understood
There is a greater good
Do unto others as you would have them do to you

Rowan Williams

LAZARUS

Rather bad quality recorded voice, as if in church, getting nearer: 'I am the Resurrection, and the Life: he that believeth in me, though he were dead, yet shall he live: And whosoever liveth and believeth in me shall never die.'

FIRST VOICE:

(Male, middle-aged, walks on, faces audience.) 'I am the Resurrection and the Life'. That's what the vicar read when the coffin came in. Some funerals are tough, this one was. Friend at work, her son crashed his motorbike, two weeks in intensive care, then he died; seventeen.

(Turns, paces.) You know how you are at funerals sometimes, things sort of come into focus because you can't concentrate too long on what's really going on. So when the vicar walked into the crem chapel, I thought, What the hell's that about? 'I am the Resurrection'. Who talks like that? Like saying 'I am the Coronation' or something. And 'the Resurrection and the Life'. You say the life *of* something, the life and soul of the party, the life of, I don't know, the life of this or that kind of thing, or 'life on earth', like the telly programme. So what's with this '*the* Life'?

(Faces audience.) I asked the vicar at the door; don't know quite what I said, embarrassing to remember now, but I sort of asked what that stuff meant, the Resurrection and the Life, and he laughed a bit and

said, Well, yes, er, it's a bit strange, isn't it? It's the old translation, we use it because people seem to like it at funerals. It's from St John's Gospel, maybe you should look at a modern version, if you're interested I could recommend…and I just said, yeah, OK, thanks, cause I couldn't be bothered, and he obviously didn't have an answer. Didn't have a clue what the question was, even. And I could see he was gearing up to have a discussion about this business of translations of the Bible. I'd never realised there was more than one, but I wasn't really interested. Wasn't what I was asking about, so I walked off. *(Moves away, sits.)*

SECOND VOICE: *(Middle-aged, female; light coming up on her, seated, not looking at audience.)* He kept on asking, 'He coming, then?' all the time he was in bed those last few days, and I just went on saying, yes, course he is, he's on his way right now. On the last day, though, he stopped asking. I remember saying, He'll be here soon, I know he'll be here soon, but he didn't seem to be listening by then.

When he came, I ran to him and it all poured out: where the hell were you, where the *hell* were you? he kept asking and asking, where were you. And he didn't say anything, he stood there and I could see he was shivering and sweating as if he had a temperature or something.

(Gets up, walks slowly downstage.) It's not as if we ever had much in the way of friends. Three people in the house, a widow, a spinster and an invalid little brother, not much to bring people through the door. When my husband died, I came back. My sister had always stayed to look after him, because he'd had fits since he was little, really frightening, and we sort of always knew that one day there'd be something we couldn't do anything about. She'd got

caught, never went out, always in the kitchen or in his room, no boyfriends or anything. And I didn't want to see anyone anyway, not after the accident. Grief makes you ugly. The house was ugly. Too much to manage. Not surprising nobody came. *(Sits again.)*

Only *he* did, just knocking on the door one day with all the rest of his friends and asking if they could sit down for half an hour, and he made us laugh as if we were ordinary and not ugly. Oh God, we wanted him so much those last days. I'll never stop hearing Lazarus saying over and over, 'He coming, then?' the words all lumpy and muffled.

Where the hell were you, I shouted. And he stood there, and then he wiped his forehead and just said, 'Well, I'm here now. Where are you? Where's he? Where have you buried him?'

FIRST VOICE:

(Light up on him, seated.) I looked it up one day, John's Gospel, in a Gideon Bible in a hotel. It was like the vicar'd said, one of these new ones, and it didn't, I don't know, it didn't sound quite the same. I sort of flicked through the pages around, couldn't make head or tail.

When I was clearing out my auntie's house a few months ago, I found her Bible. Big old thing, biggish print, I think it might have been one of those family Bibles, probably from her gran or something. I thought I'd look up this John's thing again. It took me a while to find it, and then – don't know why – I read the first bit out loud.

(Gets up, moves towards audience.) When I was little and I heard thunderstorms I used to think it was like the noise of someone moving big empty wooden boxes around upstairs, and all these heavy things falling over. That's what it reminded

me of, heavy stuff falling over in an empty room somewhere. The Word was with God and the Word was God. No idea what it meant. Only the noise of it, big hard boxes falling over slowly on a wood floor.

THIRD VOICE:

(Young, male, walking on slowly and sitting to face audience.) He started off with her, walking to the cemetery, shivering as if he had a cold or flu. And along the road he stopped suddenly and bent double and – cried, if that's the word. He wept. I don't know how to say what it sounded like, though. At first I thought it was like an animal, just one long sound tearing up out of his belly. Then I thought it's the noise Adam might have made when he first had breath pushed into him and had to push it out again. Then I thought, it's the noise a dead man waking up would make, starting to breathe again.

He wept.

(Stands, pause.) Doesn't tell you anything, that. You know – well, maybe you don't, you're lucky if you don't – you know what it sounds like when someone hasn't cried for years and it's kind of sucked up out of them? Only this was as if you were hearing weeping for the first time. As if it was being sucked up out of the ground or under the ground.

Everybody was quiet for a minute. Then I heard a bit of whispering and a laugh or two. He didn't look up or round. Then he straightened up and walked on. I could see her pointing to the grave.

He stopped again. There was quite a lot of noise by this time, but I could just hear him, whispering the dead boy's name. Then just, 'Come'. Like that, flat, short, dropping like a stone on the dust. 'Lazarus, come forth'. I can't remember if it was loud or quiet or what. It just – dropped there.

SECOND VOICE: *(She gets up and walks towards the THIRD VOICE.)*
You hear about noises starting a landslide, don't
you? One stone drops and then the hillside starts
moving?

They'd moved the grave slab aside – lots of frowning
and complaining over that, and it was there,
balanced against the hillside, and it started shaking,
just like him, he was still shivering, and then it fell
over and slammed on the dry rocks.

(Quietly.) And he came to him. *(Pause; she speaks
with difficulty.)* He came to him, and he said a
strange thing, he said, 'Let him go'. He was very
still now, he'd stopped shivering. They were both
very still, and I thought, 'Things come to him when
he calls'. *(Still laboured, feeling for words.)* The stone
plug comes out of the grave hole, the breath comes
to him – from the, from the end of the earth and
he breathes it into the grave *(Faster.)* and the dead
bodies come to him and the words come to him out
of the dead bodies and, and *(She grasps the sleeve of
the first speaker.)* –

(Lets go, moves away.) When the stone fell over, I
thought it was a storm starting. And sure enough
the rain suddenly came up and we were all running
back indoors, with all those folk who'd turned up to
see him not sure what they'd seen.

FIRST VOICE: *(Looks/moves toward SECOND VOICE.)* I had a
nightmare after that time looking through my
aunt's stuff. I'd been to her funeral too, and I was
back there in church looking at the coffin, and I
went up to it and the lid started slipping off and
I could see her face moving, like it was starting to
breathe again, her mouth opening. And I was scared
out of my mind that she'd – say something. Or that
when she opened her mouth there'd be something
inside it that I couldn't bear to see. There was a

noise like rain beginning to hiss on a pavement when it starts to pour down, hissing getting louder and louder, more like a steam engine after a bit, and then the lid of the coffin just slid on the floor, a big loud wooden sound, and I sort of panicked and knocked the whole coffin over and it fell off the stand thing and clattered and echoed, and I woke up sweating like a pig. I realised it was a thunderstorm starting outside. Of course.

THIRD VOICE: *(Abstracted, to herself at first.)* The rain came stabbing down. Washing the rocks, leaping off the rocks, white limestone turning black. I stood there for a long time. I felt my mind was like the rocks, soaked and streaming and turning dark. I am the Life, he said.

The rain strips the earth away and what's left is the rock. When he…when he wept, something, I don't know, something stripped the covers away and what's left is the life. Whatever's alive underneath it all. And you stand there, streaming with the darkness pouring over you, and he says, I'm what's left. You may go away, I won't. The water keeps on coming.

FIRST VOICE: *(Wanders towards audience.)* Someone just back from a trip to China said he'd been to some kind of cultural event and they had this wooden gong. You think, 'Wooden gongs?' He tried to describe it; he said it's like a hollow clap, you feel the emptiness all round; it sort of clears a space in your brain. I thought of that when I tried to think about this nightmare and the sound of falling boxes upstairs and the…the words I'd read. The sound before the rain comes and streams down the windows, and then you can see what you didn't see before. The Word was with God and the Word was God. Then the rain comes.

Sounds bloody daft like that, doesn't it? But I had this picture in my head, water scouring off the soil and the rock coming through. And all those big plain words just sitting there; only not rocks but more like – what? Some big patient animal, something alive. Like you think you're looking at a rock in the sea or a mound of earth in a wood and suddenly you notice it's looking at you. *(Sits.)* Something alive. The life that's left.

SECOND VOICE: It was so strange later on. Serving food to a table of silent faces. Because no one had anything to say. How could they? We sat and listened to the rain. We listened to the rain. It was a long time. After a while, you could feel people settling back, as if all there ever was to do was listen to the rain. He was lying on his elbow, very pale, and his breath seemed to be coming slowly, and his eyes kept meeting Lazarus's eyes, as if he knew Lazarus knew something and knew he couldn't say it, and only the two of them would understand if he ever opened his mouth. I think – I think we were afraid at the thought he'd open his mouth…that either of them would open their mouths. Rain and the sounds of laboured breath and silence. Sometimes the big wooden noises overhead and the sudden light. *(Slowly moving towards audience.)* And when the rain stopped at last, he got up slowly and smiled at us all and said it was better for him to go away. And he went away.

FIRST VOICE: 'I am the life'. I'm what's alive here. That's what I was hearing. The hollow clap, then the rain, the flood. Words heavy enough to splinter the floor of the sky. Or whatever. You run out of things to say, you want to go back to the beginning, before…

SECOND VOICE: *(Pacing.)* He never asked me if I wanted Lazarus back. Never asked Lazarus, if it comes to that. You think about it, and why would you want to come back? *(Still for a moment.)* No, that's not right, though, it's more that – well, you think the best thing is to sort of rest, really, specially when you think about what people go through. What Lazarus went through. No, he never asked. Like he couldn't *ask* permission to be – what he is. Whatever he is. So he weeps. It rains. The thunder makes great hollow noises. The words tumble over and roll downhill, lie around in the wet.

THIRD VOICE   *(Moving towards SECOND VOICE.)* There they lie. I climb over them, I look to see if you can build something out of them. My fingers slip off them. *(Turns away, then round to audience; pause.)* Even the world itself could not contain the books that should be written.

Silence: the three speakers stand still, looking at each other. Then the recorded voice again, reading 'I am the Resurrection and the life'. Pause. A wooden gong struck three times.

Lachlan Mackinnon

ACTS

The readers (1, 2, 3) need have nothing in common in terms of age, sex, ethnicity or accent. Clarity of diction is paramount.

Except where pauses are indicated, speeches run on continuously, governed only by syntax. Pauses within speeches may be used to serve either sense or clarity. Biblical or liturgical echoes should not be distinguished in any way. The only relationship between the readers is vocal; they neither look at, nor respond to, one another in any other way.

The set consists of three lecterns, built or draped so as to conceal all but head, arms and upper torso. The lecterns are in a straight line facing the audience, with a gap of six feet separating the first from the second and the second from the third.

Reader 1 stands behind the central lectern, reader 2 behind that on stage right, reader 3 behind that on stage left.

Costume: black roll-neck pullovers, black trousers or skirts, black socks, tights or stockings, black shoes. Glasses as required.

Enter the readers. If from stage left, in the order 2, 1, 3; from stage right, 3, 1, 2. They stand behind their respective lecterns and look straight at the audience. They do not move. Pause.

2:	another letter
1:	the usual
3:	more of the same
1:	the usual
3:	wigging about
2:	fornication
1:	the closing
2:	hope this find us
3:	as it leaves him
2:	sealed
3:	in the name of the Lord
1:	after the travelling
2:	creak of timber
1:	the salt smell
3:	snagging his senses
2:	you'd think he'd
1:	lay off retire
3:	to contemplation not
2:	a bit of it
1:	for the acts were all his
2:	that made us
1:	that made and sustain us
3:	his
2:	he was not of Jerusalem
1:	the blessed
3:	though a proud Jew
1:	he was not of Jerusalem
2:	not of the fortunate

1:	who had touched
3:	heard
2:	smelt
1:	and known Jesus
2:	more than Messiah
1:	the itinerant God
	Pause.
	almighty
	Pause.
	he had not seen
3:	though he would see him soon
2:	in broad daylight
1:	an intensification
3:	a fist of light
2:	swirling about him
1:	staggering
3:	blinded
1:	why do you
3:	Saul
1:	to become Paul
3:	when he outfoxed a wizard Saul
2:	recognised Jesus
1:	he must have known him
2:	seen him
3:	or perhaps only
2:	by the heart's light
1:	heard him the Lord God
3:	and in those first times
2:	turned away
1:	unknowing
3:	not knowing

1: what he would later preach

2: to the slave girl who had never

3: heard of Messiah

2: who had never

3: dreamed of such things

1: such things

2: were possible

1: possible

2: for the busy man

1: in his toils

2: for all the spent the broken

3: freedom had come

1: had walked among us

2: freedom

1: and left us these things

3: faith

1: hope

2: charity

1: and the greatest of these

2: is charity

1: the Christ who spoke to him

3: out of the white light

1: why do you persecute

2: me

3: the scene changes

   Pause.

1: at the moment the light

2: failed in the Christ

3: and he found himself God-

1: forsaken he went

2: down into hell

3:    and there was no God the veil

1:    in the temple

2:    was ripped apart

1:    and there was no God

2:    until he rose again

1:    in humble

3:    and thankful triumph

1:    it was like that for Saul

3:    when the light struck him

2:    no God

1:    and suddenly God

3:    was talking to him

1:    explain

2:    as you will the long years

1:    of silence following

3:    the slow insinuation

1:    vein

2:    by vein

1:    of what he must become

3:    transfiguring

2:    before the boyish years

3:    of derring-do

1:    prisons escaped from

2:    angels assisting

3:    driven

2:    by the force of the God who

1:    rejected God

2:    to undergo

1:    all suffering

2:    to know

1:    all suffering

2:      in whose footsteps Saul

1:      through hell

3:      coming at last

2:      to Jerusalem

1:      being received

3:      by James

1:      James

2:      who was keeping the whole thing

1:      together the

2:      show on the road

1:      James

3:      the bewildered

2:      the resolute

3:      man-manager

1:      behind whom

2:      the ever-chastened Peter

1:      poor Peter

3:      slow on the uptake

2:      to whose limitations

3:      God accommodated

1:      himself

2:      Peter

1:      the servant

3:      of the servants of God

2:      who thrice

1:      denied Christ

3:      and three times refused

2:      to believe a Gentile

1:      was equal to a Jew

3:      then knew

2:      quite suddenly

THE ACTS OF THE APOSTLES

1:	all he had ever assumed
3:	was wrong
1:	and must be made new
2:	by contrition
1:	by grace
	Pause.
	those years of waiting
3:	waiting and wondering
1:	whether Messiah
2:	would return in his splendour
1:	to raise the kingdom
3:	out of its impotence
1:	or whether the word
2:	was to the present and meant
1:	only do good
3:	Peter
1:	servant of the servants
2:	lodged here and there
1:	living the word
3:	within him then suddenly Paul
1:	appears among them
2:	ready to handle
3:	all the overseas business
2:	entrepreneurial Paul with his
1:	new energy
3:	they take him on
1:	the letters follow
3:	letters
2:	of anxious management
3:	preventing quarrels
2:	disdaining pride

1:        though Paul is a proud man

3:        terrified

1:        by the thorn in the flesh

3:        in his flesh

2:        lust

1:        who will never accommodate

3:        God to the human

1:        in that

2:        sense a fanatic

1:        there follow

3:        the boy's own years

1:        of split water

3:        bubbling at the bow

2:        like a slow fire

1:        the fire that was in them Paul

3:        and his companions

1:        taking the sea road

3:        like young men

2:        with the fire that is in them

1:        preaching wakening

2:        enlightening unchaining

3:        loving attending

1:        to the first

2:        flutterings of the soul

1:        the freshly woken soul

2:        as it chips at its shell

1:        attending

3:        to the last flutterings

1:        like the itinerant God

3:        among the ships

2:        the olives

THE ACTS OF THE APOSTLES

1:   in the thick of the smell

2:   of new bread of fresh fish

1:   without a care

3:   chipped toenails

1:   and remembering one

2:   who dropped off

1:   during a late-night sermon Paul

3:   banging on as he will

2:   who dropped off the window-sill

1:   into the void

3:   whom Paul

1:   restored to life

2:   Paul

3:   would baptize a lion

2:   he did

1:   another story

3:   the sleeper's son

1:   became a bishop

2:   Eurychus

1:   was the name

3:   the treasured

2:   recorded name

3:   of the weary sleeper

1:   to whom God stooped

Pause.

   Paul

3:   rarely depends

2:   seems to pay his own way

1:   fruit of the silent years perhaps

3:   foreign sales manager

1:	of the first global enterprise
3:	itinerant God
1:	we never saw
2:	watch over him
3:	itinerant God
1:	we never heard
2:	watch over him
3:	itinerant God
1:	we never touched
2:	watch over him
1:	as you watch over us
3:	despite the police
1:	the knock in the night
2:	the flames the torturers
1:	but Paul was there when they stoned Stephen
3:	you have seen
2:	stoning
1:	how they wrap the head in a cloth
3:	and stone the cloth
1:	until the cloth stops moving
3:	O man of blood
2:	man of horrors
1:	you came
2:	to us
1:	to ask
3:	forgiveness
1:	this
2:	is our test
1:	you would throw it all off
2:	and go carefree about the earth
3:	like the itinerant God

1:      in whose footsteps

2:      know you not he is God

1:      people say

3:      he is the Christ

2:      why do you persecute God

Pause.

1:      almighty

Pause.

      and then

2:      the Wanderjahre

3:      the voyaging

1:      the water-cleaving keel

2:      wind in their faces

3:      salt

2:      in their eyes in their hair

3:      groaning of wet

2:      and warping wood

3:      sailors

2:      in terror

3:      the sunny patches

2:      the gliding over

3:      clarity down to sand

2:      the making fast

3:      the shore leaves

1:      and the incessant letters

3:      from points unknown

1:      making us what we are

Pause.

      what is happening what is this

2: press of people

1: a stranger look

3: some gadabout preacher

1: is holding forth

2: wanting to quicken

1: a hallelujah hubbub a head

2: nods here and there a head nods

1: as with a quickening

3: of the true life this

1: is enough this

2: is more than enough

1: to be doing these things

2: and going carefree

1: to and fro in the earth

2: until they come to Rome

3: with the word that is heard

2: on the shores of lakes

3: in marketplaces

2: in city squares

3: upper rooms

2: in fearful secret

3: in open forum

1: giving the word

2: to Rome

1: Rome Paul

3: had always longed for Rome his

2: other Jerusalem

1: Rome

3: so proud a citizen

1: where the fade-out begins

2: two years

THE ACTS OF THE APOSTLES

1:        in his own house

2:        Paul

1:        never dependent

2:        do not believe Peter servant

1:        of the servants of God

3:        would not have made him welcome

1:        it is evening in Rome

2:        fading from history

3:        lost

1:        anonymous

3:        the torturers are waiting

2:        where they shall both die

3:        as though a mist

2:        covers the last days

3:        when they shall die

2:        horribly die

1:        in the name of the Father

2:        and of the Son

3:        *(Speaking as if more were to follow.)* and of the Holy Ghost

They do not move. Pause.

Amy Rosenthal

THE MAN WHO CAME TO BRUNCH

A living room in North London. BERNICE and JONNY sit on the sofa. BERNICE is about forty. JONNY is in his mid thirties, handsome and charismatic.

BERNICE: Sorry about this.

JONNY: Absolutely not a problem.

BERNICE: I should have told them we were coming.

JONNY: If they're anything like my parents, they'd have got caterers in.

BERNICE: I'm beginning to think they have.

JONNY: Relax. I'm not in a hurry.

BERNICE: Thanks, Jonny.

JONNY: No need.

BERNICE: For coming with me.

JONNY: Hey. To some extent I'm responsible for this, remember.

BERNICE: I suppose to some extent you are.

JONNY: Quite a large extent, if we're honest.

BERNICE: True. It's basically your fault.

They smile radiantly at each other. HOWARD, BERNICE's father, late sixties, enters with a tray piled high with food.

HOWARD: Right. Your mother's bringing the tea. She's also made some coffee if you prefer coffee, Jonny, we didn't know.

JONNY: Wow, Mr Hayman, you didn't need to go to all this trouble.

HOWARD: It's not every day we get a visit from our girl. And it's certainly not every day she brings a fella with her! Not by a long shot.

ELAINE, mid-sixties, enters with a teapot, a cafetière and cups on a tray.

ELAINE: Here we are. Sorry it took so long. Howard refuses to let me slice a bagel with a knife.

JONNY: What do you use?

HOWARD: I found this device, Jonny. Ingenious. Did you know, in 2008 alone 1,979 New Yorkers were admitted to A&E with bagel-related injuries?

JONNY: I didn't know that.

ELAINE: Who knew? He reads these things online –

HOWARD: The *Wall Street Journal*, excuse me.

ELAINE: And he orders this thing. 'SafeBagel'. Two bits of plastic and a wire.

HOWARD: 'SafeBagel'! It's called SafeSlice. It's ingenious.

ELAINE: It's ingenious in every way except you can't slice a bagel with it.

HOWARD: A hundred times I've shown her, but no, she'd rather use a knife and whack the top of her finger off.

ELAINE: Sixty years of slicing, have I ever drawn blood?

HOWARD: *(Standing, excited.)* You want to see it, Jonny? The device? It's in the kitchen, I can show you…

ELAINE: Why would he want to see it, Howard? Sit down.

HOWARD: It won't take a sec.

HOWARD exits. ELAINE rolls her eyes.

ELAINE: Now, what will you have? There's smoked salmon, chopped liver, chopped herring, egg-and-onion, cream cheese. Some of the bagels are plain and some are poppyseed. Help yourself, Jonny, don't hold back.

BERNICE goes to take a bagel.

Bernice, you hold back. Just a little. *(She taps her waistline.)* Have a pickled cucumber.

JONNY: This is amazing, Mrs Hayman, what a spread.

ELAINE: Please! Bits and bobs from the back of the fridge! If I'd known you were coming…

HOWARD: *(Re-entering.)* Known he was coming? We didn't know he existed! *(Holding up his slicer.)* Here we are. She's carved up all the bagels, or I'd give you a demo.

JONNY takes it, studies it.

JONNY: Wow, I see. Kind of deceptively simple.

HOWARD: What did I say? Wish I'd invented it myself, could have gone on *Dragon's Den*. Silenced the unbelievers!

ELAINE: *(Ignoring him.)* Did you grow up locally, Jonny?

JONNY: Hendon, for my sins. My father had a practice there, so…

HOWARD: He's a doctor?

JONNY: He's retired now.

HOWARD: Would I know him?

ELAINE: Howard used to work in Hendon.

JONNY: Alan Goldfarb.

ELAINE: Dr Goldfarb…

HOWARD: Dr Goldfarb…

ELAINE: Have you followed in his footsteps, Jonny?

JONNY: No, I'm not a doctor.

JONNY and BERNICE look at each other. She gives him a small nod.

I actually work in the ministry of our Lord Jesus Christ.

BERNICE: Amen.

            A short silence.

ELAINE: You what?

            HOWARD laughs merrily.

            But – you're Jewish.

HOWARD: Elaine, he's kidding.

JONNY: Christ was Jewish, Mrs Hayman.

HOWARD: He's winding you up!

JONNY: I work for a fantastic organization called Jews for Jesus.

HOWARD: Oh, bloody hell.

JONNY: Our aim is to make the Messiahship of Jesus an unavoidable issue to our Jewish people worldwide.

HOWARD: Dear God.

JONNY: *(Smiling.)* Exactly.

HOWARD: 'An unavoidable issue?'

JONNY: That's our mission statement.

HOWARD: And how do you propose to do that?

JONNY: Good question. Basically, by talking to people directly. Getting out there, handing out our literature, spreading the word that being born into Judaism doesn't shut you out from the divine salvation of Christ.

ELAINE: But it does.

JONNY: Everything's a choice.

HOWARD: You mean conversion. You convert people.

JONNY: That's absolutely what we don't do.

HOWARD: But you're asking me, as a Jew, to believe in Jesus Christ?

JONNY: I'm inviting you –

HOWARD: Fine. I'm sure he existed. He was a nice fella, a prophet if you
           like. Kind to his mother, a good egg. But in our religion, we
           don't believe he was the Son of God.

JONNY: The thing is, some of us do.

           He looks at BERNICE.

ELAINE: Not you.

           BERNICE glows.

HOWARD: Don't be ridiculous.

ELAINE: Look at her, Howard, she's brainwashed.

JONNY: She's been saved, Mrs Hayman. Very different thing.

HOWARD: How long have you been seeing this clown, Bernice?

JONNY: *(Appalled.)* We're not –

BERNICE: Jonny's my mentor, Dad.

HOWARD: Well, how long has he been – mentoring you?

BERNICE: I found my way to Jonny six months ago, after Christ came to
           me for the first time.

HOWARD: Came to you. Where?

BERNICE: In my kitchen. Well, the utility room.

HOWARD: Saw his face in a cherry tomato, one of those?

BERNICE: I felt His presence. It filled the room. I knew that He loved
           me, and was opening His arms to me, and I'd never be alone
           again.

ELAINE: I knew it. That's what it's about. All her friends are settled.

BERNICE: A few days later, I was walking home and Jonny and his friends
           were handing out literature in the street. They were wearing
           bright t-shirts, chatting and laughing. Their happiness almost
           shocked me, it was so visible. It showed up everything around
           them. And when they told me it was possible…to be Jewish
           and still be with Christ…

HOWARD: There's only one word for a Jew who believes in Christ.

BERNICE: Please Dad, don't blaspheme –

HOWARD: A Christian! A bloody Christian! We're waiting for the
           Messiah, they think he's already been! You can't have it both
           ways.

JONNY: May I tell you a little story?

           HOWARD and ELAINE regard him with deep suspicion.

           Not long ago I saw this play about a Jewish family. A family
           like yours or mine, North London, present day. I think it was
           even set in Hendon.

HOWARD: *(Unsure.)* Right…

JONNY: Perfectly decent play, nice acting, one problem. No food. In
           the whole play not a single character eats a bite. People come
           in, go out – no one even gets a cup of tea. No, wait, I'm
           wrong! Just after the interval the mother hands round a bowl
           of peanuts. *A bowl of peanuts.* And I'm thinking, what sort of a
           Jewish family is this? No food, no hospitality, no warmth. You
           wouldn't buy it, would you, Mrs Hayman?

ELAINE: I don't see what…

JONNY: My point being, that's what it's about. What *we're* about. The
           food. The warmth. The importance of family. The culture,
           the heritage, the humour. These are the things that matter.
           And I'm here to tell you – *none of this changes when you join
           our organization.* It's in our blood. It's who we are. We still
           eat fishballs, we still shrug. We still laugh at Woody Allen –
           the early stuff. Hand on heart, go and sit in my car, I've got
           Streisand singing Sondheim on a loop. *Nothing is lost.* We're
           not sacrificing one single element of our Jewishness, we're only
           gaining something. The eternal love of Jesus Christ our Lord.

BERNICE: Amen.

ELAINE: Stop it, Bernice.

HOWARD: Woody Allen? Fishballs? *That's* what it's all about? And there was I, thinking it had something to do with *God*!

BERNICE: (*Suddenly.*) 'I have great heaviness and continual sorrow in my heart. For I could wish that myself were accursed from Christ for my brethren, my kinsmen according to the flesh, who are Israelites.'

ELAINE: She's possessed.

HOWARD: Now what's she on about?

JONNY: St. Paul's letter to the Romans. You should read it, it explains so much.

HOWARD: Thanks, I've still got two Harry Potters to get through.

BERNICE: 'Brethren,' he says, 'my heart's desire and prayer to God for Israel is that they might be saved. For I bear them record that they have a zeal of God, but not according to knowledge. For they being ignorant of God's righteousness, and going about to establish their own righteousness, have not submitted themselves unto the righteousness of – '

HOWARD: All right, that'll do. Anti-Semitic codswallop.

JONNY: Paul was Jewish, Mr Hayman.

HOWARD: Self-hating! Self-hating! He didn't like what he was but you can't get away from it, can you? It's on your face, in your name, in your trousers.

HOWARD is still holding his bagel slicer. He waves it at JONNY.

I'm assuming you're circumcised, are you?

BERNICE: Dad!

JONNY: I don't think it matters. As Paul says, it's a circumcision of the heart that matters, not of the flesh.

HOWARD: So you've found a way of being it and not being it. Embracing it and rejecting it. I know your type. Even seen you in the mirror, now and then, when something's made me ashamed of what I am. I know what self-hatred feels like. But I fight it. You – you piss in your own chicken soup. Aaargh!

He roars with pain. He has cut his thumb on the bagel-slicer.

ELAINE: What have you done?

BERNICE: *(Simultaneous.)* Dad!

JONNY grabs HOWARD's thumb and holds it tightly high above his head.

JONNY: Keep it up in the air! Let the blood run the other way!

HOWARD: Little bastard!

BERNICE: He's trying to help!

HOWARD: Not him, the bloody bagel-slicer!

ELAINE: Let me look at it.

She takes HOWARD's thumb from JONNY. She frowns.

HOWARD: *(Weakly.)* Is there much blood?

ELAINE: There's no blood.

HOWARD: No blood?

JONNY: Oh…

HOWARD: But it was agony.

ELAINE: You got a shock.

JONNY: Well, wow. Thank God.

HOWARD slowly sits down, inspecting his thumb. Silence. JONNY looks at his watch, clear his throat.

Well…

BERNICE: Don't go. Please. You said you'd stay.

JONNY: It's going to be fine, Bernice.

BERNICE: I need you to keep me strong.

JONNY: Christ will keep you strong. His Love will surround you. I said I'd meet Camilla in Caffé Nero.

BERNICE wilts.

Mr and Mrs Hayman, I know this is hard. But it gets easier. My parents struggled for a long time but we've moved into real acceptance now. In fact my dad and my twin sister have just been baptised –

HOWARD: Bugger off.

JONNY: Absolutely. Bernice, I'll text you.

BERNICE: OK.

JONNY: And thanks again for the wonderful spread.

He leaves. The door slams, off. Silence. All three lost in thought. Eventually:

ELAINE: I suppose I should clear this away.

HOWARD: Hardly touched it, did we?

ELAINE: Are you hungry?

HOWARD: Not really. I feel a bit sick.

ELAINE: Are you, Bernice?

BERNICE shakes her head. Pause.

HOWARD: Seems a waste though.

ELAINE: How about half a bagel.

HOWARD: I'll have half a bagel with you.

ELAINE: Plain or poppyseed?

HOWARD: One of each?

ELAINE: One of each.

HOWARD: You can use –

ELAINE: I'm using an ordinary knife.

ELAINE cuts the bagel halves into quarters, tops them with cream cheese, smoked salmon etc., and arranges them on three plates.

BERNICE: *(Suddenly.)* 'Nay but, O man, who are thou that repliest against God? Shall the thing formed say to him that formed it, why has thou made me thus? Hath not the potter power over the clay, of the same lump to make one vessel unto honour, and another unto dishonour?'

ELAINE hands one plate to HOWARD and one to BERNICE. She speaks almost to herself.

ELAINE: Eat. Don't worry. It'll sort itself out. These things happen. We get through. We survive. Don't think about it any more. Eat.

All three start to eat.

The End.

Matt Charman

WITHOUT LOVE

JO: We borrowed an eight-year-old to come and stay for the weekend. Neil said it was the toughest age to control and it would therefore be the best test of whether we had 'parental instincts' or not. I reminded Neil of the period in a child's life known as the 'terrible twos' but he said it was a fallacy that kids were any trouble at two and that it's actually at eight years old that the cracks begin to show in a child's personality.

Neil called it a 'road test' and even though I asked him not to I still heard him refer to it as a 'road test' to his brother on the phone. The kid was called Isaac and we picked him up on a Saturday morning from a colleague of Neil's.

I was hoping for a little boy who didn't say very much and was nervous, whose life we could have a huge impact on in one day. In fact he was very talkative and quite dominating conversationally.

Neil was certain by the time we got home that he and Isaac were incompatible and that this wouldn't be a fair trial of his parental skills. He asked whether I would mind if he observed me with the child instead, to see if I had what it took to be the parent of a difficult eight-year-old, something he foresaw as a worse case scenario.

I was terrible with Isaac.
Aware Neil was watching me from the lounge I allowed the child too much autonomy in the kitchen and he cut his hand with a vegetable knife.

339

739 people a year are injured by watering cans.

431 by clothes pegs and 493 by cakes or scones.

It took us five attempts to get the answer machine message right when we first moved in together.

Finally, I wrote it out and underlined Neil's part because I wanted us to each say a bit of the message, so that what people heard when they called was both of us together, in our home.

When you consider that some people don't change their answer machine messages until they change their actual phone then it might be that a message is used for three or four years so it's worth getting right.

Neil calls from work when he thinks I'm not in, to hear my voice on the answer machine and then he hangs up.

I dial 1471.

Ali, my sister, won't leave a message on the machine because she says she hears Neil's voice and it doesn't feel private.

Ali is a year younger than me and from a different father, and she's a Gemini.

Ali is independent and classically difficult to be around.

She and Neil have never got on well and had a fight on our third wedding anniversary about whether we should celebrate wedding anniversaries at all.

I sided with Neil because I happen to agree with him that celebrating anniversaries is an important testament to fidelity and longevity in a society where more people fall apart now than stay together.

Ali has a difficult streak and has never liked Neil.

She said to mum when I got engaged, don't expect me to marry a man like Neil, and she meant it.

She brought 'Steve' to our wedding instead, who had a tattoo on his hand of three little dots shaped in a triangle.

At the reception Steve told Neil that he was an idiot for settling down at such a young age and then he pointed at the three dots on his hand and said it was his mantra, the three F's.

Find them, Fuck them, Forget about them.

Neil said he didn't have a mantra so Steve borrowed a biro and drew three dots on his hand and said 'Now you do'.

Neil washed them off and told me all about it.

Steve took money from my sister before he disappeared which must have been difficult because she didn't have any.

Mum died and Ali said it's just you and me now.

I told Isaac over lunch 'not to lick your knife you fucking little pig'.

I wanted to tell him that.

I didn't tell him that.

His little plaster started to bleed from the accident with the vegetable knife.

I'm worried that if we ever had one, I'd hurt our baby.

A few months ago when Neil got a little bit fat because we're contented and I'm aware that happens to couples, I used a screwdriver and took the bathroom scales apart.

With the stickers you get when you buy a blank video I changed the numbers on the scale so that 13 stone now read 14 stone.

Neil soon became concerned at his weight gain and we designed a diet together, which proved successful.

When he began losing weight I moved the numbers again, as the ideal weight for Neil's height is actually ten and a half stone and I knew he would get down to eleven stone then stop.

When he reached ten stone I adjusted the scales so they now read twelve stone.

I got him down to nine and a half stone with this method, which is, I realise, technically a stone underweight for Neil but I thought it was probably a good thing for his all-round health.

We took Isaac to the cinema in the afternoon because he wouldn't go bowling because of his asthma.

We watched a film with Johnny Depp in it, which both Isaac and I loved and bonded over on the way home.

Neil watched me in the rear-view mirror, impressed with the rapport I was building with Isaac I think.

While I walked, out the corner of my eye I saw a street performer juggling fire along by the river.

I stopped and watched him because it was getting dark and the flames looked impressive at dusk.

A crowd gathered and he sent these sticks up higher and higher until one got away from him and landed in the hood of a girl in the crowd who was a tourist.

The flame from the stick didn't burn for long because it's designed not to but it still burnt her pony tail and all up the back of her neck was blistered.

People hung around and waited until an ambulance came and the whole area stunk badly of singed hair.

The performer waited as well, feeling terrible and making conversation with people.

When the ambulance finally came, I left.

Ali went abroad which I found out from a postcard she sent me.

She was in Thailand then a month later she was in Cambodia.

She said she gave up her job and eBayed everything for her ticket including things I'd lent her, which I thought was a joke, but might have been true.

I don't use eBay, I don't know.

Don't get business cards printed from a machine in a service station even if they are in colour.

Neil did when he lost his job and it held him back for weeks.

He was stubborn and he wouldn't admit that the card was thin and cheap and that the font wasn't sophisticated enough for the responsibility level he was applying for.

He said the card was more 'a tick in a box than anything' and the quality of it really didn't matter much, but if that's what you leave behind in people's hands after an interview, then the quality matters most of all.

It's like the aftertaste of something, I said.

It doesn't matter if you've enjoyed the meal, in this case the interview, if the aftertaste, in this case the card – is bad, if the card is bad it makes you re-appraise the meal, the interview.

We rowed a lot about that.

They drilled open the lock on a flat in Bethnal Green and found a pile of post dating back to December 2010.

Ali was in arrears with her rent and they wanted to kick her out.

I didn't even know she was back in the country.

Inside, the television was on and Ali was laid out on the carpet by a homemade Christmas tree with presents underneath.

They used her teeth to identify her.

All the bulbs except two had burnt out on the Christmas tree lights because she'd been lying there like that for eight months and it was summer now.

Late in the afternoon, when I was bored of talking about Johnny Depp and Isaac seemed to be slowing down, Neil joined us at the table.

He had a suggestion for a game that wouldn't aggravate Isaac's breathing but that might be more boisterous and therefore boyish compared to the 'low-key activities we'd done till now', his words.

The 'men' went outside and while I pretended to be casual about it I rushed upstairs to look at them from the bedroom window.

Neil began by showing Isaac our small garden and then how to re-pot a plant.

Neil was good with Isaac.

He was encouraging, with a tone of voice I'd never heard him use before.

A little bit like when we move furniture together but less patronising.

I realised then Neil could make a good father and that the 'road test' had been a good idea.

Eventually Isaac got wheezy and had to stop but it didn't change my feelings of how Neil had handled their half an hour together.

The lonely deaths officer asked if we were a close family, Ali and me.

I had to say no.

A lonely deaths officer is a horrible job title.

It's hard to think of a worse one.

She helped me clear out Ali's flat.

Neil was in Scarborough, getting up to speed on a training course for a new sales job but I didn't want his help anyway.

He would have wanted to do things too fast and fill up bin
bags and get home and I wanted to take my time.

I didn't want the lonely deaths officer's help either, but she said
I looked fragile which is to say she thought I might break at
any moment.

Ali left a pile of clothes and a book she was reading, which
mentioned a Frog in the title, and a bunch of unprocessed film
that I knew would be of her because she loved taking photos of
herself with the camera I gave her second hand after Neil made
the switch to digital.
And she left a Bible.

Which was strange because I didn't think Ali was religious
unless she had found God in Cambodia.
But it looked like the book hadn't even been opened.
The ribbon bookmarker was on a page that said 1 Corinthians.
I kept the Bible.
I took it home with me.
I read 1 Corinthians and it didn't make any sense.
I phoned the company that was printed in the front because I
wanted to know what page they usually put the ribbon book
marker on when they sold this particular Bible and they said
that it varied.
I asked if they ever put it anywhere near 1 Corinthians and
they said it was unlikely but possible.

We returned Isaac to his parents' house in the evening.
I didn't get a glimpse of his father but I waved at his mother
who waved back at me.
We drove home pretty contented, Neil and I.
We talked about it in bed.

How it had all gone.

Neil had warmed to Isaac but he still didn't altogether trust him although he realised that wouldn't be an issue with his own baby.

Lightning strikes, Neil said, the same spot sometimes.

And the things that happen aren't my fault.

Losing our baby wasn't my fault.

Nor was what happened with Ali.

I can be a mother.

He said that and then he switched off the light.

Curtain pelmets injure 129 people a year.

No one should lie there for eight months without anyone knocking on the door, especially not my sister.

She said I was trapped but I think it was her who was trapped because everything disappointed Ali.

Nothing ever lived up to her expectations.

I miss my sister.

1 Corinthians says 'Absent in body, but present in spirit'.

Did she mark that page, so I would see?

Was there something she wanted me to see?

Something.

So I would understand?

'Without love we are nothing', it says that.

Is that it? What she wanted to say…

I came here on the bus, sat in the pregnant seats.

I sat behind a girl with a scar on her neck and short hair and I wanted to tap her on the shoulder to see if she was the girl who got burnt that night by the river, by the man juggling fire.

I sometimes look for that girl, if I ever walk down by that stretch of river, which is stupid because I'm sure she was a tourist and even so the chances of her being there, at that moment, with me are so remote.

But I still look.

I'd like to know if she's alright.

Wena Poon

THE WOOD ORCHID

The first Chinese arrived in England in the seventeenth century. They were kept as pets.

'They were not!' said Edward, laughing.

'They were, they were,' said Saffy determinedly, typing on her tiny laptop. It had a pink cover. 'I read it on Wikipedia, therefore it must be true.'

She wore a pink lace slip. Her hair was long and spread all over his couch. If the Pre-Raphaelites were still alive, they would have painted her. But he was too old to have such thoughts. He was thirty-eight, which according to Saffy, twenty years his junior, was to be 'just about dead'.

'What are you writing now?' he asked. He was packing for Dubai. Edward lost his job three years ago during the financial crisis in London. Things were slowly picking up. He was offered a post by his previous bank to head up a new Middle Eastern division. It was a two-year posting. In his last month in London, he decided to let out his townhouse in Islington to university students.

'A new play. For my theater group. They never have any roles for Chinese girls. I decided to create my own. I'll be a pet.'

'Saffy,' he put on his coat. 'I've got to go and sort out my work visa at the bank. I'm expecting a potential tenant, a young chap who might be interested in taking out the middle floor. He might drop by at noon. Can you take care of him?'

She looked up. 'The Chinese guy?'

'I think he's Chinese. Can't tell from his email,' Edward checked his phone. 'Max Tam. Is that a Chinese name? Sounds like yours.'

'Does not!'

'He's a student.'

'Probably business student,' she said in disdain.

'Least he'll have a job.'

'I hope he's not fresh off the boat.'

'Like you?'

'Shut up! Why are you taking Chinese tenants?' asked Saffy, suddenly interested. 'Do you have some kind of Oriental fetish?'

'No, I heard that Chinese students are very clean. I don't want people to trash my house when I'm in Dubai. I'm not going to come home much.'

Saffy pouted. 'I'm not clean. I'll stick Hello Kitty stickers on the walls when you're gone. You'll never get them off.'

'You lie, Saffy, you're neat, I looked into your room,' he retrieved an umbrella from the hallway.

'When?'

'Yesterday, when you were in class. I think the house will be in good hands.'

'Can I give Max Tam a cleanliness test?'

'Please do.' As he shut the front door behind him, Edward found himself grinning. He wished he didn't have the visa appointment. He wanted to be around when the new tenant met Saffy Tang.

*

'Hi, I'm here to see the house. Is Edward around?'

Saffy looked him up and down. He was a young man wearing a narrowly tailored black suit and a thin black tie. His shoes looked expensive. 'What's your name?'

'Max Tam.' He offered his hand.

'Are you Chinese?' she said suspiciously.

'Yes. As a matter of fact.'

'From?'

'Hong Kong.'

She let him in. 'I'm Saffy. Edward's out. He wants me to show you around. Come on.'

They stood in the living room. 'This is the ground floor,' she said listlessly. 'Obviously. Common area. And this…is the basement. That's Edward's bedroom and bathroom, which is off limits. Broom closet. Dunno what this is, don't have the key. Probably full of dead babies. Washing machine. This is where you can hang up your laundry, there isn't a dryer, which sucks. This is the kitchen. Obviously.'

'This is nicer than I expected,' said Max, looking out into the sunny backyard. 'He must have money.'

'He's a banker. He's going to Dubai. He doesn't want the house to be empty 'cos there are break-ins sometimes.'

'If he's rich, is the rent negotiable?'

'How much is he charging you?'

Max named the price. Saffy shrugged. 'He charges me more, but that's because I have the top floor, which is the nicest.'

'Oh really?'

'I'll show you your floor.'

They climbed the blue-carpeted stairs. Max tried not to look at Saffy. She was still wearing the see-through pink slip, although her hair was so long it covered all the most interesting spots.

'Is he gay?' asked Max suddenly.

'No. He's divorced though. His ex-wife's ugly.'

'You met her?'

'No, I spied on his old photos the week I moved in. When he was out.'

'Interesting. He keeps old photos of his ex?'

'In a special drawer. I was hoping to find dirty mags, but he hasn't any.' Saffy opened the bedroom door. 'You get these two rooms – study and bedroom, and your own bathroom.'

'And where do you live?' he asked.

She pointed at the last flight of steps in the narrow house. He could see sunlight flooding in from the skylight on the roof. On the top of the steps, there was a row of colorful stuffed animals forming a barricade. They held a handwritten sign: NO BOYS ALLOWED PAST HERE.

'How old are you?' asked Max.

She stared. 'You're so rude.'

'I'm sorry, I just find it rather funny.'

'I live to entertain.'

'May I point out an error?' he climbed up to the toy barricade. 'You've got their shirts on wrong. This is Kiki. This is Lala.'

'No!' She watched in horror as he undressed and re-dressed her Sanrio toys.

'I don't know how to break it to you, but Kiki's the boy, Lala's the girl,' Max stepped back, satisfied at his handiwork. 'You mean you didn't know? Where did you grow up?'

'California.'

'Pity. Americans just don't understand Sanrio.'

When Edward came back from the office, he found Saffy hiding in her bedroom. He knocked. 'Well, did that Max bloke come?'

'Yes,' she said from behind the door.

'Did you give him your cleanliness test?'

'He left you a cheque. If you say yes he moves in on Monday.'

'He's alright then?'

'Yeah. He's doing some fellowship at the university. Hong Kong. Stuffy. Cambridge grad. Like you.'

'Interesting. You'll get along, then?'

She grunted, then turned up the music in her room. Serge Gainsbourg, with Jane Birkin sounding like she was having an orgasm.

Edward was suddenly sorry to be leaving for Dubai.

*

Saffy made it absolutely clear that she was not going to cut Max Tam any slack just because they happened to belong to the same race.

'You didn't put the milk back in the fridge last night,' she said accusingly when he came down one morning. She was wearing another pink slip with pink feather pom-poms at her wrists. Max was disappointed that this one wasn't translucent.

She said, 'Edward says we must be neat.'

'Sorry. It's not as if he would check.'

'I file reports with him weekly. I give you ratings.'

Max yawned. 'Can I give you ratings too?'

Saffy scowled and turned on the radio for the morning news.

'Your last name is Tang?' he said, filling the kettle.

'How do you know?'

'Your letters were on the doormat.'

'What about it?' She was on Facebook, eating a piece of toast.

'Are you Teochew?'

'So?'

'My mum's Teochew,' said Max.

Saffy shrugged.

'Speak it?' he asked.

'No.' She added jealously, 'Can you?'

'Sure. I'm a linguist. I study it. Can you read Chinese?'

'Yes. Mom forced me.'

'Simple or complex script?'

'Complex,' Saffy said, making more toast. She glared at him, he glared back, and grudgingly she inserted another piece of bread into the toaster for him. 'Are you satisfied with my Chinese qualifications now? Want my birth signs?'

'I've never met a Teochew before in England. Most of them are in France. It's interesting. You're an actress?'

'Can't be an actress if no one will offer you any roles,' she handed him his toast.

'Why are you in London to study drama then, if you know they don't have roles for Chinese girls?'

'I want to get away from my mom.'

Max finished his breakfast. 'I've been volunteering at a Teochew Chinese association every Saturday. If you're interested, you can come along and check it out.'

'What's that?'

'It's a clan association. Don't you have them in America?'

She wrinkled her nose.

*

Max was up before her the next morning. 'You left your toy in the living room.'

'Did not!'

He held up the doll. 'We're even.'

Saffy took back the doll. As she stamped upstairs, he said, 'What *is* that doll? She looks like Barbie's evil twin.'

'Mulan.'

'From the Disney movie?'

'Yep.'

'That's really pathetic, Saffy,' he called after her. 'She doesn't even look Chinese!'

'Shut up. She's my role model.'

*

Dear Edward,

The stinky plant in the garden is getting stinkier now that it's spring. The flowers are in full bloom. I refuse to water it, hoping that it would die, but it keeps getting bigger. Yesterday Max Tam made dinner. I thought he was going to make something fobby and Chinese, but he made brown bread, salmon, and haggis. He was very scientific and stood for hours at the stove, observing and taking notes. He said he had a Scottish roommate at Cambridge and they had perfected haggis. I lost a bet with him, so I had to eat one spoonful.

Edward was in a conference room in Dubai watching as lawyers drafted a document on a big screen. The Swiss lead banker was droning on and on. He reached for his Blackberry and typed under the table:

What was the bet you lost?

Her email reply came back instantly.

I said there was no such thing as Miss Happy. He said there was, that she looked just like Mr Happy except she had a ribbon. The dispute was settled by Google. Tonight, we are going to argue about your sexuality by looking in your wardrobe. P.S. Max only wears black suits. He is so boring.

'What do you think, Edward?' asked the Swiss banker, his hands poised over the laptop. 'Should we say 'use best efforts to cause' or 'use best efforts to *reasonably* cause'?'

'The latter,' said Edward absent-mindedly.

The young American lawyer objected. 'Isn't that a split infinitive?'

'We'll see if the investors are paying attention,' said Edward.

*

'Oh good,' said Max appreciatively. 'If you could take that thing off your head, you would look almost presentable.'

He had told her to dress conservatively. Saffy came downstairs in what looked like a nun's outfit – black, with a small, white Peter Pan collar and large white cuffs. Her head was almost obscured by a gigantic bow of black satin.

'Won't take off bow,' she said. 'Bow comes with us.'

They stood at the bus stop.

'Are you making a film?' asked an old lady.

'No, we're going to see a Buddhist monk,' said Max amiably.

They got on the bus and rode it to Soho. They stood outside a shop. The sign was of black lacquered wood and had big gold Chinese letters carved into it.

'Read,' said Max, pointing.

'Teochew Clan Association of London,' said Saffy. She gave him a superior look.

'Very good. Come on in. My class is starting in ten minutes.'

*

'*While we look not at the things which are seen, but at the things which are not seen: for the things which are seen are temporal; but the things which are not seen are eternal,*' said Max. He was reading a passage from the Bible. He looked up. 'Okay, questions? Yes, Duc?'

'New word,' said one of the students. 'Temporal.'

'What word does it most look like?' asked Max. 'You already know it.'

Another student volunteered, 'Temporary?'

'Right. 'Temporal' is from *tempus*, Latin for 'time'. It has a similar meaning to 'temporary'. The opposite of that word also occurs in this line. What is it? Mei Ling?'

A girl spoke, 'Eternal?'

'Correct. He's saying something very beautiful here. What does he mean? Anyone?'

The class was taught in an empty auditorium in the basement of the clan association. There was a proscenium stage at one end, with red velvet curtains carefully pleated and held with golden ropes. An elderly Buddhist monk in a grey suit and black cotton shoes was on stage, showing Saffy Tang around. She stood with her hands behind her back, staring primly at the black and white photographs that hung backstage.

'My grandmother was a Teochew opera singer,' she said noncommittally. 'In Indonesia.'

'Oh?' The monk was surprised. He looked her up and down. He had not pegged her for a member of his dialect group. She looked extremely foreign to him. 'Is she still alive?'

'No.'

'I'm sorry. We could have invited her to give a recital here. Our older members donate money each year and we bring in a troupe from China to perform. Do you know anything about Teochew opera?'

'No,' said Saffy, a little scornfully. 'I'm an actress though. I'm taking French postmodern drama. And fashion.'

The monk unlocked a door backstage. 'Our women members always like looking in here.'

She stared at the racks of glittering costumes, zipped in clear plastic bags.

'We used to have an opera troupe in London. Many years ago. When they disbanded they donated their things to our association.'

'Teochew opera?'

'Teochew, and some Peking, Cantonese stuff. A good collection. A museum wanted to buy them, but I kept them here, so they could still be used by actors. I'm not sure if I've made the right decision.' His cellphone rang. The monk excused himself. 'Feel free to look around. You can try them on. Max's class won't be done for another thirty minutes.'

Saffy was left alone in the airless room. She opened one of the windows, sneezed at the dust, and began taking pictures of the costumes with her camera phone.

*

Dear Edward,

Saffy Tang tells me that she reports to you weekly about the overall condition of the house, and that she has made up some kind of 'points scheme' to rate my performance as a tenant. I trust that as long as my rent keeps being deposited into your bank account, you will not really care too much about my points. However, to humor Saffy, I am supposed to show considerable anxiety over my performance, so I am writing you, at her request, to beg you to reveal to me how my points compare to hers. May I say that, as she is awarding points to both herself and me, that her system is quite suspect. I believe the correct expression is 'leaving the hare in charge of the lettuce.'

The water boiler has broken again, but I made sure it was promptly repaired by the man you told us to call. It is probably because Saffy takes hour-long baths. I thought about asking her to pay for her pro rata share of the heating bill, but as she informs me that I consume double her share of Marmite toast each morning, I decided it was not worth pursuing.

I hope all is well in Dubai. How strange it is that all three of us are not living in the countries of our birth. Saffy says you read English Literature in Cambridge. I did Linguistics. Last night Saffy and I argued about which of our degrees was the most useless. I think I win.

Max Tam

*

'*A night and a day I have been in the deep. In journeyings often, in perils of waters, in perils of robbers, in perils by mine own countrymen,*' Max broke off and looked up at his students. Their eyes were busily trained on the page, their mouths moving soundlessly, trying to form the letters. Where had they all come from? Duc, a Teochew from Vietnam. Mei Ling, from China. Sylvester, an orphan from Cambodia, who had named himself after his favorite cartoon cat. Mr Ng, retired, recently arrived from Penang, who already spoke English but came because his grandchildren left him alone in the daytime and he wanted to be with people.

His students began looking at Max curiously.

'This is a beautiful passage,' said Max. 'Sylvester, would you like to continue reading? Slowly please. Pay attention to forming the consonants. I want to hear you pronounce the 'l's.'

'*In perils by the heathen, in perils in the city, in perils in the wilderness, in perils in the sea, in perils among false brethren…*'

'Thank you. Duc, please continue.'

'*In weariness and painfulness, in watchings often, in hunger and thirst, in fastings often, in cold and nakedness…*'

'Thank you. Try to stress the front syllables. 'Ness' is always soft. In *wea*riness and *pain*fulness…in *cold* and *nak*edness…'

'This part has a nice sound,' said Mei Ling. 'Like a ship going up and down in the sea.'

*

Besides the theater in the basement, which also functioned as a classroom, the clan association had a ground floor which was divided equally into a secular section and a religious section. The secular section had a rosewood dining table, eight chairs, a tea service, a television, and a receptionist's desk. The religious section was a one-room Buddhist temple. A sign reminded visitors to remove their shoes in order to enter the temple. People walked softly on the cold tiles in their socks. Gold buddhas lined the walls. During the day, several monks and lay members could be found chanting softly to religious music issuing forth from a CD player.

The clan association served vegetarian food on Saturday afternoons. Made of simple, inexpensive ingredients, it was often delicious. After Max's class, Max took his students and Saffy upstairs for the free meal.

'What I don't understand is,' whispered Saffy, standing in line with a paper plate in her hands as a volunteer heaped noodles on it with a pair of tongs. 'Why are you teaching them Bible class in this Buddhist place?'

'My dear Saffy,' said Max, unperturbed. 'I'm not volunteering to teach Bible class.'

'You're not?'

'I'm teaching English as a Second Language.'

'But why use the Bible?' said Saffy, as they sat down at the communal table.

The monk overheard. He leaned over. 'We needed free English language books. The church down the street was more than happy to send over a box of brand new Bibles.'

Saffy stared.

'The Chinese are practical people,' said the monk. 'Anyway, if immigrants are seen reading the Bible on buses, they are less likely to be harassed.'

Saffy opened her mouth to argue. Max said, changing the subject, 'Saffy here believes Hua Mulan is a Disney character.'

The monk raised his eyebrows.

'I know she was a real person,' said Saffy angrily. 'I'm not stupid.'

'Did you know the first records of Hua Mulan exist in the form of a poem?' said the monk.

'No,' sulked Saffy.

The monk wrote three Chinese characters in a vertical string on a napkin with a blue fountain pen. 'Can you read?'

'*Wood. Orchid. Resign?*' said Saffy. 'The Wood Orchid's Farewell?'

'Ah, you would not understand the last word, it's an old literary word. *Mu Lan Ci. The Ballad of Hua Mulan*. It's almost a thousand years old. You should read it.'

'I suppose it's some long and musty scroll?' said Saffy scornfully. 'Lost in the mists of time?'

'Oh no,' said the old monk briskly. 'It's quite short. You can print it off the Web. That's where I read it.'

*

Dear Max

Great to hear from you. Dubai is absolutely rotten. Sand storms and no good films. You and Saffy are my sole source of entertainment.

As of last Friday, your Merit Points amounted to 82. Twenty points were deducted because you did not replenish the loo roll after using it in your own bathroom. I told her it was your bathroom which was none of her business, but Saffy apparently conducts spot checks throughout the house.

Saffy's Merit Points are 74,210. To be fair, she's been there a little longer, so she's chalked up more Merit Points. She is quite honest. Last week, she deducted 1 point for leaving her Mulan Doll (whatever that is) in the common area overnight, which you complained about.

Thanks very much for fixing boiler and for forwarding my letters.

I am glad you are getting along with Saffy. I think she's lonely (do not on the pain of death quote me). Has she found a play to act in yet?

English Literature has been marginally useful in banking. Most bankers cannot form an English sentence. I end up writing a lot on their behalf. Most of it is fiction anyway, so I rather fancy myself a novelist at times.

Edward

*

Max came home from the university one evening and found Saffy in the living room resplendent in a glittering Chinese opera costume. She admired herself in the hallway mirror, waving her flowing white sleeves about and making little cymbal noises in accompaniment.

'Where the hell did you get that?'

'Clan association. *Chiang!* Monk said I could use. *Tup-tup-turrup-tup-chiang!*'

'What are you doing?'

'*Chik-chik-chiang!* Practising for my play.'

'You finally found a part?'

'Found a part? *Chiang!*' she repeated, swishing her embroidered robe behind her. 'Found a part? *Chiang!* I *made* the part. I wrote my own play.'

'What are you supposed to be?'

'Mulan, of course. Monk gave me advice. Look, he even lent me this pink feather duster thing. The feather duster's the stage version of a horse. You walk like this, and hold it out, like this, and it's like you're riding a horse! A pink horse!' She demonstrated elegantly, sweeping across the room.

Max cleared his throat. 'I don't think just because the tassels are pink means it's a pink horse, Saf.'

'It's a pink horse. I *love* it. And the best part is, nobody will know whether I'm doing it correctly, because guess what? *Nobody at my school is Teochew.*'

'You look absolutely ridiculous,' said Max, folding his arms, smiling.

*

'O ye Corinthians, our mouth is open unto you, our heart is enlarged,' read Max. 'Ye are not straitened in us, but ye are straitened in your own bowels. Can anyone explain?'

The class giggled nervously.

'Right. Your English must be very good then, because you realize it's funny.'

The students exchanged glances and grinned.

'Actually I'm starting to think your English level far exceeds what I would expect of ESL students. May I ask why do you keep coming every week?'

'Free food!' chorused the class.

*

He heard her weeping.

'Saf?' Max picked his way through the barricade of stuffed animals and knocked on her door.

'Read sign. Obey.'

'I'm sorry, Saf. What's the matter?'

'My step-dad left my mom. He's gone to live in Shanghai with another woman.'

Max tried to recall the little he knew about her family. 'I thought you always said he should leave her.'

'Well, he *should*, she's such a bitch. But she's now saying she wants to go back to Taiwan. She's selling our house in Palo Alto. When I graduate, I will have no home to return to. All my friends – ' she broke off, sobbing.

'I'm sorry.' He sat down outside her door, troubled.

'I can't live in Taiwan. I *can't!* I am American! I don't even like living in London! They spell funny!'

'You're Chinese, Saf. The Chinese live everywhere. Everywhere is home.'

'Lie.'

'No, it's true. Look, there are so many of us in Hong Kong.'

'Never been.'

'Do you know the biggest population of Teochew Chinese are in France? Don't you like Serge Gainsbourg? You could live in Paris.'

'Don't want.'

'You know what Teochew means?'

'No.'

'Think of the characters. *Chaozhou*. Tide province. We are people of the tides, Saf. The world is our home. It's like the Big Bang theory. In the nineteenth century, there was a big bang in southern China, and our people fanned out across the South China Sea, in every conceivable direction, wherever the ships would take them: to Vietnam, Cambodia, Thailand, Hong Kong, the Philippines, Indonesia, Malaysia, Singapore. And then from those places, they just kept on going, except their children, their children's children, could go even further, because now there were planes. So they flew to France, to England, to America. One day we'll be on the moon. You know that clan association's been around for a hundred and fifty years. Why do you think there is one? For people like you. Think of all the people there, every weekend. They got together so they won't be alone. And that's just people from one province! Wherever you are, Saf, you will find us. We have 1.3 billion people in this world. Doesn't that make you feel a bit better?'

'No.'

He leaned his head against the wall. 'I was getting pretty homesick before I moved here. I've really enjoyed living in this house with you.'

She went on crying. Just as he was about to get up and leave, she opened the door. 'Thanks,' she said, sniffing. 'You're not so stupid after all. For a Chinese guy.'

'You're welcome. You're not so weak, after all, for a Chinese girl.' Max looked down and poked a doll on her floor with his shoe. 'Remember, she's a wood orchid. She's beautiful but she doesn't just lie around limply. She's tough, a steel butterfly.'

'Yeah.'

'Have you read the Mulan poem?'

'Yeah. I was thinking of using it for my play.'

'Well?'

'It's kind of boring. I can't use it. I've decided to rewrite the whole story.'

'Like Disney?'

'No. Better than Disney.'

He went back downstairs. Halfway down, he turned and said, 'Hey, do I get any Merit Points for making you cheer up?'

'Five.'

'Ten!'

'Seven and a half.'

'Eight!'

'Alright. Eight. Goodnight Max.'

*

Edward applied for his annual leave from Dubai. At Max's advice, he timed it so that he could go with Max to watch Saffy's play at her university.

'She doesn't have any family to come watch and show moral support,' said Max on the phone. 'It'll mean a lot to her if you can come.'

'I did not want to say this on email,' said Edward, shutting the door to his office. 'But how is it possible that you have not had any sexual relations with her?'

'Have you ever seen her bedroom?'

'I know. It's pink.'

'And her bed! It's full of stuffed toys. You feel like a pedo in there.'

'I remember it had a *few* stuffed toys on it.'

'She's gotten worse. She buys them online. I see the packages. Now there are so many, you can't even see the bed beneath them! Honestly. *Where* does she sleep?'

'*On* them?' chuckled Edward.

'I suspect she sleeps on the floor, actually.'

'I'll come,' said Edward, checking his calendar. 'I think I can take that week off. It's a big Islamic holiday and nothing will get done anyway.' He proceeded to enter Saffy's play in his calendar. '*See Saffy Play.* What's it called?'

'It's a one woman soliloquy. *The Battle of Hua Mulan.*'

*

A glittering red figure stood in the middle of the bare stage, illuminated from above by a single spotlight. She wore an ornate helmet, bristling with pearl orbs, silver filigree and colorful felt pom-poms. Two long pheasant tail feathers, tiger-striped, arched high above her head like soft antlers.

'Where did she get that?' asked Edward.

'Soho,' said Max.

Four yellow and red flags rose behind her shoulders like wings, symbolizing that she was fully armored. Her long hair hung behind her back, tied at the nape of her neck with a thick band of red silk. She clutched a spear with a quivering red tassel at its tip.

'Is she playing a man?'

Max smiled. 'No. We are looking at *Dao Ma Dan*. Sword Horse Woman. Unlike Western opera, in Chinese opera, the role of the woman warrior is part of the official repertoire. She rides horses and leads armies to battle. She is your most beautiful nightmare.'

Cymbals crashed. Offstage, a drum began rat-tat-tatting furiously, played by students from the school orchestra. She swept across the stage in fierce, swift gestures, lifting her feet high, showing off her thick, elevated shoes and flicking her embroidered skirt tails.

'Where did our Saffy learn all that?'

'YouTube.'

The actress posed in the front of the stage, balancing on one foot, her spear extended as the plaintive wail of an old string instrument came from behind the stage. Her traditional shoes made her much taller. She turned her head sharply, and her feathers and shoulder pennants quivered with warrior arrogance. She could have been a Mayan high priest, a shaman of the Inuit. There was no trace of the familiar beneath the thick pink and white paint on her face. She raised her chin and began to speak.

Deirdre Kinahan

THE TRANSGRESSOR

Characters

KEVIN – a choreograper from Dublin, 30

DAMIEN – a struggling heroin addict from Dublin, 34

Setting

A Theatre

363

DAMIEN is waiting for KEVIN. He is agitated. KEVIN enters

DAMIEN: She's gettin' her tits done!

KEVIN: Sorry?

DAMIEN: She's gettin' her tits done Kev.

                    Amanda!

KEVIN: What?

DAMIEN: Chris's Ma.

KEVIN: Chris's Ma?

DAMIEN: Chris! Me son. Me son Kev!

KEVIN: O. Yes. Chris.

DAMIEN: And his Ma's gettin' her tits done.

KEVIN: O…?

DAMIEN: She's goin' to some counsellor…apparently. Says she's psycho coz she's always felt inferior so she's getting her tits done on the social.

KEVIN: On the social?

                    I don't thinks so…

DAMIEN: Yeah, well you never lived with her!

KEVIN: No I mean I don't think you can get your… I don't think you can get an enhancement done on the social.

DAMIEN: What Amanda wants, Amanda gets.

                    You don't know her Kev!

KEVIN: No I don't.

                    No I don't know her Damien and I'm actually in rehearsal.

DAMIEN: You're what?

KEVIN: I'm in rehearsal!

                    I'm in work.

DAMIEN: O the dancin'!

KEVIN: Yes of course the dancing.

DAMIEN: But you said I could call you.

KEVIN: Did I?

DAMIEN: In an emergency.

KEVIN: And is this an emergency?

DAMIEN: You said we could re-connect…that's what you said!

KEVIN: And we have…we are. I mean we are reconnecting Damien but I can't just drop…I can't keep dropping everything with every new crisis…because I've explained to you I'm under pressure…

DAMIEN: Yeah, but.

KEVIN: And this show, my show.

DAMIEN: Wha'?

KEVIN: My dance show, well…success is crucial.

DAMIEN: O yeah…crucial.

KEVIN: Yes, crucial.

DAMIEN: Right.

KEVIN: And we open in ONE week!

DAMIEN: I know I got me ticket.

KEVIN: And in this environment Damien, well, with this recession… the pressure, the pressure on the artist is unreal, it's all about success…

DAMIEN: It has to be good like?

KEVIN: Whatever 'good' is!

DAMIEN: Coz the last one was shite.

            Pause.

KEVIN: Ill-judged.

DAMIEN: What?

KEVIN: Not successful!

DAMIEN: O…yeah.

KEVIN: So I need to focus Damien, that's what I'm saying, I need to focus right now, on this. On my show and on my rehearsal.

DAMIEN: But I thought I was helpin' you.

KEVIN: You were…you are.

DAMIEN: Get back to the 'raw'!

KEVIN: Yes

DAMIEN: To the basic…the base.

KEVIN: Your talk was inspirational…

DAMIEN: I know. Them dancers were blown away…

KEVIN: They were…but now we have to rehearse.

DAMIEN: The moves is it?

KEVIN: Yes, yes…the moves.

DAMIEN: Right…

KEVIN: Thanks.

DAMIEN: It's just that…

KEVIN: I have to get back Damien.

DAMIEN: Okay…jaysus, don't stress!

KEVIN: I am not stressed

DAMIEN: Ya sound stressed!

KEVIN: Please. You can ring. You can just ring me next time and we can arrange…

DAMIEN: But I did ring. That's just it Kev, I was ringin' all mornin'. They even let me ring from the methadone clinic but ya didn't answer.

KEVIN: Because I'm in rehearsal!…

DAMIEN: I mean she never even consulted me Kev!

KEVIN: Who? who never consulted you?

DAMIEN: Amanda!

KEVIN: O God! Right. Amanda.

DAMIEN: I had to hear it down the clinic…

KEVIN: But you're not even an item are you?

DAMIEN: Fuck no! She has me barred three years.

KEVIN: So why are we even having this conversation?

DAMIEN: Because….
            Because Kev. You don't go messin' with yourself.

KEVIN: You don't go what?

DAMIEN: You've got the face that God gave you!
            Or in this case you've got the tits that God gave you. And you
            should be happy with that…with them…

KEVIN: I really…I just don't know what you're talking about Damien.

DAMIEN: It says it in the Bible!

KEVIN: It says it in the Bible?

DAMIEN: Yeah

KEVIN: 'Thou shalt not get your tits done'?

DAMIEN: No!…other stuff…other stuff about skinnin', skinnin' dicks,
            hackin' bits off, stickin' bits on, sure it's all the same isn't it?

KEVIN: Is it?

DAMIEN: Of course it is.
            He says it in a letter.

KEVIN: Who says it in a letter?

DAMIEN: God! For God's sake.
            There's an ex-priest down the clinic.

And he told me.

KEVIN: A priest?

DAMIEN: He's on the phy.
80 mils and in recovery.
We're all in recovery.

KEVIN: Well, of course you are.

DAMIEN: O, do I detect a note of sarcasm there?
A note of cynicism?

KEVIN: No.
No…I'm sorry.

DAMIEN: I hope not. From me own brother!?

KEVIN: Step-brother.

DAMIEN: O right…here we go…always with the 'step'.

KEVIN: No.

DAMIEN: Removin' me.

KEVIN: No look I'm sorry Damien.

DAMIEN: And I wouldn't mind but it was you that put me on to it.

KEVIN: Me?

DAMIEN: Yeah.

KEVIN: Put you on to what?

DAMIEN: Me body.
Me 'essence' as you put it.
And 'acceptance'.

KEVIN: Me?

DAMIEN: 'The body is a gift' you said.

KEVIN: Well it is a gift

DAMIEN: 'A mechanical triumph of tissue and bone and blood and gut'.

KEVIN: True.

DAMIEN: Not something to be messed with!

KEVIN: But…

DAMIEN: But nothin'. I mean look at me Kev. I've abused! I've abused
            and used…debased!…but this body still walks, this body still
            stands. And it was you that made me see that Kev. You and
            your dancin'…this body is me! It's part of me soul, and that's
            something beautiful that is…something to cherish.

KEVIN: O right…
            Good…

DAMIEN: So I think we should say that to Amanda.

KEVIN: We should what?

DAMIEN: Because she needs to love herself Kev!
            She needs to accept the woman she is and be thankful. That's
            what I've learnt, and that's what I'm learning Kev…at the
            clinic…and here. There's healing in what you do Kev…you
            should say that to them critics because I mean I like tits as
            much as the next man but there's too much pressure on birds!
            Skinny ass, boobs, no hips…it just doesn't add up. We want
            them like Barbie but Barbie's plastic…so what's real…what's
            really real Kev?

KEVIN: What's really real?

DAMIEN: Exactly!
            Now you're the good influence, you were always the good
            talker. I should a listened to you, stuck with you Kev, like Da
            always said…then I never would have hit these depths…

KEVIN: Da?!

DAMIEN: He was proud of you.

KEVIN: He referred to me as the 'puff'.

DAMIEN: Now when are you going to let that go?

KEVIN: Let it go!…my own father?

DAMIEN: He was old school…

KEVIN: He loved you more.

DAMIEN: Not true Kev.

KEVIN: It is true.
And then he blamed me...for your...your...disastrous life!

DAMIEN: I don't think so Kev.

KEVIN: He did! Even at the end. He hadn't a word for me...on his
dying breath, it was just you. 'Help Damien! Save Damien!'

DAMIEN: Because he knew you had it sussed.

KEVIN: I have nothing sussed!

DAMIEN: But you do Kev.
You've all this!

KEVIN: It's a theatre!

DAMIEN: And a way of livin'.

KEVIN: O look, I don't, I can't...I just don't have time for this right
now.

DAMIEN: I know.
I understand that Kev.
You have your work.

KEVIN: I do.

DAMIEN: So I'll get Amanda down after rehearsal.

KEVIN: What?

DAMIEN: I'll get her down through Chris, I'll swing it with Chris.

KEVIN: No!

DAMIEN: She likes you Kev.

KEVIN: I've never even met her!

DAMIEN: But she knows you've been on the telly.
And that counts.

KEVIN: No. no. I'm not getting involved in this...

DAMIEN: But she could get hurt!

KEVIN: She won't get hurt.

DAMIEN: There are dangers Kev…in any kind of surgery…risks! In lascerating yourself! And then some of that silicone can leak! Me mate said that down the clinic…Leak! and float off into your glands…your heart…cause breast cancer!

KEVIN: I don't think so.

DAMIEN: And where does it stop? Where's does it stop Kev? That's what I want to know. A boob job here, a nose job there, tummy tuck, arse tuck, slop out me thighs tuck. This shit is addictive…and I know addiction.

KEVIN: Look, she's her own woman Damien…

DAMIEN: O don't give me that Kev. Don't give me that!

KEVIN: It's her choice!

DAMIEN: Choice! Choice! To disfigure herself! Split herself! You don't just wrap that up in feminism Kev – in choice! Because it's panderin' is what that is. Pandering to the age old objectivity of women!

KEVIN: Jesus!

DAMIEN: And they're not just objects – women.
They're people! They're Mothers!

KEVIN: Right.
Well…

DAMIEN: Well…

KEVIN: I never knew you felt that way.

DAMIEN: No, and there's a lot you don't know about me Kev…coz I've got thoughts.
…opinions!

KEVIN: Yes.
Right.
Of course you do.

DAMIEN: So you'll help me here…?

Pause.

KEVIN: Help you? How?

DAMIEN: She's going to Spain Kev.

KEVIN: What?

DAMIEN: Amanda.
She met some bloke. Some bloke called Barnabas and he likes big tits…so she's gettin' her tits done and movin' to Spain… with Chris.

KEVIN: O.

DAMIEN: For permanent.

KEVIN: O.

DAMIEN: And he's me son.

KEVIN: Well of course he is.

DAMIEN: And I don't have much. In fact I have fuckin' nothin'…but he's still me son.

KEVIN: Yes.

DAMIEN: So will ya talk to her Kev?

Pause.

Will ya fuckin'…will ya help me? Coz if she goes…if she goes Amanda…and then Chris! Well, that'll be it then won't it. I'll never see him…and I know I'm fuckin' useless and I know I've never paid nothin' but…I'm tryin'…I'm tryin' now Kev…I'm at the clinic…and we're reconnectin'…and it's something new…I'm tryin' something new.

KEVIN: Okay.

DAMIEN: Wha?

KEVIN: Okay! Okay. I'll try.

DAMIEN: You'll talk to her?

KEVIN: I'll talk to her.

DAMIEN: O that's fuckin' amazin' that is.
That's amazin' Kev

KEVIN: *(Sigh.)* Right.

Can I go now?

DAMIEN: Absolutely...absolutley dance man. Back to them mirrors...
back to the floor and keep it groovin' yeah?...keep it raw!

He does a dance move.

KEVIN: Right

DAMIEN: I'll get her here, get her here for after...

KEVIN: Six.

DAMIEN: Yeah! Six. Coz she'll listen to you Kev...
And if you're goin' that tit angle, I got leaflets...!

KEVIN: Goodbye Damien

DAMIEN: Coz it's not right.

KEVIN: I'll see you at six.

DAMIEN: Six Bro!
...and...thanks.

KEVIN is gone.

End.

Laurence Marks and Maurice Gran

EPHESUS-SHMEPHESUS

ST PAUL'S HOUSE, TARSUS. 25AD – DAY

The large ground-floor room in a middle-class two-up-one-down in Roman-occupied Turkey. The room is both kitchen and living room, with a stove, a small table and chairs and a rickety cupboard. ST PAUL's care-worn mother, MIRIAM, is stirring the chicken soup on the primitive stove. She tastes it, adds some salt and stirs again. She crosses to where we imagine the stairs to be, and shouts up them.

MIRIAM: Saul, you coming down?

There is no reply.

MIRIAM: Saul! Your supper's on the table.

ST PAUL: *(Offstage.)* I'm not hungry, and my name isn't Saul! How many times have I got to tell you, you stupid woman!

MIRIAM: But it's my special chicken soup, your favourite.

ST PAUL: *(Offstage.)* It's not my favourite!

MIRIAM: Since when?

ST PAUL: *(Offstage.)* Since I went to that all-you-can-eat shellfish restaurant in Damascus. The *Plateau de Fruits de Mer* is to die for.

MIRIAM: I am not making lobster, it's not kosher! *(To herself.)* If your father was alive... What you doing up there anyway?

ST PAUL: *(Offstage.)* An epistle.

MIRIAM: In your room?!

ST PAUL: An epistle's a letter.

MIRIAM: Oh.

ST PAUL: Now leave me alone.

There's a knock on the door. MIRIAM opens it to admit RABBI MORDACHAI BEN WARRIS, an ancient, stooped sage, only a little older than his beard.

MIRIAM: Rabbi, thank God!

RABBI: Who else should you thank? *(Sniffs.)* Is that chicken soup I can smell?

MIRIAM: What else should you smell? You want to stay for supper?

RABBI: Do I want to stay for supper? Is the Emperor Roman? You sure you've got enough?

MIRIAM: Enough? I've got more than enough. Especially if his majesty refuses to come downstairs.

RABBI: So what is it? Again with the women's clothes?

MIRIAM: Worse.

RABBI: You want me to speak to him?

MIRIAM: No, I want you to knock some sense into him with a big stick!

ST PAUL: *(Offstage.)* Who you talking to down there?

RABBI: *(Drops voice.)* Don't answer him.

ST PAUL: *(Offstage.)* Mother!? Have you got a man down there?

RABBI: *(To MIRIAM.)* Shhh...if he thinks we're talking about him he'll come down.

ST PAUL: *(Offstage.)* Right! I'm coming down.

RABBI: See?

MIRIAM: You're so wise.

We hear the slap of sandals on the stairs, and ST PAUL enters (though he's not yet a saint, of course, because he's not yet dead).

He's in his early twenties, but already his hair is thinning. He's grown a goatee beard to make up for it. He wears a Roman-looking tunic and, as we said, sandals. He is taken aback to see the rabbi.

ST PAUL: Oh. Rabbi...

RABBI: Saul, your mother's very worried...

ST PAUL: Don't call me that!

RABBI: Call you what, Saul?

ST PAUL: That! Saul.

MIRIAM: I'm sorry Rabbi, I should have warned you. He's changed his name. To Paul.

RABBI: Why Paul, Saul?

ST PAUL: Paul!

RABBI: Sorry, Paul. So what's wrong with Saul, Paul?

ST PAUL: Saul's too Jewish.

MIRIAM: But you are Jewish!

ST PAUL: Yes...and no.

MIRIAM: *(To RABBI.)* See? I've had this all week!

ST PAUL: But then He appeared to me.

RABBI: Who?

ST PAUL: He! Him! With a capital aitch. Our Saviour. On the Road to Damascus.

RABBI: Why were you going to Damascus?

MIRIAM: That's the irony of it, Rabbi. He and his friends were on their way to smash up one of those Christian synagogues...

RABBI: Very commendable.

ST PAUL: They're called churches! And one day they'll name one after me! A big one. With a dome.

RABBI: So if you're not Jewish any more...?

ST PAUL: I didn't say that. I'm still Jewish, but I'm more than Jewish. I've transcended Jewish.

MIRIAM: Can you believe this mishigas?!

ST PAUL: I wasn't talking to you!

MIRIAM: Hear how he speaks to his mother?

RABBI: And this is all because you think you saw Jesus on the Road to Damascus?

MIRIAM: I don't think! I saw Him!

RABBI: You do know the Road to Damascus is the number one mirage location in the whole ancient world?

ST PAUL: It was not a mirage. He spoke to me. He told me to change my name and spread His word. He's the son of God, you know.

RABBI: We're all God's sons and daughters Saul, Paul.

ST PAUL: No! He's the Lord's actual begotten Son. He sits on the God Almighty's right hand.

MIRIAM: Doesn't that give God Almighty pins and needles?

Both men stare at her disapprovingly.

RABBI: Miriam, I expected better of you.

MIRIAM: Sorry Rabbi, but I'm under a lot of pressure here.

ST PAUL: Mother, you've got to say twenty Hail Marys or you'll go to hell.

MIRIAM: Hail who? What's he talking about? You see what I'm up against, Rabbi?

RABBI: I'm confused. If He told you to spread the word, why did you come straight home and lock yourself in your room?

ST PAUL: I've been traumatised! I went blind for three days.

MIRIAM: Blind drunk. They call themselves Disciples – I call them piss artists.

ST PAUL: It wasn't the drink!

RABBI: Ah. I see. Then perhaps the blindness was the Lord with a capital L punishing you for the sin of Onan?

ST PAUL: That's disgusting. I never spill my seed! I'm repelled by all manifestations of the reproductive process. No, I was blinded by the splendour of His golden crown, His gorgeous raiment and His bounteous countenance. *(To MIRIAM.)* His mother was a virgin you know, unlike some I could mention.

RABBI: We are talking about the same Jesus?

ST PAUL: What do you mean?

RABBI: Because I knew him, in Nazareth, in the old days. He was always talking big, but between you and me, everyone thought he was just a very naughty boy.

ST PAUL: He's not a naughty boy, he's The Messiah!

ST PAUL crosses himself frantically and repeatedly.

RABBI: So he said. There were lots of them around back then. You couldn't throw a stick without hitting some self-proclaimed Messiah. I told him, I said Josh, you're entering a very competitive field.

MIRIAM: Josh?

RABBI: Josh, Joshua, that was his Jewish name.

MIRIAM: Jesus was Jewish? His poor mother.

RABBI: Jesus is just a Latinized version, like Paul. Anyway, he asked me to become an Apostle, but I had to pass...

ST PAUL: He asked you?!

RABBI: He asked everyone. Do you think the twelve he got were the twelve he wanted? But people with good jobs, mortgages to pay, families to feed, they weren't about to go tramping around the Empire with some firebrand. Plus between you and me he had personal hygiene issues. Dirty robes, unkempt beard, matted hair. He could raise the dead, but he couldn't comb his hair? And as for his toenails – don't ask! It's all very commendable washing the feet of the poor, but his could have done with a soak once in a while.

ST PAUL: He was forty days and nights in the desert.

RABBI: So? Moses was in the desert for forty years, and the sages tell us he had the feet of an angel.

MIRIAM: As a matter of interest, Rabbi, did Jesus ask any women? You know, to be disciples?

RABBI: Sure, loads. He liked women.

MIRIAM: *(To PAUL.)* See?

RABBI: But none of them fancied going on the road with a randy bunch of farmers, fishermen and fixers. Can you blame them?

MIRIAM: Only Saul, sorry, Paul tells me women aren't up to it. Women can't be leaders, only followers.

ST PAUL: Exactly. Women should be wives, slaves and handmaidens. For as He saith...

MIRIAM: Saith? Suddenly you've got a lisp?

ST PAUL: He saith verily that a wife should subjugate herself to her husband.

MIRIAM: What do you know about wives? What do you know about marriage? *(Third person invisible.)* He sees a girl, he runs a mile If it was left up to him the human race would die out. *(To ST PAUL.)* You may not be spilling your seed but you're definitely bottling it up.

ST PAUL: That's not fair. Didn't I say it's better to marry than to burn?

MIRIAM: When did you say that?

ST PAUL: I think I put it in my epistle to the Corinthians. I've got it somewhere.

PAUL looks around for his tract.

MIRIAM: See Rabbi? He'd rather write to Gentiles than talk to his mother!

RABBI: Don't worry, I'll knock some sense into him. You stir the soup.

MIRIAM moves aside to stir the soup. The RABBI takes ST PAUL by the arm.

RABBI: You happy now? You satisfied? What about 'Honour Your Father and Mother'? Is that no longer the law? You abolishing the Ten Commandments?

ST PAUL: Of course not Rabbi. I don't want to upset her.

RABBI: But?

ST PAUL: But I had a profound revelation and I need to share it.

RABBI: So share it with me.

ST PAUL: But you don't believe.

RABBI: Try me.

ST PAUL: All right. Jesus told me that He was sent by His Father to save mankind, that He was crucified and rose again, that...

RABBI: Hold on, you've lost me already. If he's the Son of God, how can he be executed?

ST PAUL: He died for our sins.

RABBI: How can you kill the Son of God? Isn't the Son of God God?

ST PAUL: Of course the Son of God is God, but God sacrificed his Son to show how much he loves us. And if we all follow Jesus we'll be saved to experience life everlasting.

RABBI: You can guarantee that? Because if you can...?

ST PAUL: It's not for me to guarantee. You've got to have faith, faith, faith –

MIRIAM: The soup's ready. *(Fills three bowls.)*

RABBI: And then all I have to do is stop being Jewish?

ST PAUL: I didn't say that.

MIRIAM: Come and sit down.

ST PAUL: You can be Jewish. But you don't have to be Jewish.

MIRIAM: You want cold soup?

ST PAUL: That's why I was upstairs. Writing a letter to the Ephesians.

RABBI: You've lost me now.

ST PAUL: You see, the word is the Ephesians like the idea of Christianity – mercy, forgiveness, life everlasting – but they don't want to have to become Jews first.

MIRIAM: Typical. What's so special about the Ephesians?

ST PAUL: Ephesus is the second largest city in the Empire. If I can make it there I'll make it anywhere...

MIRIAM: Ephesus Shmephesus, eat your soup.

ST PAUL and RABBI sit to eat.

RABBI: This is great soup Miriam. You don't want to send these Ephesians a letter Saul, Paul, you want to send them some of this soup.

MIRIAM: But I thought Christianity was a branch of Judaism?

ST PAUL: *(Long-suffering sigh.)* Not any more, mother. That's what I was telling the Rabbi. Christianity is a religion of love and forgiveness. Judaism is a religion of fear and obedience. Which one do you think has more chance of going viral?

MIRIAM: Who did you ever love or forgive?

ST PAUL: On top of which, we've got all these rules and regulations which seem frankly ridiculous to sophisticated people like the Ephesians.

RABBI: Sophisticated? They worship Artemis, a multi-breasted virgin huntress!

ST PAUL: How do you know that?

MIRIAM: He's a sage, he knows everything.

RABBI: I've seen engravings. The Temple of Artemis is one of the Seven Wonders of the World. Beautiful building – stupid religion.

ST PAUL: Exactly. They're ripe for conversion. As long as we ease them into it.

RABBI: How do you mean, ease?

ST PAUL: For example, Ephesus is by the sea. They love shellfish, which aren't kosher. Should the grace of God be denied them for the sake of a prawn cocktail? And another thing. Circumcision.

MIRIAM: Not at the dinner table.

ST PAUL: Do you have any idea what a turn-off that is to the average Gentile?

RABBI: But circumcision is our covenant with the Lord.

ST PAUL: You know that, I know that, but the Ephesians are very attached to their foreskins...

MIRIAM: Right, that's it Saul, go to your room!

ST PAUL: Suits me. I'll get on with my epistle.

RABBI: Miriam, with respect, you called me here to get him out of his room.

MIRIAM: Not so I'd have to listen to this filth.

ST PAUL: It's not filth, mother. It's the future. Imagine a world in which we can all pray together, all live together, all eat together.

RABBI: But we don't want to eat with them! We're the Chosen People!

ST PAUL: Who chose us?

RABBI: Your imaginary friend's Father chose us. To be an example to the world.

ST PAUL: And we will be an example. Because the Jews will be the first to embrace the new truth. And then everybody will follow the teachings of Jesus Christ and there will be peace everlasting.

RABBI: I'm not following the teachings of Jesus Christ!

MIRIAM: Neither am I.

RABBI: What's going to happen to us?

ST PAUL: All right, so there'll be a handful of obstinate Hebrews who refuse to see the light. Does it matter?

RABBI: Of course it matters, because as soon as you persuade all these Gentiles to join your club, they'll turn around and look for a handy minority to persecute. And guess who'll they'll pick on?

ST PAUL: Not necessarily.

RABBI: Trust me, it's always the Jews who get it in the neck. The Egyptians, the Babylonians, the Syrians, the Greeks, the Romans, everyone gives us a hard time.

ST PAUL: Maybe we could persecute the Zoroastrans. There aren't many of them.

MIRIAM: There's more than you think. The Asabanas at number 17 are Zoroastrans. Lovely people. I speak to them all the time and what they believe in isn't so different from what we believe in.

ST PAUL AND RABBI: So?

ST PAUL: This would all be academic if you would just accept Jesus as your Lord and stop swimming against the tide.

MIRIAM: I like the Lord we've got.

ST PAUL: You can still have that Lord too. He's the Father, Jesus is the Son, and then there's the Holy Ghost.

MIRIAM: He's seeing ghosts now!

ST PAUL: No, the Holy Ghost. He's the third part of the Trinity.

RABBI: I've heard about this Trinity. I've never understood it.

ST PAUL: It's simple. God exists as three persons but is one God, meaning that God the Son and God the Holy Spirit have exactly the same nature or being as God the Father in every way. The Father isn't the Son, and the Son isn't the Holy Spirit, yet they are all God.

MIRIAM: That doesn't make sense.

RABBI: That's what I said to Josh.

ST PAUL: It's not supposed to make sense. It's supposed to be mysterious. If it made sense it wouldn't be much of a religion, would it?

MIRIAM: You said it was simple.

ST PAUL: It is simple – as long as you don't think about it.

RABBI: I prefer 'Hear oh Israel, the Lord our God, the Lord is One.' At least you know where you stand. We're monotheists and that's the end of it.

ST PAUL: We're monotheists too.

MIRIAM: How can you be a monotheist with three Gods?

RABBI: I think we should all calm down. Can I have some more of this wonderful soup, Miriam?

MIRIAM tops up ST PAUL's soup.

MIRIAM: Of course. Better than lobster, eh Rabbi? Saul, Paul, some more soup?

ST PAUL: No, I've got to finish my letter to the Ephesians. There's a camel-train leaving at day break.

ST PAUL heads for the stairs.

RABBI: Do you think I could take a look at it first?

ST PAUL: You? Why? So you can mock it?

RABBI: I'm an enabler, not an iconoclast.

MIRIAM: *(Admiringly.)* Such words!

RABBI: I'm your old teacher. I know you have trouble with spelling.

ST PAUL: And you won't laugh? Because this could be a life changing event for the Ephesians – and for me. *(Exiting.)* If I play my cards right I could become a saint. *(Goes.)*

MIRIAM: A what?

RABBI: *(Shrugs.)* No idea.

MIRIAM: You really want to read that nonsense?

RABBI: Better safe than sorry. Don't worry. It's probably just a fad. Last year it was the chariot racing, the year before it was the fasting in the desert –

ST PAUL returns with his letter on a long scroll. He hands it to the RABBI, a bit nervously.

RABBI: 'Dear Ephesians, you don't know me so let me introduce myself. My name is...Raul?' Who's Raul?

ST PAUL: I put Saul by mistake, and tried to change it to Paul, and then the nib broke –

MIRIAM: Never mind boobala.

ST PAUL: 'My name is Paul, and I bring you greetings from Judea. How's the weather where you are? It's hot here and very dusty. We had a sandstorm the other night, buried three camels. But anyway, that isn't why I'm writing. The other day a funny thing happened to me on the way to Damascus...'

The RABBI takes the scroll from ST PAUL and continues reading to himself.

He mutters the odd word.

RABBI: Lobster...circumcision...polygamy...

MIRIAM: Polygamy?

ST PAUL: We're a broad church! So what do you think of it so far?

RABBI: Well...it's very, yes, it's not bad...colloquial, chatty, informative...I think you're onto a winner.

ST PAUL: Really? That's wonderful! I think I'll just rewrite the first inch. Don't want to go down in history as Saint Raul. *(Exits.)*

MIRIAM: History! Sure he'll go down in history – as Saint Nudnik. You can't let him send that letter.

RABBI: Why not? It can't do any harm, it's drivel.

MIRIAM: Exactly! I can't bear the thought of those idolatrous Ephesians laughing at my little Saul.

RABBI: It's Paul.

MIRIAM: Not to me.

RABBI: What do you want me to do?

MIRIAM: Help the boy. It's just a letter. At least put it into decent Hebrew for him.

ST PAUL returns with his missive.

ST PAUL: Done it.

RABBI: On second thoughts Raul, Saul, Paul, maybe the tone is, well, a bit too...chummy? After all, you don't know them, they don't know you from a hole in a bagel, you got one shot at changing the culture of the entire Mediterranean Basin...

ST PAUL: What do you mean?

RABBI: Just get some fresh vellum and a new nib, and I'll dictate something.

ST PAUL: Really? Oh thank you Rabbi.

ST PAUL finds what he needs somewhere in the kitchen.

ST PAUL: Ready.

RABBI: Right. Take this down. *(Making it up as he goes along.)* 'Paul, an Apostle of Jesus Christ by the will of God, to the Saints which are at Ephesus...'

ST PAUL: That's smart, calling them saints, get into their good scrolls...

RABBI: '...and to the faithful in Christ Jesus. Grace be to you, and peace, from God our Father, and from the Lord Jesus Christ...'

ST PAUL: Hold on, I've broken my nib. *(Changes nib and then scratches away with his quill pen.)*

RABBI: Put the kettle on Miriam, I think it's going to be a long night.

Curtain.

Chris Goode

THE LOSS OF ALL THINGS

One.

A slightly run-down classroom in a second-rate private school. Present day, but you can't necessarily tell that straight away. At first glance this might be the 80s, say.

A little after the end of the regular school day. Late spring; natural light floods the room.

On one wall, a Times map of the world. It's seen better days.

In a corner, an old human anatomical model showing the muscles and internal organs of the body.

An old-fashioned blackboard covered in chalk writings. Most of the board is taken up with notes from a maths lesson on linear subspaces; it looks much too advanced for secondary school. Traces of previous lessons pertaining to the Industrial Revolution and First World War poetry can still be made out, but these have mostly been erased or obliterated.

There are three people in the room:

MARC, a schoolmaster in his late thirties. Dynamic, focused, a future headmaster in the making.

PAUL and TIM, two year 9 pupils, both thirteen years old, sitting together at desks in the centre of the classroom.

PAUL's breaking the rules on school uniform. He's dressed almost entirely in black: a black shirt, tight black school trousers, heavy black boots, a black-and-white check bandana around his wrist. The only colour is his red and dark green striped school tie; what would conventionally be the front part of his tie is tucked into his shirt so only the smaller half is visible. A crucifix dog-tag around his neck on a thin black cord, worn next to his skin, but we can't see that.

TIM's uniform is by the book, neat, a little stuffy even. Plain white shirt, a grey v-neck sweater that he must be hot in. Only his tie is a little awry.

PAUL and TIM are in detention.

MARC stands behind the teacher's desk at the front of the room, leaning on the desktop. His clothes are sharp, not expensive but immaculate.

Silence. A battle of wills.

Finally:

MARC: Gentlemen, it's your own time you're wasting.

PAUL shifts in his chair.

...Sorry, Paul. I know how you abhor the cliché.
But I want to be absolutely clear. No one's going home until we've got some answers. I'm not going anywhere, you're not going anywhere. It's totally up to you. If it takes all night, it takes all night.

No response from the boys.

Boys, I thought you were smarter than this.
Tim?

No response.

Paul?

No response.

You know, normally I can't shut you up, can I, Paul? And then, not infrequently, we meet here, don't we, in detention. And then I can't get a word out of you.

A sort of scornful grunt from PAUL.

Oh hello. What was that? Little sign of life. Was there something you wanted to say?

PAUL gives him a contemptuous look.

No, come on, let's hear it. You've obviously got something to get off your chest.
Come on, Paul. Spit it out.

Beat; then PAUL puts his right hand out in front of himself, palm up, and, watching MARC all the time, he spits into his hand.

Well there's clever.

PAUL offers the spit in his hand to MARC.

No I think I'll pass, thanks.

Still staring at MARC, quite slowly PAUL sucks the spit out of his palm.

It's a pity. I was rather hoping to get home at a reasonable hour tonight.
Not too much marking tonight. I was looking forward to having dinner with my partner.
I was going to cook.
You'd like my partner.

Pause.

PAUL: What's his name, sir?

MARC: You see! I knew it! I knew you wouldn't be able to resist that one.

PAUL: Where did you meet him, sir? At a club?

MARC: That's the spirit.

PAUL: Was it love at first sight?

MARC: Very good.

PAUL: Or was it more of an animal thing? Just lust was it? Just animal desire?

MARC: Good yes. Very good indeed, Paul. Her name is Jo.

PAUL: No, Joe's a man's name, sir.

MARC: Jo for Joanne.

PAUL: You sure she's not a man?

MARC: Yes.

PAUL: Joanne the Man.

MARC: She's five months pregnant, actually. So...

PAUL: Fair enough. If you insist. Just I always assumed you were a homosexual.

MARC: 'A homosexual'? ...No, well, I'm not.

PAUL: Everyone's a little bit homosexual, don't you think, sir?

MARC: I don't think so.

PAUL: I am. I'm a bit homosexual.

MARC: All right.

PAUL: Quite a big bit. Sir.

MARC: Well, good. But we're straying off topic rather.

PAUL: What did you want to talk about again? I can't remember. I don't think I received a copy of the agenda. Did you Timmy?

MARC: I think we both know what –

PAUL: What were you going to cook, anyway? For your partner Jo. Your lady partner. Your female lady partner.

MARC: Let's talk about the past week. Shall we?

PAUL: Tsk. Always the past, sir! Your fixation on the past. Me and Timmy are the future. The children are the future. You know that song, sir. Whitney Houston.

MARC: Paul —

PAUL: So but what do you want to talk about? From the past week? Is this general behaviour? Or are there specific things you wanted to discuss?

Like did you want to talk about the fire we started? In the bin by the sports hall?

Or the fire alarm. The following day, when there wasn't a fire.

Or singing that hymn too loud and I might, I totally admit, I might have got some of the words a bit wrong. Language is tricky, isn't it, sir? It's a minefield. AT THE NAME OF JESUS EVERY KNEE SHALL BOW and then after that it's all a bit unpredictable. I got a bit confused.

Or did you want to talk about me getting sent out of biology for bleeding everywhere?

Or when I pissed in the shower after games. And piss may have gone on some other people. And it turned out this was all being watched by the head groundsman. He didn't stop me, sir, which I thought was interesting. He just watched until I'd finished and then he shouted at me. I think he thought I didn't know he was watching. So that's sweet of him really, isn't it? In a way.

Or was it me kissing that autistic kid.

Or standing up in geography and not being prepared to sit down again.

Or praying in French. I mean in French class but actually also in French, I prayed out loud in French, which ought to be, whatever the word is. Mitigating.

Or this afternoon when I got a little bit hot doing linear subspace and I had to undo the buttons on my shirt and Miss saw my nipple, sir. She glimpsed it. And she seemed disturbed. Distressed, might be a better word. So you'd have to ask her about that. I mean I'm thirteen, sir, and Miss is like forty, so I feel like that might have been probably illegal, but I'm the one who's in trouble. So, but that's all right.

And then Timmy was getting bullied, weren't you.

Weren't you, baby.

TIM: Yeah.

PAUL: Yeah. And I knocked some heads together.

We've had a busy week, haven't we, sir? Come to think of it. Lots to talk about.

Ah, look, you've loosened my tongue, sir. It's running away with me. My tongue.

Maybe you should call your partner, sir. Maybe he or she should order a takeaway. You said yourself, sir, this could take all night.

Two.

An hour or so has elapsed.

The light has changed: it's a little gloomier out.

MARC's jacket has been placed on the back of the chair behind his desk. His sleeves are rolled up now, his top shirt button undone. He sits on his desk. His manner of engaging with the boys is more eager now but also a little frayed.

PAUL: I was thinking about AIDS, sir.

MARC: Hang on –

PAUL: I was thinking, I was wondering. Like, if I had AIDS. Like not proper full-blown AIDS but, like, HIV. If I had HIV, if I was HIV-positive. Do you think you'd like me more, or less?

MARC: Paul –

PAUL: Or about the same? Like, so I'm not completely dying. I've just got this thing inside me. But I'm doing my work, like a good boy. Head down over my work. A picture of concentration. You know what I'm like when I'm actually being, you know, stretched. When something is stretching me, when I'm being stretched, sir, and I'm hard at work. That snapshot, sir. And you're looking at me in that moment, sir. Sir can I call you Marc?

MARC: No thank you.

PAUL: Maybe it was a blood transfusion. It probably wasn't though, was it. But you're looking at me in that moment, Marc, and you're thinking about your lady partner who's a woman and I've got this virus. Under my skin. And you're thinking, wow, like, wow, that boy's got AIDS. Or HIV. No, AIDS. Just basically AIDS. Like wow he might die. And it probably wasn't a blood transfusion. Do you, I mean, would you like me more? Do you think? Or less?

PAUL reaches his hand out and runs his fingers through TIM's hair.

Or about the same?

Pause.

PAUL moves his hand down over TIM's face and puts his finger up TIM's nose.

TIM giggles.

TIM: Stop it!

PAUL doesn't stop it. TIM continues to giggle and squirm.

MARC: Leave him alone, Paul. Come on. I don't understand what this has to do with the matter at hand.

PAUL: ...Yeah, what...

MARC: We were talking about uniform. I was reminding you of the last conversation we had on this subject, which you seem to have forgotten.

PAUL: No, sir, I remember exactly what you said. *Exactly.* You said I had to make an effort to come to school wearing appropriate uniform.

MARC: Yes I did.

PAUL: Yes sir you did.

MARC: So what happened?

PAUL: *(Gestures towards himself, his clothes.)*

MARC: You look like a stormtrooper.

PAUL: This is my uniform. These are my work clothes.

MARC: But the whole point of the rule about uniform is that you're supposed to look like everyone else.

PAUL: I appreciate that.

MARC: So?

PAUL: So everyone else will come round. Given time.

MARC: *(Smiles, genuinely.)* Funny. But I'm afraid I don't think the school rules are going to come round to your way of thinking.

PAUL: This isn't about the rules, though, is it?

MARC: I'm afraid it is, Paul. Even clever boys like you have to obey the same rules as everybody else. Tim doesn't seem to have a problem wearing the correct uniform. Do you Tim?

No response.

Tim is there anything you'd like to share with us? Any... insight? Perhaps you can inspire your friend to move past this rather trivial rebellion?

Silence.

Tim? You're very quiet. Is there anything you'd like to say?

Silence.

Talk about?

Silence.

How are things at home?

Pause.

Mm?

Pause.

	Tim?
TIM:	All right.
MARC:	All right. How's your mum?
TIM:	...Still dead.
PAUL:	*(To MARC.)* Well done.
MARC:	Sorry. – Tim, I'm sorry, I got confused. It's been a long day. I'm really sorry. How's your dad? How's he doing?

Pause.

All right?

Pause.

Tim?

PAUL:	He doesn't want to talk.
MARC:	Tim?
TIM:	I don't really want to talk. Actually.
MARC:	OK.

Pause.

TIM:	Nothing to say.
MARC:	No?
TIM:	No point saying.
PAUL:	Timmy do you want to tell him what you told me before?

Pause.

TIM:	Yeah OK.
PAUL:	OK.
MARC:	OK, what's that then?
TIM:	...I said to Paul that I love him.

Pause.

MARC: OK.

 Pause.

 OK well that's nice.

 Pause.

 Even though he does all these naughty things? Gets you in trouble?

TIM: *(Very quietly.)* I'm just always in trouble.

MARC: What's that?

TIM: I'm always in trouble anyway.

MARC: Not always. And anyway, you know, we all know, you're not a bad person really, are you?

TIM: Yes.

MARC: No. You're just...

PAUL: 'Easily led.' – Wow, you were actually going to say 'easily led'.

MARC: I was going to say 'impressionable'. I don't think that's unfair, is it? *You've* evidently made quite an impression on him.

PAUL: If he was that easily led, he wouldn't be here in detention with me, would he? All day there are people like you in positions of authority telling him what to do, when to be where, what clothes to put on, what to think, what to feel, and want, and... If he was that easily led, he'd be no trouble at all.

MARC: He at least recognizes that the smart thing to do is play by the rules.

PAUL: Sir, put me in a place where the rules are worth playing by, and I'll follow them closer than anyone. Give me something I can conform to with any pride or dignity and I'll conform with all my heart and soul. Seriously. I'm longing for that. We're all longing for that. I'm not the only one who wears this uniform, sir. That's why it's a uniform.

 Oh yeah this is how we got on to AIDS.

MARC: Is it?

PAUL: Because we seem to spend a lot of time talking about what I'm wearing and it seems like maybe in your imagination you're thinking all the time about my clothes, are you?

MARC: No I'm not Paul. I'm really not.

PAUL: And my body. My clothes on my body. My skin underneath. You know how sometimes you can feel like between your clothes and your skin there's just a kind of static electricity. I really hate my clothes sometimes. Hate my body, hate my clothes. Hate my breathing, like a machine. In and out like a machine. ...So I was thinking maybe you were thinking about my clothes and my skin.

MARC: I'm really lost now.

PAUL: Well that's exciting. That you're lost, sir. Do you want to come and sit with us, sir? We're lost too, sir.

MARC: I think... Don't call me sir. If you're going to do it like that.

PAUL: Can I call you Marc again?

MARC: No.

PAUL: What then?

MARC: Nothing. Don't call me anything.

PAUL: Oh! You *are* lost. Go on. Come and sit with us. You poor man. Come on.

          Pause.

          Are you jealous of Miss, sir? Seeing my nipple like that?

MARC: Paul, what did you say in your careers interview?

          Pause.

          Look there's a certain protocol that kicks in when you say things like that. Even as a joke. I've told the Headmaster I'm certain you were just trying to shock, and he's agreed not to take it any further. But you can't say things like that. Even as a joke.

Was it a joke?

Because most people don't think suicide is a suitable subject for jokes.

PAUL: ...I'm not going to talk about it in front of Timmy. It's not fair.

MARC: Well I'm afraid –

PAUL: It doesn't matter.

Beat.

It's all right, sir, if you are. Jealous of Miss. I don't mind. It's nice to be looked at. Glimpsed, even. Illegally, even.

I'm thirteen years old, sir. I mean Marc. I mean nothing. Thirteen.

My clothes, my skin. What's under my skin. Can't stop thinking about it.

Pause.

That's correct, isn't it, sir?

Pause.

A car alarm goes off outside, several streets away.

A dog barking at the alarm.

Three.

Late evening. Deep blue dark outside, slightly unreal.

MARC is sitting with PAUL and TIM. His manner suggests that he's been drinking, though there's no evidence of what, or how come.

MARC: You know the part I would have liked?

PAUL: What's that, sir?

MARC: Peeling the potatoes. I love it, for some reason. *Love it.* Don't tell Jo-Jo, she'll make me do it all the time. But I do like it. It's very satisfying.

Put the radio on; stand at the sink and look out through the blinds into the street.

Everyone that goes past, you really love them, if you're inside peeling potatoes.

PAUL: Well I'm sorry you're missing dinner because of us.

MARC: ...No, no, you're quite right. No one goes home until we've got some answers. That's what I said, that's what we'll do.

PAUL: If it takes all night –

MARC: If it takes all night, it takes all night. Exactly. *Exactamente.*

Pause.

What were you going to have for dinner?

PAUL: Me? ...I don't know. It doesn't matter.

MARC: What's your favourite?

PAUL: I don't like food.

MARC: You don't like food?

PAUL: It all tastes like...excrement. It's disgusting.

MARC: You don't make it easy for yourself, do you.

Silence.

I was peeling potatoes on Sunday and I cut myself and I thought of you.

PAUL: That's sweet of you, sir.

MARC: What you did in biology. With the scalpel.

PAUL: But yours was an accident.

MARC: Yes. ...Was it? ...You know, now that I think about it, I'm not sure.

(Showing them.) Just there on the tip of the thumb. It was ever so sore. In an interesting way. Where was yours? I wasn't told.

PAUL: ...I'd have to take my shirt off.

MARC: Oh no, don't. This is... I'm probably in enough trouble as it is.

           Pause.

           My mother used to sew her fingers together. She'd sit there of
           an evening in front of the telly and sew her fingers together.
           Watch *This Is Your Life.*

           Pause.

           I am sorry about your mum.
           Tim.
           I'm sorry about your mum.

           Silence.

           Can I put your thingy on? Paul?

PAUL: What?

MARC: On your wrist. I can't remember the word.

PAUL: My bandana? Yeah.

           PAUL starts to take off his bandana.

MARC: I wish I'd had the guts to look like you when I was thirteen.
           You try it for the first time at thirty-eight there's no way you're
           not going to look like a knob. I'm about to look like a knob. Is
           everyone all right with that?

           *PAUL gives MARC his bandana. MARC wants to tie it over his
           face like a mask. It's a clumsy process but eventually he succeeds.*

PAUL: Looks good. Sir.

MARC: Call me Marc.

PAUL: Yes sir.

           MARC goes over to the window to check out his reflection.

MARC: *(Singing.)* 'I am an anarchist... I am...' ...No, I can't even get
           the bloody words right. Oh I look like a knob. ...Do I?

PAUL: You look... Great. You look really sexy.

MARC: Sssh. Don't. What does this remind me of? It's a cartoon or a pop video or something. I can't place it. There's a man going out after dark. With a something-like-this, like a mask or a veil or something. And it's dark and he's walking the streets and it's dark and it's dark and it's dark. Like he's lost but he still knows where he's going. But you think he's never going to get there, wherever it is. And then there's another man. Very beautiful. And they lie down together. It's in a castle or something. There's a close-up on their faces next to each other. He hasn't got his mask on any more, the first one. And the other one, his hair against his forehead. And the two of them sleeping together. One has his head on the other one's chest. And then it's the morning. And there's a close-up of... Ah. Lilies. ...How funny.

PAUL: What's funny?

MARC: If it's a girl we're going to call her Lily.

          Pause.

          We're going for an ultrasound on Friday afternoon. Twenty weeks. They should be able to tell us the sex of the baby. I don't know if I want to know. Jo wants to know. We sort of have to agree to know or...or to not know.

          Beat.

          I'm going to take this off now.

          MARC takes off the bandana and hands it back to PAUL.

          I like not knowing.
          I mean... I like knowing it's a baby.

PAUL: What if it's a deformed one? Would you know by now if it was deformed?

          Long pause.

MARC: That's not very kind.

PAUL: I'm not saying I hope it's deformed. I'm just saying would you know?

Long pause.

MARC: I think I just...want to just... Wait and meet it.

Beat.

Can I ask you... Listen. When you... You know when you prayed. In French. In French.

PAUL: Yeah.

MARC: What did you pray for?

PAUL: Honestly?

MARC: Yeah.

PAUL: ...I prayed for you to try on my bandana.

MARC: *(Laughs.)*

PAUL: *(Laughing too.)* I did! I prayed for you to try on my bandana. And then I prayed for you to want to see what I did with the scalpel. So I'd have to take my shirt off. I'd say I didn't want to but you'd say I had to. You'd say I'd have to do as you say. And you'd say please. Please. So I'd take my shirt off. And you'd cry. And you'd put your fingers on the lines. And you'd kiss the lines.

Not like kissing something better. Like kissing it like you loved it. Like kissing it like it was pregnant with your child.
And I prayed that Miss would be like watching from the doorway.
And the head groundsman would be watching through the window.
And Timmy would be watching on the internet, it would be streaming on the internet, and it would be something that he'd never forget. Like the lines on my body becoming lines in his mind. Like if you scratched your eye, forever.

Beat.

TIM: Yeah I thought that's what you prayed for.

I'm not very good at French but I thought that was it.

Silence.

MARC: What time is it?

Four.

The middle of the night in the classroom.

MARC is slumped in front of the teacher's desk, sleeping.

TIM and PAUL are watching a video on PAUL's phone; the sounds of it can be faintly heard. TIM is rapt but also overtly amused. PAUL is pleased by TIM's reaction.

MARC is talking violently but incoherently in his sleep.

MARC: slut kick harm

The sounds of the video. TIM is beaming.

PAUL: It's good, isn't it.

TIM: It's amazing.

PAUL: Yeah.

TIM: It's really funny.

PAUL: *(Laughs.)* It's not meant to be funny, baby. It's porn. It's meant to make you hard.

TIM: Yeah.

PAUL: You got a little hard on?

TIM: Yeah a little bit.

PAUL: Yeah?

MARC: stray shame

PAUL: Oh for –

MARC: strip light

PAUL: He's doing my head in now.

TIM: Can you show me that one of Jamal?

PAUL: What?

TIM: You know the one you took of Jamal. In the toilets.

PAUL: Yeah. In a bit. Do you like Jamal?

TIM: He's got a good body.

PAUL: Yeah. ...Are you sleepy?

TIM: No.

PAUL: Do you want to see something else?

TIM: Yeah.

PAUL: All right, hang on.

          PAUL looks for a saved video clip on his phone.

MARC: damage you so completely

TIM: It was good what you said before. About AIDS.

PAUL: Yeah?

TIM: That was cool.

PAUL: Good.

TIM: Do you think you'll get AIDS?

PAUL: I don't know.

TIM: ...I think if you had it I'd want it.

PAUL: Baby.

TIM: I think that would be cool.

PAUL: Yeah. That would be amazing. ...Look, here.

          PAUL shows TIM the video clip on his phone. Again, its
          soundtrack can be faintly heard.

So this isn't porn, this one. This is... Can you see?

TIM: Yeah.

They watch the video together.

What does that mean?

PAUL: So this is a place called Lausanne in Switzerland.

TIM: Who lives there?

PAUL: ...I dunno. Loads of people. This is a... So there's this, like, it's called G8, it means Group of Eight, it's eight countries, eight governments, the eight biggest, and they all get together every year for a big meeting. They talk about, you know, money and terrorism and stuff.

So this is a few years ago and all these people, yeah? are like really angry with the G8 because the world's in such a mess. And they're, look, they're angry so they're protesting and smashing stuff up and they've got bandanas and masks and stuff.

TIM: Cool.

PAUL: It's good isn't it. ...You know what that sign means?

TIM: No entry.

PAUL: Yeah, no, the, what he's spraying over the top of the no entry sign?

TIM: No.

PAUL: It means anarchy.

TIM: Oh.

PAUL: It means no one can tell you what to do.

They watch for a while.

TIM: That makes me feel sad.

PAUL: What?

MARC: stain

TIM: That idea.

MARC: kick you so

TIM: That no one can tell you what to do.

MARC: shut down

PAUL: Well... It doesn't matter anyway.

PAUL takes the phone back and stops the video.

TIM: It's good though. I liked it.

MARC: stop to it

PAUL: I'm going to... Seriously.

Beat.

I'm going to wake him up.

PAUL gets up and starts going over to where MARC is sleeping.

TIM: Don't.

PAUL: He's getting on my nerves.

TIM: Don't be mean...

PAUL: Baby I'm not going to be mean, I'm just going to wake him up. He sounds like he's having a bad dream, doesn't he?

PAUL takes a lighter from out of his pocket. He squats down in front of MARC and holds the lighter flame in his face.

TIM: Don't hurt him.

MARC: hurt it out

PAUL: I'm not hurting him, baby, it's a gentle little wake-up.

MARC: stamp on the
            face is
            face is fire
            room's on fire
            disgust bitch

kick it out
room's on fire

MARC yelps, chokes, wakes himself up.

Jesus! The room's on...

PAUL: It's OK.

MARC: Too bright! Take it – ...Jesus!

PAUL: It's OK.

MARC: Take it away. Jesus. ...What time is it?

PAUL: It's really late, sir.

MARC: I was asleep.

PAUL: Yeah. Are you all right? You were saying things.

MARC: What?

PAUL: You were saying things.

MARC: What time is it? Christ. Is the fire out?

PAUL: Fire's out.

MARC: What was I saying?

PAUL: There was a lot of kicking. I think.

           Beat.

MARC: Jesus. Oh God. I... Are you all right?

PAUL: We're fine.

MARC: I need to call her.

PAUL: That's fine.

MARC: I'm going to go... Just need a moment. Into the corridor. Call
           Jo-Jo.

PAUL: Yep.

MARC: And then I'll come back in and we'll get you home, we'll get,
           should I call your parents, or we'll just get a taxi. We'll get you

a taxi. No I can drop you, what am I talking about.

PAUL: He can stay at mine. It's OK. It's all OK. You go and call Joanne.

MARC: Yes.

MARC gets to his feet. He is still a little disoriented.

PAUL: Call Jo-Jo.

MARC: Yes. It's OK. Don't be scared.

PAUL: We're fine. We're not scared.

MARC: Yes.

PAUL: Nobody's scared.

MARC is obviously scared.

MARC: Yeah it's OK. I'll be right back. I just...

MARC goes out. PAUL goes back to sit with TIM. A moment of quiet. PAUL smiles.

PAUL: You all right Timmy?

TIM: Yeah.

PAUL: It's been quite fun, hasn't it?

TIM: Yeah.

PAUL: Don't be sad.

TIM: I'm not.

PAUL touches TIM's face.

PAUL: I think you're so pretty.

TIM: Thanks.

TIM's face is twitching, as if he is going to cry.

PAUL: What's happening in your head, soldier?

Pause.

TIM smiles.

TIM: I was just...wondering. I've been thinking.

PAUL: Yeah.

TIM: You know... When you like... Kill yourself.

PAUL: Yeah.

TIM: Are you still going to do that?

PAUL: Yeah. ...Might not be soon. Might not be for ages.

TIM: Yeah. Yeah only I was thinking...

PAUL: Yeah.

TIM: Maybe instead... I could just, like...

Maybe I could, instead, I could just, like, have you.

Beat.

PAUL: How do you mean, baby?

TIM: I mean... You could come and live with me. In my house. There's like a room at the back of the cellar where my dad just keeps old wood and stuff. I thought you could go in there. And it would be sort of like being dead but I could just, like, have you.

Like to do stuff with.
You could have a little bit of water and a little bit of food if you wanted. But you wouldn't have to eat it. You could get really, you know, skinny, really. I wouldn't mind.
I'd take your clothes away so...you wouldn't have to worry about that.
You could just be there and I could come and visit you and...
You couldn't say anything because you're basically like dead. So I could, like...
Do what I wanted, really.
Like, do... Sort of... Experiments, in a way.

I don't know.

Only cos when I was younger, couple of years ago, and my mum was starting to get ill, my mum and my dad got me a dog. I'd wanted a dog for ages and they said I could have a dog as long as it was me that took care of it and everything.

It was called Shreds. It was a lab retriever. Friendly. Good personality. There were two of them, Shreds and Patches. And they got split up because the owner couldn't cope any more. She had a, um...nervous breakdown.

And it was fine, for a while, having Shreds around, and then I started thinking about how it would be interesting to have a dog that was like a ghost or something. Like it would still follow you around but it wouldn't quite be alive exactly.

So I got this notebook, you know, and I started doing drawings of ghost dogs and weird sort of not-quite dogs and dogs that were made out of rubbish and stuff.

And I drew this one that was like a skeleton dog. But it still worked. You could see its heart or whatever. And I started to think, you know, how much of a dog could you actually get rid of and it would still work.

I was looking it up on the internet and stuff. Like, what's like actually inside a dog?

And there were pictures from like scientific experiments and stuff where there's only, there's not quite a whole dog. It's like, some of it's been cut away. Like when you've started eating a chicken and it's in the fridge the next day.

So I did sketches of these like science dogs. And you could see their skulls or whatever. Their ribs with a heart. Shaped like a proper heart.

Anyway.

It was quite lucky that my mum started getting really ill, in a way, because no one was thinking about Shreds. So I could just... No one was like, where's Shreds?

And then I read this thing about where you take the bark out. Like you can actually debark them, surgically. Or not necessarily exactly surgically exactly. But so then it's just... Because it's easier after that.

But I wouldn't do that to you. Necessarily. But you'd have to promise to be quiet.

But then we could live together. And you could still be basically dead.

You'd be like a ghost but not exactly. Because you'd still have a body. For as long as you wanted. I mean as much as you wanted. Or like just enough or whatever.

It's just a thought. I mean you might not want.

But because otherwise it's a waste.

Silence.

PAUL: Well.

Pause.

We'll see.

TIM: Yeah.

Pause.

PAUL: Thank you for telling me about it.

TIM: Yeah.

PAUL: It's really exciting. Don't be sad.

TIM: I'm not sad.

PAUL: No, well, don't be.

Anyway we can do lots of cool stuff before we start thinking about all that. Can't we?

You can come back to mine tonight if you want and see what we want to do.

Silence.

MARC comes back in. He is still very discomposed.

MARC: Right let's get you home. Come on.

Pause. No response.

Come on. This is... We can't do this. We... This has been really

	wrong.
	We've got to get in the car and go. It's the middle of the night.
PAUL:	Sir. Are you all right, sir?
MARC:	I'm just a bit...

Beat.

	I woke Joanne up. She wasn't very happy.
	And I...
	Just had a, just had a very vivid, um...
	I can't stop shaking.
	But we're just... It's against the rules. So we're just going to get in the car.
PAUL:	Are you sure you're all right to drive, sir?
MARC:	No.
PAUL:	Would you like me to call someone, sir?

Beat.

	Marc?
MARC:	I don't know what to...
	I can't stop shaking. I physically can't stop shaking.

Beat.

PAUL:	You don't have to.
MARC:	I can't stop trembling.
PAUL:	You don't have to. You can just...

Beat.

TIM:	Just tremble, sir.
PAUL:	It's OK.
MARC:	I can't stop shaking.
PAUL:	You don't have to stop.

Beat.

MARC: Boys I can't stop shaking. It's not good.

PAUL: It's OK. We're here.

MARC trembles violently.

The two boys sit together and watch as he trembles.

PAUL reaches his hand out and runs his fingers through TIM's hair again. TIM cuddles up to PAUL.

MARC: I don't know why but...

PAUL: You don't have to stop.

TIM: Don't stop, sir.

Beat.

PAUL: Don't stop, sir.

TIM: Don't stop.

Beat.

PAUL: Don't stop.

Beat.

Blackout.

Zukiswa Wanner

UNCOOL RELIGION

Zukiswa Wanner, a writer, to Paul – wherever you may be.

So I was talking to my Catholic priest friend Caspar, and he tells me, twenty centuries later, there still seems to be some dispute that you may have written this letter to try and proselytise the Christian faithful at Colosse. Be that as it may, I shall respond to that letter as though you did in fact write it.

This will probably be a long response as I have to put a few things in context for you. It has been a long time since you were around after all. We travel on these winged birds called planes now and other vehicles called cars. The chariots of your days? Gone. Only ever used for some royal weddings. As the undisputed guy who brought religion to the Gentiles, you would have reached more lands and perhaps converted more people to Christianity in a shorter time than it took you back then.

And now that I have talked about Christianity, let me jump right in and enlighten you because I suspect that you are curious to know whether the Christian religion you started to spread managed to go very far.

I have to tell you Paul, you did a brilliant job. If you were in contemporary times, I would totally want you as my head of state because if you could make as great an ambassador for my country as you did for that religion we now call Christianity, my country would be a super power I tell you. And power Paul, as many contemporary heads of state would tell you, is sweet. But I digress. I was commenting on the success of your venture. Christianity did so well it managed to come all the way to the country I am writing from – a country called South Africa which is about 3000 kilometres south of Egypt, a place you perhaps heard of during the course of your journeys. The religion is in fact, worldwide. The faithful at Colosse who you wrote the letter to though, are not such great Christians as the Africans, Asians and South Americans. Perhaps it is because they are economically better off (although the Greeks currently have their financial issues. Maybe they will return to your Christianity?). It is very strange Paul. The poorer the people the more they are likely to believe in God. So many poor people are Christians then? Nuuh. There are two other monotheistic religions Paul. For starters, the majority of your fellow Jews never really bought into the whole Christianity thing. Perhaps Peter was just not as good a proselytiser as you were, dude? Oh and the third religion? A few centuries after your death, a new one sprung up. They believe Christ was a prophet but they believe the greatest prophet is a guy called Mohammed. And like the Jews, they do not eat pork. They clearly never read your letter to the Colossians. That bit about 'let no man judge you in meat or in drink' Paul? Spot on.

So anyway, now we have these three major religions: Judaism, Christianity (yours Paul), and Islam. They all really have the same root believing as they do in one God who they call by different names – Yahweh, God, and Allah but I tell you if you were here now you would not believe it. In your native Palestine Paul, the Moslems and the Jews are killing each other on a frequent basis (to be honest the former are being killed more than the latter) and here in Africa where both religions came later than elsewhere, Christians and Moslems are constantly and sometimes senselessly killing each other. Some guy in some European country draws cartoons of Mohammed? Hey, another reason for Christians and Moslems to slaughter each other in Africa. I tell you Paul, it is this type of behaviour makes me say, 'thank God I am agnostic.'

Sometimes when I read your letter Paul, I cannot help but think how prophetic you were. Maybe you sounded so prophetic because history repeats itself? I keep thinking about that 'beware lest any man spoil you through philosophy and vain deceit,' how did you know that Dawkins would be coming? Wow. I am impressed in spite of myself.

But at other times I realise what ancient times you lived in. 'Servants, obey in all things your masters according to the flesh...' and, 'Wives, submit yourselves to your husband' ...Really Paul, really?

And yet I must tell you too that although much has changed on the workers' rights and gender front, we still have far to go. Many servants have corporate companies as their masters and you would be amazed at how much those corporates own them so perhaps, the servants are still listening to your injunction although I would be hard-pressed to find many who have read your work. From the cleaner in a car assembling plant in South Africa, the coffee picker in South America, to the call centre worker in India and the stockbroker in New York, some of the conditions these workers are under are terrible. It is when I hear some of these horror stories that I, for one, am glad to be self-employed although every now and again, my empty fridge beckons and makes me want to give in to being a servant.

And now for the wives submitting to their husband bit. Oh dear. Many a woman who has done that on this continent and elsewhere has ended up dead, Paul. There is, you see, this big disease with a small name that is doing the rounds. Men may sometimes work in cities while their women are in the villages. During their times in the cities, they go around with women of the Mary Magdalene variety, possibly contract this disease and when their wives 'submit' on return to the village, tragically we have nations of orphans. Nay Paul. If you were writing today I would tell you to change that to 'wives, do not submit yourselves to your husbands except through your own choice.' Because you see Paul, like I mentioned earlier, the greatest followers of this Christianity of yours are poor people and they quote you verbatim. In fact, if I had a Rand for every time some Christian has said, 'According to Paul,' guy, I would never have an empty fridge.

Oh and you may want to know…that is not the only place where sexism exists. Whereas I, as a woman, am writing this response to you which may be read and performed on stage and listened to by people of all genders, the Church that you left behind – that is now called Catholic, does not see it fit for me (or any woman in case you are remembering my agnostic claim bit) to do the same in front of a congregation. Not only that, but that same Church does not recognise love between people of the same sexes, and insists that married women should not use contraception despite the limited resources the world has (Ehhh, contraception is something that people use to prevent pregnancy. It may sound strange to you but from your letter twenty centuries ago, I am pretty sure if you were to wake up today, you would catch up in no time). There is more I could say about the way Christianity is interpreted by the different Christian branches but you would need to be here to believe it Paul.

If Father Caspar is wrong and you for one have no dispute about having written that letter to the Colossians or indeed any of the Christian faithful of the world, I am curious to know how you would write it today with the little information that I have given you above. What would be your stance on women, on workers and employers, on Christianity itself? Because you see Paul, though this letter of yours was written while you were in prison in the 1st Century, it has, since its discovery and incorporation into the book that is known as the Bible, served to be a prison of its own for many human beings. Do you have any regrets?

This salutation by the hands of Zuki. Remember our bonds you wrought the world through your letter to the Colossians.

Amen.

DC Jackson

PAUL'S FIRST VOICEMAIL TO THESSA

This is a piece to be spoken but is an audio only experience. So either the audience are in the dark or it's a pre-record or live actors hidden or some other more inventive device. This is not a play for the eyes. Sound only.

PAUL: Fucking voicemail. It's just her voicemail.

THESSA: Hi you've reached Thessa. Sorry I can't take your call just now. But if you leave your name and hat size I'll get back to you. Bye bye big head!

PAUL: Thessa? Thessa it's Paul. It's Paul. HELLO! Sorry. You're sleeping. I shouldn't have called. I hope your phone is on silent. I hope I didn't wake you. You always have your phone on silent when you're in bed anyway. I'm sorry you're in bed. Sorry. Start again. HELLO! I'm sorry you're sleeping. What time is it?

Checks.

Oh it's late.

I just wanted to say that I'm so lucky to have you baby. I fucking love you. I fucking love you and I am so lucky that you love me. I am the luckiest man in the street. HELLO!!! And I'm not alone even though it's late – the street's not empty it's busy – Tim's here and Silas. And Tim's here with some bird.

TIM: Julie.

JULIE: Marie.

PAUL: Julie. Tim's here with Julie and Silas is here too.

SILAS: Hello Thessa!

PAUL: Everyone here misses you. And it's not just us I don't mean just us – there's a *black* man on the other side of the street. I don't know if he misses you but he would if he did know you. Because you're amazing. I love you so much. We've just had a kebab and I wanted to phone you and say…

I know that we're so far apart, geographically, and I know that it isn't ideal. I mean, I know that it's shit, it's shit to be apart isn't it? But you know that I'm always thinking about you. Always. And if you're always thinking about me then that means we'll be okay. You are always thinking about me aren't you? Always? Because baby you know that I'm a good man and I behave in a good way. You know that I'm not running around cheating on you or anything like that and you know that I never would. And I know that sometimes you think I'm being a bit controlling or whatever but it's only because I care about you so much baby and I just want the very best for you.

SILAS: Come on Paul. Let's get a cab.

PAUL: Fuck off Silas.

You're not cheating on me are you baby? Because you're the only one for me. You're my girl and I love you. More than love you. I'm devoted to you. And I don't think you are cheating on me, I mean, I'm pretty sure that you're not cheating on me.

TIM: Seriously mate let's make a move.

PAUL: Fine, fine, alright Tim. Just hail one and I'll hang up when it gets here – alright? Is that okay with you?

I know you're not cheating on me baby. Because when would you have time, with your job and everything and your evening classes. You're too busy growing to be cheating. You're improving yourself and I am so proud of you doing that baby, I am proud of you. And I trust you so much. You're not cheating though are you? No. I know. I know.

You haven't seen that Gavin recently? I know he's just – like –

your gay mate but that guy wants in to your pants. Seriously. I totally don't mind you having a gay mate, honestly – it's the nineties – I'm not prejudiced or anything but I do think that your gay mate should actually be gay and Gavin isn't is he? He's poofy – sure he's poofy but he isn't actually homosexual.

And I fucking know that he fancies you.

Oh. Bollock. I've hung up.

THESSA: Hi you've reached Thessa. Sorry I can't take your call just now. But if you leave your name and hat size I'll get back to you. Bye bye big head!

PAUL: Sorry I hung up, it was a mistake. My fat cheeks pressed the disconnect button. And I'm sorry I've been getting all crazy about that Gavin. Why wouldn't he fancy you? You're beautiful. You're amazing. And I know that he is just like a little weasel or something...

...but look – shit – sometimes those weird weedy weaselly guys manage to score. Look at that fucking Lembit Opik.

Oh god, listen, listen, baby please, I do realise I am sounding like some kind of paranoid lunatic but it's just that I'm so crazy about you. I love you so much. And I don't mind if you still see that Gavin, it's fine. I don't mind. I know that he's your pal, I know that, and I know that there is nothing going on between you two. I'm sorry, I'm being possessive. But I'll work on that baby, I promise you, I'll work on that and stop being a possessive lunatic.

I wish you were awake.

TIM: Hello Thessa. We all miss you.

PAUL: Oh, Marie doesn't look too pleased at that – she's got a face on her. Cheer up Marie.

JULIE: It's Julie.

PAUL: Alright Marie – she doesn't give a fuck love.

Hi – it's me again...oh fuck, I've just hung up again.

THESSA: Hi you've reached Thessa. Sorry I can't take your call just now. But if you leave your name and hat size I'll get back to you. Bye bye big head!

PAUL: Sorry abut that. Sorry. I'm a bit drunk. Listen I just wanted to make sure that you were alright. After my last visit. I'm sorry I had to go. Stuff keeps getting in the way. You know that I am CONSTANTLY thinking about you. We belong together. Just be patient baby. We are going to be together for ever. And it's going to be perfect. So just hold tight. And go to work and keeping doing your evening classes…

          …and baby? Please don't drink – I can't stand drunk women, it makes them look so unattractive and it loosens their morals.

JULIE: Fuck you. Dick.

PAUL: Oh all right Marie. You're actually just proving my point there.

TIM: Steady on mate.

PAUL: CAN EVERYONE JUST PISS OFF AND LEAVE ME ALONE FOR A SECOND, I'M TRYING TO SAY GOODBYE TO MY GIRLFRIEND.

SILAS: That's us got a cab Paul.

PAUL: I love you baby. OH FOR FUCK SAKE, I'VE HUNG UP AGAIN. DO I HAVE TO HOLD THE PHONE ABOUT A MILLION MILES AWAY FROM MY FUCKING CHEEKS OR WHAT?

TIM: Come on Paul, get in the taxi.

THESSA: Hi you've reached Thessa. Sorry I can't take your call just now. But if you leave your name and hat size I'll get back to you. Bye bye big head!

PAUL: Sleep well baby. I love you. Goodbye.

SILAS: Finally.

PAUL: Fuck off Silas. I've warned you.

TIM: Right – can we please go?

PAUL: Uh hu, right.

             PAUL's phone rings.

SILAS: What is wrong with you pair?

PAUL: Hi baby. I thought you were asleep. I'm so glad you're up. I
             really wanted to speak to you. I LOVE YOU BABY.

THESSA: Don't ever phone or contact me again.

PAUL: What? What are you talking about? Thessa? Baby?

             I must have disconnected by mistake again.

             Come on, come on…

THESSA: Hi you've reached Thessa. Sorry I can't take your call just now.
             But if you leave your name and hat size I'll get back to you.
             Bye bye big head!

PAUL: Her phone's off now.

SILAS: Fuck it, plenty more fish in the sea.

Christopher Shinn

FALLING AWAY

Characters

TOM

ANNA

Time

Now.

Place

A public place. Others are nearby.

…that day shall not come, except there come a falling away first…

1.

TOM: It makes you wonder.

ANNA: What.

TOM: How narcissists get to these positions of power. I mean, when it's so transparent.

ANNA: Isn't it that the people above them are narcissists?

TOM: Yes, you're right.

ANNA: And so they choose in their image.

TOM: But this gulf. Between the narcissists and everyone else. How do you explain that?

ANNA: Why are some people self-centered and others not?

TOM: Yes. It seems so extreme. I mean, to be told to do something by someone – and then three hours later for her to have forgotten what she told me to do and begin berating me for something I didn't therefore have time to do – I mean, I just can't understand.

ANNA: Understand what?

TOM: What goes on in her brain. Obviously she's competent. She's charming. But these are severe cognitive limitations. Forgetting – flying into a rage – basic lack of empathy –

ANNA: It's mysterious. The way I try to learn about it is to pinpoint the moment things fall apart.

TOM: What do you mean?

ANNA: When I'm styling a model – it can take time and because at that moment I'm the centre, this relatively insignificant person – people can begin to act out. The photographer says something inappropriate, the model begins to sulk, someone begins talking loudly on their phone or interrupting with nonsense – it's all going on, but it hasn't exploded – and when it does explode I try to understand why, what happened in that moment –

TOM: You mean what prompted it.

ANNA: Yes. Because there are so many narcissists there! And I wonder why a certain moment will cause one of them to decide that's it, they now have to act out extravagantly –

TOM: Well you're in fashion, which has a different hierarchy than what I do. In the investment group, there's one boss. The rest of us are not allowed to be narcissists. In what you do –

ANNA: Do you think that's why you aren't, though? Only because you're not allowed?

TOM: No, I'm not like that. I know I'm not.

ANNA: – Do you have to go?

TOM: I do.

ANNA: We've been here a long time I just realized –

TOM: Well there's something I've been wanting to say to you.

Pause.

I'm not trying to manipulate you by anything I'm going to say. As your friend I have to tell you that you don't seem well to me –

ANNA: I'm all right –

TOM: Things are obviously not improving –

ANNA: I'm all right –

TOM: You haven't said a word about him. The relationship is not working, clearly. You're throwing your life away. I'm right here. We're in love with each other.

Pause.

ANNA: I did want to see you. I think you – knew the parameters.

TOM: I know what you must still be telling yourself they are. But I can't believe that's all you truly want. To have some desiccated friendship when we both feel the passion we do.

ANNA: I know. I'm sitting here and I feel it again, I still feel it. I want it. I do.

Pause.

TOM: I understand that you love him and that you are a good person. I think by now you've established that – no one could say you are not that –

ANNA: Things are not changing.

TOM: No? He's still depressed?

ANNA: Yes. And he hasn't been able to find work – and he's not presenting himself well –

TOM: So it's even worse.

ANNA: Yes. He's started to become very mean.

TOM: How?

ANNA: He's become contemptuous.

TOM: In what way.

ANNA: Subtle ways. He won't do dishes, won't look after the cat. Leaves things lying around…

TOM: You said contemptuous… There must be more –

ANNA: He claims I don't love him. That I'm going to leave him, that it's obvious –

TOM: My God. When you have stuck by him –

ANNA: Yes. Or he says that my job is easy so I can't understand what it's like for him –

TOM: Your job is not easy – all those crazy people! Meanwhile he has no job at all –

ANNA: He feels being an artist, even if you're not working – is a job.

TOM: He's an actor.

ANNA: He considers that an artist.

Pause.

It's so painful to see you. Which is why I asked that you not contact me anymore the last time we saw each other… But when you emailed me yesterday… I just became happy. Something inside me that is just not within my control, just – and I wanted to follow it.

TOM: Keep following it. Why don't you?
You've been so good to him. You've given him every chance.

ANNA: It's only been one year –

TOM: One year!

ANNA: I've had rough periods –

TOM: Not like this. A few weeks I imagine – at most a month or two. Am I right? Did he meet anyone when you went through those periods? No, he didn't – because in those times I bet you were still caring and loving towards him –

ANNA: We met because – you think you and I met because –

TOM: Because of his retreat from you, yes. You're a good person. You wouldn't have opened up to me that day if he hadn't shut something down in himself, in your relationship –

ANNA: No. There was something in me that wanted – that has always wanted. It wasn't just because he –

TOM: So you mean that every day of your life you went around wanting and never acted on it – and then one day, randomly you decided to act on it, for no other reason than –

ANNA: I don't know.

Pause.

TOM: With how much – when we talk about the selfishness and greed in the worlds that we're in…and we're two people who have worked so hard to not – for decency in ourselves – to deny yourself the love and care we could give to one another –

ANNA: I know. I know.

Pause.

TOM:	But you say that and I can't tell what you mean. Are you resigned? Are you pondering?
ANNA:	I want you so badly. I don't think I've ever wanted something so fiercely in all my life.

Pause.

TOM:	That's new to me. You know you've never said that –
ANNA:	I know.

Pause.

TOM:	I know at one point he was good to you. For a long time. I think – however long you want to take. To do it. Would be fine with me.
	Even if it were – I don't know how much time you think you would need. Because I know you don't want to hurt him –
ANNA:	I love him. He is a caring man, I think he is a good man, I do –
TOM:	Of course. And he would be distraught I'm sure – I know it might take a long –
ANNA:	He is distraught. He is.
TOM:	He – you mean – you told him? You told him about your feelings for me?
ANNA:	I felt I had to.

Pause.

TOM:	When? Why didn't you tell me you told him?
ANNA:	I don't know. I…felt it might give you hope. Last week.
TOM:	It – I think it gives me the opposite. You told him – what – that –
ANNA:	That I had met someone in a coffee shop a few months ago – that I'd fallen in love with.
TOM:	So now he can get better. He can treat you better. Now that

there's competition.

Pause.

ANNA: There was no reason to tell him other than feeling it was the honest thing to –

TOM: Why. We never touched each other, we never even kissed – everything was up front and spoken about, everything was appropriate –

ANNA: He could feel something and it felt cruel to not validate –

TOM: Why do I care why – you did it. You told him.

ANNA: I don't believe it's changed anything. He's still – that's your worry – that now he'll –

TOM: Who cares what my worry is. Why do you care what – I don't understand what you're saying to me now, I don't understand the point of these communications.

ANNA: I just want you to know – I told him because I felt he should know. Not to motivate him –

TOM: And you didn't tell me because you didn't want to give me hope. Then you told me.

ANNA: Initially – I thought – that you might think that it was the first step.

TOM: To your leaving him. No. I feel like that's the kind of thing you tell someone to come clean, to be able to move forward with them.

Pause.

Anna. We have an opportunity to love each other, to bring each other joy. To truly care for one another. I've never felt this way about anyone in my life, anyone on this earth.

He will never get better. I know him. I know men like him. They only become more spiteful. They seem decent, then something breaks in them and they never come back.

	I would wait for a very long time. If you feel that you owe him that. If you owe it to him to see him through –
ANNA:	Do you know how much I want it.
TOM:	– Why do you ask that?
ANNA:	It's important to me that you know. Because it affects me – when you tell me you want me more than anyone you've wanted. I want you to know that I know what this is like –
TOM:	I've lost. It's clear to me now. I'm not going to beg you. I really – I will simply say that part of me will be expecting you to come and will wait for you for a long time. All right? You need to know that. Because I do love you and I sympathize with everything you are going through. Can I ask you just one question. It won't impact that I'll wait for you. I'll wait anyway –
ANNA:	Yes.
TOM:	Is there a chance.
ANNA:	That I'll leave him for you?
TOM:	Yes.

Pause.

ANNA:	No. I'm sorry.
TOM:	Tell me why. Not why you won't leave him, but why no chance. If he's to get worse – if you're to become even more miserable –
ANNA:	I don't know if I can say why –
TOM:	You have to. This is life. Why!

Pause.

ANNA:	I don't believe it's because I'm a masochist. I know you think that's it –
TOM:	I don't.
ANNA:	Well –

TOM: I think you love someone – I understand that you love him –

ANNA: That's why I can't – … I imagine my life… I imagine leaving this person –

TOM: I know he's suffering –

ANNA: I don't know what I think life should be. Or is. I don't know what – that what you say we'll do for each other – sometimes I think – the same thing could happen –

TOM: No. It would never. Never with me –

ANNA: Even if it would never. I don't… I don't think this is life.

TOM: This…what we feel –

ANNA: No. I think it's something else.

TOM: What then. What is this.

ANNA: It might feel like love…but I think it's – closing something down.

TOM: Closing – what down?

ANNA: Closing – what I thought of life as – what I think it is, what I believe about commitments and trust and care… And instead choosing something so much smaller –

TOM: Smaller? What? It would be forever. It would be huge. It's love! I would marry you –

ANNA: I have to not go down this road. I have to go back. I have to accept that that is what life is.

TOM: Even. Even if it were to get worse.

ANNA: It might get better.

TOM: I don't say this to be cruel, it's just a fact. It won't.

ANNA: Even then.

TOM: You would rather it get even worse. Miserable as you already are. Because of your beliefs about what life is.

Pause.

All right. I've heard all that. I understand it. But I'm going to ask you one more time. Because sometimes good people think things and say things because they're good people, not because it's what they really feel. I want you to tell me what you really feel.

Is there ever a chance. Anytime. At any point. Is there a chance that you will come to me and tell me you love me and wish now to be with me?

Pause.

ANNA: No.

David Edgar

CONCERNING FAITH

Paradise is three gold chairs on which sit three sixteenth-century Bishops: Hugh LATIMER, Matthew PARKER and Cuthbert TUNSTALL. PARKER and LATIMER hold books, TUNSTALL a file of letters.

LATIMER: Good friends. Men oftentime ask the true fruit of the scripture. For you – as godly men, as yet still trapped and bonded by the flesh – such fruit is sweetest sustenance. We herein shew a true example of a man of faith. We speak of Master Thomas –

PARKER has raised a finger, indicating that the three men should introduce themselves.

PARKER: Forgive me. You are Master Latimer.

LATIMER: I am so.

PARKER: You were Fellow of Clare College, Cambridge, University Preacher and Chaplain, and latterly Court Preacher to King Edward the Sixth.

TUNSTALL   And Bishop of Worcester.

PARKER: Verily. For all this, you are best remembered for your last words.

LATIMER: *(Tapping the book on PARKER's lap.)* As they were herein set down.

A wry look between the three men.

PARKER: *(A look to TUNSTALL.)* Whereas...

TUNSTALL: My name is Cuthbert Tunstall. My study was mathematics, theology and law at the Universities of Oxford, Cambridge and Padua. I was Canon of Lincoln, Archdeacon of Chester, Lord Keeper of the Privy Seal, Bishop of London, and of Durham.

PARKER: Under three monarchs.

TUNSTALL: Under four.

PARKER: An accomplishment, in the middle years of the sixteenth century.

TUNSTALL: Indeed.

Another wry look.

For all this I died in prison.

PARKER: Whilst I am Matthew Parker. I was Fellow and later Master of Corpus Christi, Cambridge, Chaplain both to King Henry and Queen Anne, Prebendary of the Cathedral Church of Ely, Vice-Chancellor of Cambridge, Dean of Lincoln, stripped of my appointments under Queen Mary, preferred to the Archbishopric of Canterbury by her sister, Queen Elizabeth.

TUNSTALL: And yet, for all this preferment...

PARKER: I died in my bed.

LATIMER: We speak notwithstanding of a man who will likely be less known to you.

PARKER opens the book.

PARKER: Master Thomas Bilney.

TUNSTALL: Little Bilney.

LATIMER: Or rather as I knew, loved and thought him, no lesser than Saint Bilney.

Pause.

Slight in stature, slender of body, taking commonly but one meal a day, giving the remains to those in prison, sleeping but four hours a night, abiding no swearing nor singing.

PARKER consulting the book.

PARKER: A man like all of us brought up in the University of Cambridge.

TUNSTALL: Profiting in all kinds of liberal sciences.

PARKER: But at the last, having gotten a better schoolmaster,

LATIMER: Even the holy spirit of Christ,

TUNSTALL: Under circumstances he was latterly to reveal,

PARKER: He converted many unto that cause.

TUNSTALL: Amongst them, Master Latimer.

PARKER and TUNSTALL look to LATIMER.

PARKER: *(Prompting, from the book.)* Being at that time...

LATIMER: Being at that time as obstinate a papist as any was in England. Insomuch that when I was made bachelor of divinity, my whole oration went against the Lutherans and their opinions. Young Bilney heard me at this time, coming to me afterward in my study, and desiring me, for God's sake, to hear his confession. I did so; and, to say the truth, by that confession I learned more than before in many years. So from that time forward I began to smell the word of God, and forsook the school-doctors and such fooleries.

PARKER: Shortly after the which time, Bilney forsook the university, going rather into common places, teaching and preaching, within doors and without, shaking and reproving the excessive pomp of the clergy, and plucking at the authority of Rome.

LATIMER: For which he aroused the ire of Cardinal Wolsey, and,

PARKER: being pulled from a pulpit at Ipswich,

LATIMER: was arrested,

PARKER: and summoned before the said cardinal and a great number of bishops,

LATIMER: Amongst them, Master Tunstall.

PARKER: Who received from him a letter...

TUNSTALL takes out a letter and reads.

TUNSTALL: 'Most reverend father in Christ, I think myself most happy that it is my charge to be called to examination before your Reverence, for that you are of such wisdom and learning, and such integrity of life, which all men do confess to be in you'.

PARKER: Whereupon the Cardinal inquired of Master Bilney whether he had preached or taught to the people the opinions of Luther, contrary to the determination of the church: whereunto Bilney answered that wittingly he had not preached or taught any of Luther's opinions.

TUNSTALL: Whereupon the Cardinal did call witnesses against Thomas Bilney and, being otherwise occupied about the affairs of the realm, committed myself and my lords the Bishops of Rochester and Ely to proceed against him.

PARKER: *(From the book.)* Asking if he believed the assertions of Luther justly and godly condemned, and that Luther was a wicked and detestable heretic? And whether images of the saints christianly set in churches ought to be observed? And that we are bound unto obedience to priests, as to our parents? To all of which he answered affirmative.

TUNSTALL: *(Taking the book.)* But bringing also witnesses, who swore that he had preached that it was a great iniquity to petition saints, and a great folly to go on pilgrimages, and that there had been no good Pope in five hundred years.

LATIMER: For which cause you did pronounce him convicted of heresy.

TUNSTALL: And did beg him to consider that he might revoke these sayings.

LATIMER: Commanding him to confer with his 'dear friends' on the matter.

TUNSTALL: Hoping thereby to spare his life and soul.

PARKER: And succeeding.

TUNSTALL: Verily, in that on the third day he returned and answered that he had been persuaded by his friends that if his life was spared, he could do greater service to the Lord, and so recanted.

LATIMER: Thereby proving that it is better for a godly man to abjure his friends, for it is they that shall undo you.

TUNSTALL: And was enjoined that for a penance he should walk bareheaded to St Paul's,

LATIMER: Carrying a faggot upon his shoulder,

TUNSTALL: And to abide in prison for two years, from whence he came again to Cambridge.

LATIMER: In agony. Overcome with remorse. Taking no comfort. In such anguish that his friends were afeared to let him alone.

TUNSTALL: But yet alive.

LATIMER: Until, one evening at ten o'clock, he did gather up his friends together. His true friends. And told them that he had resolved to give over his life for the confession of that truth which before he had renounced. Being determined that, like one rising from the dead, he would 'go up to Jerusalem'. And so he set forth once more to preach in houses, amongst simple people, in the fields.

PARKER: Saying: 'Put away your golden gods, your silver gods, your stony gods, and leave your offerings, and lift your hearts up to the sacrament'.

LATIMER: For which 'offence' he was once more taken,

PARKER: Thrown in prison,

LATIMER: Examined and condemned,

PARKER: Degraded from his office,

LATIMER: According to the custom of their popish manner.

PARKER: Which done, he was immediately committed to the lay power, and to the two sheriffs of the city, and was confined at the Guildhall,

LATIMER: there to remain until a writ might be precured to burn him.

TUNSTALL: Where many friars and religious men resorted to him, labouring to persuade him not to die in his opinions.

LATIMER: Some of whom were reclaimed to the gospel's side.

PARKER: And on the night before the day determined for his end, I was among divers friends who resorted to him at the Guildhall. Where, finding him eating of an ale-brew with such a cheerful heart and quiet mind as he did, some said that they were glad to see him at that time, so heartily to refresh himself. Whereupon he answered that he but followed the example of the husbandmen, who having a ruinous house to dwell in, yet bestow cost so long as they may hold it up, and so did he now with this ruinous house of his body. Whereupon some others put him in mind, that though the fire, which he should suffer next day, should be of great heat unto his body, yet the comfort of God's Spirit should cool it to his everlasting refreshing. At which word he put his hand toward the flame of the candle burning before them, blackening it unto the first joint thereof, and then did say: 'I am only trying my flesh; tomorrow God's rods shall burn my whole body. But yet I constantly believe that howsoever the stubble of this my body shall be wasted by it, yet my soul and spirit shall be purged thereby; a pain for the time, whereon notwithstanding followeth joy unspeakable'.

Pause.

LATIMER: And the next day...

PARKER: And the next day came the officers of execution, as their manner is, with their glaves and halberds, to lead him to the place of execution, without the city gate, commonly called the lollards' pit. And he was apparelled in a layman's gown, with his sleeves hanging down and his arms out, his hair being piteously mangled at his degradation, being a little single body in person, but always of a good upright countenance. And when they came to the stake, he rehearsed unto the people the words of the common creed, and confessed to have run into the disobedience of the Church by preaching to the poor when prohibited. This said, he put off his gown and went to the stake. And while he thus stood on the ledge, certain friars, doctors and priors who had been present at his examination and degradation, came to him and said: 'O Master Bilney, the people be persuaded that we be the causers of your death, and thereupon it is likely that they will withdraw their charitable alms from us, except you declare your charity towards us, and discharge us of the matter', whereupon he spake with a loud voice and said 'I pray you, good people! be never the worse to these men for my sake, as though they should be the authors of my death: it was not they'. Then the officers put reeds and faggots about his body, and set fire on the reeds, which made a very great flame, which deformed the visor of his face. And he held up his hands, and knocked upon his breast, crying sometimes 'Jesus!', sometimes 'Credo!'. But the flame was blown away from him by the violence of the wind, and so, for a little pause, he stood without flame, the flame departing and recoursing thrice ere the wood took strength to be the sharper to consume him; and then he gave up the ghost, and his body, being withered, bowed downward on the chain. And then one of the officers, with his halberd, smote out the staple in the stake behind him, and suffered his body to fall into the bottom of the fire, and so he was consumed.

Pause.

LATIMER: Truly should we ask, why should this man be so blithe to such a sharp correction? When he might readily have abjured his heresies, and lived thereby to do – as spake his friends – 'greater service to the lord'?

Pause. To TUNSTALL.

For which answer, that in the springtime of his age he bought a book. Wherein was a New Testament in Greek. Which he took into his rooms and read. As he did write to you.

TUNSTALL takes out another letter and reads.

TUNSTALL: 'I bought it' – this the Testament – 'even by the providence of God, as I do now well understand and perceive. And at the first reading – as I well remember – I chanced upon this sentence of St Paul – O most sweet and comfortable sentence to my soul! – the first epistle unto Timothy'.

LATIMER opens his book: the Tyndale New Testament.

LATIMER: In which he might have found:

He hands the book to PARKER who reads a verse.

PARKER: 'Godliness is great riches, if a man be content with that he hath'.

He hands the book to TUNSTALL who reads a verse.

TUNSTALL: Or 'covetousness is the root of all evil'.

The testament continues to go round.

LATIMER: Or 'Yea and a bishop must be faultless, the husband of one wife, sober, discreet, not drunken, no fighter, not given to filthy lucre'.

PARKER: Or 'Let the woman learn in silence with all subjection'.

TUNSTALL: Or 'Exercise thyself unto godliness. For bodily exercise profiteth little'.

LATIMER: Or 'drink no longer water, but use a little wine for thy stomach's sake'.

PARKER: Or, 'Let as many servants as are under the yoke, count their masters worthy of all honour'.

TUNSTALL: Or 'despise not the gift that is in thee'.

LATIMER: Or 'fight the good fight'.

PARKER: But what he did find was chapter one, the fifteenth verse: Wherein he learned that all his travails, all his fasting and watching, all the redemption of masses and pardons being done without trust in Christ, was nothing.

LATIMER: *(With the Testament.)* In the verse Paul writes: 'Christ Jesus came into the world to save sinners, of whom I am the chief and principal'.

Taking TUNSTALL's letter and reading from it.

'Which did so exhilarate my heart, being before wounded with the guilt of my sins, and being almost in despair, that immediately I felt a marvellous comfort and quietness, insomuch that my bruised bones leapt for joy'.

Pause.

TUNSTALL: Good little saintly Bilney.

Pause.

LATIMER: But that he had read these words, he might have died a-bed.

TUNSTALL: And not only he.

PARKER: Master Hugh Latimer. Having been mightily admonished by the Cardinal, cruelly imprisoned for sedition in King Henry's latter years, preferred by his son Edward, arrested under rule of his papist sister Mary, tried, condemned, degraded, and brought with Bishop Ridley, to a ditch over against Balliol College, Oxford, for their execution.

Reads from the book.

'They then brought a lighted faggot, and laid it at Dr Ridley's feet upon which Master Latimer said, "Be of good comfort, Master Ridley, and play the man; we shall this day light such a candle by God's grace in England as I trust shall never be put out".'

Closes the book.

Master Latimer, who might too have died a-bed, save for Paul's words to Timothy.

LATIMER: *(Gently.)* As you did, Master Parker.

A moment then the three BISHOPS stand.

PARKER: 'O Timothy, keep that which is given thee to keep, and avoid unghostly vanities of voices and oppositions of science – '

TUNSTALL: ' – falsely so called – '

LATIMER: 'Which, some professing, have erred concerning faith'.

They go out, leaving the three chairs behind them.

James Graham

HAND-ME-DOWNS

Characters

PAULINE
Woman, mid forties–mid fifties.

PAULINE arrives in a bit of a flutter, but smiling at her audience still, greeting them with a nod and a 'hello', carrying in a box of clothes, jumble and accessories.

Matchbox 20's 'Hand Me Down' plays on a laptop that sits by her chair.

She clicks stop on it.

PAULINE: I downloaded that – I know, mad innit. Not only that, I did it on my phone, not even the computer; on my mobile and then I just synched it up to iTunes. 'Synched it up', honestly, I know, I know, don't. I'd have laughed, the old me, a year ago – not even that; less.

Anyway, here we are, shall we have a go?

She approaches the audience with her box, and offers them items of clothing etc.

PAULINE: Who's first then, you? Little scarf, yep?

Hat for you, sir? Pop that on.

Sunglasses, there you go.

Christ, look at that – never mind, on you pop…

…handing out a dozen or so items of clothing before coming back to her seat and picking out some items to put on herself.

PAULINE: It's not that I don't like Primark. It's that I *hate* it.
Nothing against anyone who shops there, this isn't me judging, 'thou shalt not judge', 'she who casts the first stone' and all that; no it's just me, my personal what's-it, it rattles my feathers and sends me nuts, even the thought, just the thought of it – look, my arms, goose pimples, and not good ones, not like when you're…so. No.
I think it's the noise, that's one, and the rushing. It's like being at a concert, like when I went to see Take That at Manchester Arena, the doors open and everyone piles in screaming, and there's not even Gary Barlow at the other end, just knickers and a top.

Anyway when money was tight with Rachel, that's where we went of course, Pam told me about it, she said 'honestly Pauline, just get yourself down, for twenty quid you could have the whole of autumn sorted', and anyway so we went, but Rachel wasn't up to much, she was having a bad day – this is when any day ending in a 'y' was a bad day for Rachel – and I'm not saying that to be, you know, I'm just saying it, because …

You know.

But we couldn't hack it, neither of us, clothes on the floor and things being tossed about and all of the staff were crap and didn't want to know, and I could see Rachel was struggling, you know, she was sweating and looked like she was going to have one of her panics, and so I just grabbed her hand and I swore in front of her, for the first time in ages, I said 'fuck it' *(Laughs.)*, honestly I did, and I said 'let's forget this and go and get a coffee'. And so we did.

Rachel used to laugh at my thing for Gary Barlow, she says 'he's chubby and he can't dance', and she's right but he tries his best, and I think that's why he's my favourite. Because he's the most normal. You know.

That's how it began, really. Well you know in the long run. That was about a year and a half ago, but the website's only been live – hear that? 'live'? Oh yes, I've got all the lingo now, me – only been *live* about three months.

It was over a cappuccino – honest to God, my mum, if my mum were still alive, she wouldn't believe how much things have changed, she wouldn't believe how much I had changed; the kind of woman who drinks cappuccinos and does yoga? she'd just – well I know what she'd do, she'd tut and sigh and probably roll her eyes, as was her wont. But honestly, I think, the past like, what, fifteen, fifteen years, have seen the biggest, you know, the most – and this is from someone who grew up in the Sixties, the 'revolution' and all that, but honestly, maybe it's just me, but the past fifteen years, I think, the biggest changes, like lifestyle-wise, you know. At least for me,

for women of my age. The clothes and what we do and stuff.
Maybe it is just me, I dunno. I mean Pam, she was at a Scissor
Sisters gig last November, and you see that's what I'm talking
about – and me, 'cappuccinos'; honest to God I've never felt
more alive. It's probably the caffeine.

Anyway, we were sat drinking our coffees and Rachel wasn't
talking much and so I was overcompensating, rattling on at
a rate of knots, as I do, and it just occurred to me, I just said,
'well bloody hell, hold the phone, the amount of bits and bobs
I've got at home, whole wardrobes, whole boxes full, that I
never wear, let's just have a rummage through that, we'll find
you some stuff in there'.

Her look said it all, she wasn't amused, but I persevered, I said
'me and your aunties, when we were your age, we never bought
a thing, we'd just swap things around, and me being the
youngest it worked a treat, cause everything gets handed down
doesn't it?' She'd never heard that before, 'hand-me-downs',
can you believe it, she was probably fibbing. I said 'You've
never heard that phrase before?!' I said, 'I'd had been naked as a
jay bird if it hadn't been for that'. She'd never heard *that* phrase
before either. Maybe no one says it anymore. Doesn't matter, I
say it.

Right, we ready. Let's go again. Everyone swap, the people
around you. Go.

*She clicks play on the music, it plays while PAULINE encourages
the audience to swap their items with one another, joining in
herself to receive a new 'outfit'.*

She clicks off the music.

PAULINE: She left, God, what are we on now, erm…

Why do people do that? Pause, pretend they're trying to think
of something, even though they already know it in their head;
I know exactly when she left, it was seven months and two
days ago.

I don't know why I pretended I didn't, sorry.

Didn't think she could get better if she was…well 'here'.

I get emails. Used to be letters, people sent, didn't it? Although I suppose with this kind of thing, like Rachel, with letters there was always the danger of being found, what with the postmark and everything. All that palaver about catching a bus to a different town and posting it there. Exhausting.

But with an email she can send it from anywhere, and I'd have no idea.

So I suppose I'm grateful for that.

She always says three things.

She says that she's fine.

She says that she's sorry.

And she says she hopes I understand.

I know she's fine. She's strong, stronger than she – well, you know, apart from the obvious, but that can bring down anyone can't it, *has* brought down, bodybuilders, and…hasn't it. This 'affliction'. Or disease; meant to call it.

I know she's fine.

I know she's sorry.

And *of course*… I understand…

I didn't; didn't used to, that's why she says it, as her third thing. God I cringe now at some of the things I said to her, ignorant, just ignorant bloody…*things*, assumptions.

You think you know stuff, about stuff, don't you, but you don't know *anything*, it's just assumed. From magazines or soaps or the news.

But we weren't that kind of family, it wasn't in our, like DNA – whow, wait, no *(Slaps her hand.)* I've been told off about that, naughty. It *is* in our DNA, I mean it obviously *is*, isn't it, it must be in mine, passed down from me to her. This kind of…

erm…(what was the word she?)…'disposition'. Chemicals in your brain or something, an imbalance, or something, making you more vulnerable to, like, this stuff. To addiction. And things. Apparently.

This has all had to be learnt. By me. Reading up, and talking to people, but how else would I learn? I can't bear people's ignorance now, about addiction and things, their presumptions, but I forget that used to be me, they used to be my presumptions.

What's the difference between an assumption and a presumption?

Which one's worse?

I suppose it doesn't matter; they're as bad as each other.

It would be nice, wouldn't it, it would be nice to still open a letter, to sit down with a cup of tea, or a gin (more likely), nice G&T, to sit and hold it, a letter, in your hand. Because it has come from *their* hand, hasn't it, that's the point, that's why you feel a connection. They wrote on that bit of paper, in their handwriting.

Saying that, all of Anthony's letters to me, they got ruined in the loft cause of the damp we had the other year. All his… well, yes, call a spade a spade, 'love'; they were *love* letters; God, sounds so old-fashioned now. They're all gone, which is such…

God, I was inconsolable. Unconsolable? Inconsolable?

Gone forever, though.

So maybe emails are better, ey; not much chance of damp getting into the internet is there? No much chance of it breaking, you wouldn't think. So technically you have them forever then, don't you?

And I suppose you could always print them off. If you wanted to…*hold* them.

She clicks play on the music.

The swap begins again.

She sits in her new outfit and turns off the music.

PAULINE: The hand-me-down website was meant to be something we both did, distract her from her stuff, and I'm only part-time now, thanks to…

I was really surprised when I got the idea, I never thought of myself as the entrepreneurial type, I mean I like Dragon's Den as much as the next man, but there you go, I just got the idea. It was mine. When we were going through my stuff, me and Rachel. Trying stuff on. Like kids. Dressing up.

I thought, hold the phone.

And I was quite…proud.

It's the thing I like best about me. This little business. Honestly.

That and my ankles, oh yes. Very nice ankles, I've been told, me. Only person who didn't think so was my bloody husband, hah. Still there you go, maybe that's why I married him; glutton for punishment.

Beat, she covers her face with her hand, brief pause…

It's dead simple, right, you go onto the website and you look for something that you want, and we've got everything, we've got tops and shoes and bags and… God, scarfs, jewellery, shoes, I've said that, jeans, skirts, dresses, lots of dresses, anything. So you pick what you fancy and then you get sent that thing in a special bag, one of these, here *(Holds it up.)*, and then in return, you pop an item *you* don't want back in the bag and post it back to us, see, and so it's sort of like, it's kind of like, everyone's just swapping. With one another. All the time.

And I know you're thinking, wait a minute, I bet some people'll just receive what they want and not send anything back, and maybe they will, but it's a system based on trust, and I find, generally speaking, if you give people the benefit of the doubt they don't let you down, more often than not.

Never thought it'd make any money, it was just a sort of hobby, but we've got advertisers and things now, so.

Although now it's just me of course.

Although I like to think, wherever she is, that she uses it. Wherever she's gone, to get better. Away from me. The 'problem'. Huh.

I sometimes think when I'm packing something up, as I'm holding it, a sweater or whatever, I look at it and think... 'I wonder if this is you. Rachel'...

…

I don't think anyone else has cottoned on, I'm waiting for it to be stolen. Someone in America's got one, which means they got the website name, gits – I googled it, and I thought 'bugger' – but that's just for swapping children's clothes, which I think is a bit creepy, I mean I've got an open mind but come on.

Lingerie we do, too – I know what you're thinking, but we insist on them being clean, and Pam, she's got a nose like a bloodhound, she gets right in there for a sniff and if there's anything untoward, she'll catch it, and back it goes. It's no use just fabreezing it and thinking 'that'll do' – she'll have you. She's like *CSI*.

She presses play on the music.

Another swap around.

She's back in another 'outfit', music off.

PAULINE: It's obvious why people don't think of it as a disease, any of these things, these head stuff things, because you can't see them, can you; it's not like when you break your leg, you put a pot on it, don't you. Or it's not like, I don't know, something awful like cancer, it's not like your hair falls out, does it?

Although actually Rachel's did, but I think that's just because she was…sad.

And of course there's no medicine, not really, but you know, even with heroin you get that…ooh god, mind like a sieve today, that…thing, the…it, like, perks you up, it's like a smaller version of heroin; you know what I mean, begins with 'm'. And they give it to people who are hooked on it, but Rachel. She just has to try and sweat it out. And it's something that never goes, apparently, you think – I thought – once you've got over your like craving, initially, that's it, done, you're *fixed*.

But you're never fixed. Not really. Apparently. I've learned.

Long pause.

PAULINE: I had to sit there, listening. Just taking it. The onslaught.

She'd been going for sessions with this woman for about three months, and I was all for it, anything if it helped. I have a natural aversion to that kind of stuff, or at least I used to. You just picture people lying on sofas don't you. A Sigmund Freud kind of character asking questions about your childhood and going 'hmm'.

But if it helped, I was all for it.

And then Rachel asked me to come and sit in on a session, and I thought fine, I was flattered, 'at last', I thought, she's letting me in.

It felt a little bit like an ambush. I had to just sit their listening, to both of them, making it sound like my fault. They said I shouldn't take it personally, but how can you not take it personally, stuff about the way you brought your kids up, the things you did wrong. 'It's not things you've done wrong' she said. It just these…oh, what did she ca-…'belief systems', or something, that move down through the generations, ways we think we're meant to behave which we're not meant to, that trap us in negative…oh well, they have all this language, or these 'terms'. I'm learning.

I could have handled it better, I suppose, but like I say. It was all a bit. New.

I started going to meetings of my own, and I asked her to come with me to mine, which she thought I was doing out of spite but I wasn't. I wasn't.

I'm not particularly religious, it's not the, the, the…

Erm.

It's not the…

Most of it I take with a pinch of salt, but I suppose it's the idea of trusting in something that you can't see. Without ever having seen it. Without ever having any evidence. Without ever having any proof. And that's why it's called faith.

Because it's about *hope*. That even though you've got no reason to believe it's there. That something can exist, and be better, on the other side. That it's there.

That opportunity to be saved.

And I like that.

That bit.

The rest I could take or leave. Especially the clothes some of these people wear. Christ.

She presses play on the music, collects the items of clothing from the audience.

And exits.

Anya Reiss

A SUNDAY SERMON

Sunday, JEREMY, a vicar in a countryside parish, in the pulpit, full of suppressed anger. He swaps from notes to ad-libing throughout.

He goes to speak, stops, he's nervous, smiles, tries again.

JEREMY: – Hello

I have to say…it's nice to see the church so packed, a rare sight here. In fact I would say this is the largest congregation I have ever seen in my eleven years here.

Goes to his notes, new thought.

Even at Christmas.

Going back to his notes.

But I suppose any publicity is good publicity.

As the saying goes.

Today I have chosen to preach to you all from a rather unusual book of the Bible, not the most fashionable you might say, so I have to come to the conclusion that I must either be very brave or very stupid. But it seems strangely appropriate for today, to today. And I feel I may have been forced into the realms of the heroic or the inane. Hopefully I'll emerge as the former, rather than the latter, well here's hoping.

My book is Titus.

And I see blank faces before me but no matter no matter for

soon I think it will become apparent to you all this passage's relevance. To here, to today, to Nicholas, for let's not pretend that we don't all know that that is the reason the seats are filled today; not God, not Sunday but Nicholas.

Smiles sheepishly.

So far I and my colleagues have avoided addressing this rather messy...business with you, with you all.

It somehow seemed the best thing to do.

But I think I have now reached the conclusion that it is time for this be confronted. In fact I fear the time was long ago.

I think, I think, I think I should...just make my own position clear before I continue, that um...the conclusion that has been reached over Nicholas does not agree with me on, on any level. Emotionally, morally...'physically'...spiritually.

But, but saying that I would like that to be put aside, I would like that to be put that to one side because I stand here not as Jeremy I stand here as your vicar and so I...I...

You know actually I um, I asked my nephew about this, he's staying with us now at the, at the vicarage and he um, he um told me 'don't be like that Geordie bird who thinks she's it'.

Have to admit I didn't know what he meant.

However after some, um interrogation I discovered he meant Cheryl Cole off the *X Factor*, not on the *X Factor* anymore apparently he's not happy about that but um yes, yes apparently last year there was an incident with her, with er with this Cheryl Cole.

You see the thing is I don't think I can, I don't think I am able to dissuade any of you from your own feelings and beliefs as I am sure, as I am certain they are the polar opposite to my own. And it would seem foolish to attempt it. As in fact I can see most of the names on that unfortunate petition sitting before me now, in the flesh. But I feel the need to do...

Something.

However yes the *X Factor*.

She's a, she's a judge on the *X Factor* and her job is to sit on the panel and tell contestants after they have sung whether they were good or not. And there was this singer, apparently by all accounts not a very good one and was really rather disliked by the public. Nevertheless he was a contestant on the show, and sang his song, and turned to Cheryl Cole for her judgement. This is er, this is er last season, show, whatever you call it. And instead of judging him in her designated role, she berated him live on television for some comments he had made in the tabloids about her and insisted on an apology.

Which she got.

Now as an *X Factor* judge she was there to comment upon his singing and performance but instead on this occasion, backed by her own sense of moral right and indignation, she launched into an attack in an attempt to shame him into what she viewed as the correct behaviour. Now strange as it may seem and as unlikely an affinity as it is, I now find myself in the same position.

I feel backed by my own sense of moral right and indignation.

However I will not be like 'that Geordie bird that thinks she's it'.

I will not confront you live on air...I will not confront you personally, emotionally, physically because that is not my designated role but I will, I will, if you all don't mind, I will confront you spiritually.

Which somehow convolutedly leads me to Titus.

Back on notes.

Titus sets out the, for want of a better word, the criteria for how to be a good bishop. Ah I see the dawning comprehension. Shall we say the rules. I'm going to tell you the rules.

As set out by the Bible.

Not you, not as set out by the people of this Parish.

But by the Bible.

The word of God...as we have been led to believe.

A bishop must be 'a lover of hospitality'.

I challenge any one of you to stand here and say that Nicholas ever rejected anyone from his doorstep, that he turned his back on one soul, that he did not try on every level to be accommodating, kind, generous to anyone he came across. Would not share his food, his table, his home, his bed with anyone of you no no no not his bed sorry, sorry, sorry.

A bishop must be 'sober'. Well yes, Nicholas has been a teetotaller for many a year now, all he ever did was finish the communion wine at the end of the service as is in fact the common practice Miss Pryce if you had ever cared to ask. A bishop must be 'Just' *(Answering the criteria.)* yes, 'holy' indeed, 'temperate' without a doubt.

'A bishop must be blameless, as the steward of God; not self-willed, not soon angry, not given to wine, no striker, not given to filthy lucre' now a gentle mild-mannered kind and caring, generous soul such as Nicholas does indeed seem to fit this exacting criteria, better than I.

Better than any of my colleagues.

So with Nicholas so firmly adhering to Titus' exacting standards let us turn and examine ourselves.

For if you are to preach the Bible back to him, asking Nicholas to obey its every word surely you have done the same...surely...

'Aged men must be sober, grave, temperate, sound in faith, in charity, in patience'.

Grimaces.

Oh dear.

Now all you sober, grave, temperate men who are sound in faith, in charity, in patience must forgive me, in fact any sober aged men in front me, must forgive me. But I fear there are not many. I mean, it's fine, I forgive you, for who has not when drunk attempted to, uh, mark their territory so to speak even if that territory is the post office...Mr Kenny.

No sorry, sorry Mr Kenny there's no need for you to leave, there's no need for you to leave, do please, sit back down. Please...thank you.

You misunderstand my point. I forgive you, but quoting that rather excellent graffiti that I saw at Nicholas' home a few days ago 'will God forgive you?' No sorry Mr Kenny, Mr Kenny oh and Mr Edes you mustn't leave as well, Mr...*(They have left.)*

Well perhaps Mr Edes is remembering that we all know the reason he moved here, perhaps the small stint at Her Majesty's pleasure has made him lose his footing on the Everest that is the moral high ground, oh and language like that in the house of God, good to know they can still shout so loudly yes they really are 'grave, temperate and sound in faith' are they not! Oh well this really is quite the little walk out is it not.

Sorry, sorry everyone. Back to the, the uh, the thing...

Now young men you are to be 'sober-minded' I will not name names for I feel there is no reason. The stipulations I see before me are near pointless to read out as I cannot think of one man who has obeyed a single one. For Clive Hill did you truly think that, what's the term, 'bottling' Michael Bartram last winter after he beat you at a game of darts really did 'in all things shew thyself a pattern of good works'? Oh and the whole Hill family is to leave, how supportive you all are of one another.

Anyone else leaving? No good, good, I would ask you all not to, I am not, I am not trying to be...I am, I am coming to a point.

I am.

You see I just...if you would all remain in your seats for just,

just a little bit longer.

I have said I will not comment upon the truthfulness of the original allegations against Nicholas and I will not. However as *always* seems to happen in this parish, the truth has snowballed into wilder and wilder accusations and I cannot resist pointing out that the allegation involving Tootsie and Yemin the village goats is not only preposterous but physically impossible.

And so I...you see it's rather hard for me to...Titus.

Now onto the so-called gentler sex; 'aged women' I will say no more than this Mrs. Leaf-aged women are to be not 'false accusers,' I in fact address that one charge to the entire congregation; 'not false accusers'.

If you are to preach the word of God that Nicholas has devoted his life to learning and spreading you too must keep to the rules that you now preach back; 'not false accusers'.

Must I speed up for fear of losing you all, come now, have I not worked here for eleven years, do I not deserve one more minute of your precious fucking time? Sorry sorry sorry.

They've gone anyway.

You know I am asked if I believe in evil and in the past my answer has always been no. Evil choices have been made by fragile, weak people but no one is evil, evil does not exist in a pure form; the devil corrupts he does not create. However my answer has changed for I see evil.

I see evil here.

I see it in this small insignificant parish.

The wish to destroy goodness, the goodness in one man, I see evil here and I am intent on working against it.

Titus says young women you are to be again 'sober' *(Makes the Family Fortunes buzzer sound.)*, 'love your husbands' *(Buzzer sound.)* 'discreet', 'chaste', 'keepers at home', 'good', 'obedient to your husbands' and the 'word of God be not blasphemed'.

(Anger becoming clearer.) Fail, fail, fail, fail, fail.

No one here lives up to the expectations, the simple, just expectations of Titus. You cannot disregard it for this is *the Bible*. This is the word of God, but who here has met this?

The exception however does seem to be Nicholas.

Young women a question to you, the last of you if you wish to pause there by the door before you leave. Does it not seem unfair that you are told to be 'chaste' and yet young men are not, you are told to be 'discreet' and yet young men are not, and most annoyingly, most aggravatingly of course you must, you simply must, the word of Lord God our Father is that you must be obedient to your husbands. Obedient.

Now God is omnipresent, omnipotent and omniscient.

Do you really, *really* think that God, the creator of the world, of the universe, of mankind, who is everywhere, can do anything and knows all, do you really think Germaine Greer changed his mind? Do you think God moves with the fashions of the western world? That you are in some way allowed to be not obedient, that men you can get away with being not sober.

Because times have changed? I hear you say that. Times have changed. Times *have* changed, so women don't have to be discreet and sober and obedient and men don't have to be grave, temperate, sound in faith and charity and patience. Times have changed.

The Bible is lapsed, flawed and faulted. So, you all can be lapsed, flawed and faulted, but Nicholas, Nicholas cannot?

In fact times have changed so much that...if Nicholas who is absolutely everything that Titus set out, to the very letter in thought and word and heart, who is everything that he should be according to the New Testament, if Nicholas who is judged by false accusing drunken impatient excitable unfaithful waverers, if Nicholas who is better and kinder and juster than us all and God forbid may actually believe in the whole damn shebang genuinely, in God, in the Holy Spirit, in Jesus Christ if Nicholas in the privacy of his own home wants to, wants to just look at a few pictures...

Allegedly just images.

I mean come on now.

I'm not defending it, I mean it was a fucking stupid thing to do but....

It's not like...

It's not like...

I mean it's not like he's *in* any of them, is it?

A long pause.

Sorry.

I'm very sorry lost my, lost my...

Seem to have wandered away from the sermon somewhat, *(Returns to the sermon notes.)* let me find my place. Um, um, ah yes. Ah yes.

(He is much calmer, almost defeated.) Titus says we are to 'speak evil of no man'. We are to speak evil of no man and we are to remember that 'we ourselves also were sometimes foolish, disobedient, deceived, serving divers lust and pleasure, living in malice and envy, hateful and hating one another'.

I think it may have been said more succinctly elsewhere in the Bible 'judge not lest ye be judged'. And it is this philosophy, belief, that I feel should be applied to Nicholas.

Do you not Mrs Leaf?

Do you not think so?

For, at the end of the day, Nicholas is a true believer in the Lord Jesus Christ, in the death and resurrection and the second coming and in heaven and hell and good and evil and in grace and love and in the word of the Lord as set down in the Holy Bible.

And to be honest that is a very rare thing to find (in the Church of England) and surely, surely his true and utter belief in God, and his genuine desire to spread that knowledge and belief and faith to others, that rare rare selfless want, that I have yet to find in any other colleague and yet to find in my own heart, that rare want to truly help others to the best of his own abilities and always at a point of sacrifice for himself surely, surely that...surely that is all that really matters...

Mrs Leaf, surely that is all that matters?

Pause.

(A feeble joke.) Here endeth the second lesson, thanks be to God. *(As he makes to leave the pulpit, he turns briefly back.)* Thank you for staying Mrs Leaf.

And I will be finding another petition very soon, yes?

Nods as if along with her.

Against myself, yes?

Nods along again.

Well I'd like to say it was all worth it Mrs Leaf, but...but it really really wasn't, was it?

He leaves.

Kamila Shamsie

THE LETTER

'You can't keep running,' he says.

He says it, and I see myself in an orchard, the sky all above me and the scent of roses and damp soil all around me. I see myself moving swiftly through the orchard, no dogs penning me in, no bell ringing just once to send me scrambling inside away from the breeze on my face, away from the flight of swallows. I run because I am a man with limbs and muscles and strength, and forward is a direction open to me. I run to leave behind all that is behind.

He won't understand that. He sees running as a state of terror, of exhaustion, of un-belonging. He said that word to me once – 'belonging' – as if it was an apple you could bite into. He listed everything to which he thinks he belongs – his people, his country, his party, his revolution. From where I stand, it's clear he belongs to the prison guards. But he doesn't see that, and more importantly, neither do they – even the dullest among them has sense enough to know that history is turning, and soon he will leave this place; he will leave and then return again, with all the scribes of the world, to show them where he spent his captivity. The prison guards are already preparing their profiles for the photographs; I see them turn their heads this way and that when they pass by a mirror, angling their necks to avoid the double chins. So, yes, I was wrong. He doesn't belong to the prison guards – only to history. It has him in its grip, exactly where he wants to be.

I have belonged since I was seven years old. I belonged to a man whose son was killed by my father. It was an accident –

he slipped from the ladder and the cement block fell from his hands – but the boy was as dead as if it had been intentional. An eye for an eye; a son for a son. The boy's father showed clemency. He could have dropped a cement block on my head while my father watched, but instead he took me to his lands, pointed out the invisible marker, twenty paces from his house, beyond which I must never step as long as I live and then pointed out the dogs who would find me if I disobeyed.

My old master is a man with little legs; his twenty paces are fifteen of mine.

How many times I stood at that invisible boundary, and looked beyond to the rose gardens, the cotton fields, the track of earth leading away, away, away. It was the curve of that track of earth, the scent from the rose garden, the singing from the cotton fields that made me run – if they'd kept me locked in a cell, as I am here, I would have stayed.

'Where are you planning to run to, in any case?' he asks.

He is a man with a strong sense of destination. The destiny of a nation. Perhaps he believes that he is destination himself – why shouldn't he? The world will come to him, soon enough. So how can I expect him to understand that 'away' is destination, that 'not there' is destination, that 'running' is destination.

He thinks I should go back.

Today, my time here is done. The prison is over-crowded with political prisoners; they must make way for the new ones by getting rid of the petty criminals among us. There is nothing petty, let me tell you, about stealing food when you're hungry – and running for your life does make you hungry. But let that go, let it go. I'll be released today before even standing trial; so what does the reason – or the wording of it – matter?

He is sorry to see me go. I'm the only one who treats him with that precise mixture of deference and comradeship that he desires. I have served the powerful for many years. I know how to gauge their moods. I know how to read their manipulations and promises and threats to each other – even so, accustomed as I am to it, I've never seen it polished to art as in this letter. Written on my behalf, and yet...and yet....if he is the artist I am the poor man on the street corner who he's chosen as subject, not the one on whose wall the painting will hang.

Twenty-five lines. That's all it is. Twenty-five lines of which the first seven speak only of the Party and its underlying ideology, that ideology which he and my old master claim to share. (All successful revolutions, he tells me, are expansive – they make room for those already in power to see how they might maintain their power if they just join early, and eagerly, enough; in this way, they divide the powerful, and create a breach. And so it is that my old master, stalwart of the crumbling system, has lately become a convert to these new beliefs, and a rising star of the Party.)

So – seven lines to establish their mutual interests. And then, a turn – 'I could ask you to do what is necessary in the name of the Party, but instead I beseech you in the name of love.' Clever.

Then it comes to me. My name on the page, in his hand. 'I beseech you for my son.' His son! What a weight that word has when it comes from his pen. I am claimed by the bonds of kinship.

'My son – which in time past was to thee unprofitable, but now profitable to thee and me!' A moment ago I was his son, but now I'm a cotton-field in a year of good rainfall. He knows exactly what he is saying, but he also doesn't understand it at all.

'I have sent him again: thou therefore receive him.' A velvet-coated command, if ever. I have gone from son to cottonfield to a gift which must be placed on the mantelpiece and polished each day with pride, not for the value of the gift itself but because receiving it is an honour.

And so I am abstracted entirely – I am not me, I am his mark of favour. And thus, I must be forgiven everything. Not only forgiven my own crime in running, but the crime of my father. That, too, is lifted off my shoulders.

'I would have retained him with me...but without thy mind would I do nothing. Having confidence in thy obedience I wrote unto thee, knowing that thou wilt also do more than I say... But withal prepare me also a lodging; for I trust through your efforts I shall be given unto you.' He is as slippery as a fish – now the petitioner, now the man of authority, now the Party man with faith in his comrade. But the final note is this: When I am free, and take the helm of power I will come to you. So be careful how you treat this gift, this cotton-field, this son of mine.

What more can I ask of any man than this letter? Never mind that it exists to assert an old man's authority over the young upstart. It may be that, but it is something else also. It is my shield against the world. 'If thou countest me a comrade, receive him as myself.' *Receive him as myself!* If I walk into that house, my old prison, with this I will be received as a prince. And when he is freed – and he will be; soon! – I will be sent to him, as tribute. He does everything but demand it in this letter. And then he will both set me free, and ask me to stay. His right hand man.

It will work out for everyone.

So why do I hesitate?

I'll be released – what does the reason, or the wording of it, matter?

If I walk back into that house I will be received as a prince. Asked to sit at the table not stand and serve at it; given linen to sleep on, not to wash; presented with a horse to ride around the land – twenty, forty, sixty, eighty, five hundred paces from the house.

But someone will stand and serve me; someone will wash the linen I sully; someone will stop nineteen and a half paces from the house and watch me ride away;

and I will know it,

and I will know them.

He thought of everything when he wrote this letter;

everything but that.

Anthony Weigh

THE MIDDLE MAN

Characters

TIMOTHY, Older. Larger.

PAUL, Younger. Smaller.

Perhaps a bell rings in the distance at the end of each chapter. Or a gong. Or a buzzer.

CHAPTER 1

TIMOTHY, in bare feet, sat in a chair watches PAUL sleep on a narrow bed.

He smokes.

Beat.

Beat.

Beat.

Black.

CHAPTER 2

Same.

Beat.

Then.

TIMOTHY: Do you ever wonder what the world will be like after you're dead? Not for you. You're dead aren't you. No. The world. What *the world* will be like after you're dead and buried. Burnt. Whatever. Gone.

This is that. I'm dead. To all intents and purposes. Dead to the world. *Tot für die Welt* as the Germans would say. Although not actually deceased. Yet. This is the world. Without me.

Beat.

Quiet isn't it.

Black.

CHAPTER 3

Same.

TIMOTHY: I'll tell you then shall I? This morning I wrote a note.

The feel of the paper. The cold of it. The lines on it as I folded it in half and left it on the desk in the front room.

Funny what you think.

We bought it for her to do her doctorate on didn't we. That desk. From Ikea or somewhere. She'd sit there. Late into the night. All night sometimes too. After a long day of work.

Come home. Get the tea on. Bit of telly. Then I'd walk the dog while she got down to it on the desk in the front room.

I admired that about her. Admire.

I'd come in with the dog. In the hallway and hear her. Clickety, clickety, clickety. That's nails on the computer. Clickety, clickety, clickety.

Once we found out there weren't going to be any kids, seemed sensible for her to do her doctorate. May as well do something useful.

Beat.

Sucking on his cigarette. Looking at PAUL.

She's away. Hamburg. At a meeting. By train. She doesn't fly. Global warming. Otherwise she'd have been back tonight after her meeting. Over and back in one day. Getting back to the house about now. Finding the paper. On the desk.

With the train you have to stay there overnight. Hotel near the station and catch the first one out the next morning. Tomorrow morning. This way it'll be tomorrow afternoon before she gets back, by the time she catches the connection and then walks home.

I've told her not to blame herself.

In the note.

My idea is to make it as painless as possible.

Seems fair.

Beat.

Cigarette.

I'm worried about the vacuum cleaner. I've taken the hose. Pipe. The thing. Haven't I. Should have gone down the hardware. Bought some hose. Pipe or something. Garden hose. But, by now I can't really bare the thought of the hardware. So, she'll just have to get a new hose. Pipe. The bit that attaches the sweeper thing to the motor thing. They're not hard to have replaced. I saw that online.

And electricians tape. I've got electricians tape. In case the hose doesn't fit properly around the what-cha-ma-call-it. The..? Exhaust? Pipe? Is that it?

PAUL moves in his sleep. TIMOTHY watches him.

Then I drove up here. With the vacuum cleaner hose and the electricians tape. Drove around. Walk down memory lane.

Slight chuckle to himself.

Drive. Down memory lane. I suppose. Nothing's changed much from when I was a kid.

I parked in the back of a services behind a fast-food shop. Out of the way. Near where blokes and girls from around here meet to go dogging. I've heard.

I try to get the hose from the vacuum around the exhaust thing-a-me, but it won't go will it because of the shaking.

Me. Shaking. And I can't find the end of the roll of electricians tape. I bite my finger nails. See? Nothing to get any purchase with. On the tape. And I pick and pick and pick at this... this...this FUCKING roll of electricians tape, but I can't find the end.

I drive into town to...I don't know...I need a drink. Stop the shaking.

To PAUL, still lying on the bed.

Does it show? Is that why you chose me?

Beat.

Sorry about your cock.

Black.

CHAPTER 4

A noisy pub.

PAUL: My mother washed me every day of my life until I turned fourteen. On my fourteenth birthday she said I was old enough to wash myself and she threw me out of the house. I lived on the street for a bit. Just like that.

Beat.

I know. Nothing to say is there. Got a job for a bit working in a factory making boilers. Long hours. Shit money. I'm going to nick outside for a fag. You save my seat for me.

TIMOTHY: I have to –

PAUL: Thanks.

Black.

CHAPTER 5

Same.

PAUL: Saw the sign on a notice board. They wanted a cook. Up at the abbey. Real life monks they are and everything. Amazing. Anyway, I'd watched her, hadn't I. My mum. Till she chucked me out that is at fourteen. I watched her boil an egg. Fry a sausage. Open cans. Cut up bits of tomato and arrange them on a plate with bits of lettuce, a sliced onion and ready sliced cheese. That's a salad isn't it. How hard could it be?

I'm happy to cook if the monks are stupid enough to give me a bed and pay me for it.

Do a bit of washing for them as well. The monks. Robes. White. Get brown around the bottom from bending down to pick things up. Runner beans. Potatoes. They grow their own. Turns the bottom of their robes brown. I'm washing my own stuff, I might as well wash theirs. Makes no difference does it.

Black.

CHAPTER 6

TIMOTHY: Now me what?

PAUL: Your turn.

TIMOTHY: There's not a lot to say.

PAUL: What are you doing here then?

TIMOTHY: I'm. It's a conference. Type thing.

PAUL: What's your line then?

TIMOTHY: Traveling. Around. Selling.

PAUL: What?

TIMOTHY: Um. It's things isn't it. I work for a publisher.

PAUL: Books then.

TIMOTHY: No. Well, yes. Amongst other things.

PAUL: Like what?

TIMOTHY: Like. Like. Well, videos. DVDs. Magazines. Pamphlets.

PAUL: You selling porn?

TIMOTHY: No!

PAUL: You do the Bible?

TIMOTHY: Do?

PAUL: Publish?

TIMOTHY: No.

PAUL: Pity. You'd be on a real killing there if you did.

TIMOTHY: No. We do support materials. Educational. Support materials.

PAUL: And you're here on a conference.

TIMOTHY: Yes.

           To audience.

           I *had* been back here on a conference. Once. Years before.

PAUL: You're married?

TIMOTHY: Yes.

PAUL: What's your wife like?

TIMOTHY: Immutable.

PAUL: What's that?

TIMOTHY: Been the same ever since I've known her.

PAUL: Sounds exciting.

TIMOTHY: I call her 'wifey'.

PAUL: And what's she call you?

TIMOTHY: 'Hubby'.

PAUL: Cute.

TIMOTHY: You get into these. Ways. They're soothing. I suppose.

PAUL: Kids?

TIMOTHY: Can't.

PAUL: Left it a bit late did you?

TIMOTHY: No. Just, can't.

PAUL: Sorry about that.

TIMOTHY: No good apportioning blame is there.

            Black.

CHAPTER 7

TIMOTHY's car.

TIMOTHY: When we got back to my car he handed me the roll of electricians tape which was sitting on the passenger seat.

PAUL: What's this?

TIMOTHY: Electricians tape.

PAUL: Right.

            To audience.

TIMOTHY: And he asked me about the big black case on the back seat.

            I'd forgotten it was there. Samples. For my work. Selling. When I used to. Work. Selling.

PAUL: Why don't you show us them.

TIMOTHY: Alright.

            To audience.

            That big black case of samples had been sitting on the back seat of the car ever since I was sacked. I was supposed to take it back. A girl kept ringing me about it. To take it back. Her messages sounded more and more tense. More officious. She could stick that big black case of samples right up her fucking arse couldn't she.

Beat.

He didn't say anything about the vacuum hose on the floor of the passengers' side. Even though it was right under his feet. Just polite I suppose.

Black.

CHAPTER 8

PAUL's room at the abbey.

TIMOTHY: We were both pretty drunk by now.

Very drunk.

His room was small and spinning and in an ugly little wing of pebble-crete off the back of an old church known locally as 'the abbey'. Never looked much like an abbey to me. But then, what do I know about abbeys?

There was a sink in the room and a little cupboard with an electric shower inside.

He sat on the bed and smoked with the window closed.

PAUL: Show us your stuff then.

TIMOTHY: I took him through the contents of the big black case.

Pamphlets. Books. CDs. DVDs. Games. Charts. Maps. Stickers. Things for counting. Things for drawing. Picture of a cat with the word for cat written under it in French. Chat. Picture of a wolf with the word for wolf written under it in German. Wolf.

I lay it all out on the bed for him to see. He kept giggling. In the end I packed up.

To PAUL.

I don't appreciate being made fun of.

PAUL: I'm not.

TIMOTHY: You are.

PAUL: I'm not. Come here.

PAUL brushes something from TIMOTHY's cheek.

TIMOTHY: What are you..?

PAUL: It was a thing. There. Eyelash.

TIMOTHY: Right.

PAUL: You've got long ones haven't you.

Black.

CHAPTER 9

Same.

TIMOTHY: He tasted like too much cologne bought in the sales after Christmas.

I thought his nob might be, well, a bit cheesy. A bit…working class. You know. Working-class nob. But it wasn't. It gave me a shock. It was bright and pink and very clean and sprang out of his boxers to say hello like a jack-in-the-box.

It made me laugh.

I wanted it.

I asked nicely.

He gave me what I wanted.

And when he pushed it up inside of me I saw something.

Stars or something.

Yes.

Like he'd pushed my head up out of a what's it called? In a ship. Port hole. Like he'd pushed my head out of a port hole and there I was with my head stuck out the window, breeze on my face, looking at stars. Like a…like a dog with its head out the car window or something.

Black.

CHAPTER 10

Same.

PAUL is naked except for a towel. TIMOTHY sits on the single bed.

PAUL: Calm down.

TIMOTHY: Stupid!

PAUL: Calm down.

TIMOTHY: Stupid, stupid, stupid, stupid, stupid!

PAUL: This is a monastery. It's got monks and everything. If you wake them up they'll be pretty annoyed and I'll get in trouble. Might even lose my job.

TIMOTHY: I'm so stupid!

PAUL: It wasn't that bad.

TIMOTHY: No?

PAUL: I wouldn't have said anything, only I had to wash the shit off my cock didn't I.

TIMOTHY: Can you not –

PAUL: Well, I did didn't I. You were there.

TIMOTHY: I'm sorry. I don't – I'm mortified.

PAUL: Happens.

TIMOTHY: Really?

PAUL: Yes.

TIMOTHY: I feel fucked!

PAUL: You were.

TIMOTHY: Don't!

PAUL: I've only got the one towel. Other one's in the wash. You mind sharing?

TIMOTHY: I should go.

PAUL: You should have a shower.

TIMOTHY: I'm so embarrassed.

PAUL: I said it happens.

TIMOTHY: Are you sure?

PAUL: It does.

TIMOTHY: You're just saying it.

PAUL: *(Lovingly.)* I'm not, you nob. Look. Some people would say you're more or less asking for it by sticking your dick up there.

            Black.

CHAPTER 11

Same.

PAUL asleep as at beginning.

TIMOTHY: By the time I came out of the cupboard with the electric shower in it he was asleep. Like that.

            Beat.

            I watched him. Lying there.

            The force of moving about had held him together. Held his muscles together. But without that he was, well…de-animated. Flabby. Without the force of moving about. Lying there. Fat little gut. Loose. I could do anything I wanted to him. He'd not be awake fast enough to do anything about it. I'm older, yes, but I'm bigger. I do push ups.

            Beat.

            I didn't know…I mean, what's the protocol in this sort of… do I stay? Wake him? Just leave quiet? I mean. The monks are bound to be up soon.

            He sits and lights a cigarette.

            And I thought.

            He didn't care, did he? He really didn't care that he…that I… that we…and there he is. Look at him. There he is. Isn't he. Dead to the world. *Tot für die Welt.*

Beat.

Beat.

She found me. With a copy of a magazine. Those health magazines. With pictures of blokes in them. Before the gym. After the gym. Used to think I'd give it a go. Ten week challenge or whatever. Never lasted more than two. I'm not exactly good raw material. I mean. Look at me.

Look of something on her face. Not exactly horror. Confirmation? She closed the door and went away.

Later, as I came in from walking the dog, I could hear her. Clickety, clickety. It sounded louder. Harder on the keys.

Took her in a cup of tea. Went to bed. She didn't say anything.

Black.

CHAPTER 12

Same.

TIMOTHY: Then. Sometime later. Weeks maybe. We were on our way to friends. We do that sometimes. A games night. We hadn't for a while. They've got a new born. Takes up a lot of their time. Understandably.

I'm driving. She's…well she's just sitting there isn't she. Looking. And she says: 'I'd kill myself if you were gay.' Just like that.

I keep driving.

What can you say to that? You're snookered aren't you. Damned if you do. Damned if you…

Beat.

Beat.

I'm not so stupid that I don't understand what that means.

Does.

To a person.

Snookered.

Beat.

Cunt.

Black.

CHAPTER 13

Same.

PAUL asleep, as at the beginning. TIMOTHY sits in the chair smoking, as at the beginning.

Beat.

Beat.

He gets up. Puts out his cigarette. Sits again and begins to put his shoes and socks on.

TIMOTHY: Can you hear that? That noise? That…

Imitating the sound of PAUL breathing.

The mucous. Membranes fluttering in air. All that wet.

Finishing with the shoes and socks.

I can't wait any longer.

Standing up.

What to do..?

I search for a piece of something. To write on. But find nothing. Just this. By his little bed. A bible. That'll be the monks. No pen, but strangely I find a child's crayon next to his overflowing ashtray.

I seem to remember something somewhere about writing in Bibles. How it's a sin or something. Somewhere.

I open the Bible to a blank page. It's hard to find one. It's the Bible isn't it. There's a lot of…well…biblical…stuff. There's a blank one right at the back though.

I write…I write…I write…

He writes something.

Reads what he's written and smiles.

I put it by his bed.

Light comes in through the window.

Bells call the monks to pray I suppose.

I can get out the back way.

Beat.

He picks up his big black samples case.

There's a piece of paper. You understand? A note. On a desk from Ikea or somewhere in a front room. Miles from here.

While it's there. I'm dead.

I drive home.

Let myself in with my keys.

It's early morning. Frost on the windows.

First, I take the hose and attach it back onto the vacuum.

Then, I tear up the piece of paper. The note. Into little pieces. Twenty. Thirty maybe. Tiny little pieces.

Beat.

I was dead when all this happened.

Technically.

When all this happened I was dead.

He walks out of the room.

PAUL stays asleep on the bed. Breathing heavily.

Slow fade to black.

Brian Chikwava

SALVATION AND JUSTIFICATION REPRISED ANEW

Jim's word cuts with the Grace of God
Tote in carts with zest of qat;
Salvation & justification
In quarts.
    Father Mervyn,
Pointless quest if all faith
But no real estate,
We accept.
    So I *bliss'* pilgrim
Start anew,
with blazing foot on ladder.

Helen Mort

SNOW IN SHEFFIELD

PETER: There's snow outside and it's snowing inside too.
    When I was sober, the window got opened and when I was high,
    I wanted to feel the cold on my face. So it stayed like that.

    Anyhow, it makes a good picture, doesn't it? Me
    in the middle of the white bed, the white walls freckled
    with Blu-Tac and the table by the window under an inch of snow,

    the aftershave, the photograph of Sam, the old clock radio
    all white, like shapes in a wedding cake. Most days,
    I lie here for hours, trying to be a corpse.

    I let the sheet rest on my face and I don't breathe too much.
    But today, the cold's woken me up and I ache with it
    so I make myself skin up, I make myself get out of bed,

    make myself a cup of piss-weak tea. I drag myself
    into the hallway where the floor's all white too
    because I stopped opening the post a long while ago,

    the last time they let me see Sam, or further back from that,
    maybe I haven't touched it since they sent me home.
    Today, there's a new letter on top of them all.

    I notice it because the envelope is small and black
    and it makes me think of coal in the snow, coal
    for a snowman's nose, or it makes me think of a footprint

or it makes me think of a bullet hole, like most things
do, so before you know, I'm bending down to pick it up,
gentle, like I'm taking something from a vicious dog

and I hold it like a lass would hold a mirror in her hand
and as if I've forgotten how to touch, I move my fingers
over it and somehow it opens up for me. And I read:

*Remember the night you got so pissed you punched
a glass and nearly slit your wrist? Remember how the blood
pearled on your skin and all the lights began to swim?*

*Remember when you were a kid and dropped
a brick down from the railway bridge? Remember how you ran
until your lungs were sore and hid behind your bedroom door?*

*I was the glass. I was the stone you threw.
What you remember, I remember too.*

*Remember how Sofia used to look asleep and how she
didn't stir the night you walked into the street, kept walking
right beyond it all, rested your head against the carpark wall?*

*Remember when you taught your lad to smoke
and gave him rollies for a joke? And how his face was serious
and straight when you took a drag and made him wait?*

*I smoothed her hair. I stroked his hand.
I am a line crossed over in the sand.*

*Even in Iraq I followed you and watched the silent things
they made you do, and watch you train a pistol on yourself
instead and hold it still for hours against your head.*

*I am the bullet that you didn't fire.
I'm every exit you desired…*

I take out my lighter and I let the letter crumple
under the flame. I run upstairs and lock the bathroom door,
stand with my back against it, breathing like I'm done for.

I think of all the times I've stood and watched –
watched from my bedroom window, looking at the shadows of
the people
on Sheaf Street, sometimes with Sam, trying to spit on them.

Watching, down in the sand with the sun on my neck.
Crouched behind trees, behind cars, through tinted windows.
Watching on my front and on my back.

Watching everything happen from my bed, like a film:
the car headlights on the ceilings and the wall.
Sofia taking Sam's hand, taking him home for good.

Who was watching me? And I catch myself
in the bathroom mirror, the mirror dirty with black spots,
darkening everything. I notice I'm very white.

I turn away, then I turn back and have a proper look.
I meet my own stare. Very slowly, I walk towards the glass
and as I get close, it starts to mist with my own breath

only I'm hardly breathing at all now. It's fogging up
and the room is freezing, and I swear there's writing
forming on the mirror and it says

*Forget the future, screw the past. Your hair's a flower
and your skin's like grass. Even as you read, it grows
until you can't tell new from old...*

but as soon as I think I see it, its gone, the glass is dark again
so I unlock the door and I check all the other mirrors
in the flat and even as I'm doing it, I'm grinning to myself,

grinning for the first time in years, because this
is ridiculous, this is fucking ridiculous
and I'm out of my tree, stood in my boxers

in the frozen bedroom, with the sleet coming in
through the window and all the walls bare and the letter burnt
and no signs, no nothing anywhere

just me and my fingers turning blue and my daft grin
and I go over to the window now and carefully, as if I'm
signing something
I write my name in the snow.

Suhayla El Bushra

FALSE TEACHERS

Characters

ASHLEY, 16

A lanky, gangly, awkward boy. His attempts at being threatening don't mask the waves of insecurity coming off him.

AMIR, 16

A calmer, more solid presence. He has more quiet conviction than Ashley, but there's a sense that he's more conflicted under the surface.

SCENE ONE

Boys' toilets.

The stench of piss and Lynx Oriental.

Outside, a bell goes. We can hear stampeding teenagers and teachers shouting as they fail to maintain order.

AMIR is hiding in the toilet. We can hear his breathing through the door, fast and heavy at first, then gradually calming down.

ASHLEY walks in. He swaggers, smiling to himself.

ASHLEY: *(Singing.)* 'Hey Mr Taliban, give me a Bin Laden'.

He laughs, checking the cubicle door. It's locked.

Little pig. Let me in.

Oy. Ali Ababwa.

He kicks the door.

ASHLEY: Open the door.

He waits – nothing.

ASHLEY stands back and jumps at the door kicking it. He hurts his foot.

Ow.

AMIR can be heard laughing from inside the cubicle.

Come out here and laugh you little fucker.

He bangs on the door.

What you hiding for, Ali Boo-Boo?

AMIR: Stop calling me that.

ASHLEY: Never used to bother you.

ASHLEY kicks the door again.

No response from AMIR.

What you acting all scared for?

Kick.

You weren't scared the other night. You were being well mouthy. There was loads of us then.

Bang bang bang.

Why you scared now?

AMIR: Ain't scared.

ASHLEY: What d'you run for then?

AMIR: I didn't run. I don't run from no one.

ASHLEY: You come out of P.E. and you ran as soon as you saw me. You were scared.

AMIR: What would I be scared of you for?

ASHLEY: Cos you know my boys are after you.

AMIR: Your boys are pussies.

ASHLEY: Why you hiding then?

AMIR: I'm contemplating.

ASHLEY: What d'you mean?

AMIR: It means I'm fucking thinking what d'you think it means?

ASHLEY considers this for a moment.

ASHLEY: Are you having a wank?

AMIR: Oh my days.

ASHLEY: You seen that new French teacher?

AMIR: I don't go French –

ASHLEY: She's well fit.

AMIR: Ain't gone French since year seven.

ASHLEY: I don't go either but I might start now if you catch my drift. She's nice.

You could have a wank about her innit?

Silence.

Are you doing it now?

AMIR: No!

Beat.

What do they want?

ASHLEY: Who?

AMIR: Your boys.

ASHLEY: I gotta give you a warnin.

AMIR: Go on.

ASHLEY: It's from Carl.

AMIR: I'm shakin in my boots you know that?

ASHLEY: It's for Sajid.

AMIR: Proceed.

ASHLEY: You gotta call off your meeting.

AMIR: Why would we do that?

ASHLEY leans into the door.

ASHLEY: *(Quietly.)* Cos we're gonna fuck you up if you don't.

AMIR: Bring it on. You gonna be there this time?

ASHLEY: Yeah.

AMIR: Only I didn't see your face the other night.

ASHLEY: I was there.

AMIR: Didn't see your shabby trainers anywhere near my head. I was looking out for 'em. I was waiting for you, hard man. Where was you?

Beat.

ASHLEY: At the back.

AMIR: Pussy.

ASHLEY: Shut up.

Kicks the door again. He paces around, gradually coming to a stop.
Were you alright then? After.

AMIR: Yeah.

ASHLEY: Looked pretty bad from where I was standing –

AMIR: What? 'At the back'?

Take more than a few punches to hurt me.

Couple of scratches that's all.

*ASHLEY nods, relieved. A bell goes. More stampeding. It goes
quiet.*

Ash? You still there?

ASHLEY's about to answer then thinks better of it.

He waits.

The lock turns slowly.

The cubicle door opens.

AMIR comes out. His face is puffy, bruised and cut.

ASHLEY: Shit.

*He reaches out to touch AMIR's face. AMIR sucks his teeth and
moves away.*

AMIR: This is nothing.

He goes over to the mirror and examines himself with pride.
Sajid had his leg broke last summer. He was left unconscious
at a bus stop for three hours before someone bothered to stop
and call an ambulance. He coulda died you know.

Took one for the team innit?

Beat.

(Shaking his head.) 'At the back.'

He looks at himself, touching his bruises, enjoying the pain when he puts the pressure on.

In't you going Maths?

ASHLEY: Got kicked out.

Called Miss de Souza a fat cunt.

AMIR: Nice.

ASHLEY: Made her cry.

AMIR: You're a dick you know that?

ASHLEY: You slashed her tyres.

AMIR: That was in year eight.

Year eight.

In't you grown up since then?

ASHLEY: At least I've grown.

D'you remember when you nicked that car, yeah, and your feet couldn't reach the pedals –

He starts laughing. Amir chuckles despite himself.

You had to steer while Tyler did the rest. Then you crashed it in Wickes's car park.

They both laugh.

AMIR stops, suddenly.

AMIR: That was a long time ago.

They look at each other for a moment.

You should go Maths.

ASHLEY: She won't have me back in there.

AMIR: Where you meant to be instead?

ASHLEY shrugs.

They must have sent you somewhere.

ASHLEY shrugs.

Didn't they give you a letter or nothing?

ASHLEY shrugs.

Are you ever gonna take responsibility for yourself?

Where you gonna be five, ten years from now? Sat on your fat arse watching telly innit? Sipping on Tenants like your old man, covered in vomit cos you can't be bothered to get up and clean yourself. Some fat dirty wife with a loada tats and a load of fat kids, man. That's what you got to look forward to. Little fatty boom booms all waddling around in their Kappa tracksuits. Your daughters'll be knocked up by the time they're thirteen. Probably you that's made them pregnant –

ASHLEY goes for AMIR – a frenzied outburst of violence that is over as quickly as it started. He lets go of AMIR and turns away from him.

AMIR sinks to the floor, holding his head.

ASHLEY sniffs, his back to AMIR.

AMIR: Are you crying?

ASHLEY: No.

He's crying.

AMIR: What you crying for?

ASHLEY: Ain't crying.

He cries.

AMIR watches him.

ASHLEY stops crying.

He wipes his nose with his hand.

Pause.

Saw your mum the other day. She asked why I didn't come round no more.

Didn't know what to tell her.

Silence.

D'you still see Leah?

AMIR: No.

ASHLEY: I keep thinking about her.

Keep thinking about her face –

AMIR: Shut up.

ASHLEY: The way she looked.

AMIR: I said shut up –

ASHLEY: It weren't just me, you know.

You were there too.

You coulda stopped it.

Fucking put up a fight in the name of Allah, couldn't put up a fight for your girlfrien –

AMIR: She wasn't my girlfriend.

She was just…

A friend.

Was.

Pause.

She don't speak to me no more.

She's still got my hoodie. The Nike one. Blue one.

Afterwards. When I walked her home.

She was shiverin.

I put it on her.

When we got to her house she just walked right in. Didn't say goodbye or nothing. Didn't even look at me.

Can't blame her I suppose.

That was rough.

ASHLEY: It weren't just me –

You coulda done something.

She should've –

Beat.

She didn't have to do it.

She could've said no.

Silence.

She still make those samosas?

AMIR: Leah?

ASHLEY: Your mum.

I used to love them.

I don't normally like spicy food but they were well nice.

AMIR: S'all fucking microwave shit now. Chips and that.

You know what she brought home the other day?

Faggots.

ASHLEY sniggers.

Faggots.

I said what is this? Batty food? She said it's just meatballs Amir, try it. I said I ain't eating no batty shit.

ASHLEY laughs.

Then, I checked the label, right. Pork! Fucking pork. I said mum – this is pork. Not only is it batty, it's fucking haram. You know what she said? 'Amir, what does it matter anymore?'

What d'you think my dad woulda said to that?

Sajid's right man. The fucking Muslims in this country are actually worse than the English.

ASHLEY: Carl says it's alright to hate Muslims. It's not like hating people for being Pakis or whatever cos that ain't their fault is it? They can't help that. But you can help being a Muslim. You can just stop.

AMIR: You keep hating us mate. Cos the more of you there are hating us, the bigger we get.

Pause.

You don't even believe that shit. That's the trouble with you

Ash. You got no conviction.

What d'you hang around with em for?

ASHLEY shrugs. He stares at AMIR, almost pleading.

AMIR: Don't look at me like that. Faggot.

ASHLEY looks away.

ASHLEY: You think about your dad much?

AMIR: Random.

ASHLEY: I miss our chess games.

He always used to let me win, remember?

AMIR: You used to do his head in.

Seriously.

You only ever thought one move at a time. You didn't have no game plan or nothing. Just reacted to whatever he did.

It did his nut.

ASHLEY: Sorry.

AMIR: S'alright.

He liked you.

Used to think he liked you more than he liked me sometimes.

Can't blame him. I was a dick.

Theivin.

Drinkin.

Hurtin people –

ASHLEY: You hurt people now –

AMIR: Yeah, for a reason.

See, that's the difference between you and me. I'm working towards something. I got an ideology.

I was lost, before. All my dad wanted was for me to find the right path. I wouldn't listen to him. But you know what? I've found my way now.

I know what I'm doing. And he'll thank me in Heaven.

ASHLEY: He just wanted you to be good, Amir.

That's all he wanted.

S'what he wanted for both of us.

Being good.

A bell rings. Sound of a stampede.

The End.

David Eldridge

SOMETHING, SOMEONE, SOMEWHERE

JOHN and KAYE. Early forties.

A window spilling sunshine into the room.

Silence.

JOHN: You knew.

KAYE: Yes I did.

Silence.

JOHN: You knew I always.

KAYE: Yes.

JOHN: Oh.

KAYE: Yes I did.

JOHN: I've loved you very deeply my whole life.

KAYE: I know.

Silence.

JOHN: You didn't say.

KAYE: Neither did you.

JOHN: Well I.

KAYE: I know. It was perfectly obvious. To me anyway.

Silence.

JOHN: Let me hold your hands.

KAYE: Okay.

JOHN holds KAYE's hand.

JOHN: You're not well.

KAYE: You would know.

Silence.

JOHN: I suppose I should be honest.

Silence.

KAYE: I am here.

JOHN: Yes.

KAYE: Go on.

JOHN: It doesn't cause me pain.

KAYE: Well then that's good.

JOHN: It's never been a source of.

KAYE: No.

JOHN: I couldn't have.

KAYE: No, I know.

Silence.

JOHN: I know. In my own way I've tried to be honest. By writing to
            you. Friendship.

KAYE: So have I.

JOHN: Yes.

KAYE: So have I John.

JOHN: I know.

KAYE: Well?

JOHN: I still feel.

KAYE: What?

JOHN: I feel I've let you down.

KAYE: You have.

JOHN: Have I?

KAYE: Yes you have.

JOHN: Have I?

KAYE: You've let us both down in a way. We could have had a life together. But you never had the courage.

Silence.

JOHN: Yes.

Silence.

KAYE: I asked only one thing of you.

JOHN: Yes.

KAYE: One thing.

JOHN: Kaye.

KAYE: That if you loved me more than you loved her you would be with me. That was the litmus test.

JOHN: How do you litmus test a human heart?

Silence.

KAYE: No, I know.

JOHN: I wanted to do the right thing.

KAYE: Yes but. For whom? It wasn't enough that you broke my heart twenty years ago you had to come back again twenty years later and do it again.

Silence.

JOHN: I thought you wanted honesty?

KAYE: You, thought I wanted honesty?

JOHN: Well what do you want darling?

Silence.

KAYE: I want my time again, in ignorant bliss of you.

Silence.

JOHN: I have never stopped.

KAYE: I didn't want your letters. I wanted your children.

Silence.

JOHN: You've a family.

KAYE: They're his children. They look like him.

           Silence.

JOHN: I could never have given you the life you wanted.

KAYE: No.

JOHN: You wanted things.

KAYE: I wanted you.

JOHN: You wanted nice things.

KAYE: I wanted you.

JOHN: Then why did you marry a man who could buy you nice things instead of me?

           Silence.

KAYE: It was the worst mistake of life.

JOHN: Yes, it's the great tragedy of our lives.

KAYE: I'm not to blame.

JOHN: What we've both done.

           Silence.

KAYE: It's not a tragedy John. My cancer is a tragedy. Your wife's cancer was a tragedy.

           Silence.

JOHN: Is this the last time we will see each other?

KAYE: Yes.

           Silence.

JOHN: Then I must speak from the heart.

           Silence.

KAYE: Yes.

           Silence.

JOHN:	I've longed for you.
KAYE:	I've felt it in your letters.

Silence.

JOHN:	It's the kind of longing that's hollowed out my bones. Made my heart want to leave my body. It's been very powerful.
KAYE:	Yes.
JOHN:	The thought of my mouth on every inch of your body. Drinking in your neck. Being so close to you I can divine the love in my own eyes. Looking back at me in your eyes.

Silence.

KAYE:	I've never wanted any one more than I've wanted you. We were beautiful.
JOHN:	Yes.
KAYE:	It made my marriage unhappy.

Silence.

JOHN:	I'm sorry.
KAYE:	You made things seem possible when really they were impossible.

Silence.

KAYE looks in her bag. She takes out a stack of love letters tied by string. Perhaps a hundred.

JOHN:	You kept them?
KAYE:	Yes.
JOHN:	All of them?
KAYE:	Yes.
JOHN:	But I.
KAYE:	What?
JOHN:	But in twenty years. I.
KAYE:	Yes?

JOHN: I thought.

KAYE: What?

JOHN: I.

KAYE: What John?

JOHN: I thought you would read them. And destroy them.

KAYE: Why?

JOHN: Because.

KAYE: He thought they were from my Auntie Chrissie.

JOHN: And he never?

KAYE: No. I put them in a shoe box on top of my wardrobe.

JOHN: He never?

KAYE: No.

JOHN: My God.

KAYE: But you have to take them back because he'll read them when I'm gone.

JOHN: I can't believe he never read them.

KAYE: He trusted me.

Silence.

JOHN: When you're gone.

KAYE: Yes. When I'm gone.

Silence.

JOHN: Everything is suddenly very real.

KAYE: Yes it is. How long is it now since Amanda died? Is it a year?

Silence.

JOHN: Not quite a year.

KAYE: Nine months then.

JOHN: Yes.

Silence.

KAYE: I'll do my best not to go on your year anniversary. That would be cruel. You must feel fate's been hard on you.

JOHN: I often feel I'm being judged.

KAYE: Perhaps you are.

KAYE laughs.

JOHN: How can you laugh?

Silence.

KAYE: You should have just fucked me John. As time's gone by I would have liked you to have fucked me more than I loved your letters.

Silence.

JOHN: Yes.

KAYE: I suppose it's something the kids are grown up.

JOHN: Yes.

KAYE: That's something.

JOHN: Yes.

Silence.

KAYE: I read your letters again. I read them all again recently. Spent a day reading them. They're beautiful. Thank you. I'm going to tell my children about you. I want them to know about you. I want them to know the truth of my life. You're the love of my life John.

Silence.

JOHN: But.

KAYE: What?

JOHN: It's.

KAYE: What?

JOHN: Well.

KAYE: They know I don't love their father.

Silence.

JOHN: Okay.

KAYE: They know there's something else in my life. They know there's always been something else. They think I regret having them. I won't let them think that. I love them. They're beautiful. They've done nothing wrong.

Silence.

JOHN: Do you want me to talk to them?

Silence.

KAYE: All I want you to do is read your letters. What a waste.

She throws them at him.

JOHN: Okay.

Silence.

KAYE: And don't you dare sit at the back.

JOHN: Okay.

KAYE: Like I had to. When Amanda died.

Silence.

JOHN: The urge to tell the truth at the end is strong isn't it?

KAYE: Yes it is.

Silence.

JOHN: Amanda thanked me for my loyalty. It was virtually the last thing she said.

KAYE: She knew.

JOHN: Yes.

Silence.

He picks up the letters.

KAYE: John?

JOHN: Yes Kaye.

KAYE: You will come?

JOHN: Yes.

KAYE: Good.

JOHN: Your kids will hate me.

KAYE: Perhaps they will.

Silence.

JOHN: I love you Kaye.

KAYE: I love you John.

Silence.

JOHN: That's something isn't it?

Silence.

KAYE: I suppose it is.

JOHN: We spoke it.

KAYE: Yes we did.

JOHN: We've spoken it.

KAYE: Yes.

Silence.

JOHN: You can't let something like that live inside you without.

KAYE: What?

JOHN: You know what.

KAYE: Tell me.

JOHN: It becomes poison.

KAYE: Poison?

JOHN: Yes.

KAYE laughs and shakes her head. Silence.

KAYE: Rather poison than cancer.

Silence.

JOHN: You can't believe.

KAYE: I do.

JOHN: God.

Silence.

KAYE: My head was wrong. My heart was wrong.

Silence.

JOHN: Do you want life to be fair?

KAYE: I know life's not fair.

JOHN: Do you think things are black and white?

KAYE: I know they're not John.

JOHN: Well.

KAYE: It's been my life.

JOHN: And mine.

Silence.

KAYE: I should have chosen.

Silence.

JOHN: You did.

Silence.

KAYE: Oh for a certainty.

KAYE laughs. Silence.

JOHN: Your heart will soon give up.

Silence.

KAYE: Yes.

JOHN: Like Amanda's did.

KAYE: Yes.

Silence.

JOHN: Who would want their heart to account for nothing more than a bloody engine wrapped in a pericardium?

He gestures with the letters.

KAYE: Yes. I can see them.

JOHN: I have given my heart in the best way I can.

KAYE: So did I.

JOHN: Then that's something.

KAYE: Yes it is.

Silence.

JOHN: Where will you go?

KAYE: To my mother's in Jaywick.

Silence.

JOHN: I would come.

KAYE: No. I'll be with my husband. The children. We'll have time to be with each other. And talk.

JOHN: Of course.

Silence.

KAYE: I want to walk by the sea.

Silence.

JOHN: Yes.

KAYE: Reconcile myself.

Silence.

JOHN: Is this goodbye?

KAYE: Yes it is.

JOHN: Is it?

JOHN: Yes.

Silence.

KAYE: Goodbye John.

Silence.

JOHN: Goodbye Kaye.

          Silence.

KAYE: I love you John.

JOHN: I love you Kaye.

          They look at each other.

          The lights gradually fall.

          The sound of the sea gently laps around the last light in the room.

Nathalie Handal

MEN IN VERSE

This letter is the same letter. This place is the same place I wrote, *Walk with me, this land is our verse.*

I waited for him at the entrance of the old city. It was the summer of my seventeenth birthday, and I had sixty lemon seeds for us to plant. We had met five years earlier at a youth camp sponsored by the BBC for boys from both sides – and then occasionally volunteered to help. Yohanan and I were paired together to plant lemon trees. We never imagined we would have enjoyed it. Something about the smell of those lemons had us coming back. They made us giggle. Maybe it was the way the lemons kept filling the empty boxes, as if mocking history. They kept us here even if we couldn't be.

I sat anxiously on a stone waiting for him.

Dreaming again, Hanna? he asked. Of the two of us, he was the dreamer. I was too impatient to sit. Ummi said that even if she tied me up, I would find a way to run. I was the youngest of a family of nine children. Baba worked at the only Keffiyah factory left in the West Bank. When I was growing up, there were more than 120 textile factories but now it was the year 2000, and only the Herbawi Factory remained. Baba's boss, Abu Yasser, would let me help sometimes. Seeing the machine weave the black and white pattern was like witnessing a village being painted on a scarf. I also liked the red and white pattern. Older men of respect mostly wore those. They were all made of cotton. And as I placed the keffiyahs on the shelf, I thought of how ironic it was that the patterns were modeled after ears of grain and fishing nets, and we couldn't get to the sea anymore. Even getting to the factory was difficult because we lived in Jerusalem and the factory was in Hebron. It took Baba a couple of buses and sometimes two hours to get there. Once I saw him sitting in the dark looking at the palms of his hands. I didn't understand why until I saw him wipe his tears. He was opening his life to God. Yohanan never heard of a Keffiyah before he met me. And I never ate pancakes before I met him. They weren't as sweet as our Kenafeh.

There you are, look at what I have, I immediately told him, proudly opening the brown cloth bag I kept the seeds in. He instantly told me he had great news. His father was having a birthday party and he wanted me to come. In all the years we had known each other, we had never met each other's families. I don't think they ever imagined we would have stayed friends. I was constantly told not to trust him, as I am sure he was told about me.

I'm excited, he said. I asked him when the party was. *Tomorrow*, he said. *Tomorrow*, I responded, a bit surprised. We laughed and started walking. That afternoon on my way home, I wondered how I was going to tell my parents. The sole of my left shoe was slowly coming off and a few pebbles got stuck to my socks. This made me think of the day my uncle came to my grandmother's house with a toe as huge as a melon. A bee had stung him. Siti placed mint leaves on his toe. She thought mint would heal any ache. But not our neighbor's heartache. Abu Walid went to three funerals in a row – his three sons. That was during the Intifadah. I thought about the olive tree on my way to the Bethlehem market. Would it be taken away from its roots? So much was changing so fast.

While I was having that thought, Yousef, the man who made *kaak*, stopped to greet me. Everyone said he was crazy because he counted backwards, knew strange facts, and had a stutter. He asked me why I was happy, as if happiness were forbidden here. I told him I was going to a party. He fixed his eyes on mine and stuttered, *Be careful ya Hanna, be careful of them, all they do is steal, steal*. He repeated *steal, steal*. His voice lingered. I stood still for a moment, then smiled and rushed home announcing I was going to Yohanan's father's birthday. Blurting it out seemed the way to do it. My mother continued to cook the eggplants she was making. She didn't speak much. But her slow motions told us what we needed to know.

The next evening, my father and I walked to Yohanan's house. He too wasn't a man of many words. I never understood the way my parents expressed love to each other. Only later, when I was calmer, more mature, was I able to comprehend the language they spoke. It wasn't poetic but tough, resistant. And they knew when the song was breaking.

My father and I walked silently. I could not contain my excitement and he knew that. He allowed me the moment. It was his way of saying he was proud. When we got to the house gate, I said goodbye and nearly ran inside. I turned around for a second, I saw him smile, both his hands behind his back.

Yohanan came to greet me. We were happy to see each other. I couldn't wait to meet his mother whom he always spoke about. Everyone was laughing and drinking, and I didn't know their music but liked it. Yohanan introduced me to his parents and they welcomed me but never asked me anything about myself. His father patted my shoulders and told me to have fun. His mother watched me from the corner of her eyes. This made me uncomfortable. And although I didn't want to admit it to myself, I was upset that I didn't like her. Yohanan didn't resemble her, nor did he really look like his father except they were both well built with green eyes and reddish hair. Unlike me – thin and long, dark with a small scar on my chin. I could be pleasing to the eye but I didn't know how to project that confidence. A beautiful girl passed by me and interrupted my thought. I never dared approach her. Yohanan saw my eyes, knew what I was thinking. He joked, *You're too skinny for her.*

We were different but something unspoken between us was exactly the same and that made us trust each other. We stayed together the entire night except that brief moment when I went to the bathroom. While I was waiting, a widow stood beside me motionless. Her hair wasn't well combed and she had dark circles under her eyes. It was as if a huge black fan had sucked all the air in the corridor. When the bathroom door opened, I was relieved to no longer be standing next to her. When I came out, Yohanan was waiting for me, but she was gone. I asked him who the lady in black was. He shrugged.

The lights went off and everyone started to sing. All I could see were the candles on the cake. As the lights slowly came back on, I watched people's faces. They seemed joyful. Were they? Yohanan's mother blushed as she watched her husband blow out the candles. I watched another man admire the beautiful girl's hands as she held a drink. Had she noticed at all? I looked at Yohanan and remembered a conversation we had while watering the lemons trees. I told him, *If you look at the sea long enough, you will know where you are from.* He laughed. *You don't even know the Sea of Galilee.* He was kidding but suddenly it wasn't funny anymore.

People started to dance with such intensity that even the debke at our weddings seemed tamed. Maybe when Yohanan and I turn fifty we will have a party like this one. When the air is sweeter than the cake. When all people want is some funny around them.

Suddenly, a scream. It was the widow, the woman in black I saw earlier. Hysterical, she claimed someone had stolen the chain around her neck. *Are you sure you had it on?* someone asked. *My late husband gave it to me,* she said, angry. I didn't understand everything she was saying but I knew when she was cursing. It reminded me of my aunt Sahar when she would say, *Kus'immak.* People tried to calm her down. But she was looking everywhere for her chain, pointing her finger accusingly at some of the party guests. For a second, everyone seemed suspicious of the person next to them. As if we were part of this conspiracy and everyone was guilty. I thought about my aunt who always said, *Damn this place, we can never stay happy.*

Suddenly the widow was right in front of me. *It was him. Yes, it was him.* Her voice was louder, higher pitched. It was like a long echo squeezing my lungs. I never moved.

I felt the burn of everyone's stare on my body. But I was concerned only with where Yohanan was. Our eyes finally met and I knew everything was going to be fine, until I felt the widow's hand down my pants pocket. She kept pushing her hand further down. She was so close I could feel her heavy breathing on my shoulder. My heart was beating fast. I thought my knees were going to collapse. Yohanan did nothing. I stared at him. In that minute the music inside me broke in half. A burial, and I never even had the chance to close my eyes. The widow got more aggressive when she found nothing. As she reached for my other pocket, Yohanan's mother gently took her away, and gestured for him to come and get me.

We walked to the gate, side by side, where my father was waiting. That was the last time I walked with Yohanan. The dark made us all smaller.

The next day, the second Intifadah started. There was no time to think of my humiliation. No time to think about anything. A month later, while walking to the Old City I saw Yohanan. His face lit up for a second. A semblance of old times. He made one step towards me. I lowered my head.

Not long after that, I received a letter from his mother asking that I forgive her and Yohanan. Even the widow begged for my forgiveness. They said the deceivers had filled their minds with fog that night. That afternoon my mother saw me by the window, held my hand, and said, *Don't be broken – build with the ashes the shadows have left you with. There are deceivers everywhere. The only reconciliation is in the flesh.* I was already too far inside to hear her. Soon came the wall.

I was troubled with the same question for ten years – where am I? On an open hill? With a rain, unable to fall? With a bird, circling too high? Did Yohanan think I could do something like that? I was with him the entire time except when I was in the bathroom. Did that minute bring him doubt? Did we finally cave into disbelieving the spirit we saw when we planted lemon trees?

Eleven years after that night, I saw Yohanan. It was Yousef who saw him. He pointed at him, stuttering repeatedly, *1161*. Yohanan was entering a funeral car with license plates 1611. I found out his mother had passed. Yousef and I walked through the old city to get what we had come for – an attempt at forgetting. In the afternoon, I asked him to please wait for me at the entrance of the Old City.

I went to Yohanan's house, walking past the gates where a certain light once crumbled into tiny pieces of glass around me. I walked into his room. He was kneeling by his bed, his head down on the mattress. After a few minutes, he slowly lifted his head. It was as if he knew I would be coming. As if he was waiting for the day. The way we wait for God at the edge of our delusion. I knelt too. From whom were we asking forgiveness? We looked older than we were. We were face to face. No wall hiding us from one another. Peace can only be found in the flesh.

Silently we went to the lemon tree we had planted. Beside it, Yohanan started digging the soil with his hands, and put in some seeds, and I did too. We knew a tree never killed another tree – *this land is our verse*.

Yousef was waiting patiently for me on the stone where I once waited for Yohanan. He looked up at me, stuttering, *You saw John. John. John means grace*. I paused to allow him to deliver his words, *He, John – you, Hanna, 2nd John*. He smiled.

It had never occurred to us that we had the same name.

3 JOHN

Enda Walsh

ROOM 303

For Steve Rose

The listener is telephoned and what they hear is an Irishman speaking from Room 303.

MAN: Which isn't to say I wouldn't because I would – ordinarily I would. On a matter of principle I would always set out to accomplish that which needs finishing. It is in my nature to finish, to complete things. I could tell you all manner of stories from my youth that would prove to you – that I have this quality but you know this – of course you do – in the past I've spoken to you about this probably – it doesn't seem wildly important to go into that sort of detail just yet.

There are lots of words for what I am – but where I am is this room – this hotel room. At least it seems like it could be a hotel room. All indications suggest that it shouldn't be. It's been a long time cleaned certainly. I can't see the floor – the carpet – if it is carpeted – it is thick with – what exactly? I don't like looking at the floor and stay lying in the bed – or very occasionally sitting in the bed and talking on this phone – just to prove that I can sit up in a bed and talk.

I felt a twinge in my back this morning which proves that I still have a little muscle inside, unfortunately. It reminds me of the years of walking – of stepping off buses – of arriving in new towns and knocking on doors and speaking the good word to strangers – and occasionally being invited into their homes and sharing with them hot sweet beverages and of course a plate of biscuits. Always the confectionery! And I would leave their homes – leave them brimming with 'hope' – and other Apostles I would see leaving other houses and stepping back onto buses and travelling the country just like me. I had working muscles then – now I am more of a quilt in substance. Fuck it! Now I am more of the bed – belong to the bed – my country is this room – my town is this mattress – my home is my head – and ordinarily I would complete a task. Of course I would! On principle I would – I would have to – but is it possible to finish this thought – this breath – this idea of me? This is the crux – as they say – of the matter!

So yesterday there was a fly in the room – in my country, let's call it – a fat blue bottle, to give it its correct term – and it barely buzzed about – so fat it was. I could see it on the desk at the far end of the country over there. It was on my papers. It was almost like it was half-reading them – the bastard! And it panted about in an asthmatic sort of way – shuffling from one line to the next – hardly looking for Enlightenment – probably looking for food matter – In here?! He'd be bloody lucky! Anyway – he stopped his reading and seemed to be looking back at me. He then – miraculously – flew. HE FLEW!

He was Malteser in size and an azure blue in colour but even as he approached I was repulsed by this beast! How much shit had he licked in his short lifetime this fat fly!? He landed where my legs are. He licked around my quilt but all the time with the intention of making his way closer to my face – which he did! Which he did! And there was something in his fat swagger that suggested that he saw in me an equal. That after perusing my Scripture he saw in me a beast of similar ambition to him – of similar worth – of similar purpose to him – the BASTARD!

BASTARD BLUE BOTTLE BASTARD!

A pause.

It was never my intention to play out my last days being stared at by a fat arrogant blue bottle in a shitty hotel room. Dreams of dying were always dreams of friends or strangers I had talked to – people I had given the good word to in return for hot beverages and biscuits. I would be dying on a bed and these people would surround that bed and kind words would float down on me and ease me into my death and towards my God – my Divinity! This is the dream. This is what teases me in moments of lucidity. Ordinarily I am a man who completes a task! I will not allow another thought to end before finding some rest! I will not allow that fly to wither me with his arrogance!

A slight pause.

Amazingly I had enough breath in me to send him toppling over this bed and into the terrible abyss of the floor. The shit!

A slight pause.

No doubt he's feeding off the remnants 'down there'. Feeding off whatever substance there is down there!! But the breath does not lie! The breath tells me of my life – that I have a life! That I must gather something from this room!! That through the room's refuse I must find again what truth is! I must!

A pause.

What was it I stepped off buses with? The details! Come on! What was the thing that I brought into strangers houses? What were the good words that came from my mouth? This is the crux – as they say – of the matter. Of me.

A pause.

And it must be a hotel room! On either side of me I can hear voices. Televisual voices with their suggestion of a world continuing – of adventure and geographies and colour. My television ceased transmission many weeks ago. I had it running continually to drown out – difficult to put a word on it – the distraction of the television helped ease me, let's say – difficult to say what exactly is happening inside this head. Anyway the fucker broke down. Some time during Bargain Hunt it died – gave up the ghost – kicked the televisual bucket!

And it is not a theory – I have made it a fact, by the way!! It *is* a hotel room! It must be! A hotel I have often visited – we have often visited. And we would meet in the mornings at breakfast – and over our breakfasts we would again define goodness and God's Truth to one another – and we would pack our papers and step on buses and arrive in towns and knock on doors and drink their hot beverages. It began, you see, in these hotels. In your hotel! In a hotel like this one.

The theory is – the theory that must now be a fact – is that these rooms are full of us, aren't they?! Full of men like me on telephones. It was always men like me – of my colour and type and sound. Men with my words, with my amount of words. That was the way it was – and here we are – in hotel rooms that are now our countries – on telephones that are now our friends – in homes that are now our heads – unable to breakfast and talk again of what it is we believe in anymore! At least the men on either side of me have Bargain Hunt! At least they have the clatter of daytime television to stave off what I must now face here alone in the fucking silence, in the darkness with a fat blue bottle for company! My God!

A long pause and only his breath.

And it's something I don't like to do – have not done for many weeks. I must.

A slight pause.

Do it!

A pause.

I look down from the bed. Down at what was the floor…

…and pictures there of a house I was taken home to and sisters and brothers in their best clothes and a dog who once shared this house and a garden crisp in black and white and an old car and my father with sleeves and trousers rolled up, a cigarette in his mouth not yet lit and me in his arms.

And scenes in a new house with another garden and the gate that led to the open road and the feeling still of the freshly cut grass tickling the backs of my legs as I'm sat under an inflatable paddling pool with Sinead Murray kissing me or rather plunging her tongue into my mouth and telling me it was called 'kissing'.

And faster the images come and fill the floor with smells of youth and half-dreamt stories of Dollymount Strand and the sea in front and breaking hearts and pulverising livers and the smell of sex in every breath and an idea of the world and my involvement in that world and burning friendships and terrible indifference and insatiable lusts and sweet vodka and everyday boredom.

And amongst the remnants a clearer more isolated me, a broken self-hating me, an insignificant vocally retarded young man who continues to show half notions of himself and proclaims half truths of himself and sells them as gospel to others who cram together and nod barely.

And deeper now into the floor and surrounded by the clatter of my younger years is the quick burn of happiness of my later years deluded in its ridiculous importance but rescued then – briefly it seems rescued – rescued by Scripture – by His words.

And joined to others and breakfasts and bus journeys and spreading those words like new air until all there is is God's Truth and my body ageing.

A pause.

His Truth now forgotten. Gone. Completely.

A pause.

And the remnants clear a little further, fall away, evaporate around one another – the carpet disintegrating with nothing to hold it – memories disappearing as a larger breath takes them.

A pause.

I look down from the bed into the big space beneath…

…and there…

…I can see a man lying in his bed…lying beneath his quilt… And he's staring back up at me.

And he's talking fast with frightened eyes just like mine must be – and holding his telephone for a few seconds more of life like I hold on for life. And his words I can't hear.

A slight pause.

I don't know what it is he's saying. No one knows.

A slight pause.

Not even he.

The line suddenly goes dead.

The End.

Anne Carson

THE GOAT AT MIDNIGHT

They bring Jude to Guantanamo.
He had just begun a letter.
Dearly beloveds.
They like it very bright.
He had just lit a cigarette.
They are who they are.
They go where they go.
Outside inside, day as night.
Beside his bed at Guantanamo
is a bedside table.
In the table a drawer.
In the drawer a Gideon Bible.
Jude looks himself up.
For certain men, he reads.
Have crept in unnoticed.
He grows confused.
They like people confused.
Night as night.
They take away his belt.
To fashion a new belt
occupies a few hours.
He makes it out of *strange flesh.*
Just before stepping off the table
he worries about his goat, tethered by the door at home.

Kate Mosse

ENDPAPERS

A woman sits alone on a bare stage – it could be a dusty attic or a hospital room – with an old suitcase. Inside are black and white photographs, a baby's christening gown, an old-fashioned notebook and pencil, objects of significance to the narrator. The time and place are uncertain.

I

(Writing.) In the desert, there are no seasons. Each day is like the next. The endless sands stretching before and after. Footprints in the dust.

In the desert, there is no life. Only ghosts of the quick and the dead, shadows. Poets and theologians, the myth-makers and the liars. Friends, long gone. In the desert, there is no colour.

Beat.

But always, the same voices. *(Smiling.)* Saying, that beyond the highest ridge, where the rock and the water and the sky met, there was a place. A place of colour and music and life.

(Resolutely.) I stopped my ears. Closed my eyes. Did not dare to hope.

(Whispering.) There is a place, where all stories find their beginnings and their end. A place of redemption, where there is rest. After noise, silence.

I set out to see.

(Stops writing.) Was there a journey? *(Taps head.)* Or was it only here? The doctors said I was ill, but how could they know? But

they talked to me in a language I barely understood. *(Beat.)* I was a refugee. A woman in a land where women's voices were of no account. A mother, once. *(Beat.)* If I was ill, it was grief that had made me so.

(Resumes writing.) I walked for seven days. The path took me up into the mountains. The towns and villages became fewer and further between until there was only wilderness. My resolve faltered, but I did not turn back. *(Beat.)* At night, when I lay down to sleep, I dreamt of cities and spires, of forests and lakes.

Beat.

Up through the dry rock, up and on until the light began to change. The air began to change. Hints of summer after spring, autumn after summer. Colour, after the absence of colour. Sound after the absence of sound. *(Animated.)* Blue, yellow, red flowers. A chorus of birds, flocked in song, the beating of feathers against the air. *(Animated.)* On and up until I was stepping out into the sky.

(Smiling.) A place of colour and music and light.

There below me, like a flourish of green silk, was a wide expanse of grass. And in the middle of it, a fairground. *(Beat.)* A fairground.

II

I stopped. Having travelled so far, I could not go back. Yet even so.

I rubbed my eyes, blind with dust and the journey, then looked again at the tents and striped canopies, at the banners and the flags.

Was this the place?

I forced myself to keep going. I walked slowly down, cautious and careful, drawn by the faint music of the band. Bright brass, dappled, the voice of the trumpet soaring above in the higher register.

The outer stalls were arranged in a circle, with a labyrinth of smaller spirals within. Draped awnings suspended on wooden struts. Tables where a customer could wager it all on the throw of a dice. Wooden hoops, gold rings, flickering candles. Each stall displayed something of the beauty of the world. Symbols of faith and art, captured like pictures in a frame. Now I could hear the wheezing of steam and air at the heart of the fair, the antique song of the calliope playing an old waltz.

I hesitated. I was content here on the outside, safe. What need to go further?

(Whispering.) 'To end so as to begin again.'

Into the second circle. The images on the stalls were the same, though each was a little less bright. Duller. There seemed to be other people, though I could see no one. Just a suggestion in the shimmering of the air.

(Quicker.) A pilgrim on the *chemin de Jérusalem*, through the maze to the next circle, then the next. The crowds grew thicker. I was conscious of the heat of skin and the echo of voices. Hundreds or thousands or tens of thousands, I couldn't say.

Further into the labyrinth, to the fifth circle, the sixth. The bellow of the calliope grew louder, more oppressive. The images on the stalls were fading. The seventh circle, where the pictures were so faint, there was no longer anything left to see. *(Beat.)* But it no longer mattered. I had arrived.

III

I looked up at the carousel, two tiers, beautiful in the slanting, shifting light. Twelve barley twist poles set with jasper, emerald and glass, sending a rainbow dancing across the polished wooden floor.

There were four rows of creatures on which to ride. Horses, yes, but also dragons and serpents, eagles, a lion, with six wings and eyes painted, leopards. *(Beat.)* A lamb.

I looked down. On the ground, I saw fluttered scraps of yellow cloth, pink cloth, black. Some were cut in the shape of a cross, others a star, each a sign of suffering borne or condemnation or judgement. A drift of autumn leaves around at the base of the carousel, having no purpose here.

I looked up. On the underside of the roof, painted cities. Fallen civilisations, thrones and kingdoms. Drift white figures standing before triumphant gates with a sword or a scroll in their hands. And in the centre, a single figure, lit by the sun and by the moon. *(Beat.)* Silver and gold.

Yet, I hesitated. This was what I had come for, this moment of salvation. Gnosis. I had come too far to turn back. But even now, I feared what might happen if I climbed up onto the carousel. Submitted to it. Memories of darker words, the cruel certainties of prophets and preachers. Threat.

IV

Then instead of music, a voice.

(Brightly.) 'All aboard. Climb on board.'

His accent was strange and I couldn't see his face, but there was a directness and a confidence I liked. My dread faded.

'All on board,' cried the barker. 'Hold on tight, all aboard.'

I saw my hand reach up. Saw my foot lift up. Felt the movement of blood and muscle and bone as I stepped up. Committed myself to the carousel.

(Welcoming.) 'Sit wherever you want. Hold on tight, all aboard.'

I chose a horse, a grey with a gilt harness and sharp eyes of pearl. I felt the barker swing past me, hand over hand, though I couldn't see his face.

(Friendly.) 'Why are you here?' he said in my ear.

'I have heard that, here, all stories find their ending.'

'You want to understand only what has happened? That's all?'

I caught my breath. 'No.'

'What's to come, then? You think me a magician?'

'Some say so.'

Pause.

'Do you know where you are?'

'I've heard it called many things.'

'Carousel, *carosella*. It means "little battle",' he said. 'Write it down.'

Before I could answer, he was gone, hand over hand over hand.

I felt the carousel tip, as if others were climbing on board on the far side. I was aware of absence and presence in the air in equal measure. Of judgements being made.

(The barker, returning to the conversation.) 'What do you really want?'

Dialogue should be quick, back and forth.

'Peace.'

'Peace?'

'Silence,' I said.

'Are you sure?'

Beat.

'Grace.'

'Write it down. Soon, time will be time no longer. Write it down.'

I felt the touch of his breath on my face as he swept past me once more.

(Loudly.) 'Who are you?'

'Only a messenger. *Angelos.*'

'My name's Joanna,' I called after him. 'Won't you tell me who you are?'

(Like an echo.) 'To end so as to begin again.'

I shivered. These words had brought me comfort. Now they were splinters under my skin.

V

The calliope struck up a new song. A blowsy waltz in a modal key to a lopsided beat. Slow, quick-quick slow, quick-quick, slow. The carousel began to move.

I felt my spirit leap.

Now I could see my companions. Other women and men had joined the ride, each with their name written in ash on their forehead. I raised a smile, a hand, but we were disconnected one from the other. No one spoke. Everyone looked straight ahead. *(Softly.)* And I understood that although we were together in this same place, each experience was unique, solitary. Each of us was destined to make the journey alone.

The barker swung past me again, handing me a fragment of paper with a name written on it.

(Quickly.) 'No, not John,' I called after him. 'Joanna.'

'All aboard, hold on tight. Hold on tight.'

(Loudly.) 'It's Joanna!'

The paper burst into flames in the palm of my hand, scorching my skin. Bright, burning fast, the borrowed name consumed by fire. Deciding it could not matter so very much, I spat into the ashes and daubed them across my forehead, like everyone else.

VI

The carousel was picking up speed. Exhilarating at first, exciting at first. I felt my soul take flight.

But quickly, the mood darkened as the carousel turned, faster and wilder. All around us, images of our ruined world. Testimonies of suffering and judgement, grief. Retribution and consequence. The old battle between dark and light.

(With panic.) I wanted to look away, but the stories held me fast. Round and around, seeing all the world had been and all that the world was and all that the world was to become.

I held on tighter, an unwilling witness to our failed history and any attempt to explain it. Seven seals broken bringing war and famine and death and victory. The blast of seven trumpets and seven bowls emptied upon the earth. The seas turned to blood, fish suffocating upon the shore. The white bones of men on the battlefield. Blackened skies and our green world turned to dust. Mountains as they collapsed into the dead oceans.

(Whispering.) 'Now do you know the name of this place?' he said.

I did not answer.

'See, the rise and fall of cities. See, Babylon defeated.'

'I see only a woman seated upon a horse.'

'In this book of myths, it is a lie that serves. Write it down.'

(Angrily.) 'But to what purpose? I understand nothing. Less than before.'

Still the carousel kept turning. The music was discordant now, syncopated now. Around my head in the air, words, like cinders thrown up from a fire. The leaves of every book, torn and ripped from their bindings, every page despoiled. A thousand years of lessons not learnt.

'See here,' he said, 'the beast with a number upon its forehead. Another symbol that means everything and nothing.'

'I came in search of redemption,' I said, sickened by the relentless movement. 'I came in hope. You show me only despair.'

'Have faith,' he whispered. 'Soon.'

(Contemptuously.) 'Faith!'

'Soon.'

I turned my face away. Shut my eyes. But the horror was inside my head now, my mind. A roaring in my ears, the squeeze of a fist at my heart. My breath, tight, in my chest. Round and around, too fast. *(In panic.)* I was falling, falling into darkness. Then, nothing.

VII

I don't know how long I slept, only that when I woke, there was a silver light in a golden sky. Everything was the same, yet transformed. Perfect. Colour and music and life. *(Beat.)* Quiet.

The carousel was slowing. Stopping.

Still.

I looked down. There was a book in my lap. Every page covered in words I had no memory of writing.

(Gently.) 'To end so as to begin again.'

A different voice, gentle. Remembered.

'Will you tell me your name?'

'You know it.'

I began to protest, then stopped.

'I do.' *(Beat.)* 'Will you tell me the name of this place?'

'That, too, you know.'

I realised I did. A new heaven. A new earth. This, the covenant.

(Softly.) 'There will be no more sorrow?'

'No sorrow. No more tears. Only life as it moves upon the waters. As it whispers through the trees.'

'No more suffering?'

'All shall be well.'

(Beat.)

'Can I at least look upon your face?'

(Beat.)

At first, nothing. Then the slightest of movements. A catching of breath.

(Beat.)

I looked into the light. (Beat.) A single moment of transcendence. Of completion. (Beat.) Grace.

Then, silence. (Beat.)

The story had reached its end.

Silence.

(Pause.)

I opened the book at the beginning to read the title set there. I smiled.

Ἀποκάλυψις, apocalypsis. The Revelation of John.'

I changed the final letters of the name to make it my own, though I knew it would make no difference.

I had written down what I had seen. Each word was in its proper place, though each had the potential to be understood or misunderstood. Words are blunt instruments, malleable, pliable. They can be made to mean what the reader wants them to mean. What the listener wants to hear.

Nonetheless, I turned to the last page and wrote the only word that remained to be written.

(Softly.) Amen.

APPENDIX

All rights whatsoever in these works are strictly reserved and application for performance, etc. should be made before rehearsal to the relevant agent. No performance may be given unless a license has been obtained, and no alterations may be made in the title or the text of the work without the author's prior written consent. The contact details for the authors and agents are as follows:

1. *Godblog* by Jeanette Winterson
Caroline Michel: Peters Fraser and Dunlop / The Rights House, 34-43 Russell Street, London WC2B 5HA / Tel: 0207 344100 / email: cmichel@pfd.co.uk

2. *The Crossing* by Anne Michaels
The Wylie Agency, 250 West 57th Street, Suite 2114, New York, NY 10107 / Tel: 212 246 0069 / mail@wylieagency.com

3. *The Foundation* by Caroline Bird
David Godwin Associates Ltd, 55 Monmouth Street, London, WC2H 9DG / Tel: +44 (0)207 240 9992

4. *The Opening of the Mouth* by Neil Bartlett
Leah Schmidt at The Agency (London) Ltd, 24 Pottery Lane, London W11 4LZ; lschmidt@theagency.co.uk

5. *The Rules* by Maha Khan Philips
maha@mahakhanphilips.com

6. *Sole Fide – By Faith Alone* by Daisy Hasan
d.hasan@gmail.com / daisyhasan@yahoo.co.uk

7. *Beardy* by Tom Wells
Casarotto Ramsey & Associates, Waverley House, 7-12 Noel Street, London W1F 8GQ / info@casarotto.co.uk

8. *The Book of Ruth (and Naomi)* by Stella Duffy
Casarotto Ramsey & Associates, Waverley House, 7-12 Noel Street, London W1F 8GQ / info@casarotto.co.uk

9. *David and Goliath* by Andrew Motion
Simon Trewin: strewin@unitedagents.co.uk
United Agents, 12-26 Lexington Street
London W1F 0LE / Tel: +44 (0) 20 3214 0800

10. *Thus Spake Orunmila...* by Wole Soyinka
C/o the Bush Theatre, 7 Uxbridge Road, London, W12 8LJ

11. *The Suleman* by Roy Williams
Lisa Foster: Alan Brodie Representation Ltd, Paddock Suite, The Courtyard, 55 Charterhouse Street, London EC1M 6HA / www.alanbrodie.com

12. *Two Bears* by Sam Burns
C/o The Bush Theatre, 7 Uxbridge Road, London, W12 8LJ

13. *The Chronicle* by Salena Godden
Cathryn Summerhayes at William Morris Endeavor: CSummerhayes@wmeentertainment.com

14. *From Soloman to Cyrus the Great* by Tim Rice
Joscelyn Evans, Television & Radio, Corporate Capel & Land Ltd, 29 Wardour Street, London W1D 6PS

15. *The Strange Wife* by Naomi Foyle
Zeno Agency Ltd, Primrose Hill Business Centre, 110 Gloucester Avenue, London 8HX

16. *When he had been loved* by Mandla Langa
mlanga@icon.co.za / P.O. Box 2855, Houghton, 2041, South Africa

17. *Hadassah* by Jackie Kay
Charles Buchan: The Wylie Agency (UK) Ltd, 17 Bedford Square, London WC1B 3JA / Tel 00 44 20 79 08 59 00 Fax 00 44 20 79 08 59 01 / Email cbuchan@wylieagency.co.uk

18. *In the Land of Uz* by Neil LaBute
Ms. Joyce Ketay at the Gersh Agency, 41 Madison Avenue, 33rd Floor, New York, NY 10010, USA

19. *When We Praise* by Kwame Kwei-Armah
Sean Gascoine: United Agents, 12-26 Lexington Street, London W1F 0LE / T +44 (0) 20 3214 0800

20. *Notes for a Young Gentleman* by Toby Litt
Lesley Thorne: Aitken Alexander Associates Ltd, 18-21 Cavaye Place, London SW10 9PT / Tel 020 7373 8672

21. *The Preacher, or How Ecclesiastes Changed my Life* by Nancy Kricorian
Lippincott Massie McQuilkin, 27 West 20th Street, Suite 305, New York, NY 10011 / Tel: 212.352.2055

22. *The Beauty of the Church* by Carol Ann Duffy
Peter Straus: Rogers, Coleridge & White Ltd., 20 Powis Mews, London, W11 1JN / Telephone: 020 7221 3717

23. *All the trees of the field* by Ian McHugh
Fay Davies: The Agency (London) Ltd., 24 Pottery Lane, London W11 4LZ / fd-office@theagency.co.uk

24 *A Lost Expression* by Luke Kennard
C/o the Bush Theatre, 7 Uxbridge Road, London, W12 8LJ

25. *Halter-Neck* by Paul Muldoon
Muldoon@Princeton.com

26. *The Fair & Tender* by Owen Sheers
Rogers, Coleridge & White Ltd., 20 Powis Mews, London W11 1JN

27. *Oliver Lewis* by Jack Thorne
Casarotto Ramsey & Associates, Waverley House, 7-12 Noel Street, London W1F 8GQ / info@casarotto.co.uk

28. *Fugitive Motel* by Nick Payne
Curtis Brown Group, Haymarket House, 28-29 Haymarket, London, SW1 4SP

bush theatre   **At the Bush Theatre**

* Artistic Director	Josie Rourke
Executive Director	Angela Bond
Associate Director	Tamara Harvey
Assistant Producer	Sade Banks
Duty Managers	Sarah Binley, Michael Byrne
Theatre Manager	Annette Butler
Marketing Manager	Sophie Coke-Steel
Digital Manager	Stacy Coyne
Head of Individual Giving	Caroline Dyott
Technical Manager	Neil Hobbs
Development Administrator	Lucy Howe
Literary Administrator	Naia Johns
General Manager	Eleanor Lang
Head of Trusts and Foundations	Bethany Ann McDonald
Theatre Administrator and Assistant to the Directors	Fran Miller
Production Manager	Anthony Newton
Producer	Rachel Tyson
Acting Theatre Administrator and Assistant to the Directors	Laura-Jane Zielinska

Associateships, Internships and Attachments

Commercial Consultant	Nathalie Bristow
Composer on attachment	Michael Bruce
Bush Producing and Marketing Intern	Hannah Smith
Literary and Bushgreen Intern	Scarlett Creme
Pearson Playwright	Nancy Harris**
Press Representative	Kate Morley
Bushgreen Developer	Rebeka Ravikumar***
Development Officer	Leonora Twynam
Local Business Development Manager	Trish Wadley
Leverhulme Trust Associate Playwright	Tom Wells
Creative Associates	Kate Budgen, Hannah Dickinson, Oliver Hawes, Alice Lacey, Nessah Muthy
Associate Artists	Tanya Burns, Arthur Darvill, Chloe Emmerson, James Farncombe, Richard Jordan, Emma Laxton, Paul Miller, Lucy Osborne
Front of House Assistants	Benedict Adiyemi, Chrissy Angus, Devante Anglin, Lily Beck, Gemma Bergomi, Tom Brewer, Nathan Byron, Scarlett Crème, Aaron Gordon, Alex Hern, Amy Hydes, Ava Morgan, Karl Queensborough, Chloe Stephens, Gareth Walker

***Bold** indicates full time staff; regular indicates part time/temporary.
**Sponsored by the Peggy Ramsey Foundation Award as part of the Pearson Playwrights' scheme
***Sponsored by Kingston University School of Humanities through a Knowledge Transfer Partnership

The Bush Theatre, 7 Uxbridge Road, London, W12 8LJ
Box Office: 020 8743 5050 | Administration: 020 8743 3584 Email: info@bushtheatre.co.uk
The Alternative Theatre Company Ltd (The Bush Theatre) is a registered charity and a company limited by guarantee.
Registered in England No. 1221968. Charity No. 270080

Be There at the Beginning

The Bush Theatre would like to say a very special 'Thank You' to the following patrons, corporate sponsors and trusts and foundations, whose valuable contributions continue to help us develop and present some of the brightest new literary stars and theatre artists, and helped us launch the new Bush Theatre.

Lone Star
Gianni Alen-Buckley
Miel de Botton
Michael Alen-Buckley
Jonathan Ford & Susannah Herbert
Christopher Hampton
Catherine Johnson
Caryn Mandabach
Miles Morland
Lady Susie Sainsbury
John & Tita Shakeshaft
Nicholas Whyatt

Handful of Stars
Anonymous
Micaela & Chris Boas
Jim Broadbent
Sarah Cooke
Clyde Cooper
Blake & Michael Daffey
David & Alexandra Emmerson
Catherine Faulks*
Chris & Sofia Fenichell
Douglas Kennedy
James & Jacky Lambert
Mark & Sophie Lewisohn
Adrian & Antonia Lloyd
Mounzer & Beatriz Nasr
Alan Rickman
Claudia Rossler
Paul & Jill Ruddock
Naomi Russell
Eva Sanchez-Ampudia & Cyrille Walter
Joana & Henrik Schliemann*
Larus Shields

Rising Stars
Anonymous
Tessa Bamford
David Bernstein & Sophie Caruth
Simon Berry
John Bottrill
David Brooks
Maggie Burrows
Clive Butler
Matthew Byam Shaw
Benedetta Cassinelli
Tim & Andrea Clark
Judy Cummins & Karen Doherty
Matthew Cushen
Irene Danilovich

Yvonne Demczynska
Ruth East
Jane & David Fletcher
Lady Antonia Fraser
Vivien Goodwin
Sarah Griffin
Hugh & Sarah Grootenhuis
Sarah Hall
Hugo & Julia Heath
Roy Hillyard
Urs & Alice Hodler
Bea Hollond
Simon Johnson
Davina & Malcom Judelson
Paul & Cathy Kafka
Rupert Jolley & Aine Kelly
Tarek & Diala Khlat
Heather Killen
Sue Knox
Neil LaBute
Eugenie White & Andrew Loewenthal
Isabella Macpherson
Peter & Bettina Mallinson
Michael McCoy
Judith Mellor
Roger Miall
David & Anita Miles
Caro Millington
Pedro & Carole Neuhaus
Georgia Oetker
Kate Pakenham
Mark Paterson
Julian & Amanda Platt
Radfin Courier Service
Kirsty Raper
Sarah Richards
Damian Rourke
The Hon M. J. Samuel Charitable Trust
Jon and NoraLee Sedmak
Russ Shaw & Lesley Hill
Brian Smith
Nick Starr
The Uncertainty Principle
Francois & Arelle von Hurter
Trish Wadley
Amanda Waggot
Olivia Warham
Edward Wild
Alison Winter

Corporate Supporters
Spotlight
Curtis Brown Group Ltd
John Lewis
United Agents

Footlight
The Agency (London) Ltd

Lightbulb
AKA

The Bush would also like to thank **Markson Pianos**, **Westfield** and **West 12 Shopping & Leisure Centre** for in-kind support, and **UBS** for their sponsorship of Supporters' evenings.

Trusts and Foundations
The Andrew Lloyd Webber Foundation
The Daisy Trust
The D'Oyly Carte Charitable Trust
EC&O Venues Charitable Trust
The Elizabeth & Gordon Bloor Charitable Foundation
Foundation for Sport and the Arts
Garfield Weston Foundation
Garrick Charitable Trust
The Gatsby Charitable Foundation
The Goldsmiths' Company
Jerwood Charitable Foundation
The John Thaw Foundation
The Laurie & Gillian Marsh Charitable Trust
The Leverhulme Trust
The Martin Bowley Charitable Trust
The Hon M J Samuel Charitable Trust
Sir Siegmund Warburg's Voluntary Settlement
King James Bible Trust

*Supporters not receiving associated benefits

Full author biographies and further details about the *Sixty-Six Books* project can be found at:

www.bushtheatre.co.uk/sixtysix/

WWW.OBERONBOOKS.COM